The Illustrated Book of
FISHES

The Illustrated Book of
FISHES

edited by
Pamela Bristow

from a text by
Karel Pivnička and *Karel Černý*

illustrated by
Květoslav Hísek

OCTOPUS BOOKS

Edited by Pamela Bristow
from a text by Karel Pivnička and Karel Černý
Illustrations by Květoslav Hísek
Translated by Margot Schierlová

English edition first published 1987 by Octopus Books Limited
59 Grosvenor Street, London W1
© 1987 Artia, Prague

ISBN 0 7064 2985 0
Printed in Czechoslovakia by TSNP Martin
3/13/11/51 − 01

Contents

Introduction

Fish are numerically the largest group of vertebrates and account for roughly half of all vertebrate species. They live in fresh, brackish and salt water and are to be found in the depths of the oceans and high up in mountain lakes, from the polar regions to desert oases. The term 'fishes' is applied collectively here to two morphologically, anatomically and evolutionally different groups — the primitive cartilaginous fishes (Chondrichthyes) and the more advanced bony fishes (Actinopterygii). The much more primitive lampreys and hagfishes are actually in a separate class and are only included here since they live in water and have traditionally been classed together with the fishes.

About 60% of the total number of roughly 20,000 fish species live in salt water; the other 40% live in fresh water. Only a few species, like salmon, sturgeons and eels, are able to move freely between fresh and salt water. Over 75% of marine species live in the coastal waters of the sea over the continental shelf, to a depth of 200 m; about one tenth are pelagic, living in open sea, and one twentieth live in deep water.

The number of species in fresh water increases nearer the equator, but it also depends on the size of the river basin or lake and on its geological past. In Europe, the largest number of species (63) is found in the Danube, which is the largest European river after the Volga. However unlike the Volga, the Danube was not affected by the ice ages. The number of species in big tropical rivers is even larger; for instance, in the Amazon there are about 1,000 and over 500 in the Congo. Similar trends can be observed in the seas; in the White Sea there are about 50 species of fishes, in the North Sea 170 and in the Red Sea 1,000.

In recent years catches of many marine species have declined from overfishing, while fresh water species have suffered from pollution by industrial, agricultural and other forms of waste with increasing frequency. However rivers are now being cleaned up and fish are returning to them; quotas on marine fishes are helping to prevent overfishing. Some species are being artificially raised in fish farms.

This book describes and illustrates 256 European freshwater and marine fishes. The species were chosen to include the majority of economically important and biologically interesting European fishes. The reader is thus given a comprehensive survey of this important group of animals together with basic information on the abundance and diversity of the species and distinguishing features to help identify the fishes described in this book.

Fig. 1. Morphology of a hypothetical fish, 1 — upper and lower jaws, 2 — nostril, 3 — eye, 4 — preoperculum, 5 — operculum, 6 — spines of dorsal fin, 7 — dorsal fin, 8 — soft fin rays, 9 — adipose fin, 10 — barbels, 11 — gill membrane, 12 — pectoral fin, 13 — ventral fin, 14 — anal orifice, 15 — spines of anal fin, 16 — anal fin, 17 — caudal or tail fin, 18 — perforated scales of lateral line.

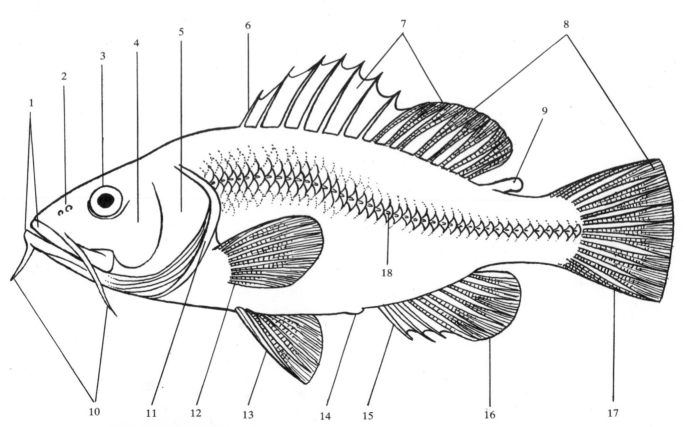

Morphology of a fish

A fish's body is divided into head, trunk and tail regions. In cartilaginous fishes the head is bounded by the posteriormost gill slit and in bony fishes by the posterior margin of the operculum. The trunk ends and the tail begins at the anal orifice. The head begins with the mouth, which may point forward (a terminal mouth), downward (a lower or inferior mouth) or upward (an upper or superior mouth).

The paired nostrils lead to a blind-ended olfactory organ, except in lampreys, in which the single nostril communicates with the branchial (gill) apparatus. The paired nostrils connect with the oral cavity in recent and extinct lungfishes and in some extinct crossopterygians. Fishes' eyes are lidless and their size depends partly on the animal's mode of life. On the head there are also the openings of the lateral line, a sense organ for detecting vibrations in the water, which in most fishes then continues down the middle of the sides to the tail.

The fins, the characteristic locomotive and stabilising organs of all fishes, include paired pectoral and ventral (pelvic) fins and unpaired dorsal and anal fins as well as the tail (caudal) fin. If the dorsal fin is very long as in the Burbot, Wolf-fish and Eel, it may be connected with the tail fin. There may be one or several dorsal fins; for example perches have two, cod have three and mackerel and tunny and a number of other species have a row of smaller fins (finlets), which probably have the function of reducing the resistance of the water close to the body.

The paired pectoral and ventral fins are homologous to the limbs of other vertebrates and are used for manoeuvring in the water. In bony fishes the pectoral fins are attached to the skull via the pectoral girdle, while in cartilaginous fishes they are anchored in the musculature by independent supporting cartilaginous elements. In most fishes the ventral fins are anchored loosely in the musculature. In some groups of fishes (for example in a number of Clupeiformes and Cypriniformes), the ventral fins are found in the abdominal region, but in the Perciformes they have shifted forward to lie below the pectoral fins and in the Gadiformes they are actually in front of the pectoral fins. Eels, however, have no ventral fins at all.

Except for the adipose fin, a small fleshy protuberance on the back immediately in front of the tail of some fishes such as salmon, all fins are reinforced by rays of bone or cartilage. Some fins have been modified to form organs of copulation for internal fertilization, as in some sharks, while in other fishes, like the gobies, the ventral fins are modified to form suckers for attachment to rocks.

The tail begins behind the anus and usually terminates in a large caudal fin. The muscular part of the tail is known as the peduncle and, together with the caudal fin, it plays an important role in locomotion and manoeuvring. The shape of the peduncle and of the caudal fin are indicative of the speed and range of the movements of the various species. The best swimmers have slender peduncles and long-lobed caudal fins as seen in tunny and swordfish, while poor swimmers have relatively short, thick peduncles and small caudal fins as in gobies. The tail also carries an unpaired anal fin, which in viviparous (those in which the young develop inside the female) fishes may be converted to a copulatory organ.

In higher bony fishes the vertebral column does not extend into the caudal fin and the lobes of the tail are more or less symmetrical, giving rise to a homocerc-

Fig. 2. Types of caudal fins. A — lamprey, B — the heterocercous fin of a shark, C — the diphycercous fin of a lungfish, D — the homocercous fin of a carp 1 — notochord, 2 — neural spines of vertebrae (in lampreys these are rod-like cartilaginous structures), 3 — haemal spines of the vertebrae, 4 — vertebra, 5 — rays of fin border of lampreys, ceratotrichia of sharks and lepidotrichia of bony fishes, 6 — urostyle.

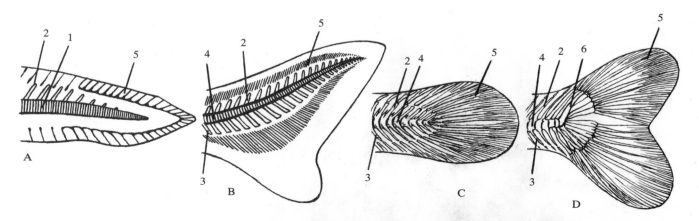

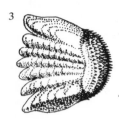

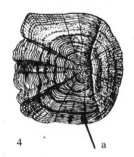

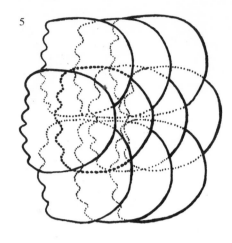

Fig. 3. Types of scales in fishes. 1 — the placoid scale of a shark, 2 — the ganoid scale of a garfish, 3 — the ctenoid scale of perch, 4 — the cycloid scale of crucian carp; a — the boundary between close and distant sclerites (the annulus), 5 — overlapping scales in a Crucian Carp.

ous tail, but in cartilaginous fishes and in sturgeon for instance, it continues into the upper lobe of the caudal fin, giving rise to an asymmetrical, 'heterocercous' tail (Fig. 2).

The skin of a fish is composed of two main layers — an outer epidermis and an underlying dermis. As well as protecting the body, the skin has respiratory, secretory and osmoregulatory functions. The secretion of the numerous mucous glands gives the body a characteristic slimy texture, designed to reduce the frictional resistance of the water.

In most fishes, the body is covered with scales which provide effective protection against injury. In the course of time, different types of scales have evolved. The placoid scales of sharks and of related species of the cartilaginous fishes are in fact cutaneous teeth covered with enamel and filled with dentine, while the rows of sharp teeth in the shark's mouth are actually enlarged placoid scales.

The oldest type of bony fish scales are ganoid scales and the modified ganoid scales, cosmoid scales, which resemble placoid scales. Bichirs (Polypterus), sturgeons and bowfins have ganoid scales, in which the uppermost layer is covered with ganoin, which gives them a shiny appearance; it is of the same origin as dentine. The thinner, oval scales of higher bony fishes (Teleostei) are not covered with enamel or dentine like the preceding types. If they are smooth, they are described as cycloid; if they are rough with spiny denticles on their protruding hind margin, they are called ctenoid. Carp and related species have cycloid scales for example, while perciform fishes have ctenoid scales.

Fish live permanently in water, an environment almost 800 times denser than air. Their bodies are therefore shaped to meet this resistance. If the maximum height of the body of a fish were more than one third of its length, the resistance presented by the water would be too great for it. Motion in water is also influenced by friction of the surface of the body against the water layer, however. Friction is directly proportional to body surface area and increases with body length.

The fusiform body is ideal for the fastest swimmers frequenting the open sea, pelagic species like the tunny, salmon, mackerel, sharks and mullet. Long distance swimmers, less swift than salmon and tunny, have long bodies, like eels, needle fishes and their allies (Beloniformes) and the Sea Burbot and sharks like *Chlamydoselachus anguineus*. Fishes that live on the bottom have flattened bodies, either flat-sided like freshwater bream *(Abramis)* and sea bream of the family Sparidae, or dorso-ventrally flattened like rays, angler-fish, scorpion-fish and bull-heads. Flat-fishes have flat-sided bodies, but since they lie on their sides they appear at first glance also to be dorsoventrally flattened. Other fishes cannot be categorized as to their mode of life by their body form, for example some puffers (globe fishes of the order Tetraodontiformes) have almost spherical bodies, whereas the giant Sun Fish *(Mola mola)* has a discoid form.

Fishes' movements

Some fishes swim with undulating movements of the entire body like eels, but most swim only by using the caudal peduncle. Some species like rays, puffers and some pipefishes use undulating movements of their unpaired fins as they swim. The members of the families Labridae and Pomacentridae and the Mud Minnow swim by producing alternate, skulling move-

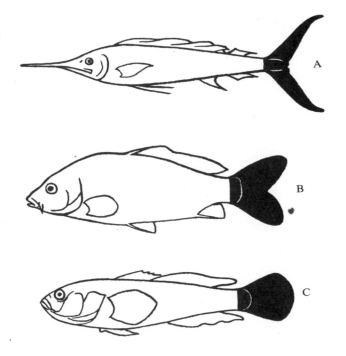

Fig. 4. Shape of the caudal fin of: A — a good swimmer *(Xiphias)*, B — a moderately good swimmer *(Cyprinus)*, and C — a poor swimmer *(Gobius)*.

Fishes' colouring

Fish attract attention by their colouring as well as by their interesting shapes, but they are not always as strikingly coloured as they appear to be in pictures or photographs in journals and books. In general, their colouring tends to be inconspicuous rather than otherwise. Fish living near the surface of the water, usually pelagic species, have dark backs and light bellies. This makes them more difficult to see both from above and below. Bottom-dwelling fishes (benthic species) have similar colouration, except that their light-coloured bellies may be almost completely unpigmented, for they have no role to play in camouflage. Many bottom-dwelling fishes have spotted bodies or can change colour to match the bottom and when they keep still these fishes are almost perfectly camouflaged.

The diversity of colouration in fishes is due to the presence of pigments in the skin or to physical reflection or refraction of light. Pigments occur in special cells (chromocytes) localized mainly, but not solely, in the surface layer of the skin. Movement of the pigment particles in the chromocytes causes changes in the intensity and type of colouration. Various kinds of chromocytes contain different pigments — erythrocytes contain light red pigments, xanthocytes contain yellow pigments and melanocytes contain dark red, brown and black pigments. Fish acquire the first two kinds of pigments in their food and melanin is a waste product of protein decomposition. Guanin crystals (guanin is another waste product of protein metabolism) occur in special cells called iridocytes. The crystals act like a mirror, reflecting the light and sending it back into the surroundings, making the fish appear silvery. All the known colours of fishes come from a combination of the basic pigments and the reflection and refraction

ments of their pectoral fins. The South American freshwater fishes of the family Gasteropelecidae are able to leave the water, actively 'flying' by 'flapping' their pectoral fins. By contrast, the 'flight' of the marine flying fishes of the families Exocoetidae and Hemirhamphidae is simply passive gliding; in these fishes the pectoral fins assume the role of a glider's wings, since they measure as much as 80% of the body length of the fish. These species are capable of gliding up to 400 metres and over, depending on the strength of the wind.

The smoothness and shape of the body both help to reduce the resistance of the water to movement. The shape of the caudal fin also plays an important role in the flow of water round the body. In the best swimmers the lobes of this fin project beyond the zone of turbulent vortex which is formed behind the maximum diameter of the body (the backwash) and can thus control direction. Thus the best swimmers, like tunny and mackerel, which can swim fast and for long distances, have very deep tails.

The maximum rate at which a fish can swim (though only for a short time) ranges from 1 m.sec^{-1} in *Gobius batrachocephalus* to 3 m.sec^{-1} in the Pike-perch *(Stizostedion lucioperca)*, 12 m.sec^{-1} in the Barracuda *(Sphyraena barracuda)* and 20 m.sec^{-1}, i.e. 70 km.h^{-1}, in the swordfish *Xiphias gladius*. The normal rate of swimming of these species during migration, for example, is much lower however.

Fig. 5. How fish change colour. A — the black pigment is concentrated in the centre of the cells and the coloured pigment (the dotted area) is dispersed — the fish is pale. B — the coloured pigment is concentrated in the centre of the cells and the dark pigment is dispersed, so that the fish becomes darker.

of light. The metallic sheen of many fish originates from the presence of iridocytes lying below chromocytes in the skin.

Most kinds of colouring can be regarded as a compromise between the need for communication with members of the same species and the need to be as invisible as possible to predators. Instantaneous changes in colouration are regulated by nerves and hormones and are triggered by the eyes. The colour of a fish changes during the reproductive period, during the care of the young, during migration and if it is in danger. It also changes during growth, with the season and in connection with environmental changes, mood and physiological condition. Young individuals generally have different colours to adults usually because they live in different environments. The most striking colour changes occur during the breeding season, when many of the males are gaily coloured. Some species like flatfishes, scorpion fishes and bull-heads can react quickly to a change in the colour of the background. For instance, if an experimental flatfish is moved from one background to another it will quickly take on the colouring of the new one. Other species also change colour to match their environment. A pike or perch lurking in clumps of aquatic plants is much more noticeably cross-striped than one in open water.

The 'poster' colouring (striking colours with sharp divisions between them) of some species living in coral reefs, like the butterfly and angel fishes of the family Chaetodontidae, is found often in territorial species, which announce by their striking presence that that particular spot is already taken. In other butterfly and angel fishes the colouring is primarily for camouflage, since they live among clumps of brightly coloured corals. In some venomous fishes and mimics, such colours are warning colouration.

The skeleton

The skeleton of a fish consists of the vertebral column, forming the axis of the body, the skull and the framework of the fins. In lampreys and hagfishes there is no vertebral column as such, only the notochord, a rod-like, flexible structure without either cartilage or bony tissue; there are no vertebrae, but only small, peg-like cartilaginous structures visible over the notochord protecting the spinal cord. In fishes with cartilage skeletons, the notochord is enclosed in cartilaginous vertebrae. Running through the dorsal part of the vertebrae there is a canal for the spinal cord, while in the body cavity area of the fish are attachments for the ribs on the ventral sides of the vertebrae. On the undersides of the caudal vertebrae is a canal containing the caudal artery and vein. Most bony fishes (except sturgeon, for example) have similarly organized, but bony vertebrae.

Hagfishes and lampreys have very primitive, cartilaginous skulls composed of a rudimentary neurocranium consisting largely of sensory capsules protecting the organs of smell, vision, and balance. Lampreys and hagfishes however, have no jaws, only funnel-shaped suctorial mouths.

Sharks, rays and chimaeras have cartilaginous skulls, which in some species are so encrusted with calcium salts that they resemble bone. In both groups the neurocranium protects both the brain and the

Fig. 6. Skeleton of a carp. 1 — skull, 2 — the fused first vertebrae (the Weberian ossicles), 3 — the vertebral column, 4 — the supporting elements (pterygiophores) of the dorsal fin, 5 — the toothed third spine of the dorsal fin, 6 — the neural spines, 7 — haemal spines of the vertebrae, 8 — the ribs, 9 — the bones of the ventral fins, 10 — the bones of the pectoral fins connected to the pectoral girdle and skull, 11 — the operculum.

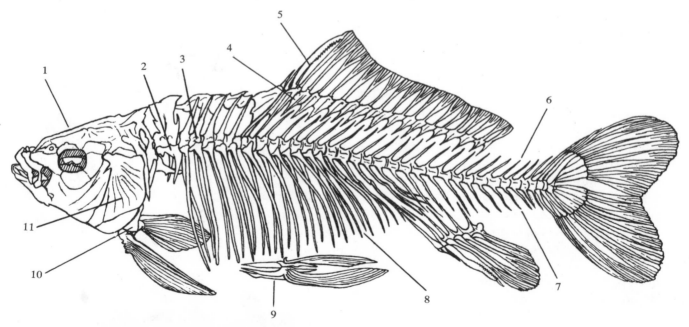

sensory organs. The skeleton surrounding the mouth and gills consists of upper and lower jaws and a support for the five or more independent branchial arches. Sturgeons have similar cartilaginous skulls, but this is believed to be a secondary phenomenon as they are thought to have had bony fish ancestors. True bone first appears in the bony fishes of the class Actinopterygii. These fishes have basically similar skulls to those of sharks, except that they are formed of separate bony plates to allow for growth and an operculum covers the gills.

The skeleton of the unpaired fins is formed of cartilaginous rays in cartilaginous fishes and of bony rays in bony fishes. In bony fishes the pectoral fins are joined to the skull via a girdle, in cartilaginous fishes to the skeleton of the gill apparatus. In both groups the ventral fins are anchored separately in the musculature, although in some fishes like the cod, where the ventral fins are attached anteriorly to the pectoral fins, they are attached to the skull.

The muscles

The arrangement of the musculature in a fish can be seen best when the fish is cooked. In lampreys and hagfishes the muscle segments are shaped like a figure 3, while in true fishes they are W-shaped, with the points of the W pointing towards the tail. The musculature may contain a quantity of tiny, thin and often forked bones unattached to the skeleton; they are only found in fishes and are formed as a result of ossification (bone formation) in the connective tissue between muscle fibres.

Muscle differentiation is greatest on the head. The eyes have six separate muscles as in all the verte-brates, for the control of eye movement and separate muscles control movement in the gill apparatus and the jaws; the fins also have their own special muscles. Movement of the body is controlled by the trunk muscles which are found in the dorsal part of the body. They are divided by connective tissue into two parts — the upper (epaxial) and the lower (hypaxial) musculature. These trunk muscles are all striped skeletal muscles which are controlled voluntarily by the brain together with the nerves to co-ordinate the movement of swimming.

In a cooked fish it can be seen that part of the skeletal musculature is dark red and part is pinkish or white. The dark red muscle is concentrated just below the skin, roughly down the flank of the body along the horizontal septum and in the peduncle. This is known as the *musculus superficialis* and it can be seen as a clear band running along the side if the fish is skinned. The contractility of its fibres is different from that of the other muscles; its colour is due to its high content of haemoglobin and myoglobin. Red

muscle can work for a long time without becoming fatigued. Consequently, species which travel long distances like tunny, mackerel and swordfish have a larger proportion of red muscles.

The lighter coloured muscles have poorer blood and oxygen supplies and are soon fatigued, but are capable of short bursts of intense activity. If they are overstressed however, they develop an 'oxygen debt' and the lactic acid concentration in the muscles rises; only when the lactic acid has been broken down and reconverted to glucose are the muscles again capable of further activity. In comparatively inactive fishes, the 'white' muscles predominate and the proportion of 'red' muscle is minimal.

Respiration

The release of chemical energy contained in food requires oxygen which fish obtain from the water by means of gills.

Lampreys have seven pairs of gill sacs, each with two openings. Through the outer openings the gill sacs are in contact with the water, while the inner openings lead into a common respiratory tube. When the lamprey is swimming it takes in water through its mouth, the water proceeds along the respiratory canals, over the gill sacs and out through the external openings. If the lamprey is attached to a host however, fresh oxygenated water is taken in through the external openings and after passing through the gill sacs is expelled by the same route.

The gills of cartilaginous fishes open into the water via five, or occasionally more, transverse slits present on the sides of the anterior part of the body in most

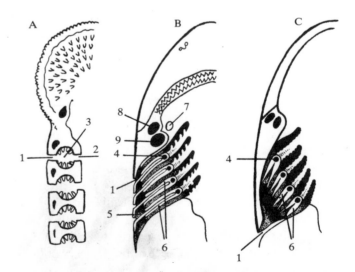

Fig. 7. Scheme of left half of gills of: A — a lamprey, B — a shark, C — a bony fish. 1 — outer gill aperture, 2 — inner gill aperture, 3 — gill sacs, 4 — the gill arches in cross section, 5 — gill septa, 6 — gill lamellae, 7 — spiracle, 8 — mandibu-lar arch in cross section, 9 — hyoid arch.

fish. In some the openings are on the under surface, as in rays. The gill slits are supported by cartilaginous gill arches. In recent elasmobranchs (sharks, rays and skates) there is a small opening visible behind the eye between the first and second gill slits; this is known as the spiracle and, in some rays, water is drawn in through it into the mouth and gills. On each side of each gill arch there is a gill — a richly branched structure well supplied with blood vessels which absorb oxygen from the water and release carbon dioxide. They also play a role in regulating the water and salt content of the body (osmoregulation).

Bony fishes have similar gills, but the gill arches are greatly reduced, so that the two half-gills are not separated from each other. Instead of several gill slits opening onto the side of the fish, there is only one opening at the back of the skull and this is protected by a bony flap called the gill-cover or operculum. In respiration, water is drawn into the mouth while the opercula remain closed. From the mouth the water flows round the branchial lamellae during which time oxygen is absorbed and carbon dioxide released. The mouth is then closed and the water flows out through the opened opercula. Particularly efficient swimmers like tunny and mackerel keep their mouths open all the time however, and a constant stream of water passes over the gills.

Some freshwater fishes can survive in conditions of oxygen deficiency by means of accessory organs of respiration. Such organs are particularly common in fish embryos, which often develop in conditions where the amount of oxygen is very variable, during the day and night for instance, or where there is altogether little oxygen. In embryos, the blood vessels of the yolk sac and of the fin border act as auxiliary organs of respiration. In some species, like lungfishes and the Weatherfish, respiration in the embryos is supplemented by the development of external filamentous 'gills'.

Some fishes are able to breathe air. Eels, for instance, can breathe through their skins and they can migrate at night, across damp grass, from one river to another. The Weatherfish can swallow air and absorb the oxygen from its intestine, which is richly supplied with blood capillaries. Lungfishes breathe by means of their swim-bladders, which have been converted to simple lungs. The freshwater fishes of the suborder Anabantoidei, which includes a number of species kept in aquaria, such as the paradise fishes, the fighting fishes and others, breathe with a supra-branchial organ termed the labyrinth. This is a collection of finger-like projections within a special cavity in the roof of the gill chamber. The cavity of the labyrinth is richly supplied with blood capillaries, so that gaseous exchange (i.e. oxygen uptake and carbon dioxide output) can take place in it.

The swim-bladder

The swim-bladder is found only in bony fishes. It originates as an evagination of the alimentary tube, to which in some species (e.g. in the orders Clupeiformes and Cypriniformes), it remains permanently connected. In other orders (e.g. Perciformes), the connection between the swim-bladder and the alimentary tube is lost during development. The swim-bladder is primarily a flotation device. The specific gravity of a fish's tissues is greater than the specific gravity of water and the swim-bladder enables the fish to float in the water without any unnecessary expenditure of energy, by reducing its specific gravity. Fishes without swim-bladders, like the cartilaginous fishes, sturgeons and some bony fishes, achieve buoyancy by deposition of oil in the body. In marine fishes the swim-bladder accounts for 4—6% of body size and in freshwater species for 7—14%. Sea water has a higher specific gravity than fresh water, closer to that of the fish, therefore marine species only need to have relatively small swim-bladders.

The shape of the swim-bladder varies. In salmonoids it has one chamber and in cyprinoids (carp) it has two, while in some species like bull-heads it is absent altogether. In cyprinoid fishes the front of the swim-bladder is connected to the ears by means of special small bones, the Weberian ossicles, which enable the fish to perceive changes in atmospheric and hydrostatic pressure. Cyprinoid fishes perceive sounds better over a wider range of wavelengths than other fishes, because their swim-bladders act as sound wave amplifiers. In some species, (like the drum fishes) the swim-bladder also acts as a resonator of emitted sounds. In gars, bowfins, the Tarpon (*Megalops*) and others it has a respiratory function.

The circulatory system

Circulation of the blood is closely associated with respiration. The red blood cells and their pigment (haemoglobin) carry oxygen all over the body of the fish. The vast surface area of the red blood cells allows the oxygen contained in 25 litres of water to be bound to only one litre of blood. Haemoglobin itself is a complex organic substance consisting of a protein component and a nonprotein, unstable and readily oxidizable ferrous complex. The amount of oxygen carried depends on the number of red blood cells present, and the amount of iron in the blood. Fast swimmers like mackerel and tunny have the largest numbers of red blood cells, inactive fish like anglerfishes, some catfishes, bull-heads and the Toadfish, the smallest.

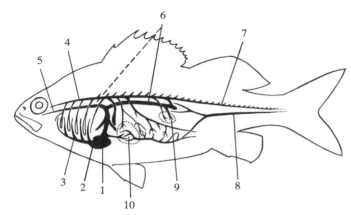

Fig. 8. Scheme of the circulatory system of a perch. 1 — atrium 2 — ventricle, 3 — ventral aorta, 4 — dorsal aorta, 5, 6 — anterior and posterior cardinal veins, 7 — caudal artery, 8 — caudal vein, 9 — renal portal system, 10 — hepatic portal system.

The blood circulates in a system of blood vessels and sinuses and in addition to oxygen and carbon dioxide it carries metabolic wastes, nutrients and hormones. The blood is kept moving by the heart, which in most fish (with the exception of the lungfishes) is filled only with de-oxygenated blood. It consists of one atrium (auricle) and one ventricle. With regular contractions the thick-walled ventricle drives the blood into the ventral aorta, which sends branches to the gills, where the blood absorbs oxygen. The oxygenated blood is then transported to the various organs. The greater part flows down the dorsal aorta from the head towards the tail, passing along branches of the aorta supplying the pectoral fins, the digestive organs, the reproductive organs, the kidneys, the muscles etc. The head is supplied with oxygenated blood by separate arteries called carotids. When it reaches the various organs, the blood releases its oxygen and passes into the veins. It is carried back to the heart via the two major veins, the precardinal vein from the head and the postcardinal vein from the rest of the body. These join to form right and left sinuses known as the ducts of Cuvier before reaching the heart. Venous blood is transported to the liver by the hepatic vein and from the liver by the portal vein. Finally, all the de-oxygenated blood reaches the atrium and passes into the ventricle, completing the circulation of the blood.

Digestion

The mouth leads into the oral cavity where there are only mucous glands, as fish do not possess salivary glands. The tongue is poorly developed in bony fishes, but well developed in lampreys and hagfishes. The oral cavity opens into the throat, the sides of which are perforated by the gill arches, and continues into the highly dilatable gullet or oesophagus. The gullet contains scattered cells which secrete a slimy mucus facilitating the passage of food into the stomach. Some groups, like cyprinoids for instance, do not have a morphologically distinguishable stomach and their gullet continues straight into the intestine and the food is digested there.

The stomach secretes hydrochloric acid to provide a pH of 2—3, the condition in which the digestive enzyme of the stomach, pepsin, works best. Food passes from the stomach into the intestines. The intestines of salmonoid and gadoid fishes have a quantity of diverticula (blind-ended processes) which increase the digestive area. The acid from the stomach is neutralized by bile from the liver. Proteins are digested in the intestine by means of the enzyme trypsin; other enzymes, lipases and carboxylases, help with the digestion of fats and sugars. These enzymes are secreted by the pancreas, which is also an endocrine gland producing the insulin necessary for maintenance of the blood sugar level.

The liver is an important organ. It produces bile, which neutralises the acid of the food coming from the stomach. Digested food is absorbed through the intestine wall and carried in the blood to the liver which acts as a 'clearing house'. Glycogen (animal starch converted from blood sugars), fat, vitamins A and D are all stored in the liver.

Flesh-eating species usually have a short intestines and herbivorous species long intestines, as plant foods are digested more slowly.

Fig. 9. The digestive systems of: A — a herbivorous fish with a long intestine, B — a carnivorous fish. 1 — oesophagus, 2 — stomach, 3 — intestine, 4 bile duct, 5 — anal orifice.

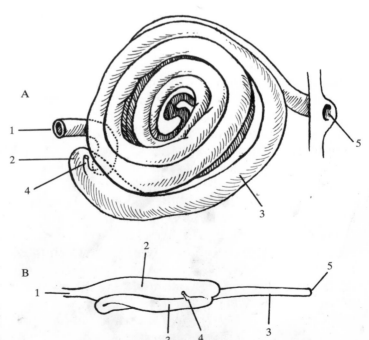

Excretion

Carbon dioxide and water are waste products formed during cell respiration when sugars are broken down to provide energy. During protein metabolism waste products are formed, mainly nitrogen compounds. In bony fishes the nitrogenous wastes are mostly ammonia (NH_3), whose molecules are so small that they can leave the body via the surface of the gills. Bony fishes consequently excrete most of their nitrogenous waste in this manner (5−10 times more than is excreted via the kidneys).

Cartilaginous fishes excrete urea via the kidneys instead of ammonia. However, they retain some urea in their bodies, increasing the concentration of salts in their own body fluids (their osmotic pressure) in relation to the sea-water.

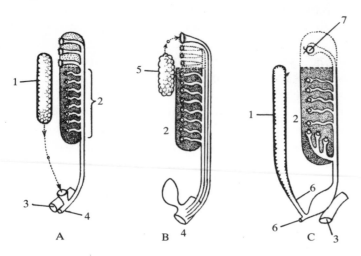

Fig. 10. Urogenital system of: A − a lamprey, B − a female shark, C − a bony fish. 1 − gonad, 2 − primitive kidneys, 3 − anal orifice, 4 − urogenital duct, 5 − ovary, 6 − secondary genital duct of bony fishes, 7 − tubule.

The kidneys are found in the upper part of the body cavity, one alongside each side of the vertebral column. They are elongate and dark red in colour. The kidneys consist of many tubules which extract the waste from the supply of blood.

Lamprey larvae have very primitive kidneys whose tubules open directly into the body cavity. After metamorphosis of the larva these kidneys disappear and are replaced by the more usual kidneys in which a tuft of blood capillaries (a glomerulus) is situated at the end of each tubule − the units from which the kidneys are formed. All true fish possess these more efficient kidneys. Urine (waste products like urea and ammonia in water) passes down the ureters and straight out of the body via the cloaca; only a few freshwater fishes possess a urinary bladder.

Osmoregulation

Fishes must maintain a stable salt concentration (osmotic pressure) in their bodies. Fishes living in salt water tend to dehydrate, since their body fluids are more dilute than sea water, while fishes living in fresh water must excrete the water which tends to be absorbed into their bodies through the gills. The process by which fishes maintain such internal stability is known as osmoregulation. Hagfishes have survived through the ages without any osmoregulation. They live permanently in sea water and their body fluids have the same osmotic pressure as the water outside.

Cartilaginous fishes (sharks, rays, chimaeras) have a very distinctive way of maintaining osmotic pressure. Since the salt concentration in their body fluids is only about one third of the salt concentration in sea water, these species would be constantly in danger of being dehydrated by the osmotically more active sea water. They therefore compensate for the salt deficiency in their body fluids by actively retaining urea, with the result that the osmotic pressure in their tissues is slightly higher than that of the surrounding water, so preventing dehydration.

Marine bony fishes make good the low osmotic pressure of their body fluids by drinking sea water all the time, retaining salts in their blood to maintain a stable osmotic balance with the sea water and actively excreting the large amount of excess salts into the outside water via their gills. The body fluids of freshwater fishes are more concentrated than the surrounding water, so they tend to absorb water through their gills; in order to get rid of the excess water which enters their body, they excrete large quantities of highly dilute urine through the kidneys (up to one third of their body weight daily).

The reproductive organs

The reproductive organs of the females are the ovaries, of the males the testes. The ovaries are generally paired glands situated in the body cavity below the kidneys and the swim-bladder (if present). Just prior to spawning they occupy a large portion of the body cavity and their weight may amount to over half the body weight of the female.

In cyclostomes the eggs are released from the ovaries into the body cavity and from there travel through the genital pore into the water. Cartilaginous fishes and most bony fishes have two oviducts, along which the eggs migrate from the ovaries into the uterus and then via the cloaca (the combined urinary/genital tract) into the water. In some bony fishes, like salmonoids, the oviducts are missing and the eggs find their way from the body cavity into the water in the same way as in cyclostomes. Most species, however, have at least short oviducts.

The testes, like the ovaries, are paired organs situated in the same part of the body as the ovaries, but their maximum weight is never more than one tenth of the male's body weight. The testes are generally creamy white, while the eggs in the ovaries are variously coloured, pink in salmonoids, black in sturgeon, for instance. The mature male germ cells or spermatozoa, familiar as milt or soft roe, are expelled from the bodies of most fishes through ducts (the *vasa deferentia*), but these ducts are missing in cyclostomes and salmonoids.

The sexes are separate in most fishes, but hermaphrodites (fish with attributes of both sexes) occur in the families Serranidae, Lutjanidae and Sparidae. Sometimes the ovaries and testes mature simultaneously, so that self-fertilization may occur; at other times they mature in succession, so that in these fishes self-fertilization is impossible. Fishes may function as females for the first part of their lives and as males later. In some viviparous fishes (e.g. the genus *Xiphophorus*), sex changes can actually be observed. It may happen that females which have already borne young are transformed to functional males. The mechanism of such changes has not been adequately investigated.

The nervous system

Concentration of the sensory organs in the anterior part of the body during the evolution of vertebrates profoundly influenced the formation of the brain, which eventually became the co-ordinating centre for all the metabolic activities. In terrestrial vertebrates the hemispheres of the forebrain have gradually taken over the central co-ordinating role, whereas in fishes the different parts of the brain are independ-ently connected with the sensory organs. The brain as a whole is enclosed in a cartilaginous or bony capsule, the neurocranium.

The forebrain co-ordinates responses to scent (the olfactory sense) and in fish with a well developed sense of smell, like sharks, it is very large. The first pair of cranial nerves, the olfactory nerves, arises from it. The forebrain also controls behaviour during spawning and the care of the eggs and offspring. The next part of the brain, the betweenbrain, is an important centre for the maintenance of the metabolic stability of the fish and is connected by way of the pituitary gland (the controlling endocrine gland) with the entire hormonal system. The paired second cranial nerves, the optic nerves, also arise from the betweenbrain and the retinas of the eyes develop from it in the larvae. The midbrain or mesencephalon is a relatively large part of the brain with two striking optic lobes. It registers and co-ordinates visual reactions to prey and movement. Fish which rely on vision have very large optic lobes. Another clearly distinguishable part of the brain is the cerebellum, which can be seen on the dorsal side of the brain, just behind the optic lobes. Its main function is to co-ordinate movement and spatial orientation. The last part of the brain is the *medulla oblongata*, from which the remaining cranial nerves (the third to the tenth) arise. It merges imperceptibly into the spinal cord, which is enclosed and protected by the vertebral column; the spinal nerves arise from the spinal cord and control a variety of involuntary movements. The sympathetic nervous system is also associated with the spinal cord. This controls the heart and viscera.

Endocrine glands

The nervous system and the endocrine glands together form what is known as the neurohumoral system, and between them they coordinate all the activities of the body. The endocrine glands secrete hormones directly into the blood and they are transported by the blood all over the body. Endocrine glands include the thyroid, whose hormones control development, and the adrenals, whose hormones participate in the regulation of metabolism and blood pressure and also in the development of the sexual glands (the gonads). The gonads themselves have an endocrine function, secreting hormones which regulate sexual behaviour, maternal care of the offspring and egg and sperm production. One of the most important endocrine glands is the pituitary, which is located at the base of the brain and produces a wide variety of hormones that, in part, co-ordinate the activities of the other endocrine glands.

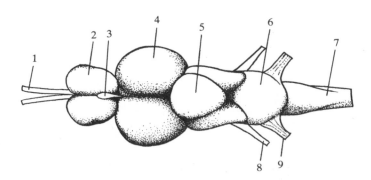

Fig. 11. View of the brain of a roach from above. 1 − olfactory (first cranial) nerve, 2 − forebrain, 3 − pineal gland, 4 − midbrain, 5 − cerebellum, 6 − medulla oblongata, 7 − spinal cord, 8 − facial (seventh cranial) nerve, 9 − vagus (tenth cranial nerve).

The senses

Fish have acute senses; these are very important for animals that live in three-dimensional environments, since they must be quick to react to predators or prey coming from above, from below or from any side. Chemicals dispersed in the water are perceived by smell (olfaction). The nostrils are found at the tip of the snout and lead to olfactory pits which are lined with sensory cells. These olfactory organs are extremely efficient and a fish will often be able to detect chemicals at concentrations of only a few molecules per litre of water.

Fishes' eyes are lidless, but occasionally, as in sharks, they may have a nictitating membrane. They focus by movement of the lens in the chamber of the eye and not (as in mammals, for instance) by a change in its shape. The eyeball is moved by three pairs of muscles. Most fish can see for only short distances (5–10 m), but they can perceive objects above, as well as in the water, within an angle of ±50 degrees from a line drawn at right angles to the middle of the body. The retina has a layer of rods and cones allowing the fish to perceive the colour of objects as well as their form. Colour vision has been demonstrated in some twenty species of fish.

Taste receptors are present in the epidermis inside the mouth and on the gill-rakers, and in some species on other parts of the body also. It has been demonstrated that many fishes have the same taste perception as mammals. Carp for example, have been shown to be capable of distinguishing all four basic tastes (sweet, sour, salty and bitter).

The ear is concerned with both hearing and the maintenance of equilibrium, including detection of turning speed, acceleration and deceleration. It is innervated by the eighth cranial nerve, which is known as the auditory nerve. The whole organ is located at the rear of the skull, in a cartilaginous or bony capsule. The inner ear consists of a labyrinth and three semicircular canals oriented at right angles to one another, leading from the labyrinth. The dilated ends of the canals (the ampullae) contain sensory cells and chalky granules (otoliths), whose movements on the sensory cells trigger nerve impulses. From the perception of these impulses the brain can co-ordinate balance. The hearing organ is a pouch in the inner ear known as the lagena, which corresponds to the cochlea in terrestrial vertebrates. The swim-bladder may also play a role in the reception of sounds by acting as an amplifier. The acoustic capacity of fishes ranges from 16 to

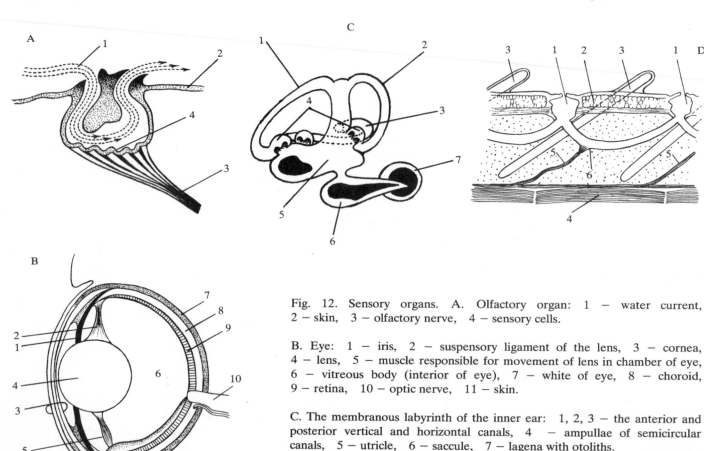

Fig. 12. Sensory organs. A. Olfactory organ: 1 — water current, 2 – skin, 3 – olfactory nerve, 4 – sensory cells.

B. Eye: 1 – iris, 2 – suspensory ligament of the lens, 3 – cornea, 4 – lens, 5 – muscle responsible for movement of lens in chamber of eye, 6 – vitreous body (interior of eye), 7 – white of eye, 8 – choroid, 9 – retina, 10 – optic nerve, 11 – skin.

C. The membranous labyrinth of the inner ear: 1, 2, 3 – the anterior and posterior vertical and horizontal canals, 4 – ampullae of semicircular canals, 5 – utricle, 6 – saccule, 7 – lagena with otoliths.

D. Section of skin in lateral line region and a lateral line scale with a pore in it: 1 – a lateral line opening in skin, 2 – skin, 3 – scales, 4 – musculature, 5 – nerve, 6 – sensory cells.

5,600 Hz. Some fishes are also able to make sounds, by the Weberian bones being rubbed together or by the activity of thin muscles and the vibrations are amplified by the swim-bladder. During the Second World War the sounds made by shoals of fish were sometimes mistaken for the engine of submarines.

The lateral line, which is innervated by one of the branches of the tenth cranial nerve (the vagus), is an important organ for detecting water vibrations found only in fishes. It runs roughly down the middle of each side and on the head it branches into a more or less complicated system of canals. In bony fishes the scales of the lateral line have openings through which the vibrations of the water are communicated to sensory cells located in a special canal below them. The lateral line organ gives the fish information about movements of predators or prey or about possible obstacles in its path.

The evolution of fishes

The oldest known vertebrates are the jawless fishes, the Agnatha, whose remains date back to the Ordovician period some 490 million years ago. These extinct species are today included in the class Ostracodermi. In the Silurian and at the beginning of the Devonian, roughly 435—395 million years ago, they could boast more species than any other group of vertebrates. They were bottom-dwellers and resembled recent fishes, but in some species the front of the body was covered with bony armour. The only agnathans to have survived to the present day are the lampreys (with about 40 species) and the hagfishes (with about 25 species).

The earliest known jawed fishes, included in the class Acanthodii, date back to the early Silurian and are thus about 430 million years old. They were small to moderately large freshwater and marine species and in the early Permian (about 260 million years ago) they gradually disappeared. Acanthodians had a similar neurocranium to placoderms (Placodermi), a large group of armoured fishes which lived at the same time.

Cartilaginous fishes (Chondrichthyes) are a very homogeneous group which today comprises about 650 species of sharks and rays and 24 species of chimaeras. They have well developed cartilaginous skeletons, teeth and paired fins. Internal fertilization is a typical feature of recent species. The first known remains of these fishes date back to the Middle Devonian and are thus some 360—380 million years old. Most fossils of these fishes come from marine rocks, whereas palaeontological finds of bony fishes come mainly from rocks formed from fresh water

deposits. Among recent cartilaginous fishes there are two quite clearly distinguishable evolutionary lineages — the sharks, rays and skates (the Elasmobranchia) and the chimaeras (Holocephali).

The largest group of fishes in the seas today are the bony fishes (Osteichthyes), whose earliest palaeontological remains date back to the Lower Devonian, when all the main groups of these fishes. lungfishes (Dipnoi), lobe-finned fishes (Crossopterygii), bichirs (Brachipterygii) and ray-finned fishes (Actinopterygii) appeared practically simultaneously.

Lungfishes, which live in fresh water, made their first appearance in the Lower Devonian and were found all over the world. Today there are only six species, living in the tropical and subtropical parts of Australia, Africa and South America. The best known species is the Australian Lungfish (Neoceratodus forsteri). The swim-bladder, which was formed for the first time in bony fishes, has been converted in lungfishes to a peculiar, but nevertheless functioning lung with its own blood supply from the heart, as in terrestrial vertebrates.

Crossopterygians were important freshwater predators in the Devonian period. The first dry land vertebrates — the ancestors of recent amphibians — evolved from one of their groups. These fish appeared during the Lower Devonian and all but died out in the Middle Carboniferous. Their only recent representative is the coelacanth, Latimeria chalumnae, discovered in 1938 off the coast of southeastern Africa. Individuals up to 180 cm long and weighing over 80 kg have been caught. Coelacanths are predators, feeding on other fish.

Actinopterygians appeared in the Middle Devonian and during the Carboniferous they steadily became more numerous, becoming the largest group

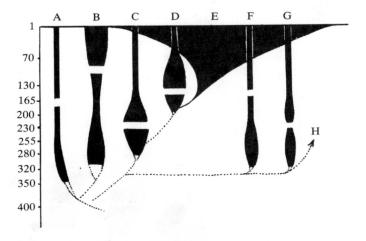

Fig. 13. Evolution of the jawless fishes and the true fishes (time scale in millions of years) A — Cyclostomata, B — Chondrichthyes, C — Chondrostei, D — Holostei, E — Teleostei, F — Dipnoi, G — Crossopterygii, H — trend of evolution to Amphibia.

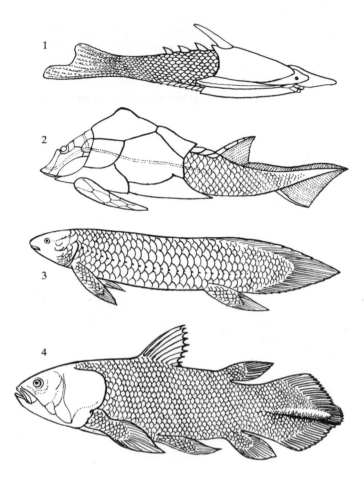

Fig. 14. Selected representatives of extinct jawless fishes (Ostracodermi — *Pteropsis rostrata* — 1) and jawed fishes (Placodermi, the genus *Remigolepis* — 2) and primitive living representatives of the bony fishes — the Australian Lungfish *Neoceratodus forsteri* (3) and *Latimeria chalumnae* (4).

of fishes, first of all in fresh water and later in the seas. They include the now extinct Palaeoniscidae, the sturgeons and paddle-fishes (Chondrostei), the gars and bowfins (Holostei) and the higher bony fishes (Teleostei). Bichirs (Brachiopterygii) are usually also ranked among the actinopterygians. Palaeoniscids appeared during the Devonian period to disappear in the Cretaceous. From the Triassic onwards they were replaced in the various strata by holosteans. Recent chondrosteans of the Acipensiformes include the sturgeons *(Acipenser)* and shovel-noses *(Pseudoscaphirhynchus),* with a total of about 25 mostly large species living in fresh and salt water in Europe, Asia and North America. Today the holosteans are represented by two orders — bowfins (Amiiformes) and gars (Lepidosteiformes) — whose ten freshwater species all occur in North America. Only eleven brachiopterygian species have survived down to recent times; they are the ten species of bichirs and one species of the genus *Calamoichthys,* all of which live in Africa.

The last and most important group of ray-finned fishes are the higher bony fishes (Teleostei), which appear to have evolved from holosteans and which made their first appearance in the Middle Triassic. One of their most distinctive characteristics is an outwardly symmetrical or homocercous tail. They have cycloid or ctenoid scales and bony vertebrae and their swim-bladders act primarily as hydrostatic organs. They are mostly small or moderately large (usually about 30 cm long), with very variably shaped bodies. The evolution of the various groups of fishes in relation to the geological periods is illustrated in Fig. 13; characteristic representatives of each group are given in Fig. 14.

When classifying fishes, scientists have various opinions with regard to the classification of the higher taxonomic units (classes, subclasses and superorders — see the Comparison of Classifications). Three simplified classifications have been given here as examples of the variation.

The systematics of fishes

Systematics (or taxonomy) is the biological science responsible for the classification of living organisms in a hierarchically organized system representing the evolutionary kinship of the various systematic groups. In classification use is made of morphological, anatomical, physiological and other characters to decide relationships. The basic systematic unit (taxon) is the species, which comprises individuals and groups of individuals (populations) incapable of fertile crossing with individual of other species under natural conditions. Other basic systematic categories (in ascending order) are the genus, the family, the order, the class and the phylum, which can be further subdivided into suborder, superorder, superfamily and so on.

Aristotle was the first to classify the animals known in his day, but the first generally acknowledged scientific classification of animals and plants was that of the eighteenth century Swedish naturalist, Carl Linnaeus. Linnaeus completed the work of a series of predecessors; for instance, he used the fish classification of his friend Peter Ardetti. The tenth edition of Linnaeus's system, entitled *Systema Naturae,* was the foundation stone of scientific nomenclature and is still largely valid today.

Linnaeus introduced and conscientiously adhered to the binomial system, in which every species was given two Latin or Greek names. The first, with a capital letter, is the generic name and the second, descriptive name, with a small initial letter, is the name of the species. In zoological publications this is followed by the name of the author (in full or

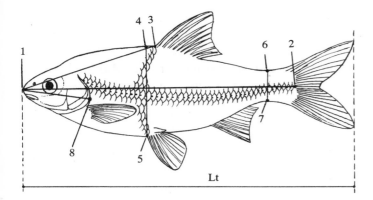

Fig. 15. Measurement of morphometric characters (body proportions): Lt − total body length, 1−2 length of body, 1−3 predorsal distance, 4−5 maximum height of body, 6−7 minimum height of body, 1−8 length of head; the scales in the lateral line and the rays in the fins are also indicated.

by exposure to an electric field when they move at different speeds. Closely related species possess very similar blood proteins.

In descriptions of individual species of fish, fin patterns are often given, spines in Roman numerals and soft, branching rays in Arabic numerals. As an example, the fin pattern of the Perch is as follows: D_1 XIII−XVII, D_2 I−II/13−16, A II/8−10. This indicates that in the dorsal fins (D_1 and D_2) there are spines, indicated by large Roman numerals and soft rays, indicated by Arabic numerals, while in the anal fin there are two spines and 8−10 soft rays. The number of rays in the pectoral fin (P) and the ventral fin (V) are sometimes given in the same way. Other features used in the identification of fishes are the number of scales in the lateral line and the number of gill-rakers on the first branchial arch; the Perch has 58−68 scales in its lateral line.

abbreviated) who described the species and the year in which the description was published. In the case of species subsequently placed in another genus, the author's name is given in brackets; for example, *Cyprinus rutilus* Linnaeus, 1758 was altered to *Rutilus rutilus* (Linnaeus, 1758).

The Latin or Greek names usually denote some morphological, anatomical or other peculiarity of the given species. For instance, the Greek generic name of the Nase *(Chondrostoma)* refers to the horny edges of the mouth *(chondros* means cartilage and *stoma* mouth); similarly, the Greek generic name of the plaice *(Pleuronectes)* means 'side-swimmer' and the Latin generic name of the Sole *(Solea)* means 'sandal'. Fishes' names may also include geographical terms, or local vernacular names may be adopted. For instance, the specific names of the east Asian salmon of the genus *Oncorhynchus* are actually the local native names of these fishes (nerka, tchawytcha, keta, etc). The names of distinguished ichthyologists also appear in the generic and specific names of fishes *(Novumbra hubbsi* was named after the American ichthyologist C. L. Hubbs and *Gobio kessleri* after the Russian ichthyologist K. T. Kessler).

When making a species description taxonomists utilize morphometric data (body proportions) and meristic characters, such as the number of scales in the lateral line, the number of vertebrae, the number of rays in the fins, etc. and relative proportions like head length, peduncle length, body height, etc. Anatomical peculiarities are more important in deciding the classification of higher taxons like families, orders and classes.

Nowadays the number and shape of the chromosomes are used in identifying fish species. Electrophoresis is another modern method used. In this technique blood proteins are separated from solution

Speciation

Every species is made up of individuals and groups of individuals (populations) living in a given area. Conditions in the area change during the course of time and the local species either become adapted to them and survive or else they do not become adapted and in time die out. Species which become adapted undergo progressive changes themselves and after a time (of the order of hundreds of thousands or millions of years) they may be quite different from their ancestors; the original species has gradually changed into another, more or less related species. In this scenario the number of species does not alter since the 'new' species is merely the transformed original species. The number of species may increase also. Populations of a particular species may consist of several varieties living in separate areas. These varieties may become permanently separated from the rest of the population, by the silting up of a lake, by changes in rivers or by the building of a dam, for instance. As a result the populations become isolated and if such isolation lasts a long time (say 10^4 to 10^6 years), isolated populations can eventually develop into separate species, which remain separate even if the cause of their original isolation is later removed. The Perch provide a good example of this, one population living today in Europe and Asia and another in the eastern parts of the U.S.A. and Canada. The originally unbroken area of distribution has split into two and the two populations are classified as separate species − *Perca fluviatilis* in Eurasia and *Perca flavescens* in North America, although not all experts recognize them as such.

Speciation can also occur as a result of ecological isolation. This occurs, for example when two or more species evolve from an original species in the same water, by living in different parts of the river or lake, by spawning in different places and at different time or by becoming isolated in other ways.

Behavioural isolation may also play a role in the formation of new species, as when different nuptial behaviour prevents mating between members of different races.

Zoogeography

The distribution of fish species is influenced by contemporary environmental conditions and by the geological and biological history of the Earth. For example, the coast of northwestern Europe is influenced by the warm Gulf Stream to such an extent that we find there warmth-loving species belonging to the families Exocoetidae, Labridae, Mugilidae, Sparidae and Mullidae.

The seas today cover 71% of the Earth's surface and contain over 98% of its water. In the ice ages however, a large amount of water was frozen in the form of ice sheets and the level of the oceans was lower than it is today. In Europe that meant that many river systems were connected (e.g. the Rhine with the Thames, the Danube with the Dnestr and the Don with the Dnepr) — a situation that facilitated the spread of many freshwater fishes.

The distribution of freshwater species is also influenced by altitude and latitude. For instance, in central Europe, at altitudes of 600–800 m and over, cold-loving species occur which are also found in northern Europe, like charr and whitefish.

As a rule, the land generally slopes down gently along the coastline into the sea, forming a continental shelf whose average width is 75 km, but which in places may be as much as 600 km. In the region of the continental shelf the sea is generally about 130 m deep, but it can be as much as 500 m in depth. The Dogger Bank in the North Sea is perhaps the most familiar of the European shallows, but the Baltic and the Barents Seas are also very shallow. At the edge of the continental shelf the ground drops away quickly into the depths. The ocean bed is broken both by deep valleys where the sea is deepest, and also by mid-oceanic mountain ranges.

The oceans can be divided both geographically by latitude and longitude and vertically, into depth zones. In this book the fishes described all come from the Boreal region, with its arctic, Atlanto-boreal, Atlanto-mediterranean and Sarmation subdivisions. Species differences in the fish populations of the various subregions are particularly marked in the shallow offshore coastal waters, where there are very pronounced temperature differences in the subregions.

The cold arctic subregion has the fewest species. There are about 130 species, most of them benthic or bottom-dwelling fishes. The most commonly represented families are Cyclopteridae, Cottidae, Gadidae, Anarhichadidae, Agonidae, Pleuronectidae, Osmeridae and Salmonidae. The economically most important species are *Arctogadus borealis* and *Boreogadus saida.*

The Atlanto-boreal and Atlanto-mediterranean subregions have the largest number of species, about 600 and 700 respectively, most of them common to both. The coastal waters of the atlanto-boreal subregion include the Barents, Norwegian and North Seas and the Baltic, while those of the atlanto-mediterranean subregion are the coastal waters of the Atlantic, from the English Channel in the north to the coast of northern Africa and the Mediterranean in the south.

The boundaries of the North Sea and the Baltic have changed several times, owing to repeated drops in their levels during the ice ages, at which time the North Sea was no more than an inlet of the Atlantic. The Baltic has changed several times, from a freshwater lake to a salt water sea, with resultant changes in the nature of its fauna. Today, the salinity of the western part of the Baltic is about 15 parts per mille, just under half the salinity of the oceans.

The fish fauna of the Mediterranean is very interesting. From the late Palaeozoic (250 million years ago) to the beginning of the Caenozoic (60 million years ago), the Mediterranean developed independently as a part of the spreading sea known as the Tethys, which stretched from southern Europe and northern Africa to Asia Minor and from there to Indonesia. The Mediterranean, the Black Sea and the Caspian Sea are all remnants of this sea. Today about 500 species of fish live in the Mediterranean. Some of them came from the Atlantic after the formation of the Straits of Gibraltar; others are original inhabitants, which have spread to the Atlantic (including members of the families Blenniidae, Gobiidae and Labridae; *Clupea pilchardus* and *Engraulis encrasicholus*). Boreo-Atlantic elements also occur in the Mediterranean (*Squalus acanthias, Raia clavata, Pagrus aurata, Pleuronectes flesus, Pleuronectes platessa, Pollachius virens, Trigla gurnardus, Scomber scomber*). In the ice ages *Salmo salar* and *Salmo trutta* lived in the Mediterranean and trout are still to be found in the streams of the Atlas Mountains in North Africa. Warmth-loving pelagic species, like *Thunnus thynnus, Xiphias gladius* and *Mugil cephalus* also frequent the Mediterranean, together with species from the Black Sea like *Acipenser stellatus* and *Huso huso*, which found their way there after the two seas were joined at the end of the Pleistocene some 15,000 years ago. In very recent times, about 14 species of fish have made their way from the Red Sea into the Mediterranean by way of the Suez Canal; this is known as Lessepsian migration, after Ferdinand Lesseps, the designer of the Suez Canal.

The recent fauna of the Black Sea, which belongs to the Sarmatian subregion, comprises about 140 species and is strongly influenced by the Mediterranean fauna. In the past the Black Sea area, like the Baltic, was a freshwater lake (the Sarmatian Lake) which reached its greatest extent in the Miocene, 20–25 million years ago, when it stretched from Austria to Lake Balkhash in central Asia. The salinity of the Black Sea today is 18 parts per mille and some of the original freshwater fishes have been driven into the northern, less salty bays of the Sea of Azov. In the Black Sea itself, only the surface layers of the water, down to 130–200 m deep, are inhabitable. There are about 30 endemic species there which do not occur anywhere else; most of these belong to the Gobiidae. Deeper in the sea there is such a high hydrogen sulphide concentration that life is impossible.

Zoogeographical subdivision of fresh water is substantially more complex than the subdivision of the seas. Freshwater fishes furnish very clear information on how the various river systems were once connected and how the recent freshwater faunistic complexes were formed.

Europe has 126 species of freshwater fishes, Canada — which is the same size — 177 species. If the whole of northern Asia is added to Europe the number of freshwater fishes in the whole area is 400. This is very little compared with North America, which is the same size but has over 700 species of freshwater fishes. The low number of freshwater species in Europe is associated primarily with the ice ages and also with the absence of big rivers. The only big European rivers are the Danube and the Volga, but the Danube was the only one unaffected by the ice ages and it became a refuge for the species fleeing from the advance of the ice-sheets. Today it contains more freshwater fishes (63 species) than any other European river. Further east, west and north, the number of species in European rivers decreases. The Dvina and Pechora in the North each have 30 species, the Elbe 40, the Thames 20 and the Volga 60.

Together with North Africa and northern Asia, Europe is in the Palaearctic biogeographic region. The region has many of the same species as the Nearctic region, which includes North America. The two are sometimes joined together as a single region, the Holarctic, and there are many species common to both, belonging to the families Thymallidae, Salmonidae, Umbridae, Esocidae and Percidae and to the genera *Petromyzon, Lampetra,* and *Cottus.*

The Palaearctic region can be divided into several subregions. In the Arctic Ocean subregion are included all the European and Asian rivers flowing north. About 80 species of fish live in this subregion in Europe and Asia and in the rivers of Europe salmon are common, together with other fishes like Bream, Bleak and Chub.

The rest of Europe belongs to the Mediterranean subregion, which is further subdivided into Baltic, Mediterranean and Pontine-Caspian-Aralian provinces. The Baltic province includes rivers flowing into the Baltic, the Bay of Biscay and the North Sea, the Mediterranean province rivers flowing into the Mediterranean, plus rivers of the Iberian Peninsula flowing into the Atlantic and the Pontine-Caspian-Aralian province rivers flowing into the Black Sea, the Caspian Sea and the Aral Sea.

Fifty-five species of fish live in the Baltic province. They include most of the species living in the Arctic Ocean subregion and warmth-loving species like the Barbel, the Silver Bream, the Zope, the Ziege and the Wels. In the Mediterranean province the total number of species is not very large and there are few salmonoid species present, mainly due to the shortness and isolation of the rivers. The genus *Chondrostoma* is represented by numerous species and fishes of the genera *Pachychilon* and *Aulopyge* only occur in this Baltic province.

The characteristic genera of the Pontine-Caspian-Aralian province are *Caspiomyzon, Clupeonella* and *Proterorhinus* amongst others and its most important rivers are the Danube and the Volga. The River Lamprey does not occur in the Danube, but the lamprey *Endontomyzon danfordi* is endemic there, like *Hucho hucho, Gymnocephalus schraetzeri, Zingel streber* and *Zingel zingel.* The Danube is sometimes classified as a separate zoogeographical province, together with the Rhine and the Rhone. The rivers of the southern European peninsulas like Italy and Spain are generally poor in freshwater species of fish: for example in the rivers of the Iberian Peninsula there are only 16 fish species present.

Ecological factors

Ecology is the science which deals with the relationships between organisms and their environment and with other organisms. The distribution and numbers of fish species are limited by the physical and chemical properties of the water, such as its salinity and temperature, the amount of oxygen dissolved in it, the pH, the amount of food and light. Complicated relationships develop between individuals of the same species competing with one another for food, shelter, a spawning site or a partner and inter-species relationships are no less complex. This leads to continual changes in the size of the various populations, which eventually result either in an increase in numbers of the species and in expansion of its distribution or a decrease in its range and possibly in its extinction.

Man influences fish populations directly by fishing and indirectly by destroying their spawning sites, by draining large stretches of wetland countryside and by changing the courses of rivers, etc. Agriculture and industry significantly affect the quality of water and thus influence the number of species and the size of their populations. Like other organisms, fish are to some extent capable of adaptation to changing conditions, but their capacity for adaptation is not unlimited. Dead fish floating on the surface of rivers and seas furnish increasingly eloquent evidence of widespread water pollution.

WATER

Water is 800 times denser than air and is consequently very buoyant; the largest animals live in water, for the water can support their weight. Whales often weigh over 100 tons — about 20 times more than the biggest terrestrial mammal, the elephant. The biggest Mesozoic dinosaurs also probably lived at least partially in water because of their tremendous weight (up to 30 tons).

Water is an excellent solvent. Sea water contains an average 33—38 parts per million of salts, chiefly sodium chloride ($NaCl$). Evaporation and ice formation increase the salinity of sea water; rain and the influx of fresh water from the rivers reduces it. With falling temperature, the density of sea water (with a salinity of 15 parts per million or more) increases down to a freezing point of −1.9 °C, whereas fresh water is densest at 4 °C. The fact that fresh water is at its densest above its freezing point of 0 °C is of great importance to freshwater organisms, because it enables them to survive the winter at the bottom of ponds, lakes and rivers, where the heaviest, non-freezing water with a relatively high temperature of 4 °C is concentrated.

Many vitally important salts are dissolved in water. Proteins (the main structural elements of living bodies) cannot be synthesized without nitrogen and phosphorus. Nitrogen is present in water as nitrates and nitrites or as ammonia; it is also present in an organic form (in amino acids). Phosphorus is important for the growth of plants and is present in water as phosphates or as dissolved organic phosphorus. Silicon and a number of trace elements present in very low concentrations are also important; they include iron, manganese and zinc, which are all important components of oxidation enzymes. Together with molybdenum, zinc, cobalt and copper, these trace elements are all essential for the regulation of the growth of plants.

TEMPERATURE

The average temperature of the surface layer of the ocean is about 17 °C; it varies from −1.9 °C (the freezing-point of sea water) to 26 °C in the tropics. At 50 degrees latitude the mean annual temperature of the water at the surface is about 5—6 °C. In fresh water the temperature varies from 0 °C to over 50 °C in some hot springs. Fresh water, especially if shallow, is far more subject to temperature fluctuation than sea water. Marine fishes in general are therefore less well adapted to temperature changes than freshwater species. Deep sea species in particular are very sensitive and often react to temperature changes of not more than a few tenths of a degree; these are known as stenothermic species.

Some fishes are adapted to survive even the extremes of temperature; for instance *Cyprinodon macularius* lives in warm springs in California, while *Dallia pectoralis,* a relative of the Pike living in Siberia and Alaska, can survive incarceration in ice for short periods of time.

Most fishes are adapted for life at a particular temperature range. They avoid temperatures of over 30—35 °C, since oxygen consumption rises quickly at these temperatures, but warm water contains less oxygen. In Europe carp grow fast only in months when the temperature of the water is over 15—20 °C and they also spawn at these temperatures. The time taken for development of the larvae also depends on the temperature of the water. For instance, Perch eggs hatch after four weeks at 10 °C, but the fry emerge after only six days at 20 °C.

OXYGEN AND CARBON DIOXIDE

Oxygen is a very important limiting factor in an aquatic environment. The amount present is regulated by exchange with the atmosphere, by the production of oxygen by green plants (chiefly diatoms and green algae) and by the breathing of animals, micro-organisms and plants. The amount of oxygen dissolved in the water is in inverse proportion to the temperature of the water and the concentration of salts dissolved in it. At 0 °C, one litre of fresh water contains 10.29 ml dissolved oxygen, but one litre of sea water only 8 ml. At 30 °C the amount of oxygen in fresh water falls to 5.6 ml and in sea water to 4.5 ml. Because of the size of the seas and oceans and the small amount of nutrients dissolved in them, sea water always contains sufficient dissolved oxygen. In fresh water however, the amount of dissolved oxygen varies considerably. Oxygen is used during the respiration of plants and animals and in the decomposition of their bodies after death. Ponds, lakes and rivers are relatively small compared to the sea and enormous quantities of nutrients from sewage and agriculture pour into them in thickly populated and farming areas. They often become clogged with algae and polluted and the oxygen levels may be very low. The decomposition of dead algae and other organic remains requires oxygen (about 1 g of oxygen for the decomposition of 1 g of organic material), so that oxygen rapidly becomes used up and the water stagnant and anaerobic. Many freshwater fishes are adapted for survival in oxygen-deficient water.

The division of rivers into fish zones is based on the oxygen requirements of various fishes. The mountain reaches of rivers and streams with a 10–130 parts of oxygen per mille gradient per km contain the largest amounts of oxygen. This is the trout zone and contains trout, bull-heads and stone loaches. Next comes the grayling zone, with a gradient of 5–20 parts of oxygen per mille, in which live grayling, chub, barbel, nase, gudgeon and riffle minnow. Fishes of the barbel zone, with a 2–15 parts of oxygen per mille gradient, include barbel, nase, vimba and chub, but also roach, dace, gudgeon, stone loach and other species. Lastly, in the bream zone, in the lower reaches of rivers with minimal oxygen are found bream, carp, tench, catfish, pike-perch, bleak, bitterling and ruffe, etc. The zones are not sharply demarcated however, and the amount of dissolved oxygen diminishes gradually from the trout zone, where the water is completely saturated with oxygen, to zero. In some parts of the lower reaches of rivers upper reach zones may be formed again, for example a trout zone may form at the foot of a dam, where the deeper layers of the outflowing water are cold and well oxygenated; such water provides a suitable environment for trout and other species normally only found in the trout zone.

In the course of the year, fresh water in rivers is thoroughly mixed and convection currents ensure mixing of water in ponds and shallow lakes; even in deep lakes the water is mixed in spring and autumn by wind and convection currents when the thermocline breaks down. Sea water is mixed similarly. In the polar regions cold water rich in oxygen sinks from the surface to the deeper layers and slowly flows towards the Equator. It has been estimated that the water at the bottom of the Atlantic last saw the light of day some 500 years ago and water at the bottom of the Pacific 1,000 years ago. The water at the bottom of some landlocked seas like the Black Sea never rises to the surface however, and is therefore anaerobic.

Carbon dioxide (CO_2) is another vitally important gas. Green plants use sunlight to produce sugars from carbon dioxide and water by photosynthesis, a process essential to the life of all organisms because it is the only way in which solar energy can be utilised by living organisms. Carbon dioxide finds its way into water in rain as a waste product of the respiration of animals, plants and micro-organisms.

THE ACIDITY (pH) OF THE WATER

The acidity of both sea and fresh water (i.e. its pH or hydrogen ion concentration) is influenced by reactions between carbon dioxide, carbonates and hydrogen carbonates. Present-day lakes and rivers are in danger of acidification through the action of acid rain, formed as a result of an increase in the atmospheric sulphur dioxide concentration and its reaction with rainwater, producing sulphurous and sulphuric acids. This has led to increased acidity of the lakes of North America and Europe and of other regions where coal with a high sulphur content is burnt. In such waters the acidity may fall as low as pH 3–4, at which point it becomes uninhabitable for fish. In the sea the pH is not at present a limiting factor for marine organisms, since the high salt concentration and the tremendous volume of water mitigate the harmful effects of acid rain pollution (the pH of sea water ranges within the limits of 8.1 to 8.3).

LIGHT

Solar energy is essential for all organisms. Green plants trap it during photosynthesis, transform it to chemical energy and in this form 'pass it on' to animals. In water however, the intensity of light diminishes very quickly with increasing depth, so that photosynthesis is possible only in the uppermost layers of the sea (down to 100–200 m). Fishes can live at much greater depths, but they are naturally inevitably dependent for their food on production at a higher level, in the 'euphotic' layer of the water. In fresh water the maximum depth of the euphotic layer is only 40 m, but if the water has become polluted or if it is too rich in nutrients, this layer may be as little as 20 cm in depth.

Variation in the amount of light during the course of the year influences the sexual cycles of fishes and also affects migration and shoal formation. Some fishes are more active by day and rest at night, others are nocturnal in their habits. Some fishes swim towards light, a fact utilized in both deep sea and freshwater fishing; herring, sprats, sardines and mackerel are all lured to light and caught in this manner. Bottom dwelling species however, especially those living at considerable depths like sturgeons or rays, hardly react to light at all and many deep sea species avoid it altogether.

Deep in the sea there are a number of species of fishes which themselves emit light (at 300 m 45% have luminiferous organs known as photophores) and fishes can detect light as far down as 700 m. Those which live at such depths have strikingly large eyes occupying up to one third of the surface of their head. At greater depths however, the eyes tend to be smaller and at depths of over 1,500 m, where the darkness is absolute, many organisms are sightless.

WATER POLLUTION

The amount of water produced daily by a city with a million inhabitants is only a little less than half a million tons and represents a river with a flow rate of about 5 cubic metres a second. A moderately large pulp mill or canning factory produces the same amount. Industrial concerns often produce toxic wastes containing salts of heavy metals, copper, lead, nickel, cadmium, mercury and others, all harmful to fish and other organisms in concentrations of only a few thousandths of one milligramme to one milligramme per litre of water. A milligramme is one millionth part of a kilogramme, i.e. 10^{-6} kg. In food chains heavy metals accumulate progressively in algae, crustaceans and fishes which may then be eaten by people. In 1956 over 40 Japanese died because their food consisted largely of fishes caught near the waste outlet of an acetaldehyde factory where mercury was employed as catalyst.

With every successive link in the food chain, the damaging concentration of heavy metals or pesticides is roughly decupled. For instance, if DDT is present in phytoplankton in a concentration of 10^{-9}, in zooplankton its concentration is 10^{-8}, in the Sprat 10^{-7} and in the Mackerel 10^{-6}.

Large scale agricultural production primarily enriches fresh water with nitrogen compounds used in artificial fertilizers and, to a lesser extent, with phosphorus compounds. This increases the nutrient value of the water and may well result in an algal bloom — the number of algae increases dramatically since nutrients cease to be a limiting factor. When the nutrients are all used up, the algae die and their decomposition often consumes all the oxygen dissolved in the water. Any fish living in it are suffocated. Phosphorus, another plant nutrient, a limiting factor in photosynthesis, is also poured into fresh water via household waste, since many modern washing powders contain phosphates.

The sea is often polluted near the mouths of large rivers, which may carry large amounts of sewage, phosphates, heavy metals and pesticides into it. Oil supertankers present other dangers, but accidents to such ships are not the only source of oil in the sea; inland sources also make a contribution, for example, about 12,000 tons of oil products flow down the Rhine into the North Sea every day.

Thermal and atomic power stations use vast amounts of fresh or sea water as coolants and there is a great danger of thermal pollution to the lake or sea to which the water is returned. The temperature may rise by 5−10 °C depending on the size of the power station. As a result, the amount of dissolved oxygen falls and important biological functions like reproduction, migration, survival and growth of the local fish populations are impaired.

Reproduction

Fishes have the most diverse forms of reproduction, each with advantages and disadvantages. Some fishes produce large numbers of eggs and fry which can quickly colonise large areas, providing there is little competition from other species and climatic conditions are favourable. Other fishes produce fewer larger eggs that develop into large strong larvae and the mortality rate of eggs and larvae is relatively much lower. Such larvae can compete effectively with those of other species for food and space. Between these two extremes there is a whole series of intermediate forms.

Some fishes are viviparous; in these the young are born alive and are immediately capable of leading an independent existence. In a number of species like gobies and sticklebacks, the parents care for the offspring during early development.

THE GERM CELLS

At the outset of the breeding season male germ cells (spermatozoa or milt) are formed in the body of the male (the process is known as spermatogenesis) and female germ cells (eggs or roe) in the body of the female (oogenesis). Each type of germ cell has only half the chromosomes of a body cell and the chromosome number is restored to its normal level by fertilization. Different species have different spermatozoa, but the commonest form has an ovoid head with a long tail or flagellum which propels the sperm cell actively towards an egg. Every egg contains food or yolk for the embryo and a germinal vesicle which fuses with the sperm at fertilization and from which a new individual develops. The egg is protected by several membranes — the vitelline (yolk) membrane and at least one other protective membrane, the secondary egg membrane. In some species, further (tertiary) egg envelopes are formed after fertilization; these are produced by accessory glands in the oviducts of the female fish. The horny capsules in which sharks' eggs are enclosed belong to this type of envelope.

Fish eggs vary considerably in size. The largest are those of viviparous sharks, which are 6−10 cm long. Salmonoid fishes also have relatively large eggs (4−7 mm) and so have sturgeons (1−4 mm). The smallest eggs belong to species which produce the largest number of eggs in relation to their size (e.g. herring, which produce eggs not more than one mm long). Within a species, middle-aged individuals have the largest eggs. The size of the larva is closely associated with the amount of yolk available in the egg to the developing embryo. A large supply of yolk means a larger, more independent and more mobile larva when it hatches from the egg. Very often large eggs are produced by fishes living in an environment with a poor food supply.

Females of small species produce fewer eggs than females of large species. The female Stickleback produces about 100 eggs, the Minnow 500—5,000 and the Common Carp — depending on its size — 100,000—250,000 eggs per kg body weight, so that a female weighing 5 kg may produce well over a million eggs. The egg output of most European freshwater fishes ranges from tens to hundreds of thousands a year. The most prolific marine species is the Sun Fish with up to 300 million eggs a year, while the Ling (*Molva molva*) produces 60 million, the Common Cod two to nine million and the Herring 100,000 to two million.

SPAWNING

Fishes generally reproduce (spawn) *en masse*. In most cases males and females release the eggs and sperm into the water without actually copulating and the eggs are fertilized externally in the water. This type of fertilization naturally involves losses, since a large number of eggs remain unfertilized. Species which care for their offspring, like cichlids and gobies, spawn in couples and the percentage of fertilized eggs is consequently much higher. The eggs of sharks and rays and also of members of the family Poecilidae are fertilized internally, since the male ejects the milt (sperm) directly into the female's genital orifice or in its immediate vicinity. These males possess special organs of copulation — the transformed ventral fins (pterygopodia) in sharks and rays and the modified anal fin (gonopodium) in the viviparous fishes of the family Poecilidae.

Most European fishes spawn just once a year, but some species spawn intermittently, laying several batches of eggs, e.g. bream, chub, rudd, mullet. Naturalized carp on Java mature when one to two years old and spawn approximately every two months, while the Black Sea Mullet (*Mullus barbatus ponticus*) produces a few eggs every day for three months. This intermittent spawning can be regarded as an adaptation to ensure optimum availability of prey, for prey species may breed several times during the warm part of the year. In waters liable to drying up or subject to flooding, intermittent spawning is one way of making good any previous losses.

Most European fishes spawn in the spring months, when the water gradually becomes warmer and the days grow longer. One of the first freshwater fishes to spawn is the Pike, which spawns as soon as the ice has melted, and its fry are therefore always larger than those of other species which spawn later in the spring and on which the pike fry feed. Perch also spawn very early, when the temperature of the water is only about 8 °C. The cyprinoid species spawn late, the last being the warmth-loving Common Carp and the Tench. Trout, salmon, whitefish and burbot spawn during the autumn and winter months and the embryos produced remain at the spawning sites until the following spring.

It often happens that members of the same species spawn in different areas of their range at different times; this is primarily associated with differences in the temperature of the water. For instance, Capelin (*Mallotus villosus*) spawn in the western part of the Barents Sea from March to May, but in the eastern part in August and September. In Australia, naturalized Perch spawn in the months of October and November. Different races of the same species may also start spawning at different times; spring and autumn races of herring, lampreys, whitefish and some salmonoids are known.

DEVELOPMENT OF THE EMBRYO

The development of an embryo is initiated by fertilization, i.e. by the union of the male and female germ cells to form a single cell or zygote. When the spermatozoon pierces the ovum (egg) it sheds its tail and the head (the nucleus) penetrates into the ovum and unites with its nucleus.

Fertilization of the egg is followed by development of the embryo; this is known as embryogenesis and generally takes place inside the egg membranes. During this time the developing individual is completely dependent for food on the nutrients stored in the yolk. The embryonic period can be divided into three phases. The first is blastogenesis, when the egg undergoes cleavage and the rudiments of the organs are formed; during this time the egg usually remains the same size. The next phase is organogenesis, during which time the organs grow very fast, with an increase in the number and size of the cells. The third phase is the free embryo, which begins when the embryo hatches and begins to look much more like the adult individual. The free embryo phase can be very long as in salmonoids or very short as in cyprinoid fishes and its duration is directly proportional to the size of the yolk sac.

As soon as the embryo is able to feed it becomes a larva. The larval period ends with the formation of the skeleton and with resorption of the fin border. This is followed by the juvenile period — at this time the fry resemble the adult fish and differ from them only in respect of their smaller size, their sexual immaturity and in many cases their colour. In salmonoids for example, juveniles have dark bands on their bodies. The juvenile period ends with maturation of the gonads and is followed by the adult period (adulthood), which may last anything from a few months, as in some members of the Gobiidae and Scopelidae, to dozens of years. Big species like the Beluga or Great Sturgeon may live as long as 100 years. Only a few individuals survive into the senescent (aging) period, when growth almost stops and the fish spawn irregularly or not at all. In most individuals of Pacific salmon senescence and death follow very quickly on from migration into the rivers and spawning which follows.

In some species development of the eggs may occur without fertilization, a phenomenon known as parthenogenesis. For instance unfertilized herring eggs can develop up to the free-swimming larval stage. European Goldfish populations generally contain only females, and males are very rare, although both sexes are represented in Eastern Asia in the original populations. In populations without males the sperm cells of another species provide the impulse for division, but do not actually fertilize the egg cells, the result being a new batch of female goldfish produced parthenogenetically.

CARE OF THE OFFSPRING

In the course of their long evolution, fish have developed a number of ways of looking after their eggs and/or their offspring. Many fishes, including members of the mackerel family, sardines, whitefish, various gadoid (cod) species, the Polar Flounder and many others, simply release their eggs into the water. During development the eggs float freely in the water; a large oil droplet is often present and acts as a flotation device, preventing them from sinking to the bottom. As a rule these eggs develop in water with a constant supply of oxygen. Consequently, neither the embryos nor the larvae of such species are adapted to oxygen deficiency. Since losses of eggs and embryos which develop in open water are very high, the females produce vast numbers of eggs.

Benthic species spawn on the bottom on plants, on stones or on sand. Eggs attached to plants have sticky envelopes, giving them a firm hold on submerged plants; some of these fishes, like the pike, favour fresh terrestrial plants just washed down in the stream and will not spawn until such vegetation is present on the spawning site. The eggs and the embryos can both survive any periods of oxygen deficiency which may occur at night as the plants respire. The embryos cling to the plants by means of special cement glands on their heads. In addition to Carp and Pike, Bream, Roach and marine species of the Labridae family all spawn on plants. In the upper reaches of rivers and on rocky coasts, bottom-dwelling fishes spawn on the stony river or sea bed. Such fishes include the Zingel, Barbel, salmonoids, sturgeons, and most of the members of the Gobiidae. Their embryos are usually photophobic (light-shy) and remain hidden among the stones until all the yolk has been used. Gudgeon, Grey Mullet and stone loaches are amongst the fishes which choose to spawn on sandy bottoms. Some species like Roach, Bream and Rudd are less discriminating in their choice of spawning site and will spawn on any one of several different substrates.

The quality of parental care can vary considerably. Salmon exert a simple form of parental care, excavating a shallow trough for the eggs with jerking movements of their bodies and keeping watch over them for a time after spawning.

The simplest nests in the true meaning of the word are plain troughs in the sea or river bed excavated and guarded by the males. Such nests are built by North American sunfishes, one of which — the Common Sunfish — has become naturalized in Europe. Some sea bream (Sparidae) also dig nests in the sand. Other species, like the sticklebacks, the Wels and the Eyed Wrasse make nests from plant debris. Members of the family Anabantidae as represented by the Siamese Fighting Fish for example, build bubble nests, while small species belonging to the families Cottidae and Gobiidae make use of hollows beneath stones or roots. The sea horses and pipe fishes of the order Syngnathiformes have a remarkable way of looking after their offspring. At the rear of their abdomens the males have special brood pouches formed of folds of skin, in which the eggs are laid by the females and where they remain until hatched. The edges of the pouch grow together and have a dense interwoven network of capillaries, so that both eggs and embryos are assured of a constant oxygen supply. Bitterling protect their eggs by laying them in the mantle cavities of molluscs of the genus *Anodonta* while some members of the family Liparidae conceal their eggs in the gill cavities of crabs.

One of the most effective methods of caring for the offspring is viviparity. In true viviparity the embryos develop in the body of the mother, without any egg membranes, and are nourished directly by her. For example, some sharks and rays possess a 'yolk placenta' — a well-defined nutritive and respiratory 'placenta' which keeps the embryo supplied with nutrients from the oviduct walls. The wall of the yolk placenta is in close contact with the wall of the oviduct, or is held fast to it by means of finger-like processes called villi. In other fishes the embryo feeds on the secretions of the oviduct walls or devours unfertilized eggs. In most viviparous fishes, however, the eggs develop in the female's body without receiving any food other than the contents of the yolk. The young hatch as soon as the eggs are expelled from the mother. This kind of reproduction is called ovoviviparity and is well known in sharks belonging to the order Squaliformes, in *Latimeria* and in some bony fishes like *Sebastes marinus* and *Zoarces viviparus*.

Feeding habits

Like all other animals, fish acquire the energy they need for growth, reproduction, locomotion etc. by feeding on other living organisms. Like all cold-blooded vertebrates, fish can go for long periods without food and in times of shortage they can survive for several months by drawing on their reserves.

Basically, fish feed on planktonic organisms, on bottom-dwelling organisms or on other fishes; only a limited number of species are parasites. The plankton is an association of organisms drifting permanently in the upper layers of the sea or in lakes; planktonic organisms are completely, or almost completely, incapable of independent movement. The term is derived from the Greek word *planktos,* which means 'wandering' or 'tossed about'. Planktonic animals are known as zooplankton, planktonic plants as phytoplankton. The nekton (also from the Greek – *nektos* means 'swimming') is an association of actively moving animals often feeding on the plankton. Fishes are the chief component of the nekton but also present are squids, turtles, whales, dolphins etc. The sea contains some 2,000 species of phytoplankton, about 1,700 of which occur in the northern hemisphere. Diatoms, dinoflagellates, blue-green algae and green algae are among the most important. These groups are also represented in fresh water, though by other genera and species.

Among the roughly 2,000 species of marine animals which can be included in the zooplankton, about 200 are crustaceans and some 400 the larvae of coelenterates and molluscs.

The gill-rakers of fishes feeding on phytoplankton are very long and thick, so that they make an effective filter. These gill filters have a high output; for example, the gills of *Brevortia tyrannus* which lives in the western part of the Atlantic, filter up to 40 litres of water per minute. Only a few fishes are adapted for a phytoplankton diet in adulthood. One of them, the Silver Carp, brought to Europe from southeastern Asia, feeds on zooplankton when young and on phytoplankton when adult. Species feeding on zooplankton also filter their food by means of thick gill-rakers. They include the marine herrings and sardines and freshwater whitefish, Bleak and also several cyprinoid fishes. Surprisingly, the two biggest recent sharks – the Whale Shark and the Basking Shark – also feed on zooplankton. The filter apparatus of fishes feeding on phytoplankton is generally much finer than that of fishes feeding on zooplankton, since the phytoplankton species on which they feed are much smaller, about ten times smaller than the normal zooplankton species.

Some fishes feed on higher submerged or floating plants or seaweeds and at the same time they eat the animals found in these plants. For example grey mullets of the family Mugilidae are seaweed gatherers which also feed on the organic debris and animals concealed in the seaweed. Nase, sometimes Roach and a number of cichlids are freshwater species which obtain their food in a similar manner. Among European fishes, Rudd and Grass Carp (introduced from Asia) both feed on higher plants.

Bottom-dwelling animals living on the bottom of the sea and freshwater lakes and rivers are another group of organisms which are prey for fishes. It has been claimed that the sea contains about 180,000 species of bottom-dwelling animals including fishes. Practically all benthic species live on the continental shelf of the sea.

Marine benthic animals include sponges, gastropods, chitons, bivalves, crustaceans and polychaete worms, while on the bottoms of lakes, reservoirs and rivers live protozoans, wheel animalcules, nematode worms, small crustaceans, insect larvae, oligochaete worms and molluscs. Fishes feeding on benthic animals are mostly species living permanently on the bottom, like rays, flatfishes, angler-fishes, gurnards and gobies in the sea and stone loaches, spined loaches and bull-heads in fresh water. Other species which look for food close to the bottom, like bream and carp, also feed on bottom-dwelling animals.

Wolf-fishes (family Anarhichadidae) feed on sea urchins, brittle stars, molluscs and crabs, whose shells they crush with their strong, sharp teeth. Puffer-fishes (order Tetraodontiformes) have teeth like paving stones, which they use for crushing corals and mollusc shells.

Many fishes are predators on other fishes. They include the marine sharks, cod, mackerel, tunny, barracuda and other species including salmon. Among European freshwater species, the Trout, the Huchen, the Pike, the Asp, the Pike-perch, the Wels and the Perch are all predatory fishes.

The composition of a fish's food changes with the time of year as well as with age. Most species of fish feed on the food most easily available, for instance the haddock *Melanogrammus aeglefinus* feeds mainly on herring eggs in the spring and on bottom-dwelling animals in the summer. Many whitefishes which feed on zooplankton will also feed on benthic molluscs in some lakes.

The jaws and teeth of fish are often specialized for a particular diet. Fishes which feed on other fishes have strikingly long, toothed jaws with teeth on the maxilla, the mandible and the premaxilla. Inside the mouth there are further special teeth on the vomer, the palate and the ectopterygoid bone. Pharyngeal teeth, if present on the last gill arch – in cyprinoid fishes, for example – are used for crushing large prey and for straining off surplus water from the food. Lampreys have funnel-shaped suctorial mouths set with numerous horny teeth.

Many species feeding on bottom-dwelling plants and animals have protrusible mouths enabling them to suck up food from the bottom. Fishes of this type include Bream, Common Carp, sturgeon and members of the Mormyridae. Barbels may be present — whisker-like tentacles around the mouth which help the fish in the search for food. Loaches and catfish have barbels. The mouths of fishes feeding on attached seaweeds often have the form of a transverse slit. The lower and sometimes the upper lips usually have sharp, horny edges (e.g. the Nase, grey mullets). Plankton feeders have relatively large mouths which can be opened very wide; their gill rakers act as sieves through which the water is strained off.

Most fish swallow their food whole without tearing or crushing it. Some predators however, like sharks and piranhas, bite pieces of flesh out of prey bigger than themselves, or like lampreys, scrape holes in their bodies and suck out the contents.

Most fishes feeding on animal food metabolize on an average 80% and excrete the rest. Species feeding mainly on vegetable food utilize only 50—60%. The greater part of the energy obtained from assimilated food is utilized for physiological processes, while the remainder is used for growth and for the production of gametes. The ratio of food intake to growth depends on the character of the food, the time of year and the size and age of the fish. In fish predators it is (5—10):1; that means these species require 5—10 kg of fish for an increase of 1 kg in the weight of their own body. In herbivorous species however, or in species feeding on animals other than fishes, yielding a large proportion of waste such as molluscs, the ratio of food intake to growth may be (10—100):1. Black Sea Mullet, *Mullus barbatus ponticus,* which consumed food amounting to 20% of their body weight in 24 hours utilized 70% of the food. Two thirds of this were utilized for physiological processes, just under one third for gamete production and only one hundredth for actual growth.

Daily food consumption varies with the size of the fish (large fish eat relatively less), with the temperature (consumption is higher at higher temperatures) and with the food supply, and it ranges from an average intake of 10—20 % of body weight in small individuals to about 5% of body weight in big fishes. Study of the food intake and of its utilization for growth is especially important for those engaged in fish-farming in ponds, where natural food consumption can be used as a guide when decisions need to be taken about whether to supplement the food supply and the necessary calculations made.

Growth

The growth of an organism is accompanied by an increase in its length and body weight. Unlike other vertebrates like birds and mammals or insects, fishes go on growing indefinitely, continuing to grow longer and to put on weight after they have reached sexual maturity. Amphibians, reptiles, molluscs — and trees — grow in the same way. However fishes do not go on growing forever at the same rate and after they have reached sexual maturity their growth rate slows down. Some species of fishes grow faster than others and some species live longer than others. Generally, larger fishes have longer life spans than small ones. Some tropical freshwater species, like the characins, familiar to aquarists, and marine species like gobies, seldom live longer than a year and never grow very big, while large sturgeons and belugas may have lived for 100—150 years, although it is not always easy to age such fish accurately. The age data on fish kept in captivity are much more exact. For instance, there are records of a sturgeon which survived for 69 years in captivity and of a carp kept for 38 years, a trout 49 years and an eel 68 years. Fish seldom live to such a ripe old age under natural conditions however, and probably the majority of species live for between one and 20 years.

The smallest fish of all is probably *Pandaka pygmaea,* a member of the Gobiidae family from the Philippines, but the gobies living round the coasts of Europe, like members of the genus *Crystalogobius,* are not much larger. Gigantic fishes like the Basking Sharks (*Cetorhinus maximus*), may grow to 15 m and more in length and Whale Sharks (*Rhincodon typus*) can measure up to 18 m. Among migratory species which live in the sea but swim upstream to spawn (anadromous migrators, as against downstream or cathodromous migrators like the eels), the biggest is the Beluga or Great Sturgeon, which grows up to 9 m long and weighs 1.5 to 2 tons. The Wels (*Silurus glanis*), a freshwater catfish some 3 m long and weighing 200 kg, is another fish which reaches a large size. Nowadays however, record-breaking fishes are becoming ever rarer, for the heavy pressure put on their populations by overfishing means that they are generally caught long before they reach maximum size. For instance, we know that in Palaeolithic times the Russian Sturgeon (*Acipenser güldenstädti*) grew to a length of 3 m, whereas present-day individuals do not grow more than 2.4 m long.

Temperature is an important abiotic factor influencing the growth of fishes. If the temperature is too low or too high, the growth rate slows down. A carp stops feeding as soon as the temperature of the water falls below 13—15 °C, so in most European countries it grows only during the summer. Most fishes also stop growing when the temperature goes over 30–35 °C.

One factor which influences growth is the total number of fishes in a population in a lake or pond. This is particularly important to fish farmers when stocking fish ponds. If there are a large number of fish in the pond they will grow more slowly than if there are a smaller number in the same area. Growth can be encouraged to some extent by supplemental feeding, but a fish-farmer must decide whether he wants a high total yield of comparatively small fishes, or a smaller yield of relatively large fishes. Similar relationships apply in open water. The influence of numbers is often masked however, by other factors like competition with other species, poor weather etc., and it is often difficult to tell which factor is actually responsible for a drop in growth rate.

In a limited space, growth is affected not only by lack of food but also by lack of space. In territorial species such as the Trout, increased population density makes it constantly necessary for the dominant individual to assert his dominant position. This makes great demands on his energy, he spends less time feeding and his growth rate slows down, even when the food supply is adequate. Very often however, growth is influenced simply by visual or chemical contact between individuals of the same species. It was found experimentally that if blennies were kept in isolation, without any visual or chemical contact with other members of the same species, they grew more slowly than when they had such contact. The fry of the American catfish *Ictalurus nebulosus* were also found to have a higher food intake and to grow at a faster rate when kept in groups.

Rapid growth is important for young fishes because their predators are often only able to swallow prey up to a certain size. This is particularly true of deep-bodied fishes like bream, which are virtually safe from predators after they attain a certain size. Rapid growth is also accompanied by faster sexual maturation and hence by earlier reproduction. In time, this may lead to an increase in the size of the population, but this will inevitably lead to a resultant decrease in the rate of growth. In this case growth rate, in association with food supply, acts as a mechanism regulating the size of populations.

DETERMINATION OF AGE AND RATE OF GROWTH

After the Second World War, biologists became very interested in evaluating the age of the individuals of various groups of animals and in the information this gave about the structure of populations and the way they changed. In many parts of the skeleton, successive rings of material are deposited every year and if

these are counted the age of the organism can be determined. In ichthyology, the scales, the opercular bones, the vertebrae and the otoliths of the ear have been used successfully since the beginning of the present century for determining the age of fishes.

A scale develops from a basic central platelet or sclerite and as it grows (together with the fish), new concentric platelets, each a little larger in diameter than the one before, are formed below it. From above, the edges of the platelets are seen as concentric circles. In winter the edges of the sclerites are close together, whereas in the spring and summer when the fish grows faster, they are further apart. The borderline between such groups of narrowly and widely spaced sclerites, an annular ring, represents a year in the life of the fish, while the distance from the centre of the scale to each ring is proportional to growth of the fish itself in each year. The scales also reflect periods of slower growth during periods of cold, food deficiency or disease and these can result in the formation of pseudo-annuli. It is not always easy to distinguish such pseudo-annuli from the true annual rings, so scales can only provide an estimate of the age of the fish, not an accurate determination.

The alternation of narrowly and widely spaced sclerites on the scales is characteristic of fishes inhabiting the temperate regions, but even in tropical and subtropical regions growth may slow down or stop during periods of drought. Concentric rings are produced by seasonal changes in the deposition of calcium phosphate and carbonate on scales, bones or otoliths, similar to those found on fish in the temperate zone and can be used to estimate the age of these fishes.

In practice, it is often necessary to verify findings on ages and lengths from past years independently, by another method not related to the scales. One good way is to mark the fish and to follow their growth from that date. If they are caught regularly every year and put back, the annual increases in their length can be measured directly.

Population dynamics

A population is usually described as a group of individuals of the same species living in a particular region and interbreeding freely with one another. It can be characterized by the number of individuals, mortality, birth rate, age structure and the spatial distribution of its members. A knowledge of these parameters is essential if endangered species are to be protected or if economically important species are to be commercially exploited.

A population with adequate food and space quickly increases in numbers (it realizes its biotic potential).

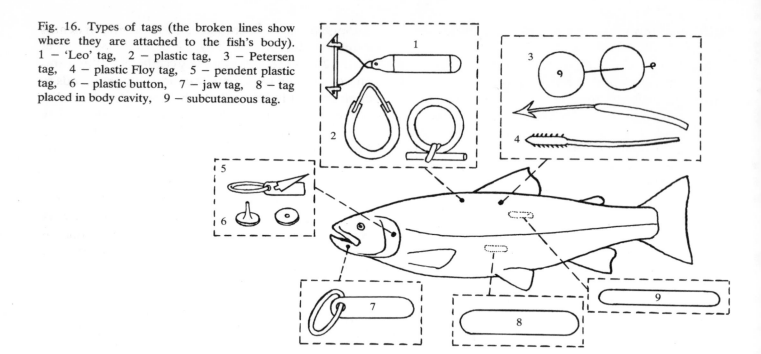

Fig. 16. Types of tags (the broken lines show where they are attached to the fish's body). 1 – 'Leo' tag, 2 – plastic tag, 3 – Petersen tag, 4 – plastic Floy tag, 5 – pendent plastic tag, 6 – plastic button, 7 – jaw tag, 8 – tag placed in body cavity, 9 – subcutaneous tag.

Food does not remain abundant for long however, and supplies decrease as the population increases until, if the population continues to increase unchecked, both food and space run out. In practice, this rarely happens as numbers are controlled by predators, disease and weather.

In some years the number of fish fry hatched is many times larger than in others. For instance, the herring fisheries in the northeastern part of the Atlantic have always been dependent on the yield from prolific years, which have formed a substantial portion of the catch over long periods. Short-term (4 years') and long-term (9–10 years') fluctuation of numbers are known. Fluctuations in the size of fish populations are determined largely by climatic factors, such as temperature and rainfall, droughts and floods, also by the food supply, degree of predation etc. Fish numbers are also influenced by the birth rate, associated with the average number of eggs produced by individual females. Stability of population size depends largely on the age structure of the spawning shoals, which usually contain several age groups. In some species, like the Caspian Herring or European Salmon, fishes spawning for the first time are predominant but in most other species fishes which have already spawned on previous occasions predominate, (herring, Polar Flounders, the majority of cyprinoid fishes and perches are of this type). This kind of spawning population is best developed in long-lived species such as sturgeon, the populations of which were once very stable as a consequence; human greed and pollution of the environment have caused their numbers to shrink, however.

Fish numbers are also associated with the condition of the eggs of the spawning females. The highest success rate for development of healthy fry is provided by eggs with the largest amount of yolk; these are usually produced during the first third to half of the reproductive life of the females.

MARKING FISH

Basic information on numbers, mortality, growth rate, migration and general fate of fish stocks can be obtained by marking the fish. The use of this important technique is not confined to fish (cf. the ringing of birds and bats).

The traditions of fish-marking go back for over a century. During this time, millions of freshwater and marine fishes have been marked and recaptured and many of the secrets of their lives have been uncovered as a consequence. Various types of tags attached to the opercular bones, or jaws, or anchored in the flesh, are used for marking. All such marks are numbered and the fish can therefore be individually identified as long as the tag remains in place. The mark should not harm the fish in any way or increase the likelihood of its death or make it easier to catch if a true picture of the population is to emerge. The fish must be handled as sparingly and quickly as possible while marking them.

ABUNDANCE ESTIMATES

With migratory species like salmon, the number of fish which pass along a river during a period of time can be counted directly. In deep sea fishing counts are obtained by comparing the size of the catch per fishery effort unit, since it was found that the size of the catch was consistently proportional to the size of the population from which the catch was made as long as fishing conditions remained the same. Marked fish

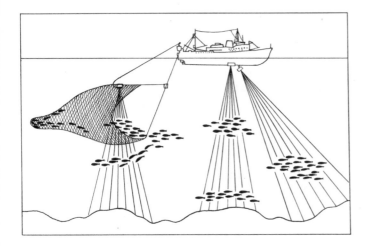

Fig. 17. A fishing vessel equipped with an echo-sounder and trawl. Shoals of fish can be detected, located and caught immediately with the trawl, using the information obtained with the echo-sounder.

can also be used for estimating numbers and during the last two decades it has become common practice to gauge the size of fish populations by means of ultrasonic echo-sounding devices. This method has several advantages. It is independent of catch statistics, is not time-consuming and produces consistently reliable results. Its disadvantage is that species cannot be differentiated and individuals just above the bottom and near the surface cannot be detected; the cost of the basic equipment is also fairly high. It consists essentially of an echo-sounder fitted with a transmitter, a converter and a receiver. The transmitter produces electric pulses which are converted to acoustic signals. The signal travels through the water and when it encounters an obstacle like a fish or the bottom, it is deflected back to the receiver, where it is reconverted to an electrical signal. A monitor displays the shape of the obstacle located. The time needed for the sound wave to reach the fish, bounce off and return is directly proportional to the depth at which the fishes are swimming. Modern computerised echo-location equipment can detect single fishes and also provide accurate counts of deep sea populations.

MORTALITY

Mortality, compensated for by the birth rate, is an important parameter regulating the size of fish populations. Predators, parasites, disease, age and a lack of food, all contribute to the mortality rate but temperature and pH changes in the water, pollution and flooding etc. can also cause deaths. These causes are all grouped together under the heading 'natural mortality' as compared with fishing mortality when fishes are caught for food. Natural mortality is highest

among the eggs and embryos. The majority of deaths among larvae occur at the time when the egg yolk is used up and the fish must begin to feed. When this phase has been overcome the mortality rate tends to diminish, but is still quite high. The lowest mortality rate occurs among adults in their prime but as they grow old it increases again. In species which do not care for their eggs or fry, 95–99% of all of young die within the first few weeks. Mortality in the period of sexual maturity among fishes which live to a moderate age, like cyprinoids, varies from 30 to 40% yearly, depending on local conditions. In fishponds where Common Carp are kept, up to about 10% mortality is normal in two-year-old stock; this is probably the minimum mortality rate, since all causes of death have been kept at the lowest possible level.

During their evolution, fish have developed a whole series of defence mechanisms for baffling predators. Protective colouring, the formation of shoals, the presence of spines on the scales and on the opercula, protection of the offspring and the utilization of hiding places are amongst the simplest. Some fishes have venom glands or poisonous flesh. In the sea, the number of species with spines and other defence mechanisms increases towards the equator, together with an increase in the number of predators. The greatest diversity is found in coastal waters, here the numbers of predators is high and almost all the prey species have some method of defence. For example, off the west coast of Africa near Dakar, up to 67% of the fish in trawler catches are 'armoured' species, while further out to sea the proportion falls to 44%. A similar situation is found in fresh water, where the percentage of 'armoured' species in the upper reaches of rivers is usually lower than in the middle and lower reaches. Furthermore, northern species have shorter protective spines than southern species of the same group; this is clearly seen in the members of the families Scorpaenidae and Cottidae.

During the course of their lives and at different seasons, predators hunt different species of fish – usually the most numerous or those easiest to catch. In times of food shortage they will feed on 'armoured' species (for example, the Pike will feed on sticklebacks if other species are unavailable).

At spawning time, predators concentrate their attention more on males, especially those belonging to species where the male guards the nest, such as the goby *Gobius paganellus* or the male Stickleback. The higher mortality among the males of such species is compensated for by a higher proportion of males in the offspring.

Fishermen compete for fish with other predators, parasites and disease. If many fishes are removed from an area of water, the remaining fishes grow faster because more food is left for them.

BIOMASS

Biomass — the total weight of all the fish in a given population or group of populations at a given time — is associated with the individual growth and number of fish. A man catching members of a fish population is using part of its biomass which would otherwise be lost through natural mortality; the part of the biomass removed in the catch is known as the yield. A fish farmer or fisherman is interested not only in the absolute size of the yield, that is in how many kilogrammes per hectare water he catches during the year, but also in how long it will be possible for him to catch that amount. There would be no point in catching so many fish every year that the population is destroyed. A sensible farmer therefore takes only a part (about one quarter to a third) of the population every year, so as to leave sufficient fish to spawn and maintain the numbers in the population, for future years.

The importance of fishes to man

Fish have always been an important source of food for man. Palaeolithic hunters exploited spawning migrations to lay in stocks of food for the winter. The problem was how to preserve and store them. Drying and salting were probably two of the first ways of preserving fish. Scales and vertebrae in the waste pits of Palaeolithic encampments provide evidence as to the species and size of the fish that were caught and eaten by the stone age people.

Fish flesh (dry weight) contains 15−30% protein, a higher percentage than the flesh of the usual domestic animals kept for meat. Fish flesh contains all the ten essential amino acids and is also an important source of iodine, phosphorus, potassium, iron, copper and vitamins A and D. Its low sugar content makes it an important item of a modern diet with its emphasis on healthy eating.

Marine fishes have traditionally been caught without any attention being paid to their husbandry. This is fishing at the same level as in Palaeolithic times when men were gatherers and hunters and it is therefore not surprising that many populations of herring, sardines and mackerel for instance, are in danger of being wiped out through over-fishing.

WORLD CATCHES

At the beginning of the nineteenth century, the total catch of fish all over the world was probably more than two or three million tons a year and even at the beginning of the present century it was still only about 5−10 million tons. However there were no worldwide statistics embracing the catches of all the countries concerned. It was not until 1947, after the Second World War and the foundation of the United Nations, that one of the latter's organizations, the FAO (Food and Agricultural Organization), which has its seat in Rome, began to publish the Yearbook of Fishery Statistics which contains data on catches of fish in salt and fresh water all over the world. Where no proper data are available, estimates are made by FAO experts. The first such estimate was made for 1938, the last year before the war, when about 21 million tons of fish and other animals and plants were estimated to have been taken from the sea and from fresh water together. In 1968 the figure was 64.3 million tons, that is three times more than in 1938, and today the total annual amount is about 70 million tons, three to four million of which is accounted for by molluscs, about two million by crustaceans and roughly one and a half million by marine plants. Fresh water organisms contribute seven to nine million tons to the total catch.

Contemporary estimates of fish production in the

Fig. 18. Diagram of the food chain in a freshwater ecosystem. 1 − green algae (phytoplankton), 2 − water fleas (zooplankton), 3 − fishes which feed on zooplankton (e.g. Bleak), 4 − carnivorous fishes (e.g. Pike).

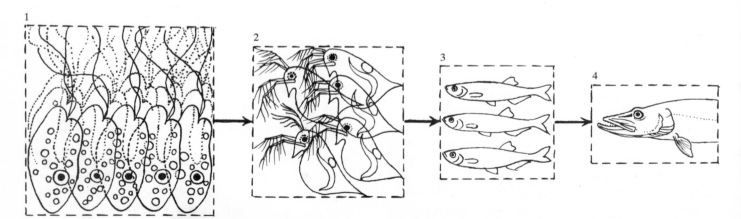

oceans are based on an analysis of the successive conversion of energy in food chains, starting with an estimate of the primary production of phytoplankton. Primary phytoplankton species are consumed by herbivores, i.e. first order consumers which in the sea are chiefly zooplankton species. Zooplankton is the food of second order consumers, which in turn are followed by higher order consumers, the result being a food chain. When food is eaten by animals, only approximately 20% of the prey biomass is actually utilized by the predator.

On the basis of primary production values, the number of links in the food chains and the effectiveness of energy transmission in these chains, fish production in the oceans, i.e. the amount of newly formed biomass per year in live weight units, can be estimated at 241.6 million tons. A large proportion of these fishes are eaten by piscivorous birds and mammals, predatory fishes and various invertebrates, however. The estimate includes all species of fish, although only about one per cent are of interest to the human population; consequently, most of the estimates of the possible long-term fish yield from the oceans (if a large number of species are caught) are in the region of 100 millions of tons a year.

The FAO divided the world oceans into 19 main regions in which the fish yields are very different. The largest catches come from regions with the highest phytoplankton and zooplankton production (the northwestern part of the Pacific, with catches of about 7–9 kg per hectare, and the northwestern and northeastern parts of the Atlantic, with catches of about 7 kg per hectare). On average, about 2.5 kg fish per hectare are caught in the Atlantic as a whole and about 2 kg per hectare in the Pacific, but in the Indian Ocean only about 0.5 kg per hectare are caught. As can be seen from the accompanying map, the open ocean is actually a desert with very low production of fish and other organisms. The greatest concentrations of fish and their prey are in the shallower continental shelf areas of the sea, or in places where ascending currents bring adequate supplies of nutrients to the surface, as off the west coast of South America, for instance where phytoplankton abound.

Deep sea fishing is concerned with approximately 200 species of fish. Almost 80% of the total catch is provided by members of the five orders Clupeiformes, Gadiformes, Perciformes, Salmoniformes and Pleuronectiformes. The record for the fish yielding the highest catch is at present held by the Peruvian anchovy *Engraulis ringeri*, over 13 million tons of which were caught in 1970; in 1974–1978, however, the mean annual catch sank to barely 2,700,000 tons, when the course of the Humboldt Current changed, and the highest catches today are provided by the Walleye Pollack (*Theragra*

chalcogramma), 4.5 to 5 million tons of which are caught every year.

UNUSED RESOURCES

It is highly probable that future catches, of the most valuable species of fish will not greatly exceed present levels and that significantly higher yields of animal protein from the sea will only come if other sources are utilized.

Invertebrates like shrimps, crabs and oysters could provide greater catches as could various cephalopods like squid and octopus. The greatest hopes of increased production from the sea, however, rest in the exploitation of krill — small planktonic marine crustaceans. In northern seas members of the genus *Calanus* form the main component of the krill, while in the Antarctic species of the genus *Euphausia* predominate. Although individually very small (their length varies from a few tenths of a millimetre to several millimetres), these crustaceans are present in huge numbers. Another possibility is to increase the catches of fishes which, for one reason or the other, have hitherto been neglected. Flying fishes of the order Beloniformes and lantern fishes of the Myctophidae could both provide much higher catches. Lantern fishes are small deep-sea fishes which spend the daytime at depths of over 500 m, but come up to the surface layers of the sea at night. At present suitable techniques for catching them have not been adequately explored and developed.

In recent years marine species are being bred artificially with increasing frequency, although the techniques are different from those of freshwater fish-farming. The grey mullets of the family Mugilidae are euryhaline and eurythermic fishes, i.e. they tolerate a wide range of salt concentrations in the water and a wide range of temperatures; they feed on plant food, plankton and debris. Their adaptability makes them ideal for fish farming and they are bred in the Mediterranean and in Indian waters. *Chanos chanos,* a herbivorous fish akin to the Herring, is another such euryhaline species which comes from the coastal areas of the Indian and Pacific Oceans and is bred in Indonesia, the Philippines and on Taiwan. Pacific salmon are also farmed intensively and they have become naturalized in regions like the Great Lakes of North America and in New Zealand.

Fishing techniques

DEEP SEA FISHING

The growing market for fish places great demands on the ships and their equipment. After the fish have been caught, it is important to prevent them from deteriorating in any way. Modern fishing-ships are small factories on which the fish can be partially processed or tinned. Factory ships also carry huge refrigeration plants holding several dozen tons of fish. As a result the ships rarely return to their home ports and can remain at sea until they have a full cargo. The size of these ships is truly imposing. For instance, a Soviet trawler of the Mayakovsky class has a displacement of 3,700 tons, is 85 m long and has a crew of about 110; it can draw behind it a trawl 38 m wide and can freeze up to 30 tons of fish per day. The biggest modern trawlers are about 100 m long and have engines with 6,000—7,000 horse-power. Modern fishing nets are made, not of the old-fashioned hemp but of strong, light, durable synthetic fibres.

A trawl is very effective for fishing in the open sea. A trawl is a large open-mouthed bag-net dragged over the bottom or in the water behind the ship. It gathers up all the fish in its path, straining the water off as it does so. The size of the catch depends on the size of the trawl and on the rate at which it is drawn through the water. When steam and diesel engines came into use at the end of the nineteenth century, they increased the pulling power of the ships and thus allowed the use of larger trawls. Echo-sounding gave the fishermen information on where the shoals were and at what depth they were swimming and the trawls

could be positioned to ensure the maximum haul. Before echo-sounding, fishermen had to rely on traditional indicators to the presence of fish like the movements of gulls or the appearance of dolphins.

Purse-seines, as well as trawls, are also used in the open sea. The success of fishing with this type of net again depends on how quickly the ship can surround the shoal. For tunny-fishing the purse-seine needs to be about 2,000 m long and 200 m deep, while for catching herring and mackerel a length of 'only' 1,500 m and a depth of 150 m are sufficient. With such nets, catches of up to 200 tons are not uncommon. A large proportion of fish are also caught with gill nets and with traps. Some trawls are fitted with electric cables and emit pulses of up to 400 Hz per second at about 600 volts. Light sources are also used for catching fishes by night; the light attracts them to the ships and they are then caught with special nets or they may alternatively be sucked up out of the water by pumps.

FISHING IN FRESH WATER

Fresh waters account for only five million square kilometres of the earth's surface. There is therefore 70 times less fresh water than sea-water but the present mean yield per hectare of fresh water is about 15 kg, compared to 1.5 kg per hectare from the oceans. This is because in fresh water there are far greater opportunities for increasing the fish yield. The yield can be increased primarily in small ponds, lakes and reservoirs covering an area ranging from 10 to not more than 100—1,000 hectares. Such areas offer the best opportunities for introducing new farming and catching technologies, for active protection of the fish and for supplementary feeding. If the fish feed on their natural prey and are also given supplemental feeds, the annual yield in warm subtropical regions can be raised to several (5—10) thousand kg per hectare a year.

Fish-farming in ponds produces its maximum yields when only one species is kept, when all the fishes of one age are kept together and segregated from other age groups, when feeding is controlled and oxygen levels are maintained.

In Europe, Carp are traditionally farmed in ponds and the annual yield varies from 100 to 1,000 kg per hectare. One possible way to increase fishpond production still further is to keep several species of fish in the pond at once, so as to achieve maximum utilization of all available natural food. Species feeding on higher plants like *Ctenopharyngodon idella* are of considerable significance in this respect, since they do not compete with the Carp.

Another way of increasing the yield is to harvest the carp when they are younger. Nowadays, three year old carp weighing about 1.5 kg and two year old

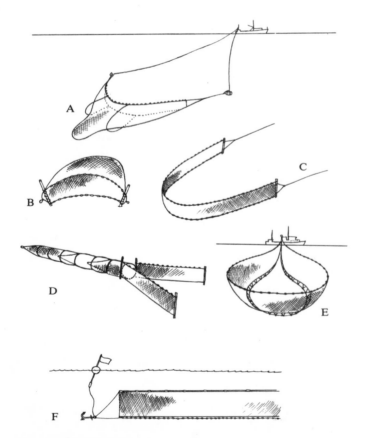

Fig. 19. Types of nets. A – trawl, B – mother-net, C – dragnet (for inshore fishing), D – fyke-net, E – purse-seine, F – gill-net.

fish weighing up to 1 kg are the most in demand. These are all sexually immature fish and a large part of the energy obtained from their food is directed into growth. If the fish are kept and fed in cages in flowing water and fed with artificial feeds, high annual yields are achieved. The trout yield from cage farming amounts to up to two million kg per hectare per year and the carp yield between one and four million kg per hectare. There are only a few species which can be farmed in this way, however. In the United States, catfish belonging to the genera *Ictalurus* and *Ictiobus* are farmed with success, while in the Near East, Africa and southeastern Asia the species of the cichlid genus *Tilapia* are used. The advantage of *Tilapia* species is that the majority of them are herbivorous and feed on plants.

At spawning time parent fish (carp, tench and catfish) are provided with spawning ponds. A few weeks after they have spawned, the fry (fingerlings) are recovered and placed in growing ponds where they are supplied with an adequate supply of natural food and grow rapidly. In the main ponds the stock fish grow to a saleable size and there are also overwintering ponds for fingerlings, stock and parent fish. Each of the separate pond systems has an outlet, so constructed that water can be let out both from the surface layers and from the bottom. A peripheral ditch regulates the inflow of water into the pond. At the bottom of the pond near the outlet, there is a catching pool where the fish are assembled in readiness for harvesting by letting the water out to the lowest level. Fish destined for the market are taken to storage ponds to await further transport to the distribution network. The stock, the fry and the parent fish are taken to overwintering ponds for the winter and in the following spring the parent fish are used for spawning and the cycle is complete.

ANGLING

In recent years angling has become an important sport for up to 10% of the populations of the countries of Europe and North America. In addition to the pleasure gained from fishing, every angler catches 10−70 kg of fish a year. In many European countries, lakes and ponds have been stocked with trout or carp in an attempt to increase the annual catch for anglers. The water is stocked either with small young fish which must grow before they are caught, or with older, larger fish that can be caught immediately. In either case the total yield is still very low and varies in the region of 110−120%; that is the increase in catch over natural yield is only 10−20%. For comparison, the yield in a carp pond is 300−400% over stocked biomass.

The angler's basic tool is a rod (made of bamboo, metal or laminated plastic), which is usually composed of several parts which can be fitted together. Along the rod there are guide loops through which runs the line. The line is wound round a reel which is of assistance when hauling in the fish, since the reel has a brake which stops the line unreeling again as the fish is reeled in. The length of the line is usually 100−200 m and its thickness 0.2−0.8 mm. At the end of the line is a hook, whose size and shape are suited to the kind of fish to be caught. For catching midwater fishes a float made of a light material is used, which is attached to the line and keeps the bait dangling in the water; the float dips beneath the surface when the fish takes the hook. In trolling, spoon lures are used, which generally look like small fish and are employed for catching predators like pike and pike-perch. Flies − specially designed lures for catching fish like grayling and trout − resemble insects floating on the surface of the water.

Most countries have their own fishing laws limiting the number of fish which may be caught on a single day; in some species like predatory fishes or carp there may also be a minimum size of catch. Other regulations protect the fish during the spawning season and restrict or ban certain fishing methods like the use of bag-nets or gill nets. Anglers are not usually allowed to sell their catches.

Tab. 1 **COMPARISON OF THREE CLASSIFICATIONS OF THE MAIN GROUPS OF CYCLOSTOMES, PRIMITIVE FISHES AND TRUE FISHES ACCORDING TO DIFFERENT AUTHORS**

BERG, 1940	NIKOLSKY, 1971	NELSON, 1976
Superclass *Agnatha* (jawless vertebrates)	Superclass *Agnatha*	Superclass *Agnatha*
Class 1. *Petromyzones* (lampreys)	Class *Cyclostomata* (roundmouths)	Class 1. *Cephalaspidomorphi*
2. *Myxini* (hagfishes)	Subclass 1. *Petromyzones* 2. *Myxini*	order: *Petromyzoniformes* (lampreys)
		2. *Pteraspidomorphi* order: *Myxiniformes* (hagfishes)
Superclass *Gnathostomata* (jawed vertebrates)	Superclass *Gnathostomata*	Superclass *Gnathostomata*
Class 1. *Elasmobranchii* Subclass *Selachii* (sharks, rays)	Class *Pisces* (Fishes) Branch 1. *Chondrichthyes* (cartilaginous fishes, sharks, rays, chimaeras)	Class 1. *Chondrichthyes* Subclass a) *Elasmobranchii* b) *Holocephali*
Class 2. *Holocephali* Subclass *Chimaerae*	Subclass a) *Elasmobranchii* b) *Holocephali*	Class 2. *Osteichthyes* bony fishes
Class 3. *Dipnoi* (lung-fishes)	Branch 2. *Osteichthyes*	Subclass aa) *Dipneusti* bb) *Brachiopterygii* cc) *Crossopterygii* dd) *Actinopterygii*
Class 4. *Teleostomi*	Subclass a) *Dipnoi* b) *Teleostomi*	Group 1. *Chondrostei* 2. *Holostei* 3. *Teleostei* various superorders and orders of higher fishes

Subclass	Group
1. *Crossopterygii*	aa) *Crossopterygii*
2. *Actinopterygii*	bb) *Actinopterygii*

Order	Superorder
1. *Polypteriformes* (bichirs)	1. *Brachiopterygii* (bichirs)
2. *Acipenseriformes* (sturgeon)	2. *Chondrostei* (sturgeon)
3. *Lepisosteiformes* (gars)	3. *Holostei* (bowfins, gars)
4. *Amiiformes* (bowfins)	4. *Teleostei* (higher bony fishes)
5. *Clupeiformes* (herring) and further orders	

Order
Clupeiformes, etc.
(herring) and further orders

The Fishes

Over 250 species of fishes, found in the rivers and lakes of Britain and Europe or in the seas and oceans around the continent, are described and illustrated in the following pages. Some are familiar fishes which are sold in wet fish shops all over Britain and Europe, many are common freshwater species which may be seen in ponds or river systems; others, perhaps less familiar, may nevertheless be found hiding in pools on rocky shores around our coasts, while some are strange and fascinating inhabitants of the deep waters of the oceans.

The fishes are arranged in a standard taxonomic sequence, beginning with the primitive jawless lampreys and hagfishes; followed by the fishes with cartilaginous skeletons, the sharks and rays; and then by the bony fishes. Each of these major sections is divided into orders and families, and at the beginning of each subdivision there is a short description of the group at the top of the page.

Accompanying the illustration of each fish is a text which includes a description of its distinguishing features, together with details of the habitats in which it may be found, and feeding and spawning habits. Also included is an indication of the economic significance of the species, if any. Additional information is given in a fact panel at the end of each description. A full explanation of the various elements in a fact panel follows.

SYNONYMS
Included here are outdated scientific names that may still be found in other books, but which have now been discarded by many zoologists. The fish may now be placed in a new genus, or two or more species may have been merged. Sometimes a scientific name is changed because it is discovered that an earlier name exists, the older name taking precedence.

SIZE
Because fishes grow throughout their lives, it is not possible to give an exact length for any one species. Given here is the normal range in length for a mature fish, measured from the tip of the snout to the base of the tail. As occasional individuals may grow considerably longer than the norm, the maximum length to which fish of this species may grow is also usually given.

WEIGHT
The weight of a fish varies considerably within a species, depending on age, time of year, habitat conditions and population density. Fishes lose and gain weight easily, many tend to weigh most at the end of summer and to lose weight during the winter, when food is scarce. Migratory fishes, like salmon and trout, are fattest just before they begin their spawning migration and do not feed while on their journey. Many of them die from exhaustion and starvation after they have spawned. Fishes living in overcrowded conditions, as in a small pond, grow slowly and put on little weight. Fishes living in conditions where they have plenty of space and food, however, grow quickly and put on weight rapidly. The normal weight range for a mature fish is given for each species. Occasionally an individual may grow much larger than the norm and weigh considerably more than the average member of the species, therefore a maximum weight is also given.

FIN FORMULA
Fin formulae are given for all bony fishes but not for the jawless lampreys and hagfishes, nor for the cartilaginous sharks and rays. In lampreys, sharks and rays, the fins are supported by many slender, horny fin rays. In lampreys the fins are covered by muscles which obscure the fin rays and in sharks and rays the fins are covered by heavy placoid scales so that the fin rays cannot be seen at all. Hagfishes lack all fins except for a small tail fin.

The fin formula of a bony fish is a very useful piece of information when it comes to identification. There are two letters used in the formula: the letter 'D' refers to the dorsal fin and the letter 'A' to the anal fin. The figures which follow each letter refer to the fin rays in the fin. All fins of bony fishes contain branched soft rays which support the fin − these are slender, segmented, pliable bones, each divided into two sections or branches; these are denoted by with Arabic numerals. In many bony fishes, such as herrings and salmon, the fins contain rays of this kind only. In a few fishes, Roach for example, the first few rays of the dorsal fin are unbranched and somewhat harder, although they cannot be categorized as spines: these are denoted by lower case roman numerals. In the spiny-rayed fishes such as perches, and in some cods, the first few rays of the dorsal and anal fins are modified to form hard, unbranched spines: these are denoted by capital roman numerals.

Thus the fin formula of a perch, which has two dorsal fins and one anal fin is:

$$D_1XIII-XVII, D_2I-II/13-16, AII/8-10$$

This indicates that the first dorsal fin has between 13−17 spines, the second dorsal fin 1−2 spines and 13−16 soft branched fin rays, and the anal fin 2 spines and 8−10 soft branched fin rays. The sequence is always the same, the first dorsal fin being the one nearest to the head, and the spines are indicated first since they are at the head end of the fin.

FECUNDITY
A statement of the number of eggs or larvae produced by a female fish in one season. Females produce most eggs in their middle years.

DISTRIBUTION
A statement of the regional occurrence of the fish. Distribution maps are also included for some species.

COLOUR PLATES

The order Petromyzoniformes (which belongs to the superclass Agnatha and to the class Cyclostomata) contains the lampreys, eel-like jawless aquatic vertebrates which retain a notochord (chorda dorsalis) throughout their lives. They have cartilaginous skeletons and their pouch-like gills, situated separately in the anterior part of their body, are not supported by gill arches as they are in true fishes. They have no scales on their skin and no paired fins. Many lampreys live in the seas of the temperate regions of both hemispheres, but migrate up the rivers to spawn. Others spend their whole lives in the sea or in fresh water. The one family, the Petromyzonidae has eight genera and twenty species.

PETROMYZONIDAE

Caspian Lamprey
Caspiomyzon wagneri

The Caspian Lamprey lives in the Caspian Sea, but at spawning time it migrates up the Volga, the Ural, the Terek and other rivers emptying into the Caspian Sea. There are two forms of migrant fish differing in respect of size and probably representing different year classes. At the beginning of September, when the temperature falls to 10−12 °C, the fishes begin to migrate upstream, arriving at their destination in December. During migration the lampreys travel some 10 km a day and the fish gradually lose their fat

reserves, so that whereas in the mouth of the Volga their tissues contain up to 34% fat, by the time they reach Volgograd they contain only 20% and at the spawning site a mere 1−2%. Spawning takes place from March to May on a sandy or stony bottom, where the Caspian Lamprey builds a nest. Most of the adults die after spawning; larval development takes at least three years.

Adult individuals are eel-like in shape, grey to grey-green in colour with lighter bellies. They are predatory. At first they attack small animals, but later they attach themselves to other fish by their rounded suctorial mouths, when they scrape a hole in the body wall with their tongue, grate the flesh and suck it out. There is one large, blunt (and occasionally forked) tooth in the upper part of the oral plate and five teeth in the lower part.

Synonym: Petromyzon wagneri
Size: 35−55 cm (large form)
20−30 cm (small form)
Weight: 0.2−1 kg
Fecundity: 20,000−32,000 eggs
Distribution: The Caspian Sea and rivers flowing into it.

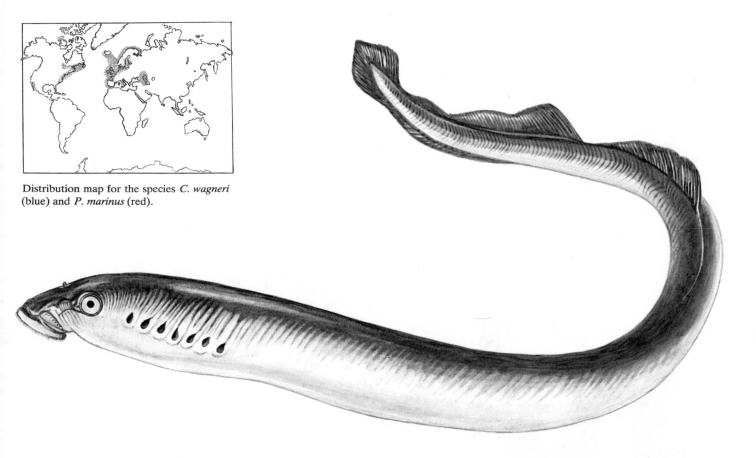

Distribution map for the species *C. wagneri* (blue) and *P. marinus* (red).

Sea Lamprey

Petromyzon marinus

This lamprey lives in the sea, generally close to the shore, but occasionally descending to depths of about 500 m and over. It is also found in brackish water in the mouths of the rivers in which it spawns. High up these rivers, in running water, the females excavate troughs up to 2 m long and 1 m wide, and lay their eggs; in doing so they may shift stones weighing up to 1 kg. This lamprey spawns several times during its lifetime and always in the spring. During spawning the fishes do not feed and they gather in small groups. The larvae develop in fresh water and after they have metamorphosed into young lampreys they migrate to the sea in search of food. The adult fish are variably coloured, their backs being mostly yellowish to greenish brown with dark and light spots, while their undersides are usually light.

They lead a parasitic existence and have suctorial mouths, with two closely adjoining teeth in the upper plate and several rows of strong, radially arranged teeth. They attack fish, to which they attach themselves by their suctorial mouths, scraping a hole in the skin of their prey with their sharp little teeth and sucking out blood and grated flesh from the wound. An anticoagulant substance which is secreted by their oral glands prevents the blood of the lamprey's prey from clotting.

Although their tasty, rather oily flesh is regarded in some countries as a delicacy, they are no longer economically important, because their numbers have diminished in recent years. This is due largely to the construction of dams and hydroelectric power stations, which in many places prevent them from reaching their traditional spawning sites, with resultant disaster to their breeding pattern.

Synonym: Batymyzon bairdii
Size: 60–80 cm, maximum 100 cm, larvae up to 20 cm
Weight: 1.5–2 kg, occasionally 2.5 kg
Fecundity: 200,000–240,000 eggs
Distribution: off European and American coasts in the northern part of Atlantic. In Europe, to the White Sea in the north and the Adriatic in the south.

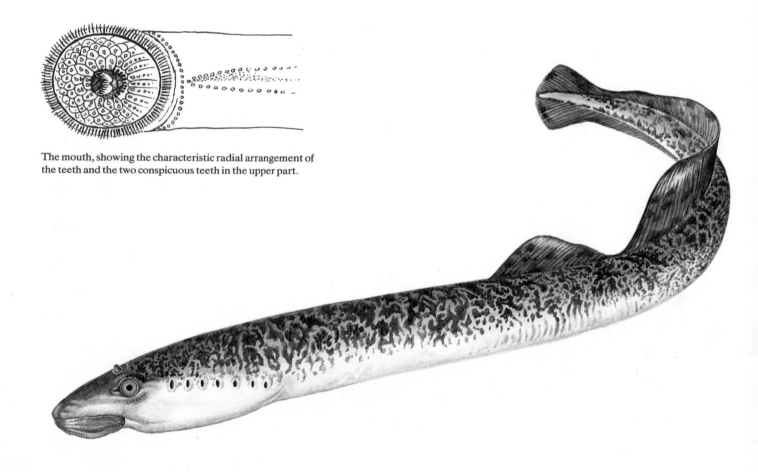

The mouth, showing the characteristic radial arrangement of the teeth and the two conspicuous teeth in the upper part.

Lampern
Lampetra fluviatilis

Lamperns are closely related to the smaller Brook Lampreys, but they have sharp teeth in their suctorial mouths, while those of the Brook Lamprey are small and blunt. Furthermore, the Lampern has two sharp little teeth on the upper oral plate of the mouth, while the Brook Lamprey has none. It has a greenish brown back, its sides are golden yellow and its underside is silvery white.

Like the Brook Lamprey, the Lampern spawns in pre-excavated pits in river beds. The newly hatched larvae measure about one mm; the adults die after spawning. The larvae live mostly buried in the river bed and their development takes four years or even more. At a length of 8.5—15 cm they undergo metamorphosis to become adult lampreys. On completing their metamorphosis the lampreys make for the sea, where they live mainly in coastal waters and spend most of their time feeding. They feed on invertebrates and dead fish but also attach themselves to healthy fish, scraping a hole in their skin and sucking out the blood, body fluids and flesh. After at least a year the fish attain sexual maturity, when they stop feeding and return to the rivers to spawn. Both autumn and spring migrations are known, but actual spawning takes place in the spring and at the beginning of the summer.

The Lampern has moist and savoury flesh and can be eaten, but because its mucus and serum are poisonous, its flesh must be thoroughly washed and all the blood removed before consumption and the fish are more often used as bait. The annual catch in recent years has been two to four tons. Lamperns have disappeared from many rivers because the water has become too polluted to allow spawning.

Synonym: Petromyzon fluviatilis
Size: 30—40 cm, maximum 50 cm, the females larger; the larvae up to 13 cm
Weight: maximum 0.7 kg
Fecundity: 4,000—40,000 eggs
Distribution: This fish is found in the rivers of northern and western Europe and in parts of southern Europe; it is also found in the adjoining seas and off the coast of North America.

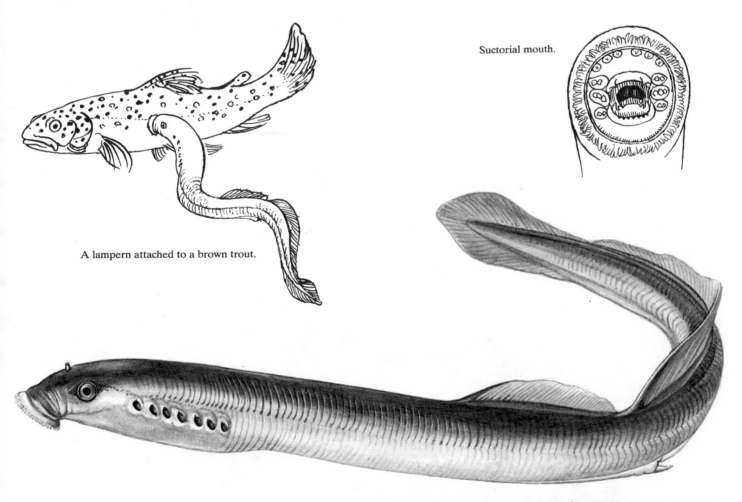

A lampern attached to a brown trout.

Suctorial mouth.

Brook Lamprey
Lampetra planeri

Brook Lampreys live mainly in the trout zone of brooks and rivers and are not migratory. The adult lampreys live only a few months, and die after spawning. During this time they do not feed and their digestive system atrophies; adult individuals are thus usually smaller than the larvae are prior to metamorphosis. Between April and June these adults excavate spawning pits in sand and gravel, rolling away large stones with their mouths. During spawning a female clings to a stone with her mouth and the male wraps the caudal part of his body round hers; sometimes he even holds fast to the back of the female's neck. The newly hatched larvae are blind with eyes overgrown by skin, they have triangular mouths with large horseshoe-shaped upper lips, gill slits localized in a common longitudinal groove and a poorly developed fin border. The larvae spend five years buried in rotting vegetation or organically rich mud in slow-moving rivers, where they feed on organic débris and small bottom-dwelling animals; they metamorphose into adults during the course of their fifth winter.

In the adult Brook Lamprey the dorsal fins are continuous, a feature which distinguishes it from the Lampern, and in the spawning season the male's urogenital papilla lengthens. The females have a swelling near the anus, the males none. The body is grey-blue to brownish green; the sides and the belly are lighter.

The Brook Lamprey is economically unimportant, although it may sometimes be used by anglers and fishermen as bait.

Synonym: Petromyzon planeri
Size: 12—16 cm, the larvae up to 18 cm
Weight: 15—25 g, maximum 40 g
Fecundity: up to 1,500 eggs
Distribution: The regions adjoining the Baltic and the North Sea, France and Ireland.

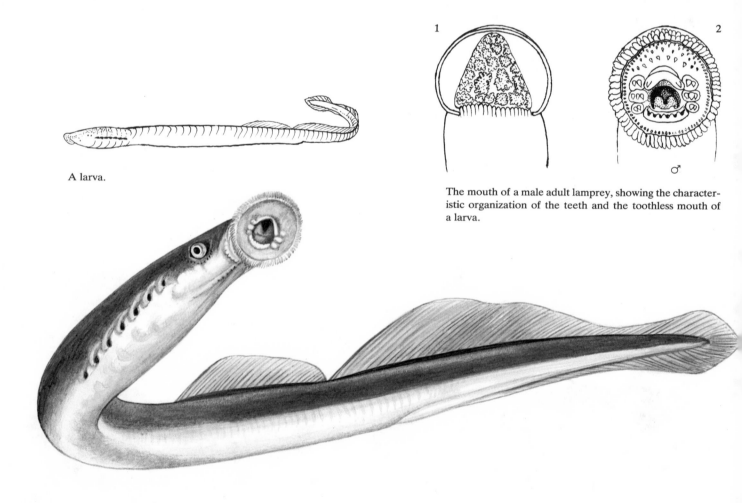

A larva.

The mouth of a male adult lamprey, showing the characteristic organization of the teeth and the toothless mouth of a larva.

Danube Lamprey
Eudontomyzon danfordi

The Danube lamprey has a typically eel-like form, a greyish blue to greyish brown back, yellow sides and a yellow or white belly. The adult lampreys attach themselves to both living and dead fish with their suctorial mouths and feed on the blood and flesh of their prey. On the suctorial mouth, between its edge and the three pairs of inner side plates, there are numerous minute teeth. These together with the tooth-bearing plates and tongue form a natural rasp which breaks up the skin and muscles of the dead fish or of the living prey.

The lampreys spawn *en masse* in the spring and it seems likely that the majority die after their first spawning. The larvae hatch after three to six days, depending on the temperature of the water. They live in the sand and mud at the bottom of the upper reaches of large and small rivers, where they feed on debris and also on small invertebrates. The Danube Lamprey is not a migratory species.

The larvae are blind for their eyes are covered with skin; they have triangular mouths and their fin borders are poorly developed. Larval development takes four to five years, after which time the larvae metamorphose. In June or July, the adults become sexually mature. However they do not spawn until the spring of the following year.

Synonym: Lampetra danfordii
Size: 15–25 cm
Weight: 40–60 g
Fecundity: 2,000–3,000 eggs
Distribution: The upper reaches of the River Danube and also in its tributaries.

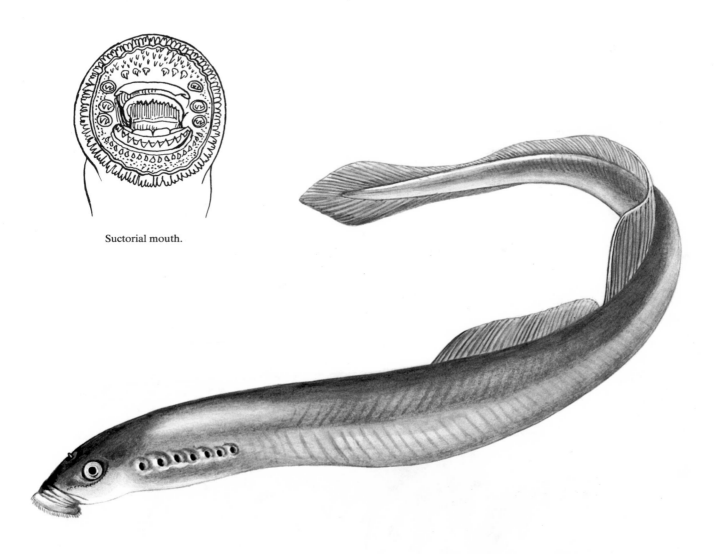

Suctorial mouth.

The jawless fishes of the order Myxiniformes have a primitive cartilaginous skeleton and no vertebrae. They live solely in the sea. They have no paired fins and even the unpaired fins are only poorly developed; their reduced eyes are hidden by skin. The mouth is encircled by fleshy barbels. The species belonging to the family Myxinidae have only one common outlet on either side for all their gill pouches.

MYXINIDAE

Common Hag

Myxine glutinosa

The Common Hag is long and eel-like and has only a single gill aperture on either side of the front of its body. Eyes, jaws and pectoral and ventral fins are absent and the body is covered with a thick layer of mucus whose secretion is stimulated chiefly by excitement. It is said that if a couple of hagfish are put into a bucket of water, they soon turn the water into a thick, slimy jelly with their mucus. The Common Hag is extremely variable in its colouration, and may range in colour from a reddish grey to many different shades of pink.

Hagfish live at depths of 20—600 m on and near the sea bed, into which they like to wriggle their bodies until only part of the head is left protruding; hags have even been found as deep as 1,100 m. They feed largely on benthic invertebrates and fish, but have a special predilection for sick fish or fish caught in nets. With its rasp-like tongue a hag gains access to a fish's body cavity and devours the flesh and viscera, often in the company of several dozen other hagfish. They are active chiefly at night.

Hagfish attain sexual maturity at a length of 25—28 cm and reproduce practically the whole year round. In some regions their depredations cause considerable damage among netted fish.

Size: 30—45 cm, maximum 60 cm
Weight: 0.5—1 kg
Fecundity: 20—30 eggs
Distribution: Off the European shores of the Atlantic from Murmansk to Gibraltar; in the western part of the Mediterranean Sea; off the North American shores of the Atlantic Ocean.

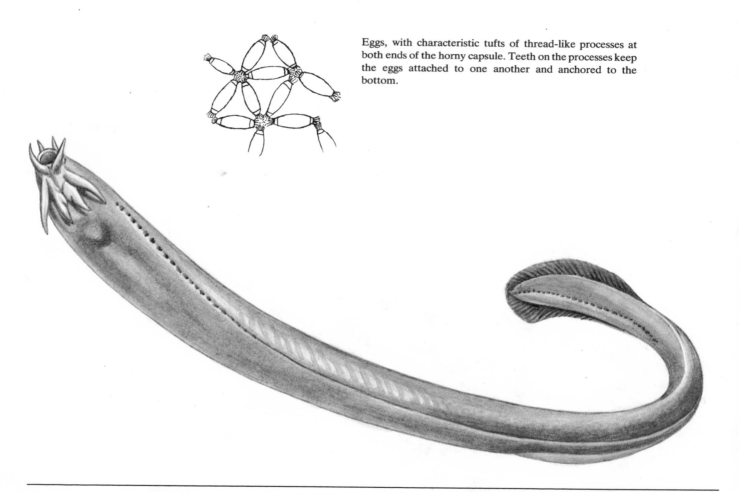

Eggs, with characteristic tufts of thread-like processes at both ends of the horny capsule. Teeth on the processes keep the eggs attached to one another and anchored to the bottom.

The following fishes belong to the superclass Gnathostomata, to the class Chondrichthyes and to the subclass Elasmobranchii. Elasmobranchs have cartilaginous skeletons and skin covered with placoid scales. On either side of the body, five to seven gill slits open on to the surface. They have jaws (usually with sharp-pointed teeth) and their gills are supported by cartilaginous branchial arches. They do not possess a swim-bladder and the main hydrostatic organ is the large oil-rich liver. In the males, the medial edges of the ventral fins have been converted to accessory organs of copulation known as claspers. The order Hexanchiformes includes primitive sharks with six or seven pairs of gill slits, a single dorsal fin and a persistent notochord. The family Hexanchidae comprises a total of six species inhabiting warm seas.

HEXANCHIDAE

Six-gilled Shark
Hexanchus griseus

The Six-gilled Shark is a deep water shark living in tropical and subtropical seas and is frequently to be seen in the Mediterranean. In years when the warm Atlantic current is particularly strong it may even visit the coast of Iceland. It can be distinguished from other sharks by its six gill arches and it has no nictitating membrane on its eyes. The single dorsal fin is situated on the posterior half of its body. It has a blackish brown or greyish black back and sides and a light-coloured belly. This shark is viviparous, bearing its young alive, and the newborn young measure 50 cm in length. It feeds on fish, especially on various codfish and flounders and on large crustaceans; in a few sharks seals have been found in their stomachs. In warm water the Six-gilled Shark can be found at depths of 200—1,000 m; in colder water it stays closer to the surface.

Its economic significance is virtually nil. In the North Sea it is usually caught in the autumn, when it can be bought in fishmarkets, but its flesh is of poorer quality than that of the Porbeagle.

Synonym: Squalus griseus
Size: up to 5 m, generally 2 m or less
Fecundity: up to 100 young
Distribution: Tropical and subtropical seas.

Distribution of dangerous sharks. Blue — water dangerous the whole year round, red — water dangerous only during the summer months.

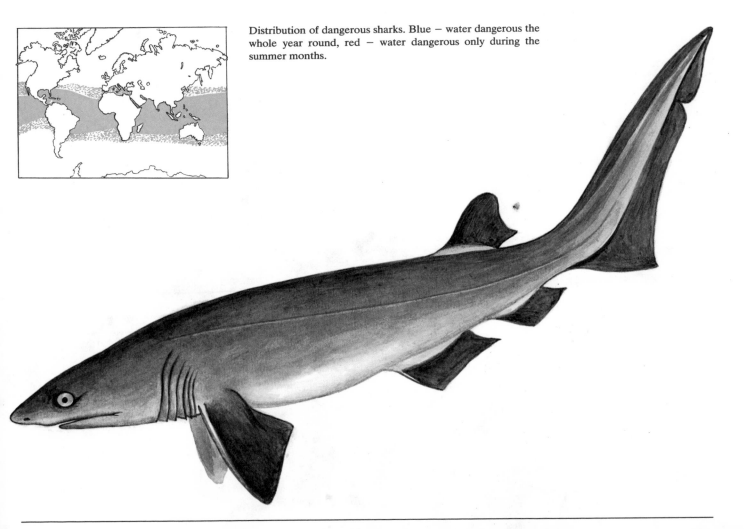

The order Lamniformes includes a large number of extant sharks characterized by two dorsal fins, one anal fin and five pairs of gill slits; the teeth in their jaws are all the same size. The family Lamnidae comprises large pelagic sharks.

Porbeagle
Lamna nasus

A big active shark, a fast swimmer with a distinct keel along each side of the tail, which helps to streamline the fish and increases its swimming speed. The first dorsal fin is much larger than the second one and often protrudes above the surface of the water. Like the belly, the posterior margins of both dorsal fins and of the caudal fins are almost white, while the back and the sides are blue-black or grey. The middle of the body is relatively deep, so that in form the shark resembles a tunny-fish. In groups of 20 to 30 the sharks accompany shoals of herring, sardines or mackerel which are the staple component of their diet. They are very voracious with large triangular teeth and they travel long distances in search of food.

Porbeagles are viviparous and, after fertilization, which usually takes place in the autumn, the female gives birth in the following summer to three to six young measuring 50—70 cm. During development the young consume unfertilized eggs in the oviduct.

Their flesh, known in some countries as 'sea veal', is relatively tasty and quite highly prized, but of late the annual catch has shown a tendency to diminish. Furthermore, since the Porbeagle attacks and feeds on economically important fishes, damages nets and also occasionally attacks human beings, it may be classified as a dangerous pest.

Commonest synonym: Lamna cornubica
Size: 3.5—4 m, maximum 5 m
Fecundity: 3—6 young
Distribution: Oceans in the temperate, subtropical and tropical belt; absent only in the cold waters of the Arctic and Antarctic Oceans and in the northern parts of the Atlantic and Pacific Oceans. Young specimens sometimes appear in river mouths.

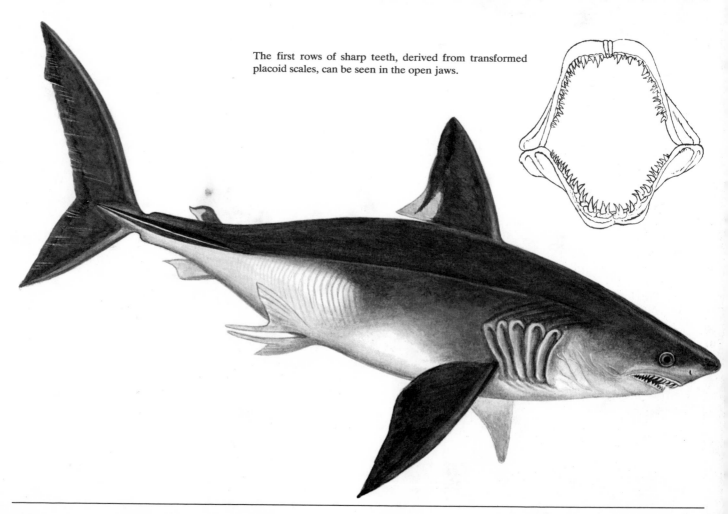

The first rows of sharp teeth, derived from transformed placoid scales, can be seen in the open jaws.

The family Cetorhinidae contains a single genus and species.

Basking Shark
Cetorhinus maximus

The sole member of its family, the Basking Shark is remarkable for its vast size and long, pronounced gill slits which stretch from its back to its throat. Large numbers of gill rakers are present on the inner surface of the branchial arches. The numerous teeth are small and blunt. It obtains its food from sea water in a similar manner to 'whalebone' whales, for it swims with its mouth open and strains off plankton from the inflowing water by means of its gill rakers. The gill rakers are shed every winter and grow again in the spring — perhaps because there is little plankton in the sea in the winter.

Basking Sharks mostly live a solitary life in the open sea, but from time to time groups of 50—250 individuals gather and migrate in search of food. The shark is greenish brown, sometimes almost black in colour, with grey spots on the anterior part. Basking Sharks are viviparous, with a three years' gestation period. About 100—150 years ago Basking Sharks were still hunted off Norway for the oil obtained from their livers and from time to time specimens measuring 7.5 m are still caught off European coasts. In large specimens the liver weighs 500—700 kg and accounts for roughly one third of the shark's total body weight. The economic significance of this species was never very great, however.

Size: maximum 14 m
Weight: up to 3.5—4 tons
Distribution: Cosmopolitan; often absent from tropical regions. One of the biggest sharks.

The commonest components of the food are crustaceans — Euphausiidae (1) and Gammaridae (2) — and small species of free-swimming molluscs (3).

The long, thickly packed gill-rakers are used for filtering off plankton (the shark's food) from the water.

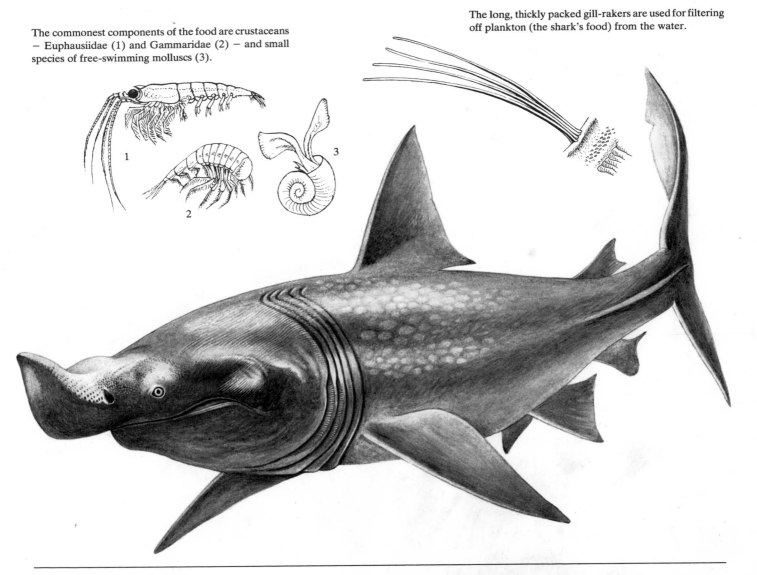

The family Alopiidae comprises a single genus with four species. The upper lobe of the caudal fin is strikingly long and the pectoral fins are strikingly large. Fox sharks inhabit every sea in the tropical, subtropical and temperate belt.

Thresher
Alopias vulpinus

A very distinctive shark, easily distinguished by its curved tail which often accounts for more than half the length of the shark. It has a greyish blue to black back, lighter sides which are sometimes mottled, greyish blue pectoral fins and a greyish white belly. The Thresher is a moderately large shark, in general females are larger than males; both sexes attain sexual maturity at a length of about 4 m. It is ovoviviparous and between two and four young sharks are usually born in the summer.

Threshers feed primarily on pelagic fishes such as herring and mackerel and also on squids and pelagic crustaceans; they may enter harbour areas in pursuit of prey. A shark is said to drive them into shoals by threshing movements of the long upper lobe of its tail and then to take its pick. The sharks live solitary lives, mostly in the surface layers of the open sea, at depths of up to 60 m, although they may sometimes be found in water as deep as 350 m, they are also occasionally seen nearer to the shore.

Its flesh is rather tough and used to be sold as 'white tuna' but its economic significance is negligible. It is not dangerous to human beings.

Size: 6 m and under
Weight: up to 300 kg
Distribution: Cosmopolitan. Fairly frequent in the Mediterranean and the temperate and subtropical parts of the Atlantic; occasionally strays into the North Sea in the summer.

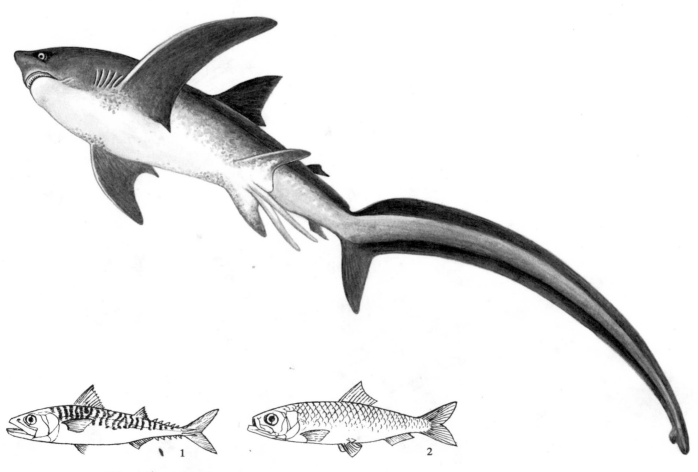

Pelagic fishes, in particular mackerel (1) and herring (2), are the commonest prey of the Thresher.

The members of the family Scyliorhinidae are characterized by the presence of a nictitating membrane in the eye and by a first dorsal fin starting posteriorly to a perpendicular drawn to the anterior edge of the ventral fins.

SCYLIORHINIDAE

Lesser Spotted Dogfish
Scyliorhinus caniculus

A typical small shark which lives in the coastal waters of the sea. It is a bottom dweller, swimming above a sandy or a muddy sea bed at depths of 15–20 m, but may descend to depths of about 100 m. It is yellowish brown to greyish red in colour, with a quantity of small dark spots and a few larger spots on its back and fins; its belly is light and unspotted: it is well camouflaged. It feeds chiefly on benthic molluscs, crustaceans and worms and to a lesser degree on small fish. The female lays up to 20 eggs up to a year after copulation. The eggs are enclosed in hard, horny capsules, about 6 cm long and provided with four long, filamentous, but strong spiral processes which keep the eggs attached to plants or to the sea bed. After eight to nine months' development inside the egg capsule the young sharks hatch out, complete with a tiny yolk sac.

Because of its small size and bright markings this shark is a popular fish in public marine aquaria. In Britain it is eaten as rock salmon or is used as bait; and other fish are dissected in schools and universities for teaching zoology.

Size: 60–80 cm, maximum 1 m
Weight: 5–10 kg
Fecundity: 2–20 eggs
Distribution: Off the coasts of Europe and Africa, from the middle of Norway to below the equator; also occurs in the Mediterranean and the Black Seas.

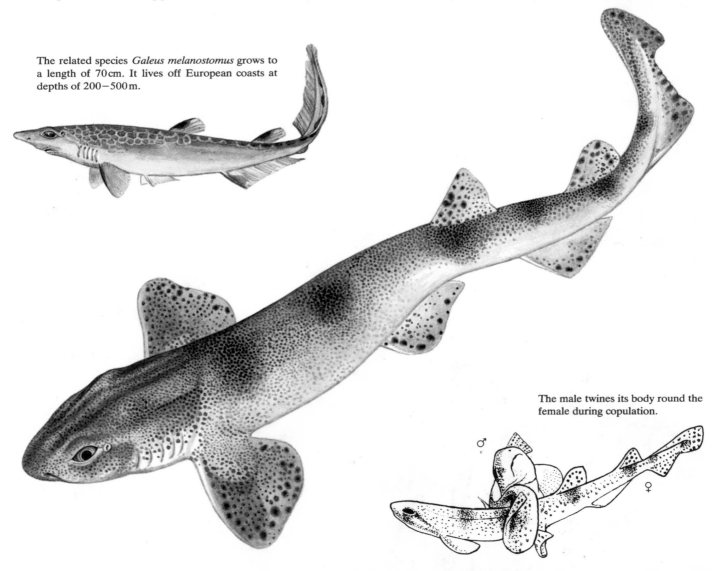

The related species *Galeus melanostomus* grows to a length of 70 cm. It lives off European coasts at depths of 200–500 m.

The male twines its body round the female during copulation.

Large Spotted Dogfish
Scyliorhinus stellaris

The Large Spotted Dogfish occupies a similar area of distribution to the Lesser Spotted Dogfish, but extends only as far as Dakar along the African coast and it is absent from the Black Sea. The two species have similar lifestyles, but the Large Spotted Dogfish has a preference for hard, rocky sea beds and it also eats more fish. The fishes can be distinguished from each other by the relative positioning of the anal and dorsal fins. In the Lesser Spotted Dogfish the second dorsal fin is situated on the base of the tail and only overlaps slightly with the posterior edge of the anal fin, whereas in the Large Spotted Dogfish it extends as far as the middle of the anal fin. The organization of the underside of the head also provides a differential character. In the Large Spotted Dogfish the nostril grooves do not lead right to the mouth, whereas in the Lesser Spotted Dogfish they do. Lastly, the markings of the two species are different, since the dark spots on the back, sides and fins of the Large Spotted Dogfish are much larger.

Breeding behaviour is similar in the two species; fertilization is internal, the females of both species can lay fertilized eggs up to a year after copulation and the eggs develop in egg cases. During copulation the male fish wraps its tail round the female fish to hold itself in place.

The Large Spotted Dogfish is not a frequent find in nets and the quality of its flesh is rather poor, so that it is economically unimportant. Because it is a small shark it is a favourite choice for inclusion in public marine aquaria.

Size: 60–100 cm, occasionally up to 150 cm
Fecundity: 20 eggs
Distribution: The Atlantic coastal waters of Africa and Europe, the Mediterranean.

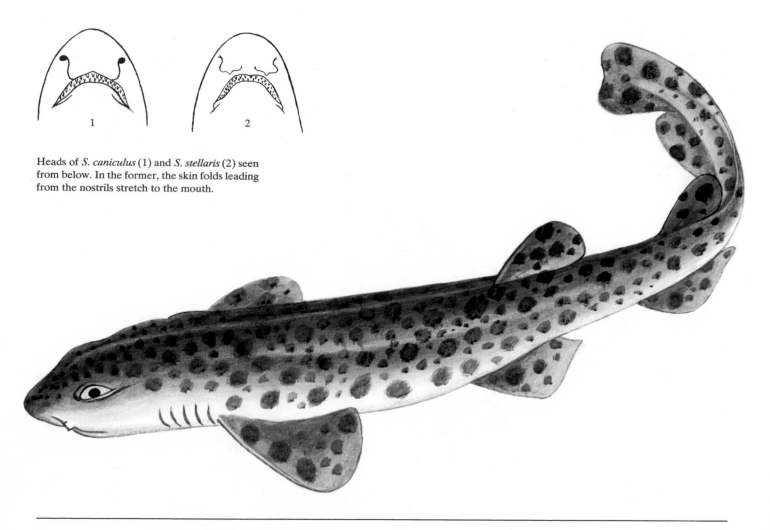

Heads of *S. caniculus* (1) and *S. stellaris* (2) seen from below. In the former, the skin folds leading from the nostrils stretch to the mouth.

The family Carcharhinidae is particularly rich in species and its 80—100 members inhabit tropical, subtropical and temperate seas all over the world. The characteristic features of this family are the position of the fifth gill slit which lies above the pectoral fin, the large upper lobe of the caudal fin and the absence of ridges along the sides of the caudal peduncle.

CARCHARHINIDAE

Blue Shark
Prionace glauca

The Blue Shark has a long, powerful body with strikingly long, curved pectoral fins. It has a dark blue back, somewhat lighter sides, blue fins and a white belly. After death it soon loses its magnificent deep blue colouring. The Blue Shark is a cosmopolitan inhabitant of warm seas where it generally remains near the surface.

In the summer the sharks undertake long migrations northwards, often accompanied by pilot-fish (*Naucrates ductor*); the distance depends on the temperature of the water and in sunny summers sharks even visit the North Sea and the southern coast of Scandinavia. They frequently accompany fishing boats and other ships and feed on garbage and the remains of discarded fish; they also hunt fish and other sharks.

Economically the Blue Shark is not very important, but it is prized by anglers. About 3,000 to 5,000 individuals are caught every year around Great Britain alone and in Japanese waters the sharks are caught in large numbers. This shark has been described as a man-eater, but its danger in this respect is grossly overrated.

It is viviparous, bearing its young alive; a brood usually consists of sixty young which are born when they are some 30—50 cm long.

Synonym: Carcharhinus glaucus
Size: up to 4 m
Weight: up to 150 kg
Fecundity: about 60 young
Distribution: Warm seas all over the world.

The related Tope *(Galeorhinus galeus)* inhabits warm water in all the oceans. It grows to a length of 1.5 m and is ovoviviparous, with a gestation period of about 10 months. This species is another fish that is popular with anglers.

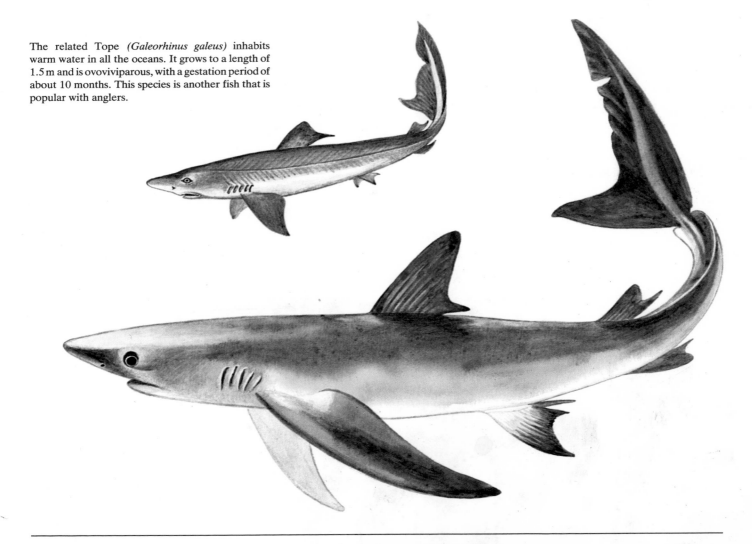

Smooth Hound
Mustelus mustelus

The Smooth Hound is much less active than many other sharks, living near the bottom of the sea on the continental shelf at depths of up to 150 m and travelling only short distances. It has two dorsal fins of almost the same size; the first is slightly larger and is situated just behind the pectoral fin, while the second is sited ahead of the small anal fin. The body of the shark is grey with a lighter belly, and there are distinctive whitish spots on the back and sides, especially in young individuals. It feeds chiefly on molluscs and bottom-dwelling crustaceans, including crabs, spider crabs, lobsters and squat lobsters, crushing their shells with its flat-topped teeth; fish form only a minor component of its diet. The teeth are so different from those of any other European shark that they form a good distinguishing feature.

Smooth Hound are viviparous; during development the embryos are nourished by way of a yolk placenta reminiscent of the true placenta of mammals. The female gives birth in autumn to up to twenty young, each measuring 15 cm. The young sharks swim into deeper water after the birth.

The shark is consumed on a small scale in Mediterranean countries.

Size: 1−1.8 m, maximum 2 m
Fecundity: 20 young
Distribution: The littoral zone of the Atlantic. It is most common in the tropical waters but in the summer its northern limit stretches as far as the southern coast of Norway. It also lives in the Mediterranean.

Distribution map of *M. mustelus*.

The related species *M. canis* found along European coasts, occurs as far as the Bay of Biscay, measures 1−1.5 m (maximum 3 m) and does not present any danger to human beings.

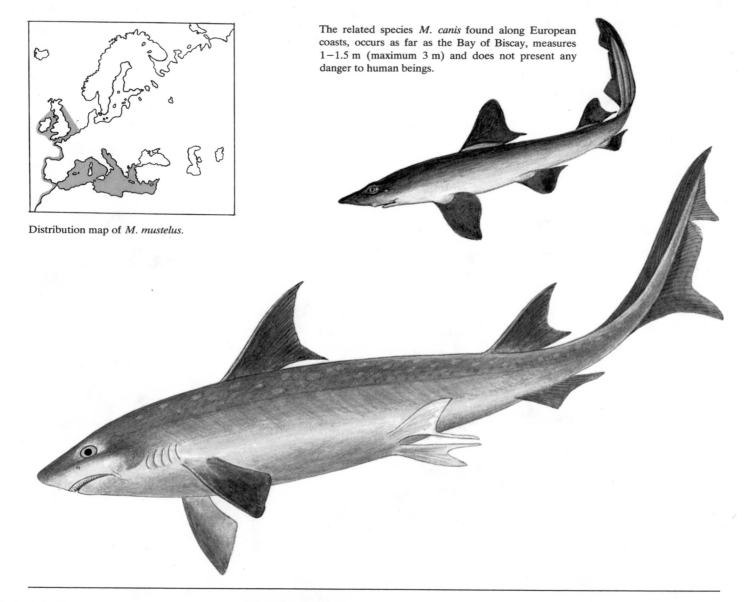

The family Sphyrnidae comprises about six species of big sharks characterized by curious lateral widening of their head to a shape resembling a hammer.

Hammerhead
Sphyrna zygaena

An extraordinary shark with its strange hammer-shaped head. Some experts consider that the head acts as an auxiliary stabilizer during swimming, while according to others it enables the fish to determine more accurately the direction from which a scent is coming (of prey or blood for instance). Hammerheads feed mainly on fish, but small individuals feed on invertebrates, especially on crustaceans.

This is a viviparous species and the embryos develop in the female's body by means of a yolk sac firmly connected to the mother, a method of develop-ment similar to that seen in mammals. The young are generally born in the second half of the summer or in the autumn.

The Hammerhead's economic value is minimal, since its flesh is not often eaten and it is not used to make fish meal, because its tough, coarse skin, like that of most sharks, would ruin the machinery. Several cases of attacks on human beings by this species are on record and it is therefore classified as a dangerous shark.

Synonym: Squalus zygaena, Zygaena malleus
Size: 3.5−4 m, occasionally up to 5 m
Weight: 150−300 kg, occasionally up to 500 kg
Fecundity: up to 40 young
Distribution: Throughout the oceans, mainly in tropical waters, but also in subtropical and temperate seas, as far north as the North Sea and in the Mediterranean.

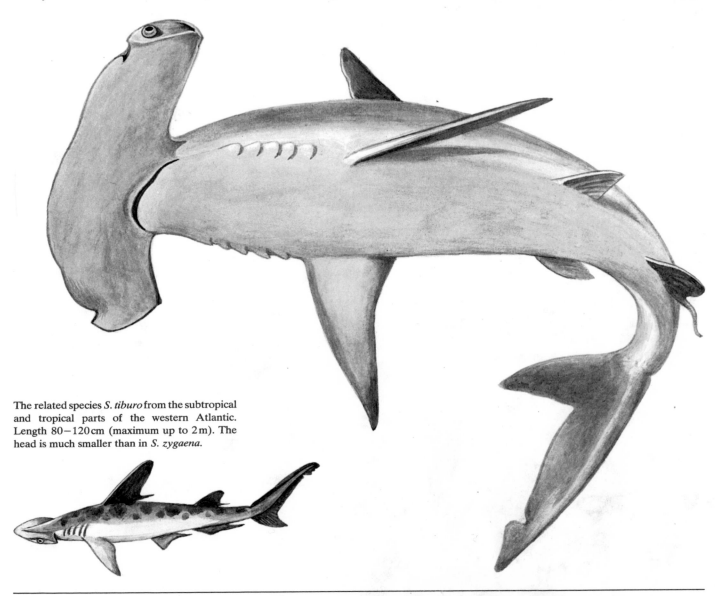

The related species *S. tiburo* from the subtropical and tropical parts of the western Atlantic. Length 80−120 cm (maximum up to 2 m). The head is much smaller than in *S. zygaena*.

The members of the order Squaliformes have no anal fin and their two dorsal fins are armed with large spines. The family Squalidae includes sharks with a slender, elongate body and no anal fin. Their most distinctive feature, however, are the free spines standing in front of each of the two dorsal fins.

Spiny Dogfish
Squalus acanthias

This is the commonest shark in the northern part of the Atlantic, where it occurs off the coasts of Europe, Africa and America. In the north it is to be found in the White Sea and off Iceland, southern Greenland and Labrador and it also occurs in the Mediterranean, the Black Sea and the Sea of Azov. In the Pacific and the southern hemisphere it is replaced by related subspecies. It has a long, pointed snout and large eyes and the upper lobe of its powerful caudal fin is distinctly larger than the lower one. It has two large spines connected with poison glands, one in front of each dorsal fin. Its back and sides are dark grey or brownish, it has a light-coloured belly and there are usually a few light spots on its sides.

These sharks live mostly in schools formed usually of fish of the same sex, near the sea bed but also in the open sea at depths of 10 to 200 m. In the spring they migrate shorewards to reproduce; in the autumn they return to deeper water. The fish is ovoviviparous, that is the young develop in egg-shells but inside the female, and after a gestation period of 18−22 months the female gives birth in the summer to about 10 young, each measuring 20−30 cm.

The Spiny Dogfish used to be persecuted because of the damage they did to catches and to nets, but fishermen now catch them instead because of the quality of the fat in the liver, which accounts for up to 20% of the total body weight. Nowadays some 30,000−40,000 tons are caught every year, partly for the manufacture of fish meal and partly for human consumption, as the flesh is quite tasty.

Size: 80−100 cm, occasionally up to 120 cm (females)
Weight: up to 8 kg, maximum 10 kg
Fecundity: 3−25 young
Distribution: Cosmopolitan.

Newborn young with remains of yolk sac.

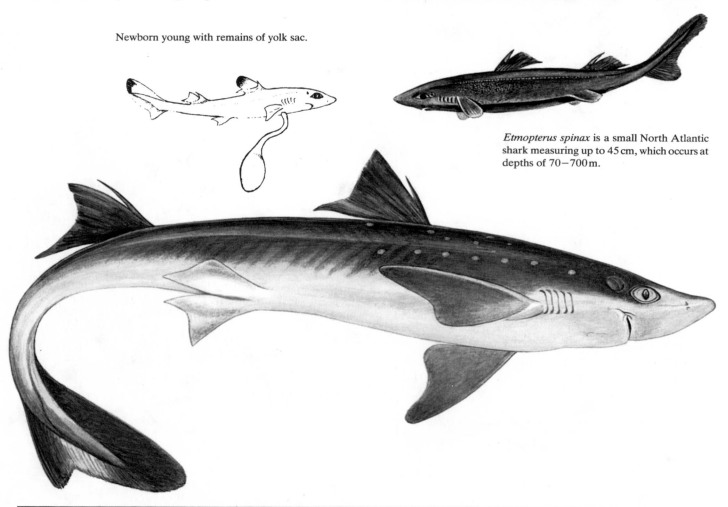

Etmopterus spinax is a small North Atlantic shark measuring up to 45 cm, which occurs at depths of 70−700 m.

In contrast to the members of the Squalidae, the sharks in the family Dalatiidae have no free spines in front of their dorsal fins. There are seven genera and twelve species in this family, distributed all over the world from the Arctic seas to the Antarctic.

DALATIIDAE

Greenland Shark
Somniosus microcephalus

Although usually a bottom-dwelling shark, the Greenland Shark often surfaces when chasing prey and it may then be hunted by Eskimoes with harpoons or with short lines. It is found most frequently at depths of 150—500m, but has been observed as far down as 1,200m. It is a long-lived and virtually omnivorous species and on a few occasions human remains — probably of drowned fishermen and sailors — have been found in its stomach. It is also a scavenger and accompanies large fishing fleets and floating 'fish factories', where it feeds on fish entrails and remains flung overboard. It is a big shark with two small dorsal fins, the first of which is situated roughly half-way along its body. The eyes and gill slits are also small compared with the length of the body. The entire body is dark blackish brown, which turns grey after death.

The data on its reproduction biology are very meagre. According to some sources, in the spring the female lays 300—500 eggs in horny capsules about 8cm long, while according to others it is ovoviviparous and gives birth to about ten young.

The Greenland Shark used to be caught in large numbers because of its liver fat, which has a high vitamin A content; its flesh was eaten dried or salted rather than fresh. In the present century the catches are decreasing and the flesh is made into fish-meal; it is said that it sometimes has toxic effects.

Size: 4—6m, maximum 8m
Weight: 250—500kg, occasionally up to 1,400kg
Distribution: Found throughout the north Atlantic, southwards to the mouth of the Seine, in parts of the Arctic Ocean and in the northern Pacific.

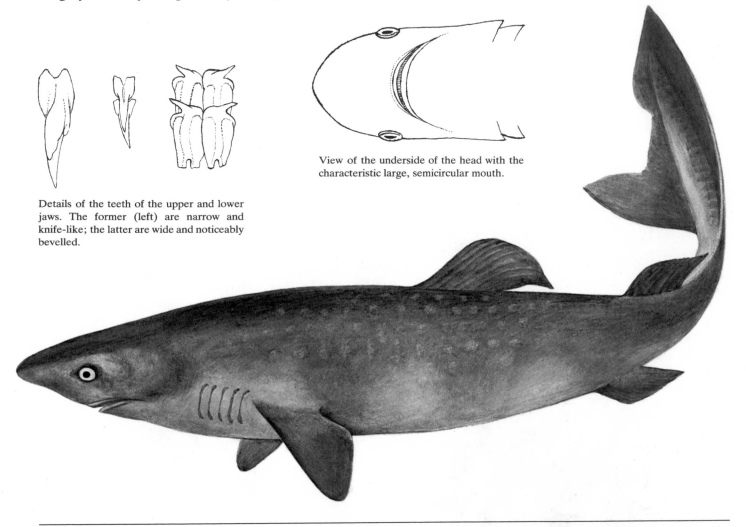

Details of the teeth of the upper and lower jaws. The former (left) are narrow and knife-like; the latter are wide and noticeably bevelled.

View of the underside of the head with the characteristic large, semicircular mouth.

The family Squatinidae is included among the sharks, but its members have many features reminiscent of rays, such as a dorsoventrally flattened body and wide, wing-like pectoral and ventral fins. However, as in other sharks the gill slits are on the sides of the head and the mouth is at the end of the body, not on the underside of the head as it is in rays.

Angel Ray
Squatina squatina

The Angel Ray is the only representative of the family off European shores except in the Mediterranean, where there are more species. It lives near the bottom of the sea at depths of 5–90 m, often almost half buried in sand or clay. Despite its flattened form the Angel Ray is a good swimmer and can cover considerable distances. It has two dorsal fins and its eyes and large spiracles are on the upper surface of its head. It has a greyish green to greyish brown back marked with small dark spots and a light-coloured belly. It feeds on bottom-dwelling fishes, chiefly flounders, plaice and rays, crabs and molluscs.

In the Mediterranean it spawns from February to April, off the French and English coasts somewhat later. It is ovoviviparous; some time after pairing (it is not known exactly how long, but usually in May or June) the female gives birth to between nine and sixteen young, each measuring about 20–25 cm.

The Angel Ray is economically unimportant, but if present in catches it is used for the production of fish-meal. Its flesh is considered edible, however it is of rather poor quality.

Size: 1.2–2 m, occasionally up to 2.5 m
Weight: 25–50 kg, maximum up to 80 kg
Fecundity: 10–25 young
Distribution: Found in the eastern Atlantic and also in the Mediterranean.

Distribution map for *S. squatina.*

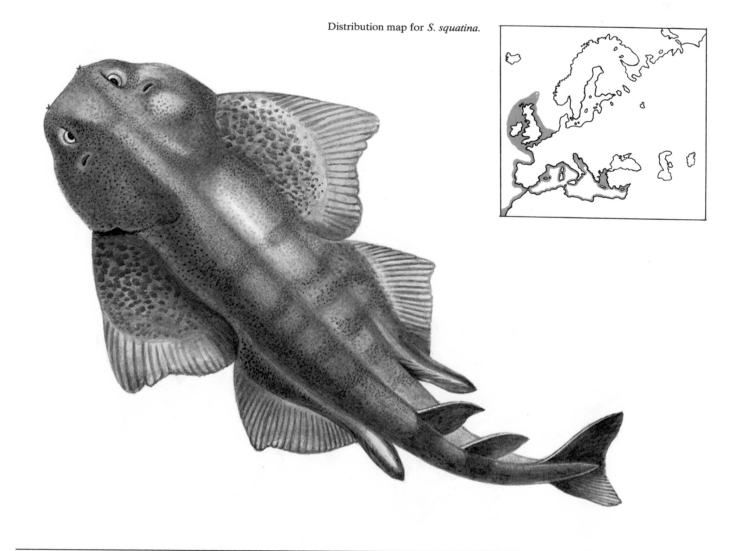

The rays of the order Rajiformes have a dorsoventrally flattened body and powerfully developed pectoral fins. The five pairs of gill slits open on the ventral surface of the body. Most members of the order are marine species. The family Rajidae comprises flattened cartilaginous fishes with wide rhomboidally-shaped pectoral fins. Most of its representatives have characteristic spines on the back; electric organs and anal fins are absent.

RAJIDAE

Thornback Ray
Raja clavata

As its name suggests, the most characteristic feature of this fish is its back which is covered with a quantity of small dermal spikes and larger spines, these latter distributed along the midline of the body and on the long tail. The spines spring from round, stud-like protuberances and are particularly large in sexually mature males. The ray is very variably coloured, but is usually cinnamon brown to light grey on the back and pale cream on the belly.

Thornback Rays generally live at depths of 10−60 m above a clayey or sandy seabed, but they occasionally venture into depths of 400 m. In the spring the sexually mature females migrate shorewards to shallow water, followed by the males. Fertilization takes place internally. The female lays eggs protected by horny capsules, each 6−10 cm long, from which the young rays − exact replicas of the adults − are hatched 16−20 weeks later. The empty capsules are often found thrown up in masses on the shore. After they have digested the rest of the yolk sac, the young feed on small crustaceans; the adult rays feed on invertebrates and fish.

Thornback Rays are caught relatively often, especially in dragnets and sometimes by anglers. They have moderately good flesh to eat and are commercially important fishes.

Size: 60−80 cm, females up to a maximum of 110 cm, width up to 75 cm
Weight: 6−10 kg, occasionally up to 17 kg
Fecundity: 5−20 eggs
Distribution: Along almost all the coasts of Europe; also along the Atlantic coast of Africa.

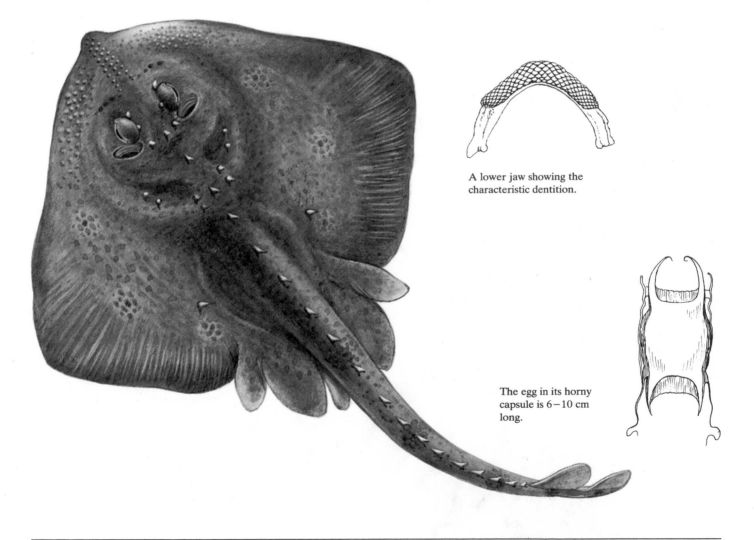

A lower jaw showing the characteristic dentition.

The egg in its horny capsule is 6−10 cm long.

Starry Ray

Raja radiata

This ray lives at greater depths than the Thornback, generally swimming just above the sea bed at depths of 50−100 m, but in the north venturing also to depths of 200−1,000 m. It can be distinguished from other rays by the 12−19 large spines running down the middle of its back and tail and the large number of somewhat smaller spines scattered over its back, which are all mounted on massive, radially toothed bosses (hence its name). It also has rather more rounded pectoral fins than other rays. It is variably coloured, but usually has a light cinnamon brown back marked with a quantity of cream or deep brown spots and a whitish belly.

It feeds mainly on various kinds of fish, but particularly on cod species, flounders, herrings and capelins, which it hunts near the bottom by smell. In its habits and reproduction it is similar to other rays.

The female matures when about 40 cm long, the male when 42 cm. The eggs and egg capsules are smaller than those of the Thornback (4−6 cm) and are laid mainly between February and June, although females containing eggs can be caught the whole year round. The surface of the egg capsule is covered with a number of long, thin, filamentous outgrowths which catch in rocks and seaweed and anchor the capsule.

The ray's flesh is not particularly good to eat and is seldom consumed fresh. Sometimes it is tinned, but more often it is used to make fish-meal.

Size: 40−60 cm, maximum 100 cm
Weight: 3−6 kg, maximum 14 kg
Distribution: This ray occurs further north than the Thornback Ray in the northwestern part of the Atlantic, off the coasts of Iceland, in the North Sea; it spreads southwards as far as the English Channel or occasionally to the Bay of Biscay.

Distribution map for *R. radiata.*

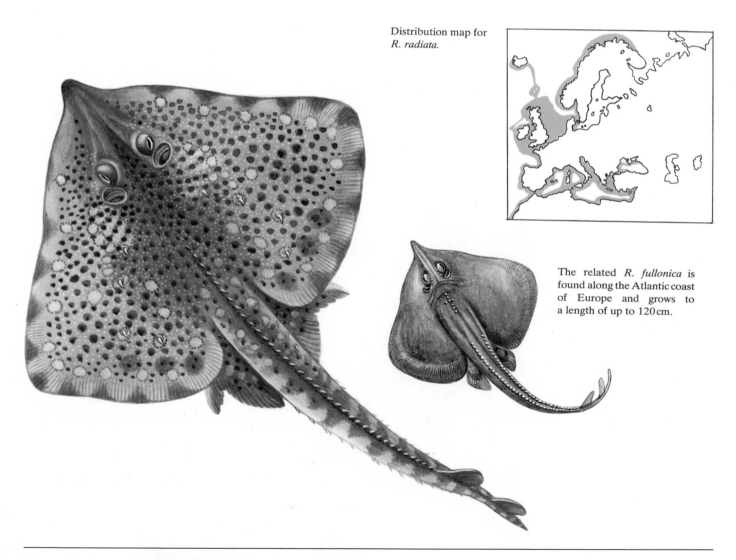

The related *R. fullonica* is found along the Atlantic coast of Europe and grows to a length of up to 120 cm.

Skate
Raja batis

The commonest and biggest ray in European waters. Its long, sharp-pointed snout measures two to three times the distance between its eyes. The back of adult individuals is strewn with small dermal teeth and there are twelve to twenty large spines running down the middle of the tail. The Skate's colouring varies from olive grey to dark cinnamon brown, usually with irregular light and dark spots; young skates generally have a pair of oval, dark-centred eye-spots on their backs, smooth toothless skin and only two pairs of spines around the eyes.

Skates live at depths of 30—600 m but young individuals can also be found in shallow water near the shore. Active predators, they feed chiefly on bottom-living fishes like small sharks, rays, angler fishes as well as crabs and lobsters and fishes like cod and herring. The females lay eggs (whose exact number is unknown) mainly between February and August. The eggs are enclosed in horny yellow capsules 14—29 cm long provided with two bundles of long, thin attachment filaments. When the young hatch out, two to nine months later, they measure 21 cm. Both sexes attain sexual maturity at a length of 1.5 m.

The Skate has savoury flesh which can be eaten fresh or preserved and oil is obtained from its liver. It is caught mainly by trawlers and in recent years the annual catch has been in the region of 2,000—3,000 tons. Nowadays big specimens are caught less often than they were forty or fifty years ago.

Size: 1.5—2.5 m, maximum 2.85 m, width up to 2 m
Weight: 75—100 kg, maximum 113 kg
Distribution: The Atlantic Ocean from Iceland and northern Norway southwards to the western part of the Mediterranean Sea.

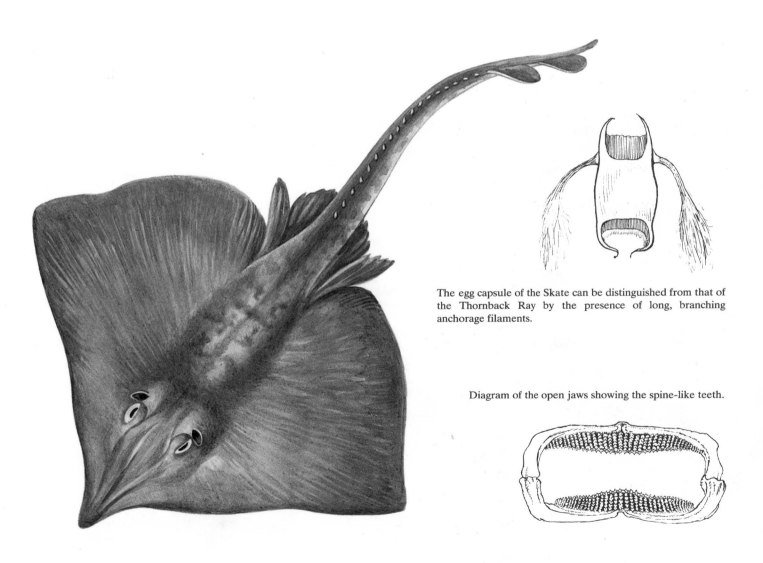

The egg capsule of the Skate can be distinguished from that of the Thornback Ray by the presence of long, branching anchorage filaments.

Diagram of the open jaws showing the spine-like teeth.

Long-nosed Skate

Raja oxyrhynchus

A striking ray which can be distinguished easily from the others by its long snout, equal to over a third of the width of its body. The skin of the back is smooth, except for a few spines on the snout and those on the tail. The fish has many sharp teeth, 32–42 rows of them in the lower jaw, all more or less the same size. The colour of the back varies from grey to brown with light brown or milky white spots, to almost black. The underside is grey, with large numbers of small marginal spots.

Like most other rays, the Long-nosed Skate lives on the sea bed in water 100–1,000 m deep, but is most often caught on a soft clayey sea bed at depths of 130–275 m. The female lays eggs in the Mediterranean in February to April, in the North Sea in June and July, the exact timing depending on the temperature of the water. The egg capsules are biconvex, with short anterior and posterior horny outgrowths; not including the outgrowths the capsules are usually 12–13 cm long and 7–10 cm wide but in the Mediterranean they may be somewhat larger. The young skates feed on crustaceans and then gradually change over to fish; they hunt small specimens of the Norway Haddock, gurnards and dragonets amongst others, and attain sexual maturity when they measure one metre in length.

The Long-nosed Skate is a common species, but its ecology is still obscure. It has some minor economic significance. Here and there it is picked up by trawlers looking for other fish.

Synonym: Raja vomer
Size: up to 150 cm, width of body disc up to 1 m
Distribution: The eastern part of the Atlantic Ocean from Senegal to Norway, in the North Sea and also in the Mediterranean Sea.

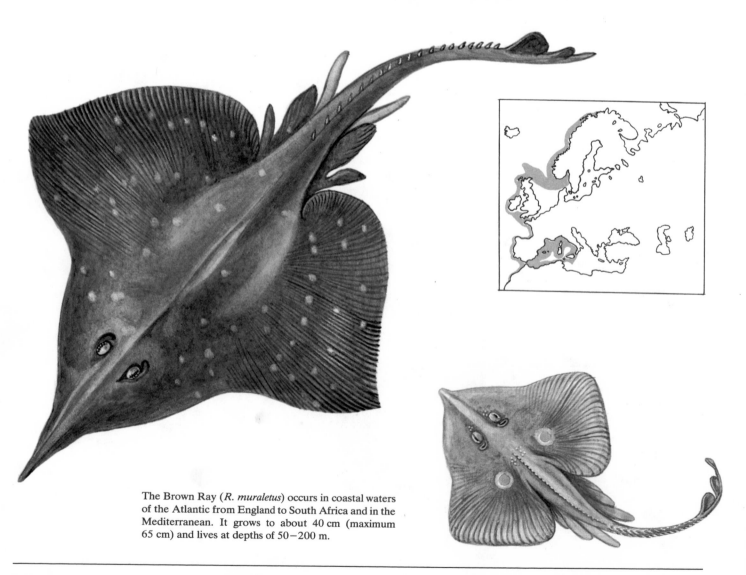

The Brown Ray (*R. muraletus*) occurs in coastal waters of the Atlantic from England to South Africa and in the Mediterranean. It grows to about 40 cm (maximum 65 cm) and lives at depths of 50–200 m.

Arctic Skate
Raja hyperborea

The Arctic Skate lives in the cold seas of the northern Atlantic at temperatures of close to freezing point. It is found over clayey seabeds, in water about 500−800 m deep, but is occasionally caught at depths of over 2,000 m, or sometimes in shallow water only 250−300 m deep.

It is somewhat similar in shape to the Starry Ray, but has a longer and sharper snout, a wider forehead and substantially more spines (22−30) down the middle of its back (*R. radiata* has only 12−19). The body disc is quite thick and the dorsal surface is usually bluish grey (sometimes brownish grey) with small dark and light spots. The underside of a young specimen is a dingy yellowish white. In an adult individual it is marked with dark spots; these sometimes join together to form dark bands which take up more of the surface area of the underside than the yellowish white ground colour. Little is known of its life and habits, because it lives at considerable depths and is seldom caught. It feeds on crustaceans of the family Euphausiidae and on fish. The egg capsules are similar to those of the Starry Ray, but are larger. They are 8−12 cm long and 5−8 cm wide and the newly hatched young measure about 15−16 cm. The number of young produced by each female is unknown at the present time.

The flesh of this ray is not good to eat and it is economically unimportant.

Synonym: Raja borea
Size: 65−70 cm, maximum 1 m
Distribution: The northern part of the Atlantic, in the area bounded by southern Norway, Iceland, Spitzbergen and Novaya Zemlya; also common off the coast of Greenland.

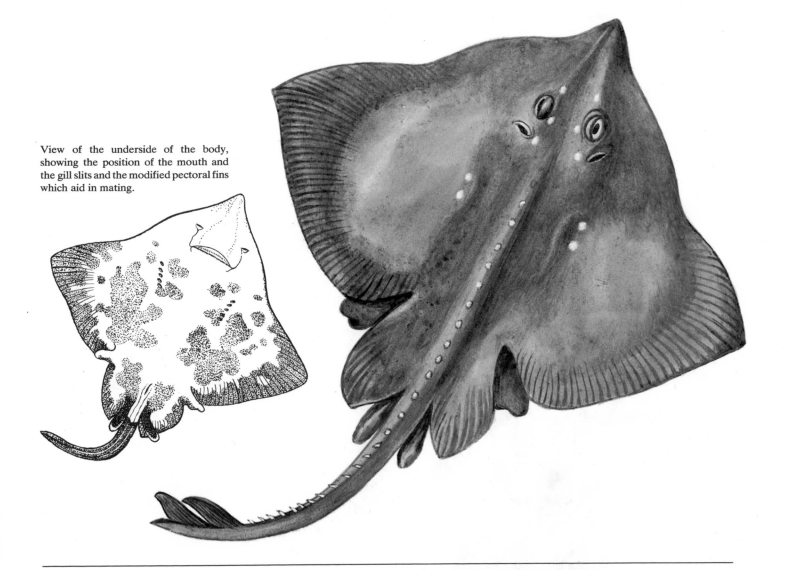

View of the underside of the body, showing the position of the mouth and the gill slits and the modified pectoral fins which aid in mating.

In the family Dasyatidae there are four genera and about thirty-five species living chiefly in the coastal waters of warm and temperate seas. The chief distinguishing feature of the family are the 'stings' — sharp needle-like spines growing from the upper surface of the tail, up to 30 m and over, which are primarily a weapon of defence against big sharks. The pectoral fins are also characteristically united at the tip of the snout.

DASYATIDAE

Sting-ray
Dasyatis pastinaca

An easily recognised ray whose characteristic feature is a spine 8—35 cm long with sharply serrated edges, about one third of the way down the back of the tail, which has grooves filled with venom glands on its underside. The ray attacks prey and enemies by whipping its tail round them and stabbing them with the spine. Such wounds are extremely painful and dangerous even to man, since the venom is both neurotoxic and haematotoxic. Some individuals have two or more such spines on their tail. The body of the Sting-ray is shorter than the whip-like tail. Dorsal and caudal fins are absent. The body is free from spines and teeth (small teeth grow down the middle of the back in large individuals only). It has a greyish olive or brownish back and a light-coloured belly.

It lives mostly at depths of 5—75 m above a sandy sea bed and often buries itself in the sand. It tolerates the brackish water in river mouths and in quiet creeks. It feeds mainly on small fish, molluscs and crabs. The Sting-ray is an ovoviviparous species, with internal fertilization. The embryos develop in the enlarged oviduct and in the advanced stages of development feed on a substance secreted by its wall. The young are born in the summer, but in addition to these the oviducts usually still contain 12—32 eggs.

The flesh of the Sting-ray is edible and the large liver (which in females amounts to up to one third of their body weight) yields oil high in vitamin D.

Size: 1—2 m, maximum 2.5 m (females)
Weight: 10—25 kg, occasionally up to 40 kg
Fecundity: 4—12 young
Distribution: The European and African coasts of the Atlantic from Norway to the Cape of Good Hope, the Mediterranean, the Black Sea and the Sea of Azov.

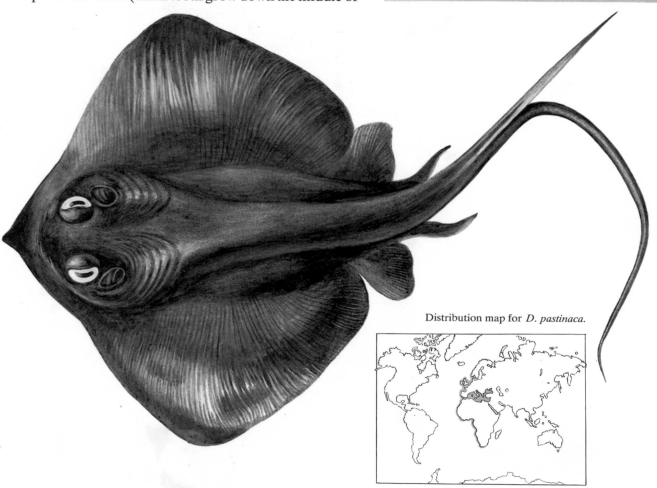

Distribution map for *D. pastinaca.*

In the members of the family Myliobatidae the head protrudes freely from the site of union of the pectoral fins, which have pointed ends. The tail is very long and in some species is armed with a needle-sharp outgrowth. There are five genera in the family with about twenty-five species inhabiting warm coastal waters in all the oceans of the world.

MYLIOBATIDAE

Eagle Ray
Myliobatis aquila

A distinctive ray with a long whip-like tail, no caudal fin, and one or two serrated spines behind the dorsal fin, supplied with venom glands and capable of causing painful injury to human beings. From above, with its long, sharp-tipped pectoral fins, the ray looks like a bird of prey — a resemblance reflected in its vernacular name in many European languages, from English to Russian and in its Latin name. The Eagle Ray has a greyish green to greyish brown back (spotted with light spots in young individuals) and a greyish white belly.

It lives in the open sea, mainly over a sandy or a clayey seabed at depths of about 100 m and prefers warm water. It feeds chiefly on crabs and molluscs, whose hard shells it crushes with the three rows of flat, tabulate teeth on either side of its mouth. It is ovoviviparous and in the later stages of development the young feed on the secretion of the oviducts.

It swims comparatively well and fast compared with other rays, sometimes near the surface, and is occasionally hunted by skin divers armed with harpoons. Economically it is unimportant.

Commonest synonyms: Raia aquila, Myliobatis noctula
Size: 1.5−2 m, complete with tail 4.5 m
Weight: 20−25 kg
Fecundity: 5−7 young
Distribution: From the coast of southern Norway north of the British Isles to the coast of South Africa. Present in the Mediterranean. Abundant off the coast of southwestern Ireland and in the English Channel.

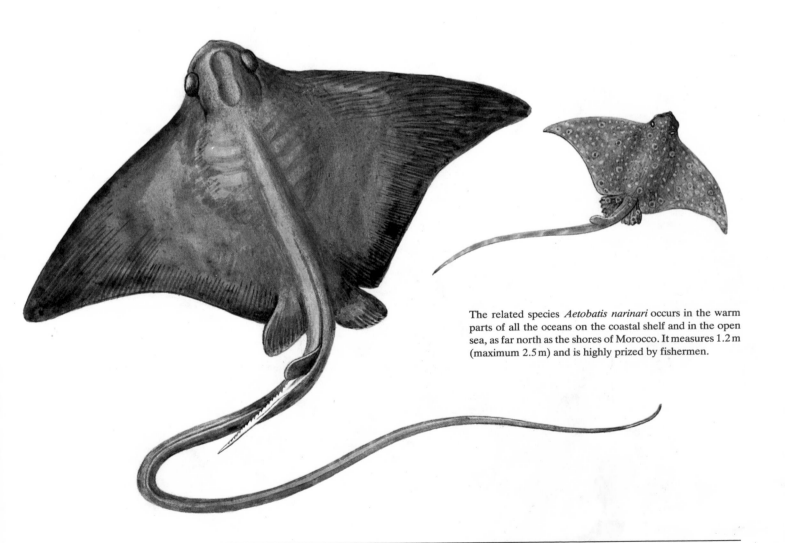

The related species *Aetobatis narinari* occurs in the warm parts of all the oceans on the coastal shelf and in the open sea, as far north as the shores of Morocco. It measures 1.2 m (maximum 2.5 m) and is highly prized by fishermen.

The representatives of the order Torpediniformes and the family Torpedinidae are characterized by a smooth skin, a well developed caudal fin and the presence of electric organs found on the anterior part of the body.

Electric Skate

Torpedo marmorata

The Electric Skate lives mostly very close to the sea bed over a sandy (but sometimes a clayey) bottom, usually at depths of 10−30 m but occasionally at a depth of 100 m. Its mottling usually makes it very hard to distinguish and sometimes it buries itself in the sand. It feeds on invertebrates and small bottom-dwelling fish, which it sometimes first of all stuns by discharges from its electric organs. The latter are paired kidney-shaped organs and are derived from muscles whose fibres have been converted to electric cells. Individually their voltage is negligible, but taken all together, up to 45−200 volts can be discharged with an amperage of 3−7 amps. In general, however, the discharges are used more for defence purposes. This Skate has a discoid body and a thick tail carrying two dorsal fins, the first of which is slightly larger than the second. It can be distinguished from the Dark Electric Ray by the spiracles, situated behind the eyes, which have fimbricated edges. The back is a dark cinnamon brown in colour with lighter mottling and the belly is cream-coloured. The fish is ovoviviparous with broods of up to 35 young, according to the size of the female.

Sometimes electric skates form a part of trawler catches, but they have no economic significance and although their flesh may be edible, its quality is poor and is rarely eaten.

Size: 60−80 cm, maximum 1.5 m
Weight: 2−5 kg
Fecundity: 5−35 young
Distribution: In the Mediterranean; in the Atlantic along the coastlines from the coast of Denmark in the north to South Africa in the south.

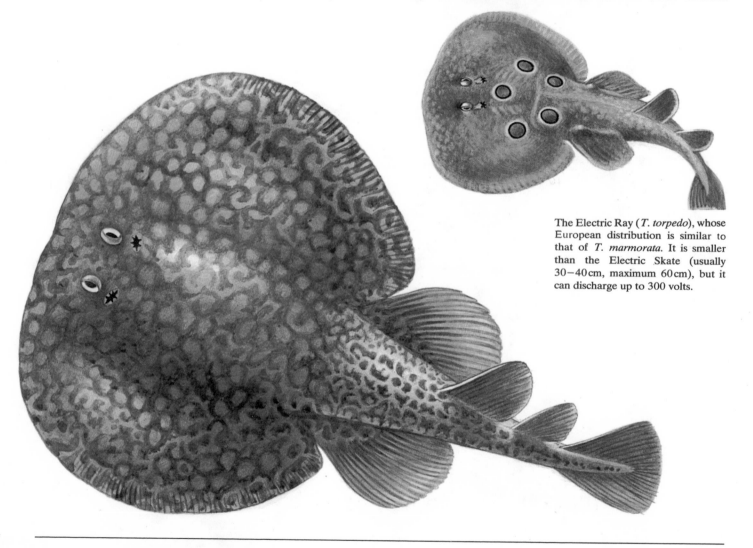

The Electric Ray (*T. torpedo*), whose European distribution is similar to that of *T. marmorata*. It is smaller than the Electric Skate (usually 30−40 cm, maximum 60 cm), but it can discharge up to 300 volts.

Dark Electric Ray

Torpedo nobiliana

The Dark Electric Ray occupies practically the same European waters as the Electric Skate, but it is more abundant in the English Channel and off the west coast of the British Isles. It lives above sandy or muddy bottoms at depths of 10–150 m (occasionally down to 350 m). It has a discoid body with two dorsal fins, the first distinctly larger than the second; the distance between them is greater than in *T. marmorata*. The pear-shaped spiracles have smooth edges, unlike those of the Electric Skate, and the fish is darker in colour; it generally has a greyish brown to dark cinnamon brown back and a pale pink belly. Dark Electric Rays are viviparous, but the size of the brood is unknown. It feeds chiefly on fish frequenting the sea bed and the remains of codfish and sharks have been found in its stomach; little is known about its feeding habits for sure, however. It has been observed to wrap its pectoral fins round its prey, to stun or kill it by electric shock and only then to eat it. Its electric organs have a higher output than the Electric Skate. The individual discharges have a voltage of up to 220 volts and an intensity of 8 amps and are thus a truly deadly weapon against either prey or enemies. This ray appears only sporadically in catches and it is economically unimportant.

Size: 150–180 cm
Weight: 40–50 kg, maximum 70 kg
Distribution: The European and African shores of the Atlantic and the Mediterranean.

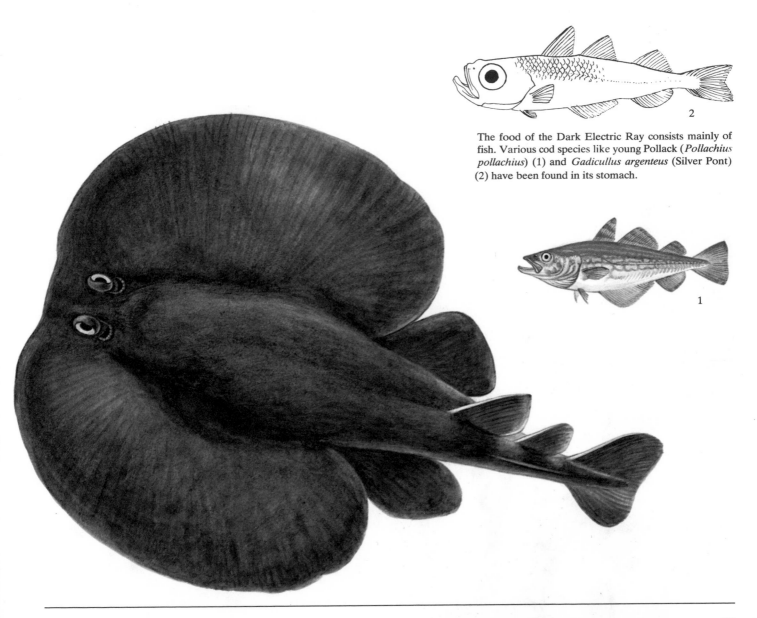

The food of the Dark Electric Ray consists mainly of fish. Various cod species like young Pollack (*Pollachius pollachius*) (1) and *Gadicullus argenteus* (Silver Pont) (2) have been found in its stomach.

The members of the subclass Holocephali are closely related to sharks and rays, but their upper jaw is fused with their skull, on either side of their head they have only one external gill slit covered by a leathery operculum. There is a single order Chimaeriformes, numbering three families and about twenty-five species.

Rabbit Fish

Chimaera monstrosa

A strange-looking fish with a scaleless, flat-sided, elongated body tapering off sharply towards the long, filamentous tail. The front of the first dorsal fin is armed with a long spine whose prick is painful but not dangerous, even though it is connected to a poison gland. The head of the males is surmounted in front by a curious outgrowth which is supposed to hold the female fast during pairing and the ventral fins have been converted to copulatory organs. The pectoral fins are often as long as the tail. The Rabbit Fish has a reddish to greyish brown back marked with dark brown spots and a light-coloured belly. The channels of its striking lateral line are very noticeable on the body and also clearly visible on the head.

This fish lives near the sea bed at depths of 300−500m, but may also be encountered at about 100m; in the winter it stays closer inshore. The main items of its diet are starfish, crabs, shrimps and molluscs; it bites off and chews single morsels, crushing the shells with its flat, tabulate teeth. Pairing takes place in the spring and summer and the eggs are fertilized internally. It is common to find rabbit fish in trawler catches, but they are not usually kept; oil may be obtained from the large liver.

Size: 80−100cm, maximum 150cm (including the filamentous tail)
Weight: 10−15kg, maximum 25kg
Fecundity: 100−200 eggs
Distribution: The Atlantic Ocean, around Iceland and from northern Norway down the entire coast of western Europe and northern Africa; also in the western part of the Mediterranean.

A rabbit fish egg enclosed in a horny capsule 15−18cm long. The oviduct never contains more than two ripening eggs at a time. The female carries them for a short time near the urogenital opening, where each is kept in place by a long, thin filament.

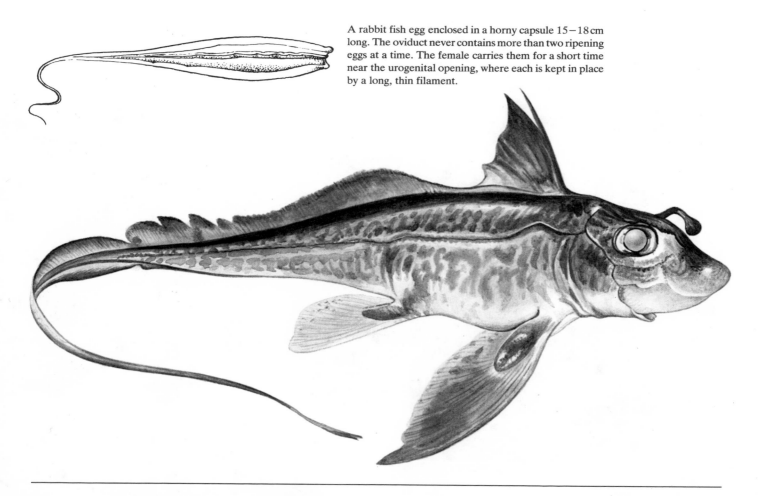

The subclass Actinopterygii includes freshwater and marine fishes with a primarily bony skeleton, gills covered by a common operculum and a swim-bladder. Sturgeons (order Acipenseriformes, superorder Chondrostei) have a secondarily cartilaginous skeleton with a fully intact notochord and a heterocercal tail, like sharks; the body is scaleless, except for a few rows of bony plates in places. The family Acipenseridae contains four genera of freshwater and migratory fishes inhabiting the northern hemisphere and displaying the characteristic features of the order.

ACIPENSERIDAE

Great Sturgeon, Beluga
Huso huso

This is the biggest member of the family, with a differently shaped mouth from the members of the genus *Acipenser*. It has a greyish black back, its belly is white (sometimes yellowish) and it has 11−14 yellow plates on its back, 40−52 on its sides and 9−11 on its belly.

It grows fast, measuring 1 m at an average age of 10 years, and can live 100 years. The males are sexually mature when about 10 years old and the females when 15. The Great Sturgeon migrates up big rivers like the Danube, Don and Volga to spawn; spawning takes place in May. The female's fecundity is enormous; it often produces several million eggs, which take eight days to hatch at 13 °C. The fry feed first of all on benthic invertebrates, but gradually change over to fishes − in the case of the Caspian Great Sturgeon mainly gobies, herring and cyprinid species; young Caspian seals (*Phoca caspica*) have also been found on occasion in the stomachs of very big specimens. Except at spawning time Great Sturgeons live in the sea, where food is plentiful. Some populations migrate upstream in the autumn (the 'autumn race'), and spend winter in the river, others in the spring.

The economic importance of the Great Sturgeon is considerable, but the catches are steadily diminishing owing to overfishing. The flesh is moist and very tasty and the large roes provide Beluga caviar.

Size: 5−8 m, today mostly under 2.5 m
Weight: up to 1,500 kg, today mostly 150−200 kg or under
Fin formula: D 62−75, A 28−42
Fecundity: 360,000−7,700,000 eggs
Distribution: The regions round the Black Sea, the Caspian Sea, the Sea of Azov and the Adriatic.

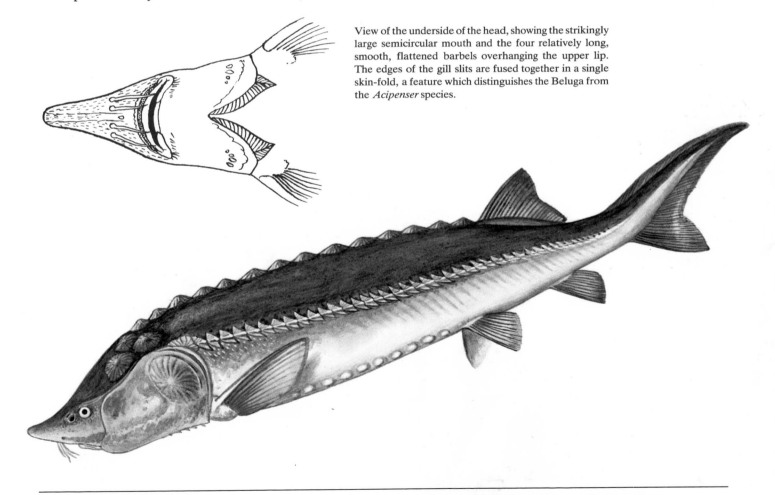

View of the underside of the head, showing the strikingly large semicircular mouth and the four relatively long, smooth, flattened barbels overhanging the upper lip. The edges of the gill slits are fused together in a single skin-fold, a feature which distinguishes the Beluga from the *Acipenser* species.

Common Sturgeon
Acipenser sturio

There are 16 *Acipenser* species living in Eurasia and North America, distinguished from each other by the shape of the mouth and the number and shape of the bony plates in the skin. The Common Sturgeon has a characteristic elongate snout with barbels closer to its mouth than to the tip of the snout. It has 9—13 scutes or bony plates on its back, 24—44 on its sides and 9—11 on its belly. The first ray of its pectoral fin is thicker than the rest. It has a greyish green or greyish brown back, a white belly, dingy white scutes and brownish fins. This is one of the biggest sturgeons, growing relatively fast and measuring about 1.5 m when ten years old.

The Common Sturgeon originally lived in coastal waters all round Europe and the east coast of North America and each year the fish migrated up the major rivers to spawn, but today only isolated specimens are caught in west European waters, none migrate up the Rhine and the Elbe any more and only comparatively few are left in the Black Sea and its tributaries. The males reach maturity when seven to nine years old,

the females between eight and fourteen. When spawning the females are extremely prolific, the number of eggs varying from one to two million. The fry feed on benthic invertebrates; adult sturgeons feed mainly on fish, but also take molluscs, bristle-worms and crabs. In the sea they probably frequent water over a sandy or a clayey bed; at spawning time they do not travel so far upstream as the Great Sturgeon. The Common Sturgeon population is today everywhere so small that its economic importance is minimal. Fishing is not the only reason for its decline and the pollution and destruction of its spawning sites together with dam construction seem to have made it almost impossible for it to increase its numbers again.

Size: up to 3 m
Weight: up to 300 kg
Fin formula: D 31—47, A 21—34
Fecundity: 800,000—2,400,000 eggs
Distribution: The Atlantic coast of Europe, the Mediterranean and the Black Sea; also present in the Baltic Sea and in Lake Ladoga and Lake Onega.

Distribution areas of *A. sturio* (blue) and *A. ruthenus* (red.)

The related species *A. güldenstädti* lives in the Black Sea and the Caspian Sea. It is smaller than *A. sturio*, grows to a maximum length of 2.5 m and weighs up to 100 kg. It has a noticeably short snout with smooth barbels.

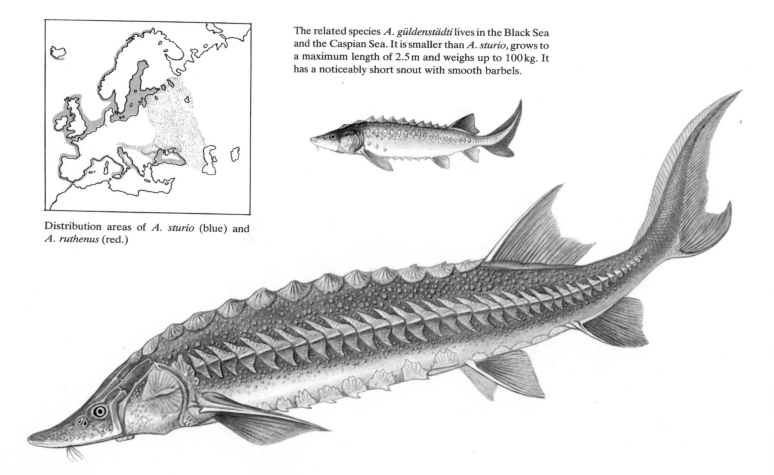

Starry Sturgeon

Acipenser stellatus

This sturgeon has a strikingly long, narrow snout accounting for 62—65% of the length of its head, with smooth barbels situated nearer to its mouth than to the tip of its snout. It has 11—14 rows of scutes on the back, 30—35 scutes on the sides and 10—11 on the belly; in addition its sides are covered with minute star-shaped platelets. The back above the lateral line is brownish black, the belly is light. This sturgeon measures about one metre in length by the time it is sexually mature at about 10—15 years old. Migration may take place in the spring from March to June, or in the autumn in October and November; autumn migrants spend the winter in the river and spawn there in the following spring. The eggs are attached to stones and if the water is warm (20 °C) the young hatch in five days. The fry remain for two to three months in the river and then migrate downstream to spend some time in the river mouth before entering the sea where they remain until sexually mature. The adult fish probably frequent the same kinds of places as the Common Sturgeon and feed on invertebrates and fish.

The catches of this sturgeon are steadily diminishing, although economically it is still one of the most important. Steps have been taken since the war to protect its spawning sites and the young fish. It has also been introduced into the Sea of Aral.

Size: up to 220 cm, average 100—150 cm
Weight: 15—25 kg, occasionally up to 70 kg
Fin formula: D 38—49, A 20—30
Fecundity: 20,000—360,000 eggs
Distribution: The Black Sea and the Caspian Sea; spawns in their tributary rivers.

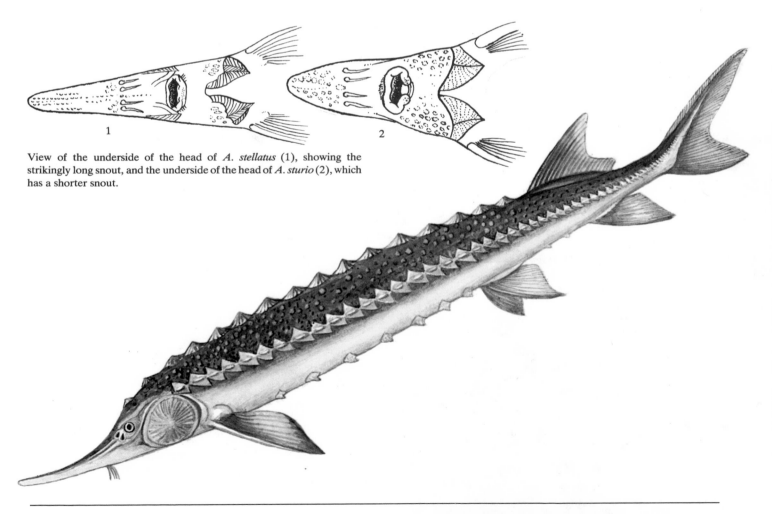

View of the underside of the head of *A. stellatus* (1), showing the strikingly long snout, and the underside of the head of *A. sturio* (2), which has a shorter snout.

Sterlet

Acipenser ruthenus

The smallest sturgeon growing to a length of half a metre by the time it is eight to ten years old. It has a dark greenish grey back, sometimes with a brownish pink tinge, and a light, slightly yellowish belly. The bony plates on its sides are also light and in young specimens they look like a white band running the length of the body. There are 58—71 small dermal plates on its sides, 12—14 on its back and 12—16 on its belly.

The Sterlet is found only in fresh water. The males mature when four to five years old, the females between five and nine. The fish usually spawn in May over a stony bottom after migrating upstream. The fry remain in the river bed, where they feed on insect larvae and insects floating on the surface of the water; large specimens will occasionally eat small fish. The adult fish live in the main channels of large rivers and approach the bank only at night, when they can be caught with dragnets.

These are highly prized fish, but their numbers are steadily decreasing from overfishing and from severe river pollution which has destroyed the spawning grounds. Like other sturgeons, the Sterlet can interbreed with related species. The advantage of such hybrids is that they stay permanently in fresh water and can be used to populate the water behind large dams. Sterlets are also kept in ponds.

Size: up to 120 cm, mostly 50—60 cm
Weight: maximum 19 kg, mostly 2—3 kg
Fin formula: D 38—49, A 11—18
Fecundity: 11,000—140,000 eggs
Distribution: Found in the rivers emptying into the Caspian Sea and the Black Sea, also in the North Dvina, the Ob and in the river systems of Lake Ladoga and Lake Onega.

Head of *A. ruthenus* from the side, showing the finely 'hairy' barbels close to the upper lip.

Head of *A. güldenstädti* (2), showing the short snout and smooth barbels.

The higher bony fishes (superorder Teleostei) are numerically the largest chordate group, of fishes in particular and of chordate animals in general. They have a homocercous (symmetrical) tail, a bony skeleton, a properly developed vertebral column and scales in the form of thin bony plates. The order Clupeiformes, with about twenty families, comprises relatively primitive and mostly pelagic fishes whose swim-bladder is connected to their alimentary tube. The family Clupeidae includes economically important marine and migratory fishes with a terminal mouth and a long anal fin. They live in shoals and feed on plankton.

CLUPEIDAE

Herring
Clupea harengus

Herrings have dark, green- or blue-tinged backs, lighter sides and silvery white bellies; sometimes their opercula and sides glisten like gold. They are one of the most important food fishes in the world. They live in the north Atlantic, swimming shorewards to spawn in March and April, to their main spawning grounds along the coast of Norway. The eggs are deposited on a sandy or clayey sea bed at a depth of 130−250 m and at a temperature of 4−7 °C; they hatch after two to three weeks. The adult herrings return to the open sea after spawning. The eggs and fry drift in the sea and are carried by the currents far away from where they were spawned. At the end of their first season, in the autumn when they measure 4−6 cm, the young herrings return towards the shore. In addition to populations which spawn in the spring there are other populations which spawn in the autumn, in shallow water further away from the shore.

The average annual catch of herring at one time was 1.3−2 million tons; today, however, it has decreased, due to overfishing of young fish.

Size: up to 45 cm
Weight: maximum 0.7 kg
Fin formula: D 16−22, A 13−20
Fecundity: 10,000−100,000 eggs
Distribution: The North Atlantic, some of the adjoining Arctic waters and along the coasts of Europe as far as the Bay of Biscay; also occurs off southern Greenland from Labrador down to the 40th latitude and in the northern part of the Pacific.

The Herring produces a number of local forms. For example, *C. harengus pallasi* lives to the east of the White Sea and in the northeastern part of the Pacific.

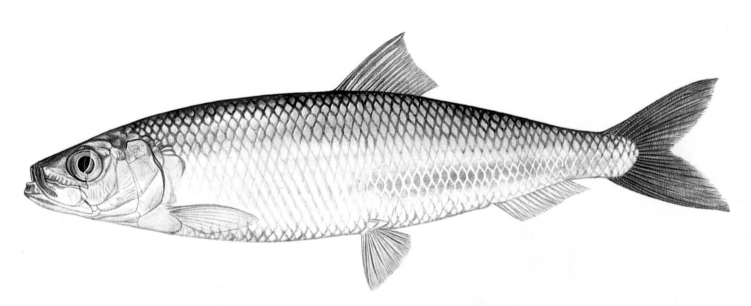

Sprat

Sprattus sprattus

A tiny pelagic fish very closely related to the Herring, but with sharper scales and a keel-like belly. The Sprat has a metallic blue or greenish back and a silvery white belly and sides, here and there with a touch of yellow. It occurs off European coasts from the Lofoten Islands to Gibraltar and is also present in the Mediterranean and the Black Sea. It is most often found in coastal waters especially in brackish water near river mouths; in the Black Sea, however, it has been described as appearing in the open sea. It congregates in large shoals and is a short-lived fish, usually living for about four years. Shoals are generally made up of individuals of the same size. The Sprat matures in its second year and it has an extended spawning period. For instance, in the North Sea spawning lasts from January to June, while in the Black Sea there is one peak at the beginning of the summer and another in October. Spawning occurs intermittently, about eight to ten batches of eggs being laid every few days. Sprats feed on zooplankton, other fishes and the fry of other species.

They are economically very important fishes, especially for the fishing industry; in some years the catch amounts to 800,000 tons. The chief European countries involved are Denmark, Norway and the USSR. Since the flesh of the Sprat is not particularly tasty when fresh, its flavour is improved by salting or marinading, but the greatest delicacy are smoked sprats, which are sold in tins.

Synonym: Clupea sprattus
Size: 13—16 cm, occasionally up to 18 cm
Weight: 50—70 g
Fin formula: D 15—19, A 17—23
Fecundity: 6,000—40,000 eggs
Distribution: The eastern part of the Atlantic from the Lofoten Islands to Gibraltar, the Mediterranean, the Baltic Sea and the Black Sea.

The distribution map of the Sprat shows that it prefers shallow coastal waters and may be found in brackish water. There is a separate Baltic subspecies, *S. sprattus balticus.*

Allis Shad
Alosa alosa

Fishes of the genus *Alosa* (shads) are distinguished from the other genera of the family Clupeidae by the very long scales at the base of the caudal fin. The various shad species are differentiated largely by the number of their gill-rakers, which are thin and are longer than the lamellae. As in other herring species, their function is to filter off plankton. The Allis Shad has a high, flat-sided body and a sharp ridge on its belly. It has a dark green-blue back and its silvery sides sometimes have a golden gleam. There is a striking large dark spot on the edge of each operculum and a few dark spots on its sides; these are particularly conspicuous in dead fish.

The Allis Shad is a migratory, anadromous species which migrates into fresh water to spawn in May, in river water with a strong current and a sandy or stony bed. The adult fish return to the sea after spawning but the fry remain in fresh water until the autumn, when they are carried by the current downstream to the sea. In the sea the Allis Shad feeds on zooplankton, in brackish water in the mouths of large rivers on various crustaceans; large individuals probably also catch fish.

These fishes used to be caught regularly in French rivers and in the Rhine in the early part of the century, but catches had already fallen practically to zero before the Second World War. This was due to the absence of any fishing controls, to river pollution and also to the destruction of suitable spawning grounds. Their flesh is very tasty.

Synonym: *Clupea alosa*
Size: up to 75 cm, mostly 30–40 cm
Weight: up to 3.5 kg, mostly 0.7–1.5 kg
Fin formula: D IV–V/13–17, A III/17–22
Fecundity: 250,000–350,000 eggs
Distribution: The Atlantic coasts of Europe and the western part of the Mediterranean.

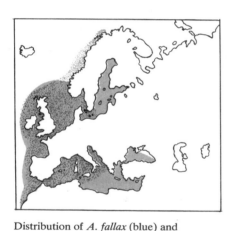

Distribution of *A. fallax* (blue) and *A. alosa* (red)

The related species *A. sapidissima,* which lives off the Atlantic and Pacific coasts of North America, measures up to 70 cm (mostly 30–50 cm) and weighs 3–4 kg. In recent years the catch has fallen to 3,000–5,000 tons per year. The flesh is good and the roe is used to make imitation caviare.

Finta Shad, Twaite Shad
Alosa fallax

The Finta Shad is a similar fish to the Allis Shad with a deep body and similar colouring. However the dark spots on the sides are brighter and the two fish have quite different gill rakers. Those of the Finta Shad are thick and rough and usually the same length as the gill lamellae. Like those of all clupeids, the scales are readily shed. The fish grow relatively quickly and at five years old measure 40 cm.

Spawning occurs in fresh water, but about one month later than the Allis Shad and in the lower reaches of the rivers, not more than 100–120 km from their mouths. The males become sexually mature at two to three years old, the females at four to five. Migrating adults do not stop for food while travelling upriver; they travel about 5 km a day, so that migration takes 20–40 days. The fry hatch about four to five days after spawning at 19 °C and are washed down to the mouth of the river by the current before autumn; there they remain until the following spring, when they swim out into the sea and remain until they are sexually mature. Young Finta Shad feed on zooplankton and adults also eat small fish.

The economic significance of this species today is negligible, owing to the small size of the various populations. The Finta Shad's flesh is drier than that of the Allis Shad and contains less fat. It is sometimes caught by anglers.

> *Synonym: Clupea fallax,*
> *Clupea finta*
> *Size:* up to 55 cm (mostly 25–40 cm)
> *Weight:* up to 1.5 kg
> *Fin formula:* D IV–V/14–16, A III/17–23
> *Fecundity:* 140,000–180,000 eggs
> *Distribution:* Along the Atlantic coast of Europe, from southern Scandinavia to the Iberian Peninsula. Also present in the Baltic and Mediterranean.

The related species *A. aestivalis* occurs off the eastern coast of North America from Florida to Nova Scotia. It reaches a maximum length of 35 cm but is mostly 25–30 cm. It has a few small, dark spots on its sides.

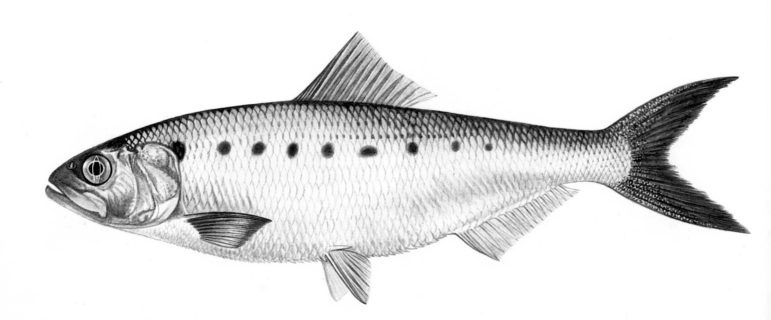

Black-backed Shad
Alosa kessleri

Seven *Alosa* species from the Black Sea, the Sea of Azov and the Caspian Sea are sometimes classified in a separate genus, *Caspialosa*. One of these has two subspecies — *A. kessleri pontica,* which inhabits the Black Sea, and *A. kessleri kessleri,* which lives in the Caspian Sea. They each have a different number of short, thick gill-rakers and the shape and size of their teeth are different. The head, back and dorsal and pectoral fins are black or violet in the spring; there is generally one dark spot on each operculum and the belly is light.

The type subspecies of the Black-backed Shad occurs in the Caspian Sea and migrates up its tributary rivers to spawn. It grows faster than other Caspian herrings; at four years old it measures 36 cm, at six years old about 45 cm and it attains sexual maturity in its fifth year. The fish migrate upstream to spawn in March and April; they travel for 10—20 days and cover 30—35 km a day. Spawning occurs between May and August, probably in the afternoons and evenings. At 20°C the eggs hatch in about two days. The fry remain for one to two months in the river and are then carried down into the sea.

The Black-backed Shad still has some economic significance, but the catches are small. Fish are caught chiefly while migrating, in the Volga delta. It has the best quality flesh of all Caspian clupeids.

Synonym: Caspialosa kessleri
Size: up to 52 cm
Weight: up to 1.8 kg
Fin formula: D III—IV/12—16, A III/16—20
Fecundity: 135,000—218,000 eggs
Distribution: The Black Sea and the Caspian Sea

Adults feed on small fish like kilkas (1), young ones on large zooplankton species like *Leptodora* species (2).

Caspian Shad
Alosa caspia

The Caspian Shad is substantially smaller than the Black-backed Shad and at three years old measures only 20 cm. The fish has a deep body, compressed sides and long pectoral fins. Its back is a very dark shade of bluish green, its sides are sometimes spotted and it has a light-coloured belly. This is an anadromous fish, migrating from the sea into the rivers to spawn. In the Danube it sometimes migrates as far as the Iron Gate, on the border between Rumania and Yugoslavia, but most of the fish remain in the river delta. In the Caspian Sea migration begins in the second half of April, when the water reaches a temperature of 7—10 °C. The second part of the population lags behind and does not start migrating until May, when the temperature of the water is 10—15 °C. Actual spawning (in the Volga, for instance) takes place at 18—20 °C and at this temperature (about 20 °C) the eggs take two to three days to hatch. The fry remain for some time at the spawning site and are then washed down into the sea to complete their development. The Caspian Shad attains sexual maturity in its second year. It feeds chiefly on planktonic crustaceans, but also on aquatic plants and algae; it is an important prey species for larger predatory fishes.

The Caspian Shad has several subspecies, the economic importance of which are small. The Caspian subspecies yields the best catches, but whereas before the war the annual catch was about 40,000 tons and in the 1960's still 32,000 tons, it has now fallen to 10,000—20,000 tons per year.

Synonym: Caspialosa caspia
Size: up to 23 cm (average about 20 cm)
Weight: up to 110 g
Fin formula: D III—IV/13—15, A III/16—21
Fecundity: 12,000—40,000 eggs
Distribution: The Black Sea and the Caspian Sea.

A comparison of the branchial arches, showing the gill-rakers which are used to filter off food particles, in two related species of the shads of the genus *Alosa. A. fallax* has thick, coarse gill-rakers (1), while those of *A. caspia* are thin and fine (2).

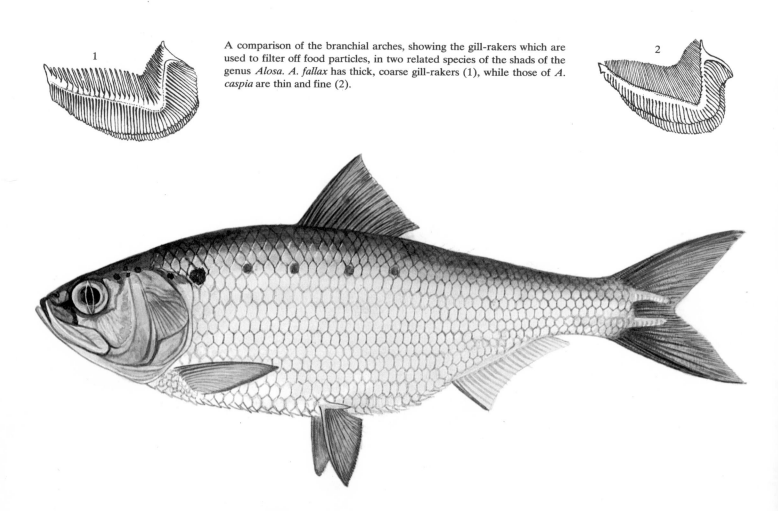

Common Kilka
Clupeonella delicatula

This fish has an elongate, flat-sided body, a sharp-edged belly with well-developed scales, a wide but elongate head and relatively large eyes. Its back and the top of its head are greyish green to bluish green and its sides and belly are silvery white or have a golden tinge. The dorsal fin and the caudal fin are grey; the other fins are lighter. This is a small fish measuring only 11 cm when four years old.

The Common Kilka is a euryhaline species, i.e. it lives and reproduces in both salt and fresh water up to 13 parts per mille salinity; in some regions it stays permanently in fresh water. Spawning occurs from April to June at a water temperature of 5−24 °C reaching a peak in May. By the end of July all sexually mature fish have finished spawning. If spawning takes place in a river, the fry are carried down by the river into the sea. Eggs are laid at intervals every few days.

At 10 °C hatching occurs after about five days, at 14 °C after three days and at 22 °C after only one day. Young fish of the current year are to be found all over the Sea of Azov or in the mouths of big rivers. The adults feed on zooplankton, the fry on phytoplankton. These fish are the most important plankton consumers in the Sea of Azov and in turn provide an important source of food for larger predatory fishes, an essential link in the food chain.

Despite their small size, their economic importance is considerable and they are still one of the main fishes caught in the Sea of Azov.

Size: up to 15 cm (mostly 10 cm)
Fin formula: D III−IV/11−13, A III/14−18
Fecundity: 5,000−20,000 eggs
Distribution: In the Sea of Azov and the Caspian Sea and in the brackish western part of the Black Sea, including the lower reaches of the tributary rivers.

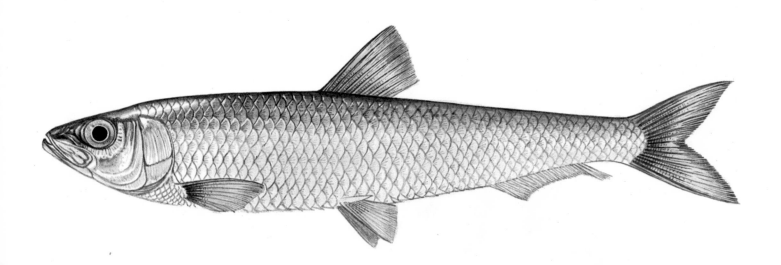

A comparison of the anal fin of three species (belonging to different genera) of the family Clupeidae: *Sardinella aurita* (1), *Sardina pilchardus* (2) and *Clupeonella delicatula* (3). There are differences in the size and shape of the last two rays in these fishes.

Sardine, Pilchard
Sardina pilchardus

The name 'sardine' is used in many languages for the members of the closely related genera *Sardina, Sardinops* and *Sardinella,* which are characterized by large scales continuing right onto the caudal fin, where they form two 'wings' on either side. Their dorsal fin lies in a kind of groove also formed of scales, which almost completely overlap its posterior end. The Pilchard is the only species of the genus *Sardina.* Its characteristic large scales sit very loosely on its body and other smaller scales are hidden beneath them. The bluish green colouring of the fish's back changes on its sides to a gleaming gold; its belly is silvery white. On each operculum there is a dark spot and there is also a line of dark spots along the upper flank sometimes with another line of spots below.

Pilchards live in large shoals in the top layers of warm (10−20 °C) coastal waters at depths of 25−100 m by day, nearer the surface at night at between 10 and 35 m. When young they feed on phytoplankton, when adult on planktonic crusta-ceans; they also eat pelagic eggs of other fishes. They spawn in the open sea at 10−18 °C, at different times of year in different regions. The fry swim shorewards into coastal waters where they stay until the winter, when they return to the open sea, swimming shorewards again in the spring. Pilchards reach sexual maturity at two years old and live for about 14 years.

In recent years the annual catch has varied from 700,000 to 1,000,000 tons, mainly of fish aged between 2.5 and 4.5 years old. The fish are caught with large dragnets and purse seines, using cod roe as bait; in Italy they are lured by the light of acetylene lamps.

Synonym: Clupea pilchardus, Clupea sardina
Size: 20−25 cm, maximum 30 cm
Weight: 0.3−0.5 kg
Fin formula: D III−IV/13−16, A III/13−17
Fecundity: 50,000−80,000 eggs
Distribution: From the southern part of the North Sea to the northwest coast of Africa: the Mediterranean Sea and the Black Sea.

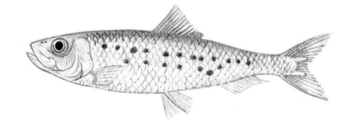

The related species *Sardinops caerulea* from the west coast of North America. Some 600,000−800,000 tons a year were caught before World War II, but after the war the yield fell disastrously, to a mere 20,000 tons.

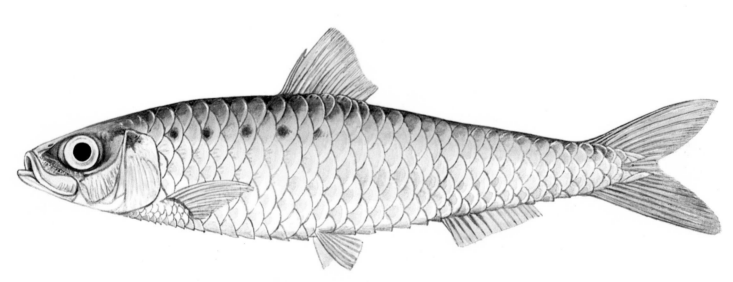

Gilt Sardine
Sardinella aurita

A sardine whose distribution area extends into the temperate belt, whereas the other members of the genus live primarily in the tropics. The Gilt Sardine's body is rounded in cross section, it has a large number of rays in its ventral fins and there are usually dark spots on the upper part of each operculum. It is distinguishable at first glance from *Sardina* and *Sardinops* species, for unlike these species it has no radial grooves on the opercula and no dark spots behind them. It has a metallic blue back, golden sides and a whitish belly.

The fishes usually live in large shoals at depths of down to 150 m, where temperatures range between 15–30 °C and the water has a salinity of not less than 34%; their average life span is six years and they reach sexual maturity when two years old. The shoals remain in deep water during the daytime, but surface at night. Moving shoals make a sound like falling rain and if they suddenly submerge they send a mass of tiny air bubbles to the surface. The young fishes feed on phytoplankton as well as on zooplankton; adults feed on zooplankton, especially on copepods. Gilt Sardines breed throughout the year but with distinct peaks in different areas, for example they breed mostly in the summer in the Mediterranean. Juvenile fishes remain in nursery areas near the coasts, joining adults in deeper water on maturity.

The annual catch of these sardines is 300,000–800,000 tons per year; part of the catch is used to make fish-meal and part for human consumption, when most of the fish are tinned. During the processing the fish are beheaded, their viscera are removed, they are washed and left for two hours in a strong saline solution; they are then washed again, dried, plunged for 2 minutes into boiling oil and placed in tins, where fresh oil is poured over them. When the tins have been sealed, they are sterilized for two hours at 115 °C.

> Synonym: *Clupea aurita*
> Size: 25–30 cm (rarely 38 cm)
> Weight: up to 0.6 kg
> Fin formula: D III–IV/14–16, A III/13–15
> Fecundity: 10,000–110,000 eggs
> Distribution: The western Pacific from southern Japan to Indonesia, the American shores of the Atlantic from Cape Cod to Rio de Janeiro, the whole western coast of Africa and the Mediterranean and Black Seas.

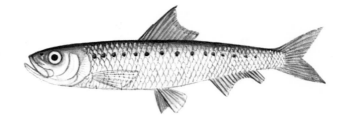

Sardinops sagax, an important species from the Pacific coast of Canada and the USA. Annual catches before World War II amounted to up to 700,000 tons, but today they amount only to 20,000–50,000 tons.

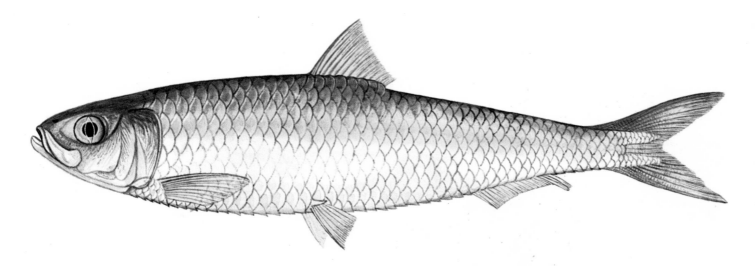

The family Engraulidae includes small shoal-forming fishes with long underslung jaws and large scales. There are approximately thirteen genera which live mostly in tropical and subtropical seas.

Anchovy
Engraulis encrasicholus

The Anchovy has an elongate body with a rounded belly and no 'keel'. Its back is green, dark blue or black, its sides are a glittering silver and its belly silvery white; its opercula are tinged with yellow. The colouring of its subspecies is very variable. It forms quite a number of subspecies over its widespread distribution area. The typical form, *E. encrasicholus encrasicholus*, lives in the Atlantic; further subspecies inhabit the Mediterranean, the Black Sea and the Sea of Azov. The Anchovy is a small fish which matures at the end of its first year, when it measures about 7−8 cm; by the time it is four years old it measures up to 12−14 cm.

Anchovies are pelagic fishes which often form very large shoals especially in inshore waters during the spawning season which lasts from May to September. They may be found in both salt and brackish water and are especially likely to inhabit river estuaries. Adults spawn two or three times in the course of their lifetime. The eggs and larvae are pelagic and the fry hatch after 24−48 hours at 18°C. Anchovies feed on small zooplankton and phytoplankton species and their food consumption is highest in the summer; in the spring when they migrate towards the shore, and in the autumn when they return to the open sea they eat less. They spend the winter at depths of 80−140 m, but as soon as the water begins to warm up to 7−10 °C they swim upwards, closer to the surface, where the water is only 6−10 m deep.

In the northern part of its range the anchovy is an economically insignificant fish but in the southern part of its range, including the Black Sea, it is an important fisheries species.

Size: up to 20 cm
Weight: up to 100 g
Fin formula: D III/14−18, A III/16−20
Fecundity: 9,000−30,000 eggs
Distribution: The Atlantic coast from southern Norway to North Africa, the Mediterranean, the Sea of Azov and the Black Sea.

The related species *E. ringens,* which lives in the Pacific off the coast of South America, measures 10−18 cm (maximum 22 cm). In 1970 it provided a record catch for any species, when over 13 million tons of fish were caught.

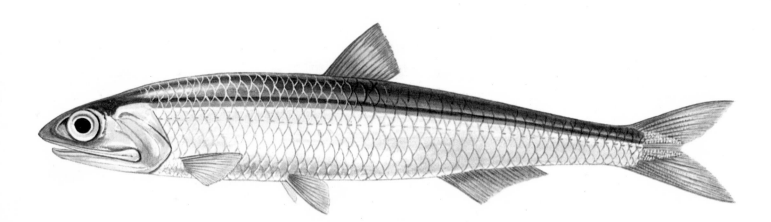

The order Salmoniformes comprises marine, migratory and permanently freshwater species; these fishes have a characteristic adipose fin and no oviduct. The family Salmonidae includes freshwater and migratory fishes of the northern hemisphere, all of them economically important. They have a fusiform body and a long upper jaw stretching to the posterior edge of their eyes. Their bodies are covered with very small scales.

SALMONIDAE

Humpback

Oncorhynchus gorbuscha

The smallest, but the most important member of the genus *Oncorhynchus,* known as Pacific salmon. The Humpback occurs in the northern part of the Pacific and in the Arctic Ocean. Years ago it was introduced into the Barents Sea and from thence some individuals found their way into the North Atlantic; since then relatively large numbers of Humpbacks have been caught in Norwegian, Icelandic and British waters. They mature when two to three years old and migrate upstream to spawn in early summer.

In their nuptial dress the males have a dark head and back and light red sides marked with greenish brown spots. The body also changes shape at this time. The upper and lower jaws grow longer and become hooked; and on the back of the fish, in front of the dorsal fin, a hump develops, from which is derived both the vernacular and scientific names of the fish (*'gorbuscha'* comes from the Russian word for 'hump'). The female lays her eggs in nests excavated in the river bed and covers them over. The spawning ground is usually in the part of the river with the strongest current and hence the most oxygen. The parent fish die after spawning. The larvae are hatched in 110—130 days; they live in the nests until spring arrives and then drift down to the sea, where they feed and grow very quickly.

The total annual Humpback catch amounts to 150,000—200,000 tons. The pinkish flesh has an excellent flavour and is considered a delicacy.

Size: 40—50 cm, maximum 70 cm
Weight: 2—4 kg, occasionally 5—6.5 kg
Fin formula: D III—IV/9—12, A II—IV/12—16
Fecundity: about 1,500 eggs
Distribution: Originally the Pacific and the Arctic Oceans; introduced into the Barents Sea and has spread into the North Atlantic.

The male of the related *O. keta* at spawning time. This species has a similar distribution to *O. gorbuscha;* of its two separate migrant forms (spring and autumn), the autumn form, which measures about 1 m, is the larger and more prolific. The catches, which amount to about 100,000 tons per year, come mainly from Japan, the USA, the USSR and from Canada.

Atlantic Salmon
Salmo salar

The Atlantic Salmon can be distinguished from Sea Trout by the thinner base of its tail, its slightly concave tail fin, its shorter upper jaw, which does not stretch beyond the posterior end of its eye, and the larger number of gill-rakers on its first branchial arch. These fishes are found both in coastal waters and in the open sea, since they undertake long migrations in search of food. However, Atlantic Salmon spawn in fresh water and so, when the fish mature at four to five years old they return to the rivers where they were spawned and swim upstream to the higher reaches, further upstream than trout. At this time red and orange spots appear on the head and sides and the belly of the fish turns pink. On their way up the river they may have to overcome obstacles up to two metres in height.

On arriving at the spawning site the females excavate nests with jerking movements of their bodies and deposit the eggs in them. Spawning usually takes place from October to December and when it is over many of the fish (especially the males) die, although, some of them take part in spawning several times. The fry hatch in the spring. They form small shoals and gradually drift down to the sea; some salmon take as many as three years to reach it. Salmon feed mainly on crustaceans and fish.

They are caught in a variety of ways, in the sea and while migrating to their spawning places. Their flesh is highly prized. In recent years worldwide annual catches have reached over 12,000 tons, but the number of salmon is steadily falling, due to over-intensive fishing, pollution and the construction of high weirs and dams which bar their progress upstream.

Size: 60—100cm, maximum 150cm
Weight: 3—15kg, occasionally up to 40kg
Fin formula: D III—IV/9—II, A III/7—8
Fecundity: 6,000—26,000 orange eggs, each 5—6mm in diameter
Distribution: The European coastal waters of the Arctic and Atlantic Oceans, coastal waters of Iceland and the south of Greenland and the eastern coastal waters of North America.

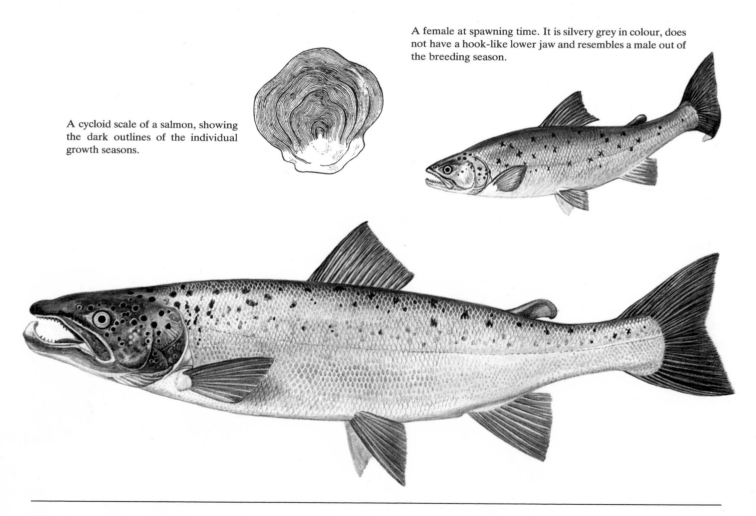

A cycloid scale of a salmon, showing the dark outlines of the individual growth seasons.

A female at spawning time. It is silvery grey in colour, does not have a hook-like lower jaw and resembles a male out of the breeding season.

Sea Trout

Salmo trutta

A migratory (anadromous) species, sexually mature when three to four years old, which generally begins its upstream migration in the spring and spawns in the upper reaches of rivers and streams from October to January. It excavates nests in the river bed in the same way as salmon. The fry develop in fresh water and then make their way gradually down to the sea, which they reach between the end of their second year and the beginning of their fourth. They remain inshore for between one and three years, feeding and growing, and after attaining sexual maturity they migrate upstream again back to their spawning grounds. Part of the migrating population (chiefly the males) dies after each spawning, largely as a result of exhaustion, since the fish do not feed while migrating. The greater part of the population takes part in spawning two or three times, however, and in some cases even more.

The Sea Trout has a straight-edged caudal fin and is silvery in colour and less brightly marked than salmon. Red spots appear on the body of some members of the migrating population and spots below the lateral line are also rare.

At one time Sea Trout were to be seen in all the rivers and streams in its area of distribution, but in many places whole populations have become extinct due to pollution and the construction of insurmountable obstacles like dams and high weirs and their numbers have dwindled accordingly. In quality, trout flesh is equal to that of salmon.

Size: 50—80 cm, maximum 110 cm
Weight: 3—18 kg, occasionally up to 25 kg
Fin formula: D III—IV/9—11, A III/7—9
Fecundity: 2,000—16,000 eggs
Distribution: The northwestern coastal waters of Europe from the Iberian Peninsula to Chesha Bay in the Kara Sea; the Black Sea region.

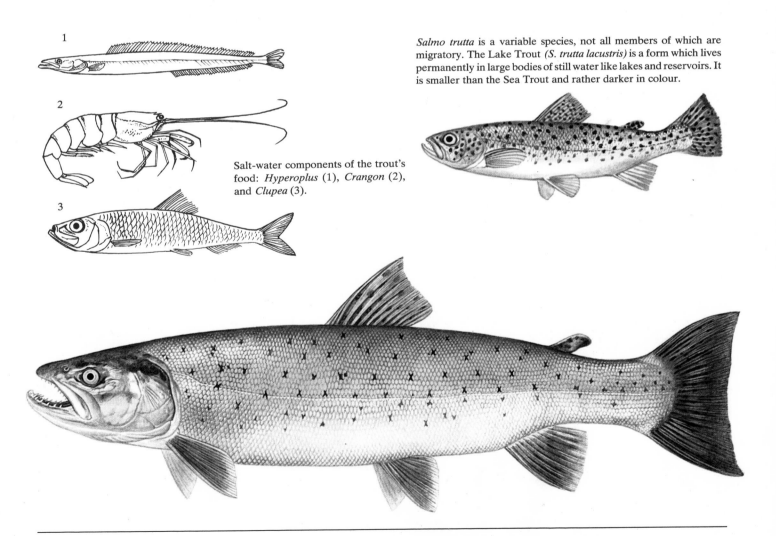

Salt-water components of the trout's food: *Hyperoplus* (1), *Crangon* (2), and *Clupea* (3).

Salmo trutta is a variable species, not all members of which are migratory. The Lake Trout *(S. trutta lacustris)* is a form which lives permanently in large bodies of still water like lakes and reservoirs. It is smaller than the Sea Trout and rather darker in colour.

Brown Trout

Salmo trutta morpha *fario*

Brown Trout belong to the same species as Sea Trout and Lake Trout but they live permanently in streams and rivers. They are smaller than the other two subspecies and more or less dark brown in colour with a greenish brown to greyish green back and lighter sides and belly, with shades varying from yellow to greyish white. The head, back and sides and dorsal and adipose fins are marked with black and red spots which sometimes have a lighter border. Old males have an upcurved lower jaw and a longer head than females. These fish live in clean cold water with plenty of dissolved oxygen. They particularly favour rocky streams with plenty of hiding-places up to an altitude of about 1,500 m. A Brown Trout defends its own territory, whose limits are determined largely by the extent of its vision. The fish feed mainly on the larvae of aquatic insects, on non-aquatic insects which fall into the water and on fish eggs, small fish and frogs. They become sexually mature between two and four years old (the males usually a year earlier than the females). Spawning takes place from October to January, but before that the trout swim upstream to the higher reaches of the rivers, overcoming obstacles up to 1.5 m high on their journey. On arriving at the spawning site the females excavate shallow troughs for the eggs, whose development takes 100—120 days. Today, however, European rivers are frequently kept well-stocked with trout by artificial breeding.

The Brown Trout is one of the most important freshwater fish to anglers; its flesh is of outstanding quality and of very high dietetic value. It is caught with rod and line, using either a fly or a troll; in the latter case a spoon-bait or a dead fish may be employed as the lure.

Size: 40—60 cm, occasionally up to 1 m
Weight: mostly 0.5—2 kg, exceptionally over 10 kg
Fin formula: D III—IV/8—11 A II—III/8—9
Fecundity: 2,000—3,000 eggs to 1 kg body weight
Distribution: The middle and upper reaches of rivers and streams throughout the whole of Europe, the Caucasus, Asia Minor, Morocco and Algeria. Introduced into Australia, New Zealand, India, North America and central Africa.

Vomers: bones in the middle of the front of the upper jaw (1), which are used to distinguish various salmonid species. Huchen (2), Sea Trout (3), freshwater form of Sea Trout (4).

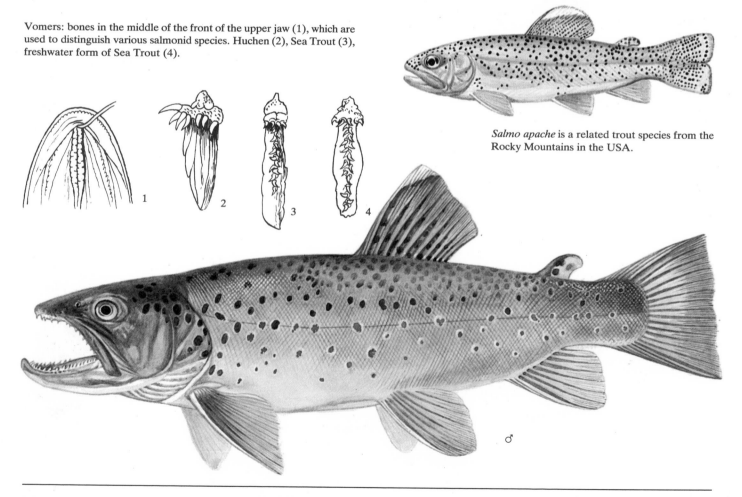

Salmo apache is a related trout species from the Rocky Mountains in the USA.

♂

Rainbow Trout

Salmo gairdneri

This species came originally from the Pacific area of North America, was introduced into other parts of North America, and then in 1880 into Europe and subsequently into other continents, first of all with the aim of enriching the fauna, but later with an eye to its economic possibilities. However, despite years of effort there are few places where the Rainbow Trout has formed populations capable of independent existence without re-stocking or supplementation from artificially bred stock. Intensive selective breeding has led to the production of different colour variants, but the characteristic feature of its colouring is still the pink or red band running down the middle of its body to the root of its tail. Its head, deep body and dorsal and caudal fins are thickly speckled with black spots. The males have a deeper colour and a hooked lower jaw, seen especially in old individuals. The long upper jaw extends beyond the posterior edge of the eye. The caudal fin is mildly concave.

Like the Brown Trout, the Rainbow Trout is sensitive to pollution but it requires less oxygen and tolerates warmer water and it does not need so many hiding-places. It feeds on the larvae of aquatic insects and on zooplankton, molluscs and small fish. It becomes sexually mature when two or three years old; under natural conditions it lives for five or six years, or it may in exceptional cases live 18 years and more. In Europe, Rainbow Trout spawn between November and May in running water and the eggs are deposited in shallow troughs excavated mainly by the females in the river bed.

The Rainbow Trout's excellent flesh has led to its being bred intensively in ponds and on special trout farms; it is also a favourite fish with anglers. In recent years it has been bred in reservoirs.

Size: 60—90 cm, maximum 120 cm
Weight: usually 1—3 kg, occasionally 6—10 kg, maximum 24 kg
Fin formula: D IV/10—11, A III/10—11
Fecundity: 2,500—8,500 eggs per kg body weight (average 4,500)
Distribution: Originally the Pacific river waters of North America, nowadays cosmopolitan.

Original (red) and present (blue) distribution area of Rainbow Trout in Europe.

The golden form of the Rainbow Trout which is to be found on some trout farms.

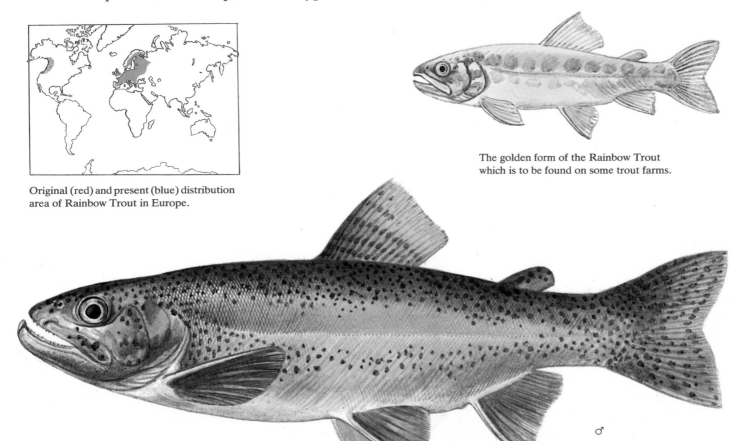

Charr

Salvelinus alpinus

Charrs present a problem for fish biologists, for there are several races, one of which is migratory, while the others are permanently resident in lakes over much of Europe and North America. The migratory form occurs in the arctic waters of the Atlantic, Pacific and Arctic Oceans; in European waters it lives in the area bounded by Iceland and by Oslo Fjord, Norway. Resident inland forms live in mountain lakes as relicts of the last glacial period.

Charrs are very similar in appearance to the American Brook Trout (*S. fontinalis*), but in young specimens and in the non-migratory form the upper jaw stretches only to the posterior edge of the eye, in the migratory form slightly beyond it; this is in contrast to the American Brook Trout, in which the upper jaw extends beyond the posterior edge of the eye. The Charr's colouring is very variable; in the migratory form the back is steely blue, while in the non-migratory forms it tends to be greenish brown. At spawning time the intensity of the fish's colouring increases and the males are the most brightly coloured fish to be found in Europe. Spawning takes place mostly in the winter, but in some localities in the spring as well. Migratory forms swim upstream to spawn for the first time at not less than three to four years old, but often not until they are six to eight years old. The females of both forms deposit the eggs in nests hollowed out in sand and gravel, usually under a sheet of ice. The young of the migratory form remain for two to four years in fresh water, where they feed chiefly on invertebrates; in the sea main food items are small fish like cod, gobies or burbot.

Economically the Charr are not very significant, but in some arctic regions they are important fish. As a rule, however, Charr are caught mainly by anglers, who prize it for its value as a trophy, for its attractive colouring and for its tasty flesh.

Size: usually 40—60 cm, maximum 1 m
(the migratory form)
Weight: 1—3 kg, occasionally up to 7 kg
Fin formula: D III—IV/9—10, A III/8—10
Fecundity: Average 3,500 eggs, maximum up to 7,500
Distribution: The arctic waters of the Atlantic, Pacific and Arctic Oceans; sporadically in cold lakes of Europe, Asia and North America.

The female is less brightly coloured than the male.

♀

♂

Brook Trout

Salvelinus fontinalis

This attractively coloured species comes from North America, where it is distributed from northern Canada to Georgia in the south. The Great Lakes and the upper reaches of the Mississippi originally marked its western limits, but now it is found in the western part of the USA, and it has been introduced into South America, Asia and New Zealand; it was introduced into Europe at the end of the last century. It can be distinguished from the Charr which it resembles, by its upper jaw which is longer than the Charr's and extends beyond the posterior edge of its eye; the lining of its mouth is black. The Brook Trout is one of the most gaily marked freshwater fishes, but its colour varies with the populations and also varies markedly during the year.

Brook Trout live in the same type of localities as Brown Trout and feed on the same type of prey. In the resultant competition the Brook Trout are generally the losers, even in their original localities in the USA, if Brown Trout have been introduced there. Brook Trout can live in the sources of streams however, where there is little oxygen, or in acid water with a low pH if it is cold enough (not more than 16 °C), and in such localities there is no competition. Brook Trout are also less dependent on streams having an uneven bottom with hiding places than Brown Trout.

Brook Trout become sexually mature when two or three years old and spawn from October to December. Like other trout they excavate a nest for the eggs, which the parent fish then cover over with whirling movements of their tails; the young hatch in about 100 days. Since the Brook Trout spawn in the same places as the Brown Trout, one can sometimes come across curiously mottled infertile hybrids of the two species. The Brook Trout has very good, well-flavoured orange-coloured flesh.

Size: in European waters 30–50 cm, in its original range up to 90 cm
Weight: in European waters 1–3 kg, in the USA and Canada up to 7 kg
Fin formula: D III/9–10, A III/8–11
Fecundity: about 2,000 eggs per kg body weight
Distribution: Originally North America; introduced to many other parts of the world.

Lake Trout (*S. namaycush*) is sometimes placed in a separate genus, *Cristivomer*. One of the biggest freshwater fishes, it can weigh up to 45 kg. It lives in Canadian lakes and rivers and is a highly prized species. In some of the Great Lakes an invasion by the Sea Lamprey, together with increasing pollution, has severely reduced its numbers.

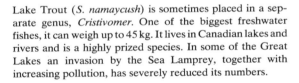

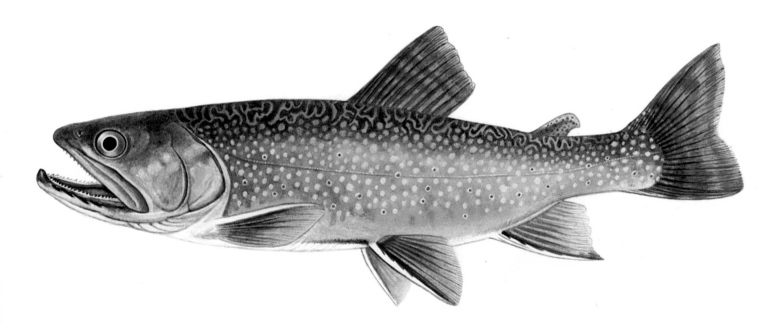

Danube Salmon, Huchen
Hucho hucho

The Huchen has a torpedo-shaped body almost circular in cross section, a large head and conspicuous toothed jaws. Its reddish brown back is marked with large numbers of dark x- or crescent-shaped spots. In the spawning season its light grey sides have a coppery lustre and red spots; its belly is white. Huchen are found only in the Danube and its tributaries but the related species *Hucho taimen* lives in Siberia, from the Yenisei to the Amur; attempts to introduce it to other areas have so far been unsuccessful. The Huchen is the biggest salmonid fish living permanently in fresh water. It grows very quickly and at five years old measures about 60 cm, attaining sexual maturity between four to six years old, depending on how fast it grows. The fish generally spawn in April, but sometimes not until May, at water temperatures of 6−9 °C; in big rivers they first of all migrate a little way upstream. The female beats out a nest in a gravelly bed for the eggs, which are then fertilized by the male; their development takes 25−35 days.

Nowadays Huchen are bred artificially. Adults are caught just before they are ready to spawn, or are kept in special reservoirs and induced to spawn artificially. When the fry measure 4−10 cm they are used to stock suitable localities. Young fish feed on the larvae of aquatic insects or on insects which have fallen into the water, while adults catch other fish.

Because of their size Huchen stay in the main channels of the rivers, at the transition from the grayling to the barbel zone. They demand clean, well-oxygenated rivers with plenty of hiding-places like big stones, roots and fallen trees. For these reasons, and because of pollution, their numbers are steadily dwindling. Huchen are considered prized trophies by anglers; the flesh has excellent flavour.

Synonym: Salmo hucho
Size: up to 1.5 m, mostly 50−80 cm
Weight: up to 50 kg
Fin formula: D III−IV/9−11, A IV−V/7−9
Fecundity: 15,000−30,000 eggs
Distribution: The catchment area of the Danube.

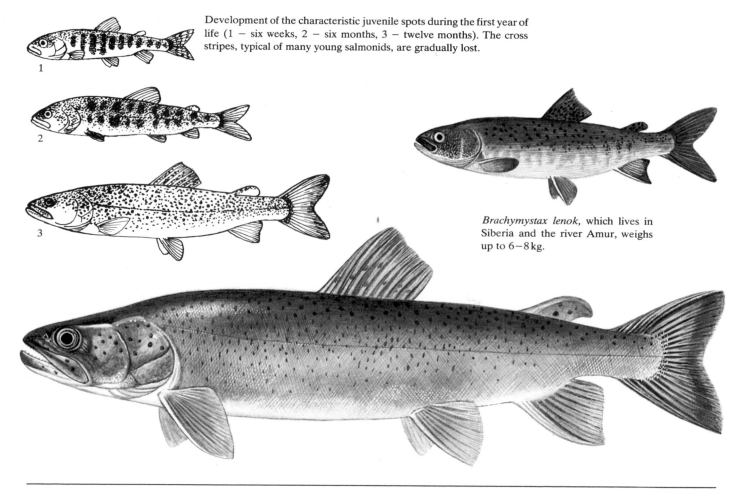

Development of the characteristic juvenile spots during the first year of life (1 − six weeks, 2 − six months, 3 − twelve months). The cross stripes, typical of many young salmonids, are gradually lost.

Brachymystax lenok, which lives in Siberia and the river Amur, weighs up to 6−8 kg.

Cisco, Inconnu

Stenodus leucichthys

The only representative of the genus *Stenodus,* which is distinguishable from the genus *Coregonus* chiefly by the different structure of the skull and the large terminal mouth with a slightly protruding lower jaw. This fish has a silvery body without any dark or light spots. It has two known subspecies, *Stenodus leucichthys nelma* inhabits the Arctic Ocean from the Gulf of Onega to the Beaufort Sea, where it frequents the littoral zone and brackish water near river mouths. It matures late — usually not until it is nine to twelve years old and never before its seventh year. To spawn the fish swim upstream to the upper reaches of the rivers. They begin migrating in June and spawning takes place from October to December. In some of the big Siberian rivers like the Ob, the spawning ground may be as much as 3,500 km away from the river mouth. The females deposit the eggs on the river bed, where they develop among the stones. The fry gradually drift down to the sea where they feed on plankton. Some of the fish prolong their stay in the river, however. From their second year the fish become piscivorous predators. The subspecies *S. leucichthys leucichthys* lives in the Caspian Sea; it matures when five to seven years old.

The members of both subspecies spawn three times at most in the course of their lives, with intervals of two to four years in between. During migration the fish do not eat and their energy requirements are met from the fat reserves they have accumulated while feeding in the sea.

Ciscos are of considerable economic importance in the USSR and Alaska; they are caught with various types of nets and with rods and lines. The catches have diminished somewhat in recent years, since dam construction and water pollution have created difficulties for migration and spawning; artificial spawning and breeding of this species have become much more important as a consequence.

Synonym: *Salmo leucichthys*
Size: 1m, occasionally up to 1.4 m
Weight: usually 6—15 kg, occasionally up to 35—40 kg
Fin formula: D II—V/10—13, A III—IV/12—16
Fecundity: 100,000—425,000 eggs
Distribution: The catchment area of the Arctic Ocean, the Caspian Sea, Volga and Ural Rivers.

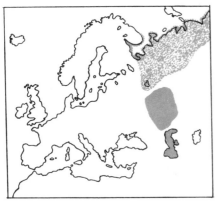

Distribution of *Stenodus leucichthys. S. l. nelma* (red) and *S. l. leucichthys* (blue).

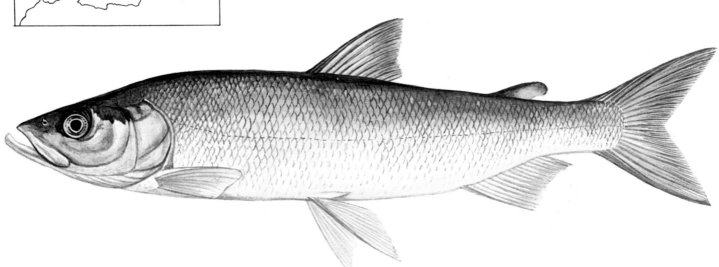

The Coregonidae are a family of salmoniform fishes, generally known as whitefishes, which live in the cold waters of holarctic lakes. Recognition of species is difficult, since there is not only considerable geographic variation between populations inhabiting different lakes, but also a high degree of hybridization between species. Most often identification depends on the size and number of gill rakers present on the first gill arch. These fish are of economic importance.

COREGONIDAE

Vendace
Coregonus albula

The fishes of the genus *Coregonus* are egg-laying fishes with relatively large scales and small mouths; accurate identification of individual species is still quite difficult. The Vendace is one of the smallest whitefish; some members of its populations mature at a length of only 8 cm. It has a slender body and a slightly protruding lower jaw, longer than the upper one, giving the fish a superior mouth. Its back has a bluish colour and its sides and belly are white. Its dorsal, caudal and pectoral fins are dark; the others are almost colourless. Vendace are found in the Baltic region, the area round Murmansk, the upper Volga, England and Scotland. The fishes reach sexual maturity when two to three years old. Lake popula-

tions spawn in shallow water in tributary rivers in November and December at a water temperature of 4−6 °C. Development of the eggs is prolonged lasting 100−130 days and can be influenced by various adverse ecological factors such as oxygen deficiency and freezing, so that the number which develop varies markedly from year to year.

Attempts have been made to acclimatize the Vendace to European fish-farming conditions, on the assumption that it would consume small plankton species and increase naturally in fishponds; these expectations were not fulfilled. The Vendace feeds chiefly on zooplankton but it may also take benthic animals like molluscs. It is caught with gill-nets, seine-nets and fyke-nets.

Synonym: Salmo albula
Size: 30−40 cm, mostly 15−25 cm
Weight: up to 1.2 kg, mostly 0.1−0.4 kg
Fin formula: D IV/8−9, A IV/11−13
Fecundity: 1,700−4,800 eggs
Distribution: The catchment area of the Baltic Sea, around Murmansk, the upper Volga, also present in England and Scotland.

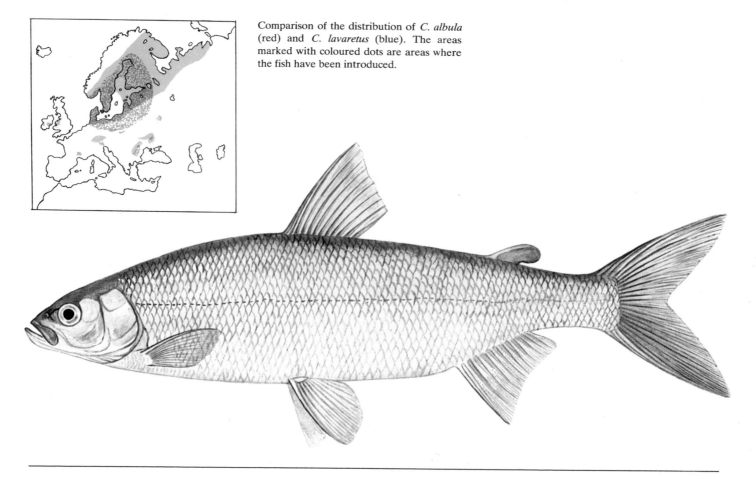

Comparison of the distribution of *C. albula* (red) and *C. lavaretus* (blue). The areas marked with coloured dots are areas where the fish have been introduced.

Tshiir
Coregonus nasus

The Tshiir is one of the biggest whitefishes. In Siberia and the River Kolyma it weighs up to 16 kg; elsewhere it weighs roughly the same as the Freshwater Houting. The fish has a deep body and the anterior part of its back drops steeply down to its head, forming a characteristic hump. The upper jaw is short and high and overlaps the lower jaw, giving the fish an inferior mouth. Its eyes are small. It has an olive brown to dark brown back, silvery sides and a silvery white belly and there are silvery yellow stripes on its scales. Its dorsal, caudal and pectoral fins are light grey, while the ventral and anal fins are almost colourless.

The Tshiir reach sexual maturity when seven years old and have a life span of about 15 years. Spawning takes place in October and November, at approximately freezing point. The fish lay fewer eggs than other whitefish species and the eggs are relatively large (measuring up to 4 mm in diameter); development takes 4—5 months.

Tshiir live mainly in rivers; in lakes they stay in the mouths of the inflowing rivers. When the fish live in small lakes, both the young and the adult fish leave the lakes in the autumn and spend the winter in the deepest parts of the rivers, but populations living in large lakes often remain throughout the winter. Tshiir are caught with seine-nets. Before the War the catches amounted to about 800 tons a year, but today they are much smaller. Introduction of this species into the rivers flowing into the White Sea is being considered at the present time.

Size: 120—130 cm
Weight: up to 16 km
Fin formula: D III—IV/9—11, A III/10—13
Fecundity: 10,000—140,000 eggs
Distribution: The Arctic Ocean region from the Pechora to the Chukotsk Peninsula; Alaska and Canada

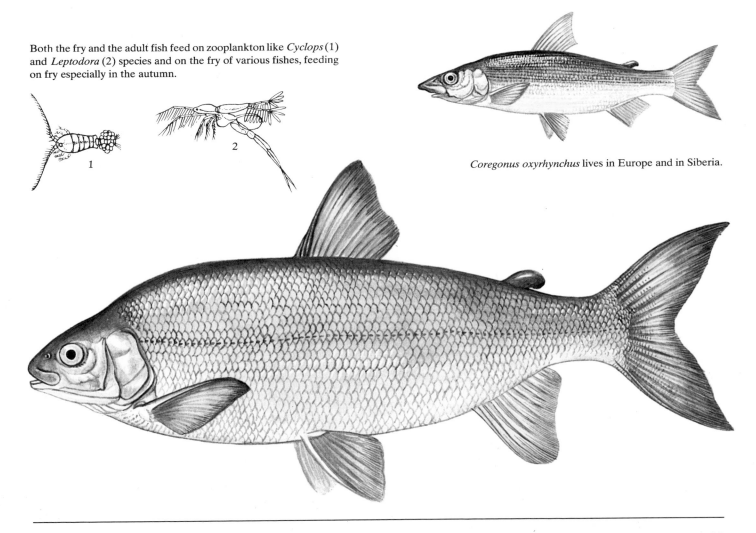

Both the fry and the adult fish feed on zooplankton like *Cyclops* (1) and *Leptodora* (2) species and on the fry of various fishes, feeding on fry especially in the autumn.

Coregonus oxyrhynchus lives in Europe and in Siberia.

Siberian Cisco
Coregonus peled

The Siberian Cisco is one of the larger whitefishes. These fish have a very restricted distribution in nature, but do well in ponds and have been introduced into East Germany, Poland and Czechoslovakia; by its second year a fish measures 35—40 cm and weighs about 600 g; in its third year it weighs about 1 kg. In nature three forms of the Siberian Cisco are known, one form lives permanently in rivers and the other two (a large and a small form) in lakes; all three feed on planktonic crustaceans.

The fish mature in ponds in their second to third year, but not in the wild state until they are four to five years old. They spawn mainly in river beds, on a sandy or stony bottom. Lake populations may spawn in lakes or migrate upstream into inflowing rivers during the autumn, in October and November. The eggs are smaller than those of other whitefish species.

The Siberian Cisco is very tolerant of temperature change and low oxygen concentrations; it tolerates a temperature range of 0 to 28 °C. This is why it has been successfully introduced — in rivers, but more particularly in ponds — in a number of northern and central European countries, where it has taken the place of the Freshwater Houting and become an economically important fish. It can be distinguished from other whitefish by its deeper body with a hump at its anterior end. The upper jaw protrudes beyond the lower jaw. The body is dark, with small black spots on head and sides and on the dorsal fin.

Size: up to 60 cm (mostly 30—40 cm)
Weight: up to 5 kg (mostly under 1 kg)
Fin formula: D III/8—12, A III/12—16
Fecundity: 5,000—105,000 eggs
Distribution: Rivers and lakes in the region of the Arctic Ocean, in Finland and Sweden. Has been introduced into other parts of northern and central Europe.

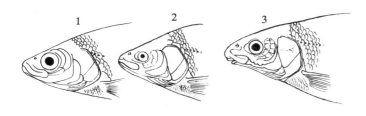

Schematic illustrations of the heads of three *Coregonus* species. 1. *Coregonus sardinella* which has a superior mouth, 2. *C. autumnalis*, with a terminal mouth, and 3. *C. lavaretus,* with a semi-inferior mouth.

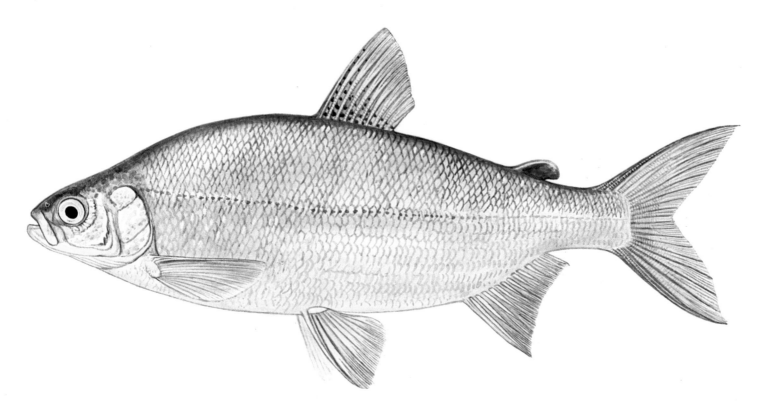

Arctic Cisco
Coregonus autumnalis

A large whitefish with a terminal mouth and jaws of roughly equal size. It has a brown back (sometimes with a greenish tinge), silvery sides and a dingy white belly. This species occurs in the region of the Arctic Ocean between the Mezen in the west and the Chukot Sea in the east; it is also found in northern Alaska and in Canada. There is a migratory subspecies, *C. autumnalis migratorius,* which spends most of its life in the sea or in river mouths, but migrates up river to spawn. The fish mature when five to ten years old depending on how fast they grow. In the Yenisei, migration begins in the middle of July, in the Lena at the end of July; the fish do not migrate up either the Ob or the Yana. While migrating the fish do not eat and rapidly lose weight. At spawning time the males are covered in a pronounced spawning eruption. Spawning takes place in the autumn, often 1,000 km from the river mouth, and when it is over the adult fish return to the sea. The eggs hatch in the spring and the fry are carried passively downstream to the river mouth, where they feed on crustaceans like Copepoda, Mysidacea and freshwater shrimps and on the fry of certain fishes (whitefishes, smelts, etc). These fish tolerate greater salinity than other whitefishes and can be caught long distances from the shore.

A separate freshwater subspecies, *C. autumnalis baicalensis,* larger than the migratory subspecies, inhabits Lake Baikal, where it forms three different populations feeding and spawning in different places. The fish feed chiefly on pelagic crustaceans, but they also feed on benthic organisms and the fry and eggs of other species of fishes.

Size: the migratory form grows up to 60 cm, the Baikal form up to 1 m
Weight: the migratory form weighs up to 2.5 kg, the Baikal form up to 7 kg
Fin formula: D III−V/8−13, A III−IV/10−14
Fecundity: 8,000−40,000 eggs (migratory form), 15,000−50,000 eggs (Baikal form)
Distribution: The catchment area of the Arctic Ocean from the River Mezen to the Chukotsk Peninsula, northern Alaska and Canada.

Distribution of *C. autumnalis autumnalis* (red); *C. autumnalis migratorius* (blue).

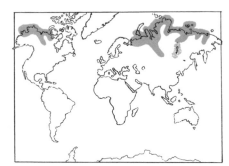

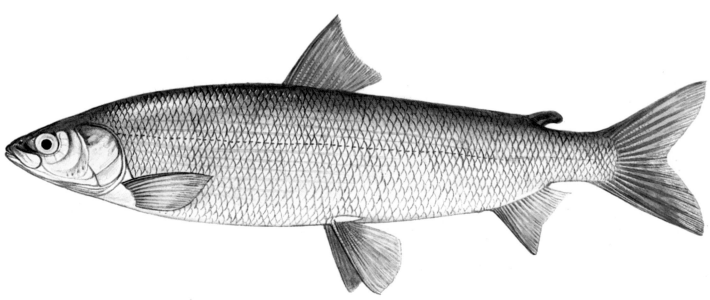

Freshwater Houting
Coregonus lavaretus

The Freshwater Houting is a large whitefish with a short, steeply slanting snout and a semi-inferior mouth, a greenish blue back and silvery sides. Its fins are grey with a touch of green and there is a pinkish tinge round its lateral line and anus. This large whitefish grows very quickly, especially in fishponds, where it may be kept with carp as a second fish. At the end of its first year it measures 20—25 cm and weighs about 100 g; in its second year it measures about 30 cm and by the time it reaches its fifth year it measures 55 cm, when it weighs over 3 kg.

In the wild, fish of river populations regularly migrate upstream to spawn. Those of lake populations may spawn on the spot in deep water in the summer, or from October to December in the shallows or following migration up the tributary rivers. Hatching occurs after approximately 100 days. In places where this fish has been introduced it is impossible to rely on natural spawning and the stock must be supplemented afresh every year from young artificially bred fry. The fish feed chiefly on zooplankton; large specimens also hunt benthic animals and occasionally catch fish fry and small fish.

The Freshwater Houting is of considerable economic importance. In fishponds it increases production, since it does not compete with the carp for food. It is caught with seine-nets and gill-nets. It has very savoury flesh.

Size: up to 130 cm, mostly 50—70 cm
Weight: up to 10 kg, mostly 2—4 kg
Fin formula: D II—IV/9—11, A III—IV/10—12
Fecundity: 10,000—50,000 eggs
Distribution: Rivers running into the Baltic and North Seas and into the Arctic Ocean as far as the River Kolyma. Also occurs as a relic of the glacial periods in lakes in Poland and the Alps.

One of the ways in which the various whitefish species can be distinguished from each other is by the number of their vertebrae. When counting them it is essential to know that the first vertebra is united with the bones of the skull (1) and is not included in the total count. The last three vertebrae curve upwards and arising from the last one is a rod-like urostyle (2), which should also be excluded from the total vertebral count.

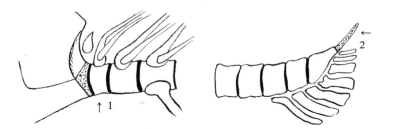

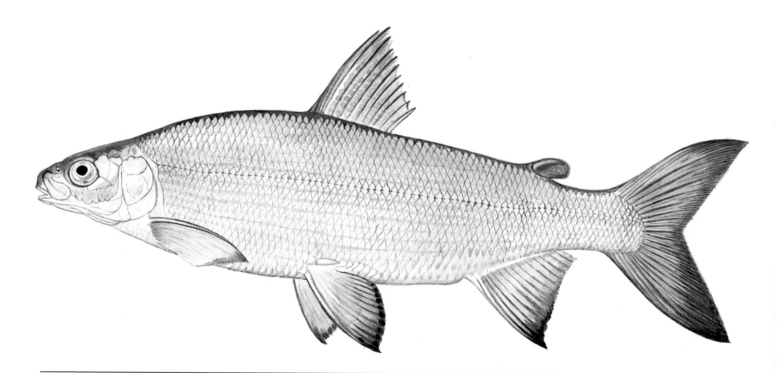

In the family Thymallidae there is a single genus of freshwater fishes living in submontane rivers and cold lakes in the northern hemisphere. The fish have a high dorsal fin and an adipose fin.

THYMALLIDAE

Grayling
Thymallus thymallus

The Grayling is similar in appearance to whitefishes and to some cyprinid fishes. Young specimens are silvery white, with a greyish green to dark blue back and iridescent sides. Sexually mature individuals are darker and have black spots on their body and the unpaired fins. In the spawning season the males in particular are brightly and diversely coloured and their characteristic wide high dorsal fins become iridescent with shades of red and violet.

Graylings live in shoals in open water, in rivers they occur mainly where slow-flowing water and rapids alternate; such stretches are known as grayling zones. The fish feed chiefly on the larvae of aquatic insects and molluscs, but also on terrestrial insects which settle on the surface. They become sexually mature when two to three years old and have an average life span of five to six years, but occasionally live up to 10 years. Grayling spawn in pairs from March to May over a gravelly and sandy bottom. Each male defends its own spawning site against other males during the daytime and does not even let sexually immature females approach it. Mature females deposit their eggs in shallow excavations and the eggs hatch after 18—20 days. The fry grow quickly and at the end of their first year measure 8—15 cm. Deterioration of natural spawning grounds has made artificial breeding necessary in some European countries.

The Grayling is very popular with anglers and its flesh has an excellent flavour.

Synonym: *Salmo thymallus*
Size: 30—50 cm, occasionally up to 50—60 cm
Weight: 0.1—1.5 kg, maximum 4.7 kg
Fin formula: D IV—VII/14—17, A III—V/8—11
Fecundity: 1,000—20,000 eggs
Distribution: Most European countries north of the 45th latitude; east as far as the Urals.

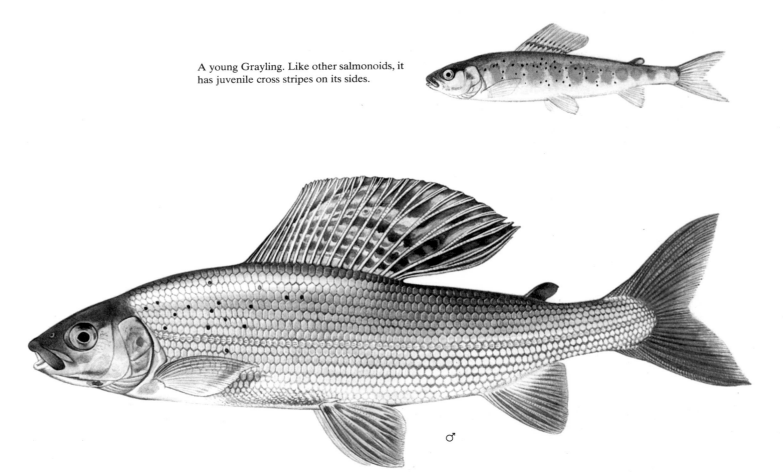

A young Grayling. Like other salmonoids, it has juvenile cross stripes on its sides.

♂

Members of the family Osmeridae differ from other Salmoniformes in respect of their stomach, which is a blind-ended pouch. They include marine, migratory and freshwater species.

Smelt
Osmerus eperlanus

The Smelt, one of six species of the genus *Osmerus,* is a small pelagic sea fish which lives in European coastal waters, but also forms freshwater races living permanently in rivers, lakes and reservoirs. The Smelt has a dark or metallic blue back and silvery grey sides and belly. Its body is covered with relatively large, loose scales. The incomplete lateral line is distinctly developed only on the anterior part of the body behind the head.

At the end of the winter sexually mature Smelts begin to collect in river mouths, in readiness for their spring migration into the brackish waters of the estuaries. They reach sexual maturity when three to four years old and have a maximum life span of nine years. At spawning time the fish lose their normal timidity. In both sexes, spawning tubercles appear on their backs and sides and their colouring is intensified. The tops of their heads and their opercula turn black and the males are altogether more brightly coloured. Spawning takes place from March to May and the sticky eggs adhere to stones and other objects lying on the bottom. The eggs hatch after about 27 days and the fry remain in the estuary for the rest of the summer, while the adults return to the sea. Young fish feed on copepods and other young fish while adults prey on planktonic crustaceans.

Like the related Capelin, the Smelt is an economically important species yielding annual catches of about 8,000—10,000 tons. Its flesh is delicious but is considered to be an acquired taste; it has a strong smell of cucumber.

Synonym: Salmo eperlanus
Size: 16—18 cm, maximum 25 cm
Fin formula: D III/7—8, A III/10—13
Fecundity: 8,000—55,000 eggs
Distribution: Coastal waters of Europe from the Bay of Biscay to the mouth of the River Pechora in the east. Also occurs in inland fresh waters.

Distribution of *Osmerus eperlanus.*

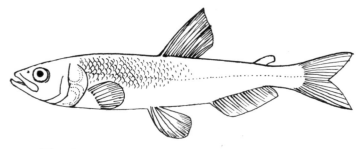

The related species *Thaleichthys pacificus,* which lives off the Pacific coast of North America, has oily flesh. American Indians used to dry it, thread a wick through its body and use it as a candle, so that today it is still known as the Candle-fish.

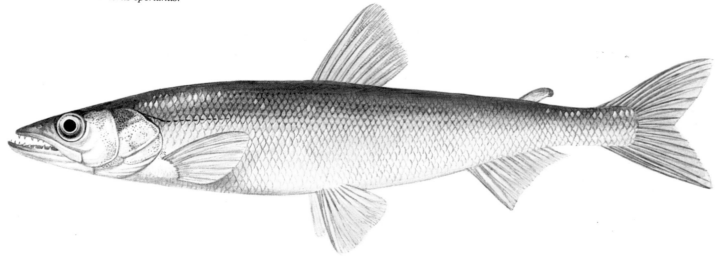

Capelin
Mallotus villosus

The Capelin is a small fish which lives in large shoals. It is the only representative of the genus *Mallotus*. It has a metallic blue or dark blue back and silvery white sides with a blue stripe running down the middle; the underside of its head and body have a yellowish (and in places a bluish) tinge.

Capelin live in the open sea at considerable distances from the shore; sometimes they occur near the surface, but generally they are found closer to the bottom, where they feed chiefly on euphausiid shrimps and other crustaceans. Before spawning the fish come to the surface and then swim towards the shore, where they spawn over submerged sandbanks at depths of 30−100 m. The spawning shoals are usually formed of fish aged between two and six years. Spawning occurs between March and September according to latitude, at a water temperature of 2−4 °C and the eggs hatch in 30 days. If the fish spawn near the shore in a strong wind the waves often carry them right up on to the beach, which may be covered for miles with layers of dead capelins. On their shoreward journey the huge spawning shoals are followed by large numbers of predators like codfish, sea-gulls and whales. They are also caught in huge numbers by fishing fleets.

In recent years the annual catch has averaged 2.9 million tons − the second largest catch for any fish species. The Capelin has very tasty flesh especially when smoked, but big catches go mainly to the making of fish-meal.

Size: maximum 20 cm
Fin formula: D II−III/10−13, A III−V/17−21
Fecundity: 20,000−50,000 eggs
Distribution: The northern parts of both the Atlantic and the Pacific Oceans, but found particularly in the Arctic Ocean.

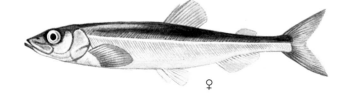

The female Capelin is smaller than the male and has a slimmer body and a less well developed anal fin. The males have filamentous outgrowths on the scales along their lateral line at spawning time.

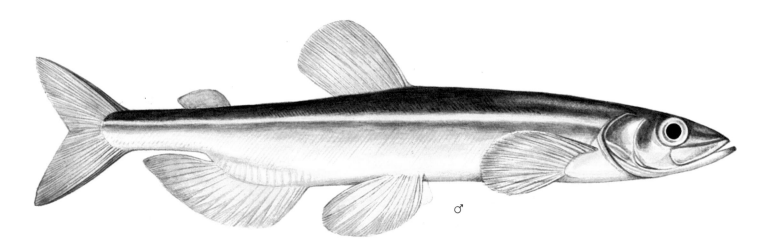

The family Argentinidae comprises twenty species of small pelagic marine fishes which may live at considerable depths in the sea. They have small mouths with no teeth in their jaws and they have relatively large eyes.

ARGENTINIDAE

Argentine, Lesser Silver Smelt

Argentina sphyraena

A small fish with an elongate body, relatively large eyes and teeth on its tongue. It has an olive green back, lighter sides with a bright silver band and a silvery white belly. It is smaller than the related *A. silus* and has fewer scales along its lateral line (*A. silus* has 64–69 whereas *A. sphyraena* has 50–54). Argentines spawn in the Mediterranean from December to April; in the Atlantic they spawn in spring and summer, beginning later further north and continuing later into the year. The eggs and larvae are pelagic. The young hatch when 7 mm long and have a characteristic pattern of dark spots on their body.

At first the fry live in water close to the surface at depths of 50–70 m, later they descend to the sea bed and older fish may live at considerable depths. Males grow faster than females, reaching maturity at 4.75 cm in their third year, females mature at 12.5 cm in their fourth year. They live for 15 or more years. Argentines are bottom feeders, living on muddy bottoms between 60 and 200 metres down and feeding on crustaceans, molluscs and fish. The related Atlantic Argentine *A. silus* is a larger, deep-water, shoal-forming fish living at depths of 50–1,000 m.

In some places Argentines are caught and made into fish-meal and they are important prey species for cod, hake and whiting.

Size: up to 26 cm
Fin formula: D I/8, A I/12–13
Fecundity: 2,000–3,000 eggs
Distribution: Along the entire coast of western Europe, from Iceland to the Mediterranean.

The related Atlantic Argentine (*A. silus*) lives in the northern part of the Atlantic, off the coasts of Europe and North America; it measures up to 50 cm.

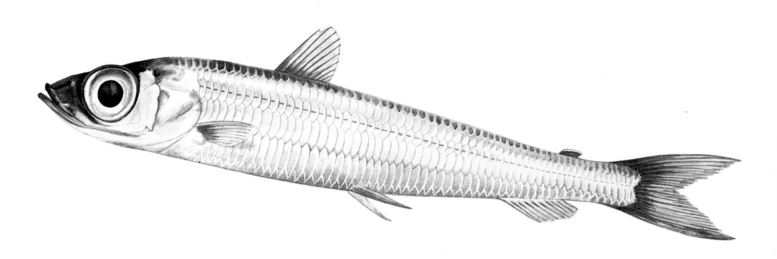

Members of the family Sternoptychidae possess light organs (photophores) and large eyes. They are deep sea species found at depths of about 2,000 m and are only seen near the surface when ascending currents bring up dead specimens.

STERNOPTYCHIDAE

Hatchet Fish
Argyropelecus olfersi

This Hatchet Fish lives in the Atlantic Ocean and is thought to have been found in the Indian and Pacific Oceans also, however, the fish in question may have been the related *A. lynchus;* it does not occur in the Mediterranean. It is a bathypelagic species frequenting depths of down to 1,000 m and ascending to lesser depths (about 200—300 m) at night. It is most frequently caught in the deep water at the edge of the continental shelf.

It has a deep body and compressed sides and its sharp-edged underside is bordered by eighteeen photophores which emit a greenish, downwardly directed light. Its adipose fin — characteristic of salmonoids — is very small. The top of its head and its back are greyish blue to black, while its sides and belly are silvery. Nothing is known of its spawning behaviour or development.

While not of any economic significance itself, it is occasionally found in the alimentary tracts of predatory species like codfish.

Synonym: Sternoptyx olfersi
Size: up to 7 cm (maximum 12 cm)
Fin formula: D VII/9—10, A III/8—10
Distribution: The Atlantic Ocean

Chauliodus sloani is a deep sea species inhabiting the oceans from the temperate to the tropical belt, generally at depths of 500—1,000 m. It is a predator with an extremely capacious mouth and is occasionally caught in the Mediterranean.

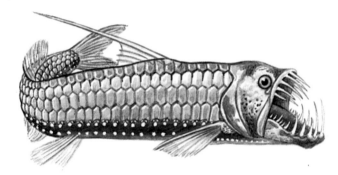

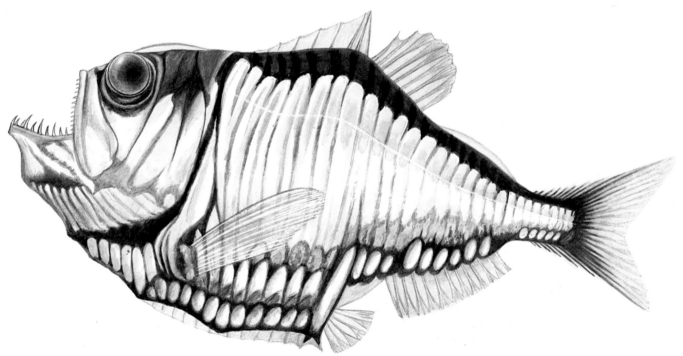

The family Esocidae includes freshwater fishes inhabiting slow-moving and still waters in Eurasia and North America. Its representatives have elongate, muscular bodies on which the dorsal and the anal fins are situated far back on the caudal peduncle. The fish have flattened heads, large, toothed snouts and small scales firmly anchored in the skin. There is one genus with five species.

Pike
Esox lucius

The Pike is a large, predatory fish which grows very quickly. For every 5−8 kg of fish consumed, its body weight increases by 1 kg and depending on the amount of food available it grows up to 12−50 cm in its first year, to 50−75 cm by its fifth and to 80−110 cm by its tenth; it reaches sexual maturity when one or two years old. It has a greyish green to markedly dark back, sometimes tinged with red or brown, greenish sides marked with yellow spots which sometimes run together to form bands, and a white grey-spotted belly.

Pike spawn very early, as soon as the ice has melted and the temperature of the water near the bank is 4−10 °C. The eggs are laid haphazardly amongst marginal reeds or other waterside plants. Development of the eggs takes 10−15 days.

Pike are territorial fishes and each defends its own hunting ground. It is most often found amongst the vegetation of still and slow-moving waters.

This is one of the most popular fish for anglers, but it is never to be found in large numbers and may be a troublesome pest in trout rivers.

Size: up to 1.5 m (mostly 0.5−1 m)
Weight: up to 35 kg (mostly 2−10 kg)
Fin formula: D VI−X/12−16, A IV−VIII/10−14
Fecundity: 40,000−300,000 eggs
Distribution: The whole of Europe except the southern peninsulas, Asia in the basins of rivers flowing into the Arctic Ocean; also found in America from Alaska to Ohio and Labrador.

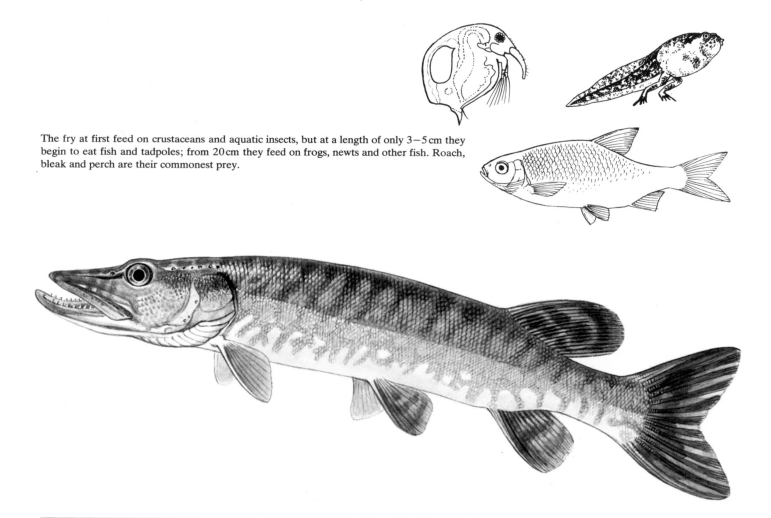

The fry at first feed on crustaceans and aquatic insects, but at a length of only 3−5 cm they begin to eat fish and tadpoles; from 20 cm they feed on frogs, newts and other fish. Roach, bleak and perch are their commonest prey.

The family Umbridae includes small fishes living in still water with dense vegetation. Their bodies, including the top and sides of the head, are covered with tiny cycloid scales. The lateral line can be seen as a light band along the side of the fish, but there are no pores in the lateral line scales. They have a typically rounded tail fin. Two of the three species live in North America and one in Europe.

UMBRIDAE

Mud Minnow
Umbra krameri

The Mud Minnow is one of the prettiest European freshwater fishes with a reddish brown body marked with large numbers of irregularly distributed dark spots. It lives at the muddy bottoms of lakes and rivers in the Danube basin but river regulation and land improvement projects, together with river pollution, have made it rare, so that in some countries it is now protected by law throughout the year.

Despite its small size, the Mud Minnow is a predatory and active fish feeding on bottom living crustaceans and on the larvae of aquatic insects. It stalks its prey by swimming towards it slowly with rowing movements of its pectoral fins and then pouncing with lightning speed. It has a life span of only three years and attains sexual maturity when one year old. Spawning takes place from March to May, when the female deposits the eggs in a shallow nest which she hollows out in the bed by means of her fins. The preparation of the nest sometimes takes two days; during this time the female does not tolerate any strange fish in her vicinity and boldly attacks intruders several times larger than herself. Two or three males generally take part in spawning with one female. Once spawning is over the female regains her aggression and defends the nest and the eggs actively for ten days.

Size: 8—10 cm (maximum 13 cm)
Fin formula: D III—IV/12—13, A II/5—6
Fecundity: 100—200 eggs
Distribution: In the flood plains of the Danube and Dnestr rivers, although not very common.

Umbra pygmaea lives in the eastern part of the USA. Unlike its European cousin it has longitudinal stripes on its sides. It has been introduced into parts of western Europe, where it grows to a length of 10 cm.

The order Cypriniformes is a very large group of freshwater fishes comprising about 6,000 species, some 3,500 of which belong to the suborder Cyprinoidei and the rest to the suborder Siluroidei. Distinguishing features of the order include the presence of Weberian ossicles, modified vertebrae and ribs which form a chain of bones connecting the swim-bladder to the ear. The bodies of the fishes are either scaleless or covered with cycloid scales. The family Cyprinidae includes over 1,500 species of fish, there are no teeth on the jaws but there are well-developed pharyngeal teeth; there is also a large swim-bladder composed of two or sometimes three segments. They live in fresh water on all the continents except Australia and South America.

CYPRINIDAE

Roach
Rutilus rutilus

This is one of the most widely distributed European freshwater fishes. It has a long flat-sided body with a moderately arched back and is covered with relatively large scales. The fish has a dark back with a bluish or greenish brown lustre, silvery sides and a light-coloured belly. The fins are mostly pinkish grey except for the ventral and anal fins which are reddish. The eyes have a red iris.

This species lives in slow-flowing and still waters, especially in large weedy ponds and lakes of lowland areas, and may sometimes be found in brackish water. It has become very common in some valley reservoirs 5–15 years after the valley has filled up. Roach become sexually mature when two or three years old and have a life span of up to 20 years. They spawn from April to June in shallow water. In the spawning season the heads and bodies of the males are covered with a granular spawning eruption. Roach spawn in large shoals and the eggs are deposited on plants, roots or on a stony or gravelly bottom. Since other cyprinid fishes often spawn in the same places the various species may interbreed. Roach feed mainly on zooplankton and to a lesser extent on insects, plants and detritus; they are most active in the day.

These fish are important prey for predatory fishes and birds and are also popular with coarse anglers.

Synonym: Cyprinus rutilus
Size: mostly 25 cm or less, maximum 50 cm
Weight: 0.3–0.5 kg, maximum 2 kg
Fin formula: D III/9–11, A III/9–10
Fecundity: 200,000–400,000 eggs per kg of the female's body weight
Distribution: European waters with the exception of southern peninsulas and part of Norway; Asian regions of the USSR, brackish waters of the Baltic, the Black Sea, the Caspian and Aral Seas.

The related *R. pigus* lives in the rivers of northern Italy and in the middle and upper reaches of the Danube and its tributaries. There are more scales in its lateral line than in that of the Roach and it has a semi-inferior mouth.

Distribution map of *R. rutilus.*

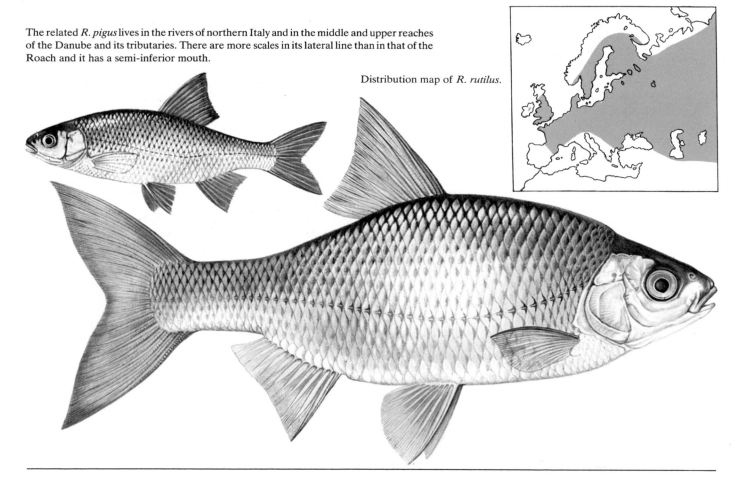

Dace
Leuciscus leuciscus

Although closely related to the Chub, the Dace is more elegantly built and has a noticeably narrower, smaller and rather pointed head, large eyes and a smaller inferior mouth. It has a greyish blue back, silvery sides, its belly is white and its paired fins yellowish. Its anal and dorsal fins are both distinctly concave, a feature which distinguishes the Dace from the Chub, since the Chub's anal and dorsal fins are convex and red in colour. The Dace's scales are fixed loosely in the epidermis and they do not have dark-borders like the Chub's.

Dace live in shoals, chiefly in clean, swiftly flowing streams and rivers, in parts of the barbel and grayling zones; occasionally they may be found in lakes or valley reservoirs. They grow slowly and have an average life span of seven to ten years. Most fish become sexually mature when two years old. The males develop spawning tubercles on their bodies and on their paired fins during the spawning season; unlike the Chub, Dace spawn only once a year, between March and May, laying their eggs on a sandy or stony bed or on aquatic plants. The young hatch after 25 days at a temperature of 13 °C. Dace-Chub hybrids are not unknown.

Dace feed primarily on algae and water weeds and on the larvae of aquatic insects, which they gather on the bottom. In the evening they surface to pick up non-aquatic insects which have fallen into the water. In hot weather dace cool themselves singly in strong currents; in the winter they retire in small shoals to deep potholes.

Dace are popular with skilled anglers for they are not easy to catch. They do not make good eating for they are too small and they have many small bones.

Size: 25–30 cm, exceptionally up to 40 cm
Weight: 0.3–0.7 kg, occasionally up to 1 kg
Fin formula: D III/7–8, A III/7–9
Fecundity: 55,000–130,000 eggs per kg body weight (total 10,000–30,000)
Distribution: The whole of Europe except the Balkans, Italy and the Iberian Peninsula.

The mouths of the Dace (*L. leuciscus*) (1) and the Chub (*L. cephalus*) (2), to illustrate the differences.

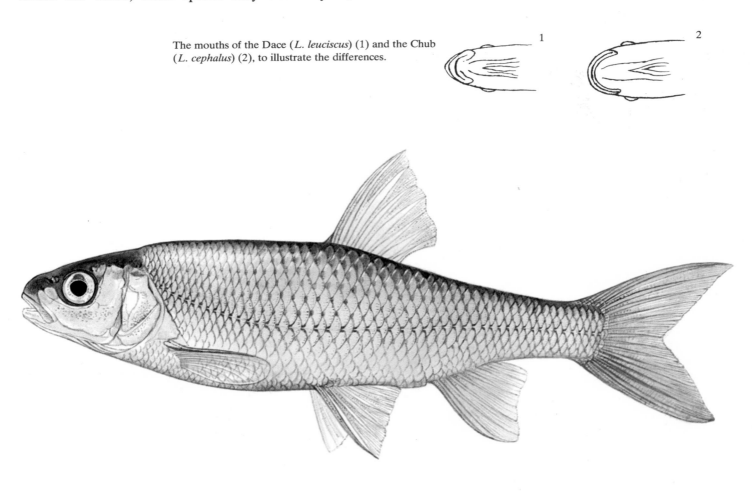

105

Chub
Leuciscus cephalus

The Chub has a robust cylindrical body and a low, wide, rounded head with a large terminal mouth which is tilted slightly upwards in profile. It has a dark grey or green back, green or blue sides and a light yellow or silvery belly. It has grey fins except for the ventral and anal fins, which are yellow or orange, and the large, dark-bordered scales give its body a reticulated appearance.

Chub live in rivers, from the lower part of the trout zone to the swiftly flowing bream zone, but they may also be found occasionally in the waters of lakes or reservoirs. They have a moderately long life span of eight to ten years, but some individuals may live to 15 years old and more. Chub become sexually mature when two to four years old and the males become covered with a white eruption at spawning time. Spawning takes place in late spring and summer at intervals of 10−20 days, the fish gathering in small shoals, chiefly in flowing water. The sticky eggs are deposited on submerged branches or logs, or on stones on the bottom. The fry hatch after eight to ten days. At first the young fish live in shoals but older Chub tend to lead solitary lives.

Chub are typical omnivorous fishes feeding on aquatic insects and other small fishes, as well as water weeds. They remain active in the winter and continue to feed in mild winters.

Although the flesh is not good to eat, with too many fine bones, they are very popular with anglers. They can be caught in various ways, but large individuals are very wily and are not easy to catch. Chub are fairly resistant to pollution and may occur near the mouth of waste pipes opening into rivers.

Size: 60 cm, exceptionally up to 80 cm, usually 20−40 cm
Weight: 3−5 kg, occasionally up to 8 kg, usually 0.2−0.6 kg
Fin formula: D III/7−9, A II−III/7−10
Fecundity: 20,000−200,000 eggs
Distribution: Over the whole of Europe (except Ireland, Scotland and part of northern Scandinavia) and in the Near East.

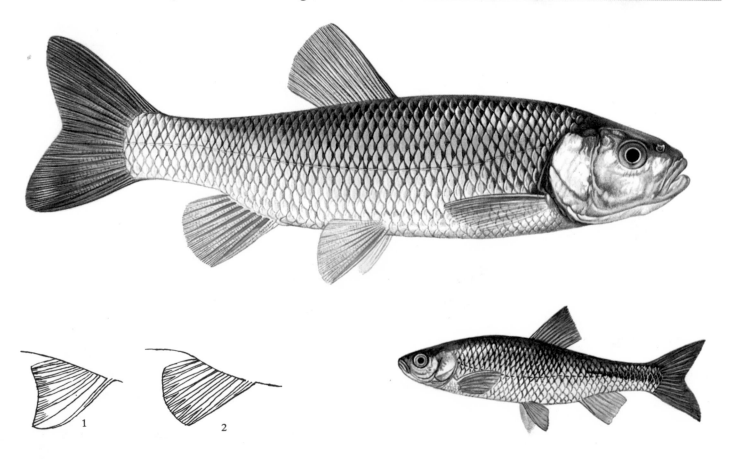

The shape of the anal fin is an important differential character in the Dace (*L. leuciscus*) (1) and in the Chub (*L. cephalus*) (2); in the Dace it is concave and in the Chub convex.

L. borysthenicus is a related species living in the southern part of the Ukraine, the Kuban region and the western part of Transcaucasia.

106

Ide, Orfe
Leuciscus idus

The Ide has a relatively deep body, a small head with a thin terminal mouth and large eyes with a brassy yellow iris. The back of this fish is dark greyish blue, while its sides are silvery and its belly is white. The dorsal fin is greyish blue while the other fins are reddish; the caudal fin is darker in colour and is deeply forked.

Ides live in shoals in the lower reaches of large rivers, in valley reservoirs and in lakes; they have also been used to stock fishponds. These fish are particularly abundant in the Danube and in the big rivers in the European part of the USSR, where they are fished commercially, and they are also found in the brackish waters of the Baltic Sea.

Ide have a life span of 10—15 years and become sexually mature when three to five years old. In the spring, adult individuals migrate in shoals to their spawning grounds. Small spawning tubercles appear on the head, body and pectoral fins of the females at this time. The eggs are laid between April and June on a gravelly or sandy bed, on aquatic plants or on fine tree roots. Spawning is a very stormy process, as the fish whirl about in their gleaming gold nuptial dress. Ides feed on zooplankton, aquatic insects, trapped floating insects, molluscs, fish fry, algae and water weeds.

They are popular with anglers and have quite tasty flesh. The Orfe, the golden variety of the Ide, is an artificially bred form (just as the Goldfish is an artificial form of the Carp).

Size: 30—40 cm, exceptionally up to 60 cm
Weight: 0.5—2.5 kg, occasionally up to 4 kg
Fin formula: D III/7—9, A III/9—10
Fecundity: 70,000—120,000 per kg body weight (average 85,000)
Distribution: Northwestern and central Europe

The Orfe, a golden variety of the Ide, is a very popular choice for ponds and lakes in public parks and gardens.

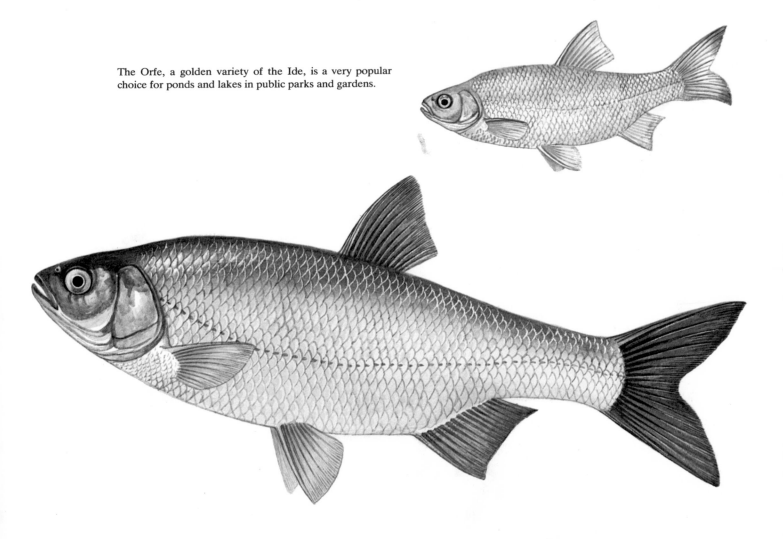

Souffie
Leuciscus souffia

A smallish slender fish resembling the Dace, for which it is often mistaken even by experienced anglers. The morphological differences between them are not obvious at first glance, so that in the past the two were not considered to be separate species. However, the number of rays in the dorsal and pectoral fins of the two species and the number of scales in their lateral line are different; the dorsal fin of the Souffie is situated a little further back than this fin in the Dace.

The two fishes are somewhat differently coloured. The Souffie has a grey to greyish blue back with orange-yellow lateral line channels, silvery sides and a white belly. It has a dark blue or black stripe on each side above the lateral line, stretching from the eye to the base of the tail. This is particularly noticeable in males at spawning time when the bases of the fins also change colour, becoming more orange in colour. When spawning is over the colours fade.

Souffies live at altitudes of up to 2,000 m. In rivers they may be found in shoals over gravel beds; in lakes they frequent the deeper layers of the water. Spawning takes place in flowing water from April to June (at high altitudes even later) and the eggs are laid on gravelly beds; both sexes have spawning tubercles on their heads and bodies. Souffies feed mainly on small aquatic invertebrates and on other insects which have fallen into the water and remain struggling on the surface. They are too small to be of any real economic significance.

Size: 12—18 cm, maximum 25 cm
Weight: 50—100 g, maximum 200 g
Fin formula: D II—III/8—9, A III/8—9
Fecundity: 5,000—8,000 eggs
Distribution: The basin of the Danube, the Rhine and the Rhone. Lives in shoals in flowing water in the tributaries of their upper and lower reaches, also occurs in a number of lakes.

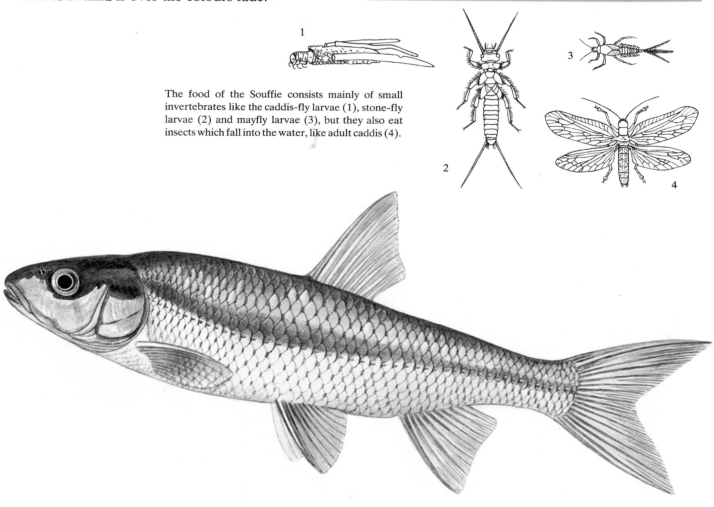

The food of the Souffie consists mainly of small invertebrates like the caddis-fly larvae (1), stone-fly larvae (2) and mayfly larvae (3), but they also eat insects which fall into the water, like adult caddis (4).

Minnow

Phoxinus phoxinus

Minnows can be seen swimming in large shoals in streams and lakes in the summer, wherever there is clean water and a gravelly bed. They are small fishes, very variable in colour, with dark spots or bands on the back and sides. At spawning time the males acquire such vivid colouring that they can be counted among the handsomest freshwater fishes in Europe. They have dark backs and sides contrasting sharply with the red anterior part of the belly, red-edged lips and red bases to the pelvic, pectoral and anal fins; the head, pectoral fins and the scales at the front of the body are all covered with a conspicuous, light-coloured spawning rash.

Minnows grow slowly and are short-lived fishes, seldom living for more than five years. They prefer clean, fast-flowing, well-oxygenated water and feed mainly on the larvae of aquatic insects, crustaceans and worms. Most fish reach sexual maturity in the second year. Minnows spawn in large shoals from April to July in gravelly shallows. The eggs are deposited on the bottom or in clumps of plants. In the summer minnows stay near the surface and close to the banks where they are hidden by water plants, but if alarmed they hide under roots and stones at the bottom, where they also take refuge in winter.

Minnows are important prey species for a variety of fishes like trout and pike and are also eaten by kingfishers, herons and otters. They are sometimes used as bait by anglers. Occasionally minnows are kept in aquaria and in the past they have been used for experimental purposes.

Size: 6−8 cm, occasionally up to 12 cm
Fin formula: D II−III/7, A III/6−7
Fecundity: 800−4,500 eggs
Distribution: In streams and the upper reaches of the rivers of northern Asia and of most of Europe, with the exception of southern Italy, Spain and Portugal, the southern part of the Balkan peninsula and the north of Scotland and Scandinavia.

The related species *P. percnurus*, which is found in eastern Europe and Asia, measures 10−12 cm and lives in small shoals in still waters.

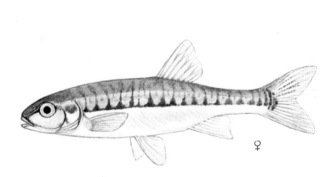

The female is less gaudily coloured.

Grass Carp

Ctenopharyngodon idella

The Grass Carp has a robust, elongate, cylindrical body and wide-apart eyes, giving it a strikingly wide forehead, and a semi-inferior mouth. It resembles the Chub in colouration, with a greyish green back, golden sides, dark-edged scales and dark dorsal and caudal fins; the other fins are light grey. The Grass Carp is a sturdy fish especially in its native haunts in Asia but it is smaller in European waters to which it has been introduced, and measures just over 50 cm by the time it is five years old. It becomes sexually mature when about six or seven years old.

Spawning occurs in the main channels of rivers and the pelagic eggs are carried along by the current; at 27−29 °C their development takes less than two days. Under European conditions spawning is carried out artificially and the eggs are incubated at about 25 °C. The fry feed at first on zooplankton, but soon change to a vegetarian diet, feeding on water weeds rather than on algae. This is the biggest asset of the Grass Carp, since it can be used to graze the vegetation in water which is excessively overgrown by aquatic plants.

The Grass Carp usually inhabits the lower reaches of big rivers but is also found in still water, if it is sufficiently warm and well supplied with vegetation. This species is often kept with Carp to improve production in carp ponds and the Chinese have bred it together with the Carp for at least 2,000 years. Since it does not breed naturally in European waters, there does not seem to be any danger of its becoming an ecological problem there, if it were to be introduced into carp ponds.

Size: 40−80 cm, maximum 1.2 m
Weight: 2−5 kg, maximum 30 kg
Fin formula: D III/7, A III/7−8
Fecundity: 50,000−150,000 eggs/kg body weight
Distribution: Originally from the Amur basin to Canton and Taiwan in the south. Introduced throughout the whole of China, the USSR, central, western and eastern Europe and in the USA.

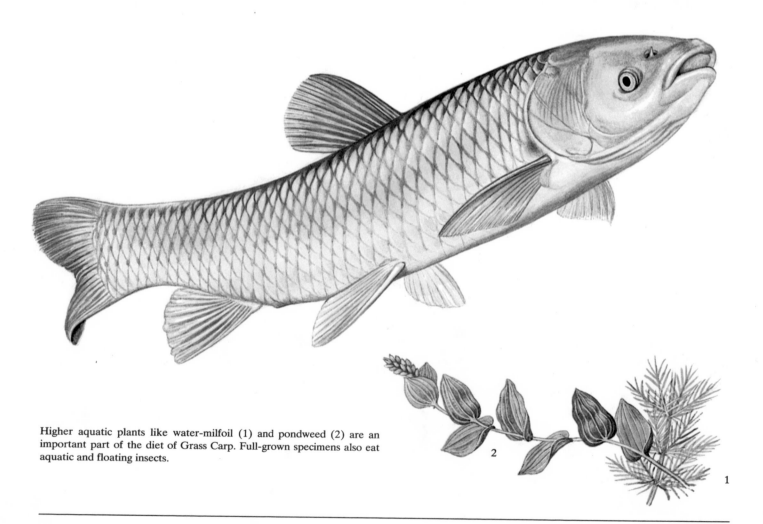

Higher aquatic plants like water-milfoil (1) and pondweed (2) are an important part of the diet of Grass Carp. Full-grown specimens also eat aquatic and floating insects.

Rudd

Scardinius erythrophthalmus

An attractive deep-bodied fish with a green to greenish brown back, yellowish green sides with a golden lustre and a light-coloured belly. The dorsal and pectoral fins are yellowish to greyish red; the others are blood red, especially at spawning time. The eyes have a yellow iris.

The Rudd has a small, upturned mouth and behind its ventral fins its belly is compressed to a sharp-edged keel covered with scales. The anterior edge of its dorsal fin lies behind the end of the base of its pectoral fins.

Rudd are found mainly in slow-moving or still waters, especially in lowland areas and form shoals which swim in the middle of the water or close to the surface. They feed on both animal and plant forms of plankton, on molluscs and on aquatic insects, and also on larvae and the fry of related species. Plants and plant débris form an important part of the diet. Sexually mature at three to four years old, Rudd spawn in small shoals from May to July. The eggs are usually laid in one or two batches on aquatic plants, but also on stones and other substrates. Rudd are known to form hybrids with Roach, Silver Bream and Bleak. In most places Rudd are present in much smaller numbers than Roach, but they are nevertheless an important prey species for predatory fishes, and at one time they were kept in small numbers in fishponds as food for larger fish. The flesh is tastier than that of the Roach but contains numerous small bones; they are nevertheless fished commercially in some parts of Europe. They are much more important as an angling species for coarse fishermen, since they are common and easy to catch.

Size: 25—30 cm, maximum 50 cm
Weight: 0.3—1 kg, occasionally up to 2 kg
Fin formula: D II—III/8—10, A III/9—12
Fecundity: 90,000—230,000 eggs
Distribution: Throughout Europe with the exception of the Iberian Peninsula, parts of Italy and the Balkans, the north of Scotland and most of Scandinavia. Also found in northern Asia.

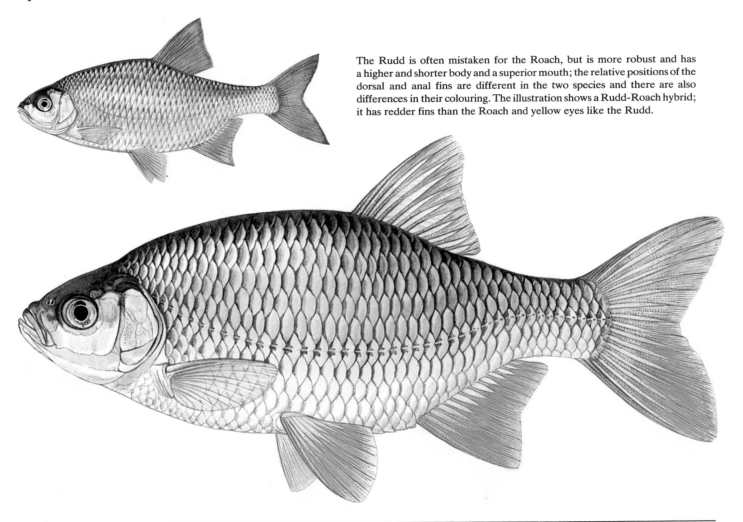

The Rudd is often mistaken for the Roach, but is more robust and has a higher and shorter body and a superior mouth; the relative positions of the dorsal and anal fins are different in the two species and there are also differences in their colouring. The illustration shows a Rudd-Roach hybrid; it has redder fins than the Roach and yellow eyes like the Rudd.

Asp
Aspius aspius

A large, predatory fish with an elongate body and a sharp ridge covered with scales, leading from the end of its ventral fin to the anal orifice. It has a large mouth extending to below its eyes. There is a thickened tip to the lower jaw which fits into a depression in its upper jaw. The Asp has a greyish blue back and silvery sides; its paired fins and anal fin are reddish, the others grey.

It grows relatively quickly and when eight to ten years old measures 50—60 cm; it becomes sexually mature when three to four years old. Spawning occurs in April, when the temperature of the water is 5—10 °C; the fish gather in small groups, in streams or rivers with a strong current and the eggs are stuck to pebbles on the bottom. The eggs hatch out after 15—20 days depending on the temperature. The fry feed at first on zooplankton but later change to the larvae of aquatic insects and the fry of other fishes. The adults are piscivorous, but also eat insects which have fallen into the water. Asp mainly live near the surface of running water, but they have also become adapted to valley reservoirs where they undertake long migrations; in rivers they have a tendency to haunt weirs and the supports of bridges.

Locally, especially in big valley reservoirs, Asp are of some economic significance. They are particularly popular with anglers because when hooked they always put up a good fight. The fish has moderately tasty flesh. Lately attempts have been made to farm it on a small scale; the fry are reared until they measure 5—10 cm and are then transplanted to natural surroundings. It is hoped that the Asp can be used to improve the ecology of valley reservoirs, by acting as a predator on other smaller fishes.

Size: 60—80 cm, maximum 1 m
Weight: 2—4 kg, maximum 10 kg
Fin formula: D III/8—9, A III/12—14
Fecundity: 80,000—100,000 eggs
Distribution: Rivers flowing into the North, Baltic, Black and Caspian seas; absent from much of western Europe, including Britain and France.

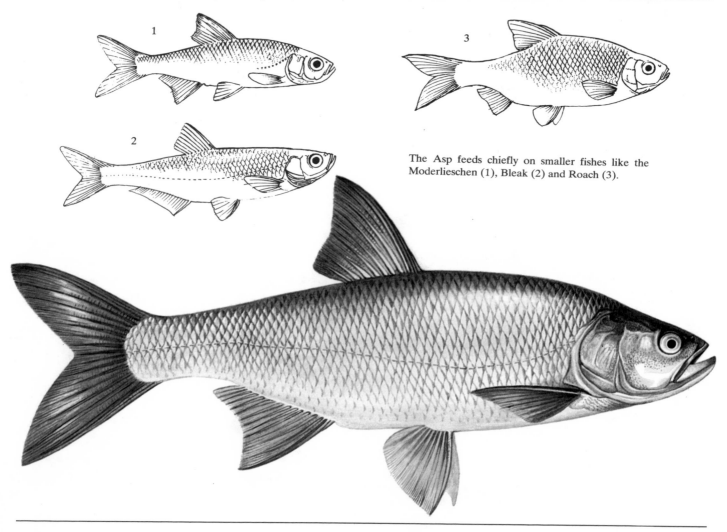

The Asp feeds chiefly on smaller fishes like the Moderlieschen (1), Bleak (2) and Roach (3).

Moderlieschen
Leucaspius delineatus

The Moderlieschen is a small, slender fish whose elongate body is covered with loose, moderately large cycloid scales. It has a brownish green back and gleaming silvery sides, along which a more or less distinct silver-blue band surmounted by a lighter line stretches from the operculum to the tail. The lateral line is noticeably incomplete. The bases of the paired fins are usually tinged red; the fins themselves are transparent.

Moderlieschen are short-lived fishes and seldom live for more than three years. They live in still and slow-flowing waters and are also found in lakes and ponds where they can survive even when the water is low in oxygen. In some localities these fish occur in large numbers and form active darting shoals. They feed chiefly on plant and animal plankton which they catch close to the surface. The sexes can be told apart from the form of their urogenital orifice, which lies in a depression in the male and has three protuberances in the female. Spawning takes place from April to June, at a water temperature of over 18 °C, and the eggs are laid in three to five batches. The eggs are colourless and minute (about the size of poppy seeds) and the female lays them in strings on the undersides of the leaves of aquatic plants, fragments of wood or roots which she has cleaned, usually near the surface of the water; the male guards them for five to twelve days until the fry swim away. These fish have little economic significance. However, they are fished commercially in a few lakes in central Russia, where they are dried for human consumption. Elsewhere in Europe Moderlieschen are sometimes used as bait.

Size: 7—9 cm
Fin formula: D II—III/7—8, A II—III/10—13
Fecundity: 100—2,300 eggs
Distribution: Central and eastern Europe; also present in parts of Denmark and southern Sweden but absent from Britain, France, Italy and the Iberian Peninsula.

Moderlieschen feed on copepod larvae (1), adult cyclops (2) and daphnias and other planktonic animals.

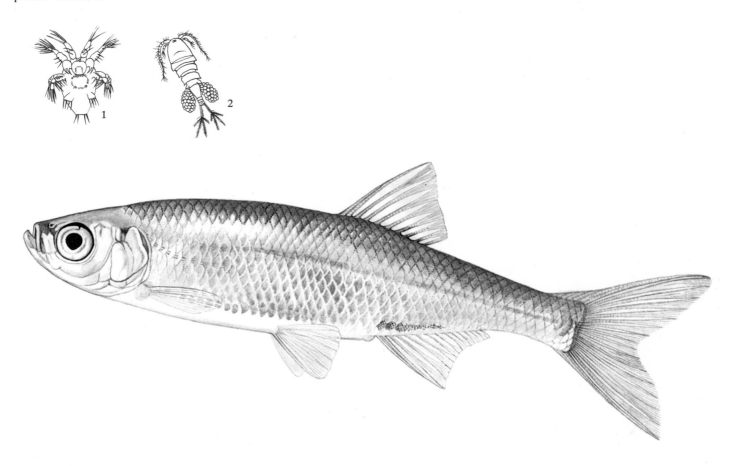

Bleak
Alburnus alburnus

These are small slender fishes with a green or blue-tinged back, silvery sides and silver belly. There is no dark band running along the sides, as there is in the similar Riffle Minnow. The dorsal and caudal fins are grey; the paired fins and the anal fin are slightly yellowish. Bleak have a life span of five to six years. They live in large shoals, swimming near the surface of the water in the middle and lower reaches of rivers, lakes and reservoirs, where they are one of the most common species. They feed on planktonic animals and floating insects.

Bleak attain sexual maturity when three years old and spawn in May or June. The females attach the eggs either to plants or to clean gravel in shallow water. The fry hatch after 14—21 days. They are short-lived fishes, rarely surviving for more than seven years. Bleak are important prey species for predatory fishes like pike and perch. In some reservoirs the fish are caught with nets and are used for making fish meal; occasionally they are caught by anglers since they have delicate, tasty flesh. Their scales were used at one time for making artificial mother-of-pearl.

Size: 15—20 cm
Weight: 30—50 g
Fin formula: D II—III/7—9, A III/14—20
Fecundity: 1,500—12,000 eggs
Distribution: Almost the whole of Europe except the southern peninsulas, northern Scandinavia, Ireland and Scotland. The subspecies *Alburnus alburnus albidus* lives in Italy and Dalmatia and the subspecies *A. alburnus charusini* in Transcaucasia; both are often regarded as separate species.

The Bleak feeds on planktonic animals and insects which have fallen on to the water; it also snaps up insects flying low over the surface like stone-flies (1) and mayflies (2).

Riffle Minnow

Alburnoides bipunctatus

A small fish, with a dark green back, silvery sides and a lateral line characteristically marked with a double intermittent line of small dark speckles. The pectoral fins are pink at the base; the other fins are grey and the anal fin is very long. Riffle Minnows live for five to six years and attain sexual maturity in the third year. They live in shoals in the shallow, swiftly flowing water in the middle and upper reaches of rivers and streams, where they live with minnows, gudgeon and other fishes. They may also be encountered, however, in the quieter lower reaches of rivers, in clean lakes and in some reservoirs. Spawning occurs in May or June when the colours of both sexes are more intense and the male bears small white tubercles on its head. The fish spawn in the swiftly flowing areas of rivers and streams on stony or gravelly beds. The development of the eggs takes four to ten days, depending on the temperature of the water. Riffle Minnows feed mainly on planktonic animals, aquatic insects and small crustaceans.

Riffle Minnows are economically unimportant since their flesh does not have a good flavour and they are bony, but they do provide food for predatory species like large trout, burbots and eels; they may also be used as bait for catching pike or pike-perch.

Size: 10—15 cm
Weight: 20—30 g
Fin formula: D II—III/7—8, A III/12—17
Fecundity: 3,000—8,000 eggs
Distribution: Western Europe eastwards to the USSR but absent from Scandinavia, the British Isles and southern Europe.

The distribution of the Riffle Minnow (red) does not extend as far north as that of the Bleak (blue).

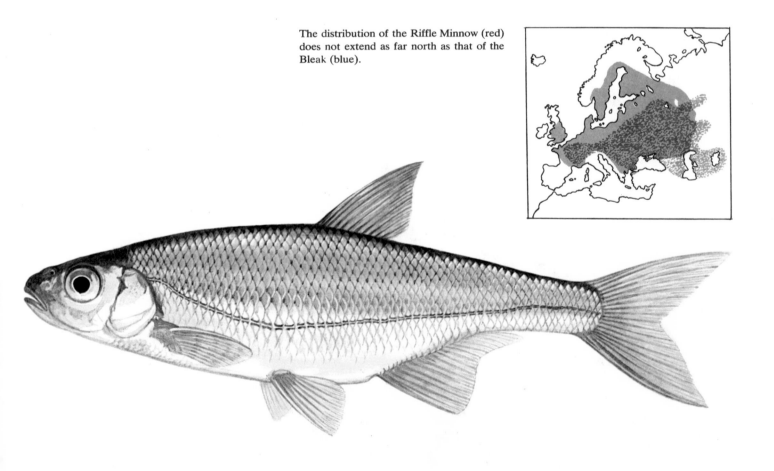

Common Bream

Abramis brama

There are three species in the genus *Abramis,* all deep-bodied fishes with long anal fins. The most important of them, the Common Bream, has compressed sides and a protrusible inferior mouth with which it can pick up food from the bottom. It has a dark brownish-blue back, silvery-bronze sides and a silver belly. All but its paired fins are greyish black in colour and the paired fins have dark leading edges. The Bream is one of the biggest European fishes, but like all fishes its rate of growth depends on the size of the population and on the number of other species competing with it for food. Adult Bream normally feed on bottom-dwelling organisms like molluscs, midge larvae and tube worms. If the number of fish is large and the food supply small the fish grow slowly and are very thin; and detritus, plant remains and mud predominate in the digestive tract.

Common Bream live in slow-flowing water, fishponds, lakes and reservoirs; they also tolerate brackish water. They become sexually mature when four to five years old. Spawning takes place from April to July; the fish gather in shoals and the eggs are laid in batches at night on stones or gravel, or more usually on aquatic plants, depending on the spawning-ground. At 18—20 °C the fry hatch in nine to ten days and feed chiefly on zooplankton.

Bream are economically important fishes, breeding very rapidly in lakes and reservoirs where they can be fished commercially. They are also popular with anglers and in some reservoirs as much as 100 kg bream per hectare are caught by anglers with rod and line every year.

Size: 35—45 cm, maximum 80 cm
Weight: 1—2 kg, maximum 10 kg
Fin formula: D II—III/7—10, A III/23—29
Fecundity: 50,000—350,000 eggs/kg body weight
Distribution: The whole of Europe except northern Scandinavia, Scotland, the Iberian Peninsula, Italy and the western and southern part of the Balkans.

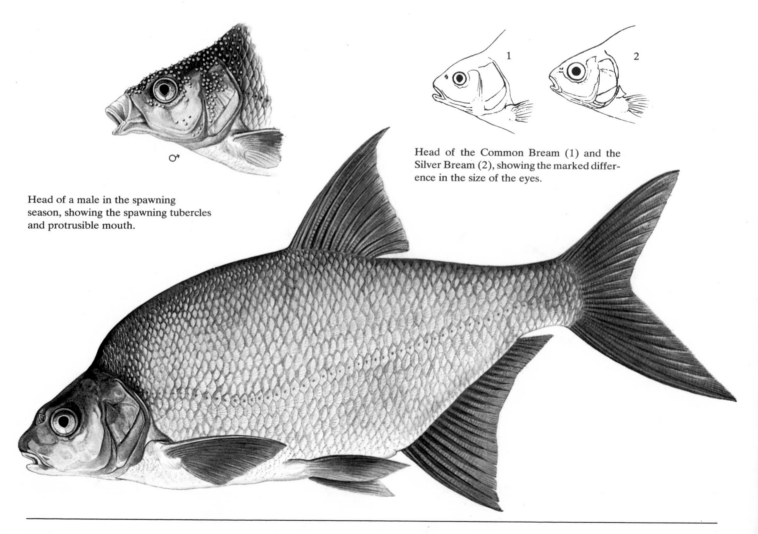

Head of a male in the spawning season, showing the spawning tubercles and protrusible mouth.

Head of the Common Bream (1) and the Silver Bream (2), showing the marked difference in the size of the eyes.

Danube Bream

Abramis sapa

This is a smallish species which even under favourable conditions grows more slowly than the Common Bream. It has a dark blue, sometimes green-tinged back and its sides are silvery grey; its fins are grey, the paired fins lighter than the others. It has a very long anal fin with over 30 soft rays, an inferior mouth and striking, relatively large, light eyes. Danube Bream live mostly in the lower reaches of rivers but never in large numbers. They become sexually mature when three to four years old and migrate upstream from the lowermost reaches of the rivers to reach their spawning grounds. They spawn in May on a gravelly bed and the adult fish then return to the lower parts of the rivers to feed and regain their strength. They feed mainly on bottom-dwelling organisms like molluscs and midge larvae, but also on water plants and detritus.

In the rivers flowing into Black Sea and the Caspian Sea the Danube Bream are of some economic significance. They are caught chiefly with dragnets and gill-nets. This Bream has tasty, though oily flesh, which is preserved by salting or smoking. It is not of interest to anglers.

Size: 15−20 cm, maximum 30 cm
Weight: 0.2−0.6 kg, maximum 1 kg
Fin formula: D II−III/7−8, A III/33−45
Fecundity: 10,000−40,000 eggs
Distribution: The rivers flowing into the Baltic, Black and Caspian seas and the Aral Sea.

The Danube Bream (*A. sapa*) (1) can be distinguished from the Zope (*A. ballerus*) (2) by its inferior mouth (the Zope has a superior mouth) and both these species can be distinguished from the Silver Bream (*Blicca bjoerkna*) and the Common Bream (*A. brama*) (4) by the strikingly long anal fin of the first two species, which has over 30 rays in both species (3).

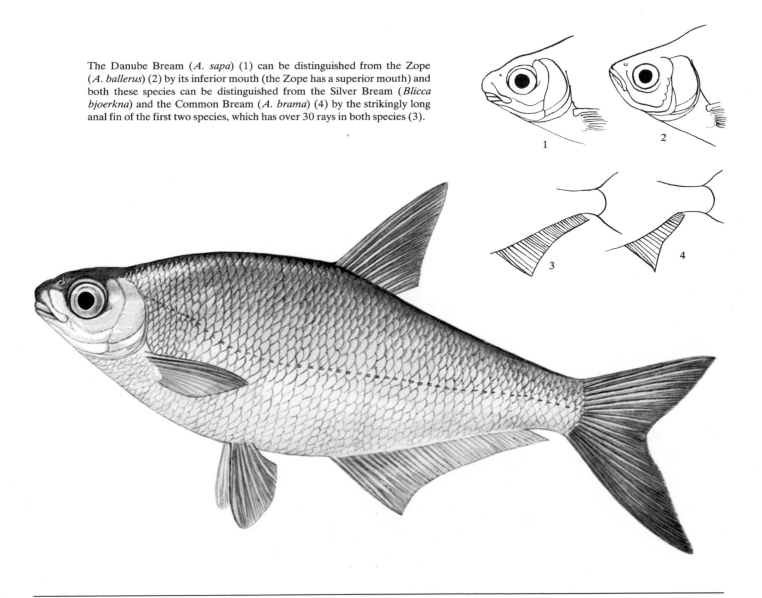

Zope
Abramis ballerus

This bream has a slender body with compressed sides. It can be distinguished from the Common Bream by its very long anal fin, which usually has over 30 soft rays, and from the Danube Bream by its superior mouth. It has small scales, over 60 in its lateral line alone. This fish has a greyish white body with an orange throat and a dark green or dark blue back, often with a metallic lustre. Its unpaired fins are grey and its paired fins yellowish with dark edges. A moderately large fish, the Zope has a life span of 18 years. It grows slowly, measuring only 16 cm when three to four years old and not reaching 30 cm in length until it is eight to ten years old.

Zope live in the lower reaches of rivers and in open water in lakes and ponds. In recent years its numbers have begun to increase in reservoirs, particularly in the USSR. The fish attain sexual maturity when three to four years old, the males generally a year before the females. They spawn at the end of April or in May in the shallow margins of lakes and in marshes, shedding the eggs on submerged aquatic plants. At a water temperature of 15 °C the fry hatch after about twelve days. After spawning the adults move back into open water while the fry remain in the shallows. The fish feed on planktonic crustaceans and other invertebrates.

The Zope is of local economic significance in the Volga and in the reservoirs of the Volga cascade, where it is caught at spawning time with dragnets. It is eaten dried and salted.

Size: 20—30 cm, maximum 45 cm
Weight: 0.3—0.6 kg, maximum 1.5 kg
Fin formula: D II—III/8—9, A III/26—44
Fecundity: 15,000—25,000 eggs
Distribution: The rivers flowing into the North, Baltic, Black and Caspian seas, from the Rhine to the Neva and from the Danube to the Ural.

Unlike other bream, the Zope feeds mostly on planktonic crustaceans belonging to the genera *Daphnia* (1) and *Cyclops* (2).

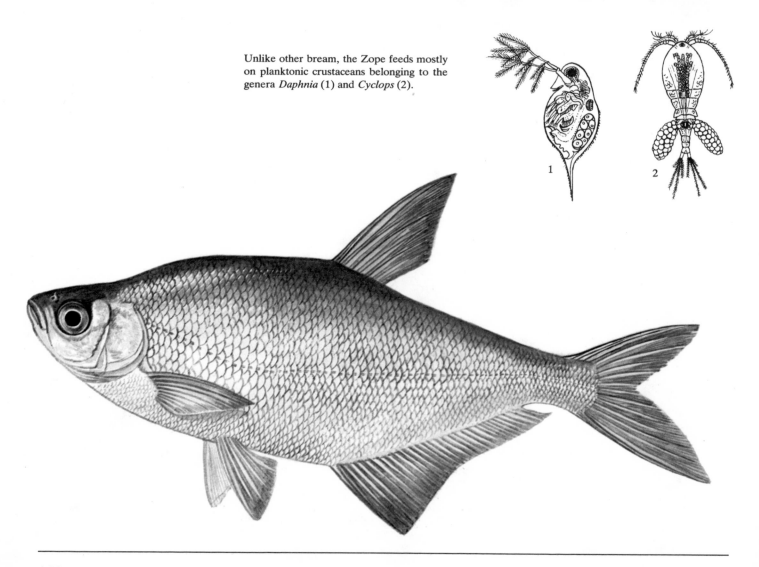

Silver Bream
Blicca bjoerkna

Silver Bream can be distinguished from the true Breams of the genus *Abramis* by its strikingly large eyes and vividly coloured paired fins. Its anal fin, which is shorter than that of true breams, begins behind the last ray of the dorsal fin. The Silver Bream has a greyish black back and silvery sides with a typical metallic bluish or greenish lustre. The unpaired fins are grey; the paired fins are red or orange at their base.

Silver Bream are quite large fish, attaining a weight of 1 kg and over in some carp ponds. They grow more slowly than the Common Bream, measuring 15 cm at five to six years old and up to 25 cm at eight to ten years old, depending on the availability of food. Silver Bream live in the lower reaches of rivers, lakes and ponds, in slow-moving or still water. Some fish, mainly males, reach sexual maturity in their second year, the others when three years old. Spawning occurs intermittently amongst dense water weeds at depths of about three metres, often in the company of other cyprinid fishes, in particular Roach, Rudd and Common Bream, with the result that hybrids of these species are not uncommon. The eggs are attached to the vegetation and the fry hatch after four to six days.

The economic significance of Silver Bream is very small although they may be caught by accident with other species during their spawning migrations in the spring, in dragnets. They are of no interest to anglers and may compete for food with other more valuable species like Common Bream, with which the Silver Bream is often confused.

Size: 15−25 cm, maximum 35 cm
Weight: 0.2−0.5 kg, maximum 1 kg
Fin formula: D III/8−9, A III/19−24
Fecundity: 15,000−110,000 eggs
Distribution: Occurs in the rivers Loire and Rhône and in the tributaries of the North Sea, the Baltic and the Caspian Sea as far as the Urals.

Distribution map of *B. bjoerkna*.

The main components of the food of the Silver Bream include pond snails (*Lymnea stagnalis*) (1) and insect larvae like those of the alder-fly (2) and of mosquitoes (3).

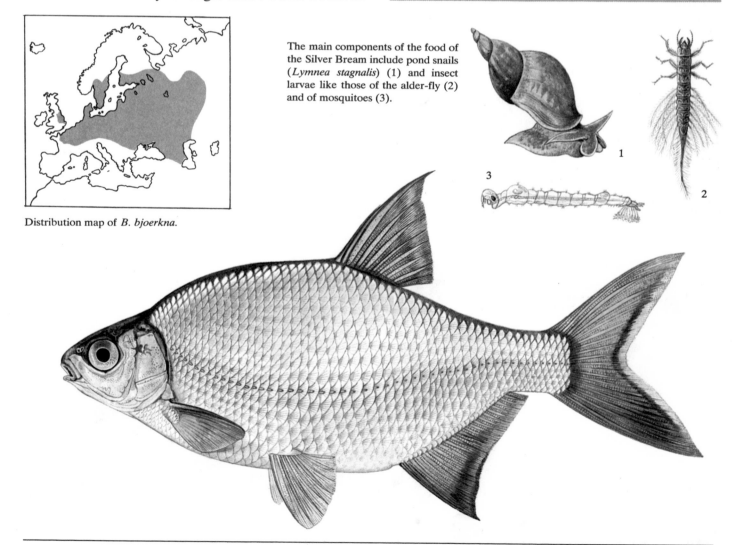

East European Bream
Vimba vimba

This fish is often mistaken for a true bream or for the Nase, but its body is less arched and more elongated than a bream's and it has a much longer anal fin than a Nase and also a rather different mouth. Its characteristic features include a sharp ridge covered with scales behind its dorsal fin and thick, fleshy lips. The inferior mouth is curved, whereas that of the Nase is straight. The East European Bream has a bluish grey back and a silvery white belly. At spawning time its back and sides become darker while the underside of its head, the front of its body and its pectoral and ventral fins become bright orange or red. When spawning is over, this 'nuptial costume' soon disappears.

East European Bream are semi-migratory fishes which live mostly in the quieter lower reaches of rivers, but they migrate upstream into the middle reaches to spawn, often covering a distance of several hundred kilometres. They are also found in lakes and in the brackish water of river mouths. In April the fish travel upstream in shoals. Spawning takes place from the end of April into July, in a gentle current in shallow weedy stretches of the river near the shore; the eggs are usually laid in two or three batches. Silver Bream feed mostly at the bottom on molluscs and insect larvae usually, but also occasionally on worms and crustaceans.

Although not very common East European Bream are popular with anglers and the fish are also netted during migration. The flesh is very tasty, especially in the winter.

Size: 25−35 cm, exceptionally up to 40 cm
Weight: 0.5−1.5 kg, occasionally up to 3 kg
Fin formula: D III/8−9, A III/17−22
Fecundity: 20,000−50,000 eggs ('trophy' females up to 300,000)
Distribution: Mostly in northern Europe, in rivers flowing into the North Sea and the Baltic.

At spawning time the fish are highly coloured. This is especially noticeable in the males, which also have a spawning eruption on the head and back.

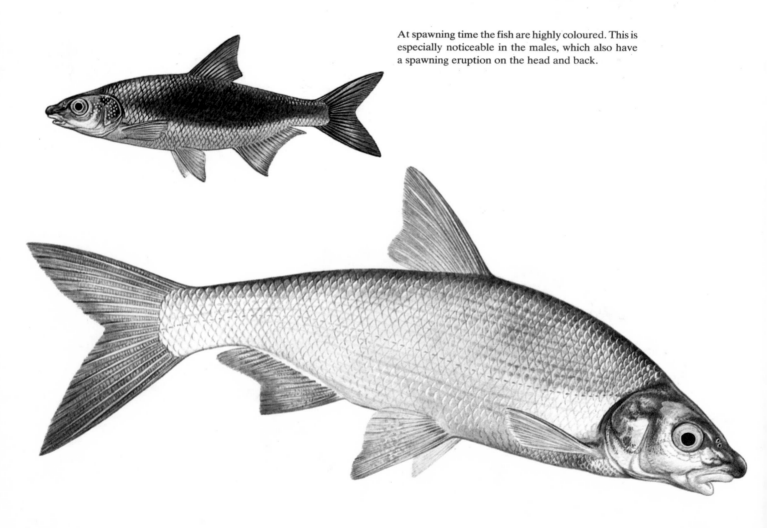

Ziege
Pelecus cultratus

At first glance the Ziege looks somewhat like a flying-fish, with its elongate, extremely flat-sided, almost straight-backed body, dorsal fin set far back on its body and curved belly forming a sharp 'keel'. Its pectoral fins are very long and it has a superior, upturned mouth. Characteristic features include loose scales and its somewhat zigzag lateral line. It has a silvery grey to bluish grey back and its sides and belly are silvery white. The fish live in large shoals close to the surface, in the brackish waters and fresh waters of the bays and lagoons of the Baltic, Black, Caspian and Aral seas. At spawning time shoals of these fish invade the big rivers and swim far upstream; some populations live permanently in fresh water. Those living in the Baltic migrate up the rivers on its southeastern side; those migrating up the Danube swim to Bratislava and beyond. The size of the populations is steadily diminishing, however — evidently as a result of the construction of dams and increasing pollution.

The fish become sexually mature when three years old, migrate in early spring and spawn between May and June. The pelagic eggs and the larvae are carried downstream by the current. The fry feed on plankton, but the adults are fast-swimming predatory fishes, which feed on small herring and cod as well as on planktonic invertebrates. The Ziege's flesh is soft, full of small bones and not very good.

> *Size:* 25—40 cm, maximum 60 cm
> *Weight:* 0.5—1 kg, rarely up to 2 kg
> *Fin formula:* D II—III/6—8, A II—III/25—29
> *Fecundity:* average 30,000 eggs, maximum 50,000
> *Distribution:* The rivers flowing into the Baltic, Black, Caspian and Aral Seas and in the brackish waters of the seas themselves.

Distribution map of *P. cultratus.*

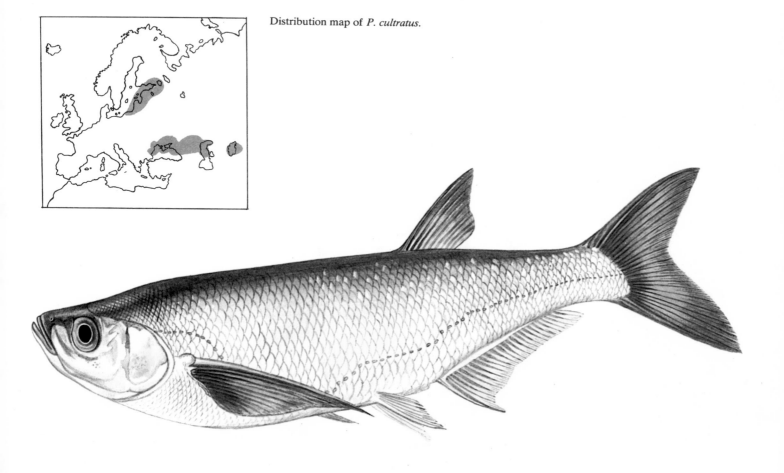

Tench
Tinca tinca

A heavy thickset fish with a relatively short deep body covered with minute scales which are embedded deep in the skin and covered with thick slime, making the fish very difficult to handle. Occasionally individuals may be completely scaleless. The Tench is predominantly green in colour with a dark green back, greenish brown to greenish grey sides with a golden sheen, a belly which is distinctly lighter in colour and dark fins. Gold and red specimens occur occasionally in fishponds.

Tench live in ponds and lakes, occasionally in the marshy lower reaches of rivers or oxbow lakes or the brackish water of estuaries or deltas; they are able to live in quite poorly oxygenated water. They spend most of their time on the bottom, where they feed mainly on benthic animals like aquatic insect larvae and crustaceans. They spawn intermittently from the end of May to the beginning of August and the sticky eggs adhere to aquatic plants. The eggs are small and hatch in six to eight days. The young fish feed on algae, copepods and water fleas. Tench spend the winter in shoals in the deepest part of the water, either just above the lake bed or buried in mud and clay. In the summer, if the water is too warm, they lie quietly on the bottom.

Tench are one of the most important freshwater fishes economically, with moist, white, tasty flesh. In a number of European countries they are bred in ponds and reservoirs as a valuable supplementary species, but they have one disadvantage in that they grow quite slowly.

Size: 30–45 cm, maximum 60 cm
Weight: 1–3 kg, exceptionally up to 7 kg
Fin formula: D III–IV/8–9, A III–IV/6–8
Fecundity: 80,000–150,000 eggs (in isolated cases up to 900,000)
Distribution: Practically the whole of Europe but absent north of the 61° N line of latitude. Has been introduced into other continents.

View of the underside of the body of a female and a male. Sexual dimorphism is evident in the ventral fins; in the male the first rays of this fish are much thicker than in the female and the fins extend beyond the anus.

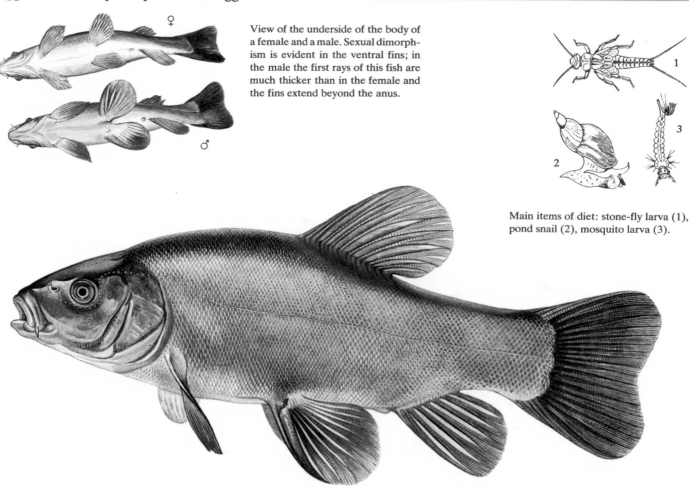

Main items of diet: stone-fly larva (1), pond snail (2), mosquito larva (3).

Nase
Chondrostoma nasus

A long slender fish, well suited to life in flowing water, with a characteristically shaped mouth on the underside of its small head. The mouth is a straight slit with sharp, horny lips adapted for scraping off algae and diatoms from stones on the bottom. The Nase has a grey to silvery white body, sometimes with a blue-tinged back, and red-tinted or red fins except for the dorsal fin which is grey.

Nase live mainly in deep, swiftly flowing water in the middle reaches of rivers often near bridges or weirs, but may also be found in lakes. They form large shoals, often numbering up to a hundred individuals, which may be clearly visible from the bank. When gathering food on the bottom the fish often turn over on to their sides betraying their presence by their flashing silvery bodies. Except when young, they feed almost entirely on algae and diatoms throughout the year. As they 'graze', they leave light bands behind them where they have stripped the stones. Nase become sexually mature when three to four years old and the males develop a white spawning eruption during the spawning season. They spawn in the turbulent parts of the upper reaches of rivers and streams between March and May after a short or long migration. The spawning shoals are large and spawning itself is stormy. At first the fry have a horseshoe-shaped mouth, but during their development it straightens out due to the uneven hornification of the lip edges.

The flesh of the Nase is not particularly tasty and it contains a quantity of tiny bones. Despite this, it is caught commercially and by anglers.

Size: 25—40 cm, maximum 50 cm
Weight: 0.5—1 kg, exceptionally up to 2 kg
Fin formula: D II—IV/8—10, A II—IV/9—12
Fecundity: 8,000—40,000 eggs
Life span: 15—18 years, maximum 20 years
Distribution: European rivers, from France to the USSR. Absent from the southern European peninsulas, from Great Britain, Denmark and Scandinavia and from the north European part of the USSR. Formerly absent in the Elbe, it has now begun to infiltrate into it via connecting canals.

The related species *C. genei* occurs in Italy, in the region round Nice and in the Rhône. It measures up to 30 cm.

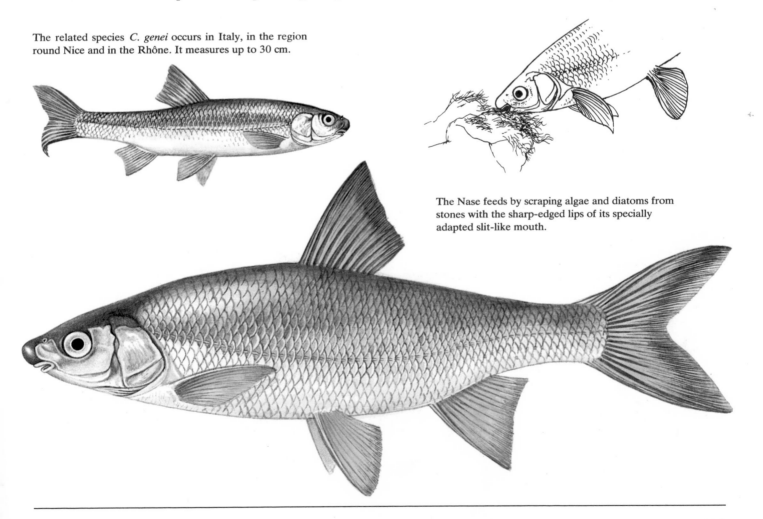

The Nase feeds by scraping algae and diatoms from stones with the sharp-edged lips of its specially adapted slit-like mouth.

Toxostome
Chondrostoma toxostoma

In shape and general appearance the Toxostome resembles the Nase, but it is smaller and lives in the higher reaches of rivers and streams. It can be distinguished from the Nase by the lower number of branched rays in its anal fin, the lower number of scales in its lateral line and, in particular, by its horseshoe-shaped mouth. It has an olive green back and on its silvery white sides, above the lateral line, there is usually a dark, greyish gold longitudinal stripe. Toxostomes are confined to the rivers of southwestern France and northern Spain. According to some experts the Spanish populations form an independent subspecies, *Ch. toxostoma arrigonus*, differing in several respects from the populations living in southwestern France.

Toxostomes tend to live in shoals in small rivers with clean, well-oxygenated, gently flowing water or in lakes. The shoals are particularly large in the winter when the fish retire to deeper water. In the spring the shoals migrate to the spawning grounds in the upper reaches of the rivers, where the current is stronger and there is a stony river bed, to spawn in shallow, gravelly areas.

These small fishes are important prey species for trout but they are of no commercial importance, nor are they valued by anglers for their flesh is oily, not very tasty and contains a quantity of small bones.

Size: 20–25 cm, maximum 30 cm
Weight: 0.3–0.5 kg
Fin formula: D III/8, A III/9
Fecundity: 500–8,000 eggs

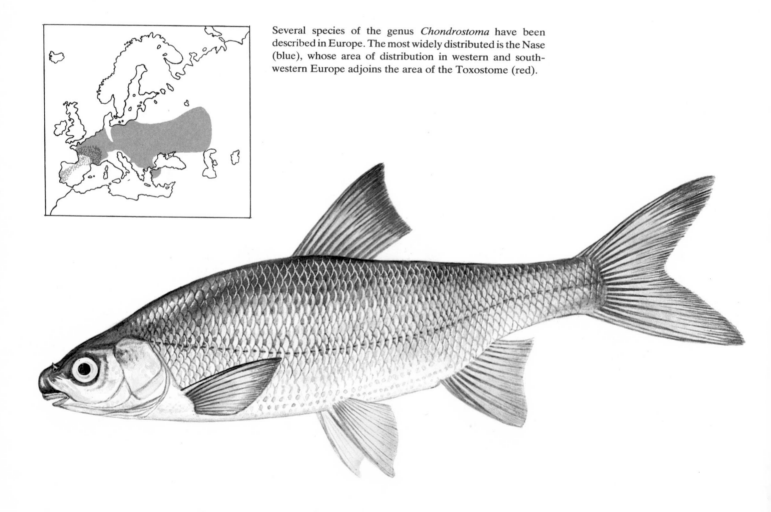

Several species of the genus *Chondrostoma* have been described in Europe. The most widely distributed is the Nase (blue), whose area of distribution in western and south-western Europe adjoins the area of the Toxostome (red).

Barbel

Barbus barbus

The Barbel has an almost cylindrical body with a long head, a short high dorsal fin, an inferior mouth with fleshy lips and four fleshy barbels. It has an olive green to brownish green back, its sides have a golden sheen and its belly is yellowish or dingy white; it has an anal fin and paired fins tinged with red, while its dorsal and caudal fins are dark. This is a large species in which the females grow faster than the males, and the fish reach sexual maturity when they are between four and six years old.

Barbels live in the deeper faster-flowing upper reaches of rivers with a stony or gravelly bottom; in fact, such parts are known as barbel zones. Barbels form shoals which hunt for food on the river bed, turning over the stones with their fleshy snouts, foraging mostly at night but in deeper water they may also be active during the day. They feed chiefly on benthic invertebrates like aquatic insect larvae and crustaceans, but they also feed on algae and larger individuals catch small fish. In the winter they are less active and spend much of the time resting. Spawning occurs after the fish have migrated upriver, intermittently from May to July in shallow water with a gravelly river bed. The eggs catch in the gravel and hatch after ten to fifteen days. The fish mature sexually after three to five years.

Barbels are caught mainly by anglers and are good sporting fish. The best time for catching them is in the evening or in turbid water after rain when they go in search of food.

Size: 30—60 cm, maximum 90 cm
Weight: 0.5—2 kg, maximum 6 kg
Fin formula: D III—IV/8—9, A II—III/5
Fecundity: 20,000—150,000 eggs
Distribution: Western and central Europe, including the Danube basin. Absent from Ireland, Scandinavia and the peninsulas of southern Europe.

The difference between the shape of the third hard ray of the dorsal fin of the Barbel and the Southern Barbel. In the Barbel it is clearly toothed, in the Southern Barbel it is smooth.

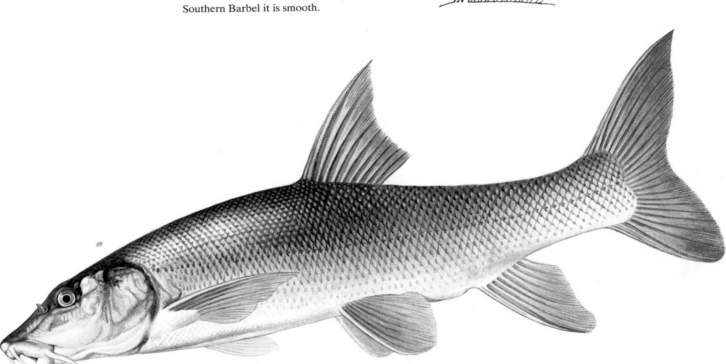

Caspian Barbel
Barbus brachycephalus

This barbel has a dark, green-tinged back; the lower parts of its sides are lighter in colour and its fins are grey. The fish live in the southern and western parts of the Caspian Sea and in the Aral Sea. The barbels are migratory. Migration begins in June and ends at the beginning of October; fish migrating upstream in August and September possess immature eggs and sperm; these fish spend the winter in the river and spawn there the following spring. Individuals which migrate in the spring have almost mature eggs and sperm and spawn in the same year. The mean weight of the barbels beginning migration is about 6 kg, but while migrating they usually stop feeding and consequently they lose weight.

Spawning takes place in April and May in the upper reaches of the rivers emptying into the Caspian Sea and the fry appear in the river deltas in August; males often remain in the rivers until after their first spawning. The males become sexually mature when three to four years old, the females one or two years later. Big females (about one metre long) have over a million eggs. The Caspian Barbel grows quickly; when five years old a fish may measure over 50 cm and by ten years old it may be 80–90 cm long. In the sea the fish feed mainly on molluscs, in particular of the genus *Adacna*. Caspian barbels caught in the river Kura are more robust than Aral populations.

Pre-war catches in the Aral Sea amounted to about 1,000 tons and in the river Kura to about 300 tons; present catches are substantially smaller.

Size: 0.5–1 m, maximum 1.2 m
Weight: 2–6 kg, maximum 25 kg
Fin formula: D III–IV/7, A II–III/5–6
Fecundity: 150,000–1.5 million eggs
Distribution: Occurs in the catchment area of the Caspian and Aral Seas.

Distribution map for
B. brachycephalus (red)
and subspecies
*B. brachycephalus
caspius* (blue).

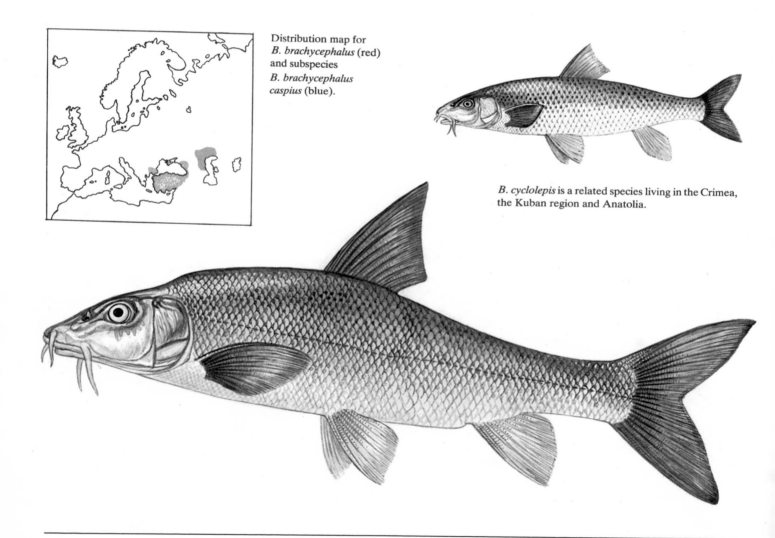

B. cyclolepis is a related species living in the Crimea, the Kuban region and Anatolia.

Southern Barbel

Barbus meridionalis

This is a smaller fish than the Barbel with a smaller straight-edged dorsal fin, which has a smooth third hard ray. It has larger scales than the Barbel and its anal fin, when folded, is longer, stretching to the base of the caudal fin. Both dorsal and caudal fins have rows of distinct dark spots. It has a brownish green back, dingy yellow sides, a dingy white belly and yellowish paired fins; its back and sides are covered with many dark brown spots. Like the other barbels, the Southern Barbel has four barbels, two on the snout and two in the angles of the mouth. In the Southern Barbel, like the Caspian Barbel, the barbels are long.

The Southern Barbel frequents the flowing water of small swift streams at middle altitudes, but may also be found in the lower reaches of rivers; it is found chiefly in the grayling zone or sometimes in the barbel zone in the summer months. Adult specimens hide among stones or under overhanging banks. Like the Barbel it first migrates upstream to spawn in gravelly shallows. The fry collect in shallows where the water is quieter; like the adult fish they feed on bottom-dwelling animals.

Wherever it occurs the Southern Barbel forms very large populations but it is not economically important or of interest to anglers because of its small size and its limited distribution. It is an important prey species however, particularly for salmonids like large trout and Danube salmon. Where it occurs together with the Barbel the two species interbreed.

Size: 25—35 cm, maximum 40 cm
Weight: 0.2—0.4 kg, maximum 0.6 kg
Fin formula: D II—III/8—9, A II—III/5
Distribution: The south of France, northern Italy, the Balkans, the northern part of the Carpathians and the Visla, the Danube and the Dnestr.

The present distribution of the Southern Barbel is restricted to a few areas of southwestern, southern and central Europe, evidently the remains of what was once a much wider area of distribution.

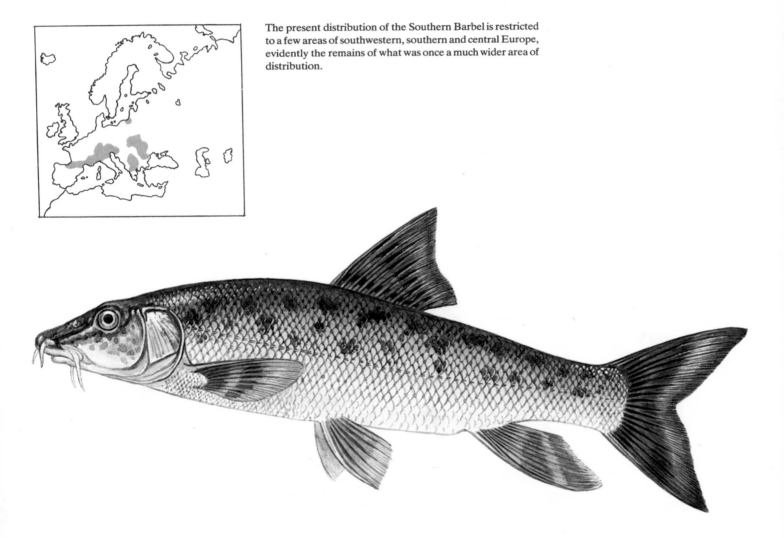

Gudgeon
Gobio gobio

One of the most widespread and numerous species of the genus *Gobio,* this small fish has an elongate, fusiform body and an inferior mouth with a single barbel at each corner of the mouth. It has a brown, sometimes green-tinged, back and dingy greyish white sides, sometimes with a yellowish tone. Its dorsal, caudal and pectoral fins are greyish yellow and are marked with a few rows of dark spots. The Gudgeon grows slowly and when five or six years old measures 10–15 cm; it becomes sexually mature when two or three years old.

Gudgeon live in shoals throughout many rivers and in ponds and lakes, usually in deep water near the bottom. When disturbed, they take shelter under an overhanging bank or amongst stones and roots. In carp ponds they sometimes form very large populations which compete with the carp for food. Spawning takes place from April to June at a water temperature of 12–18 °C, in either flowing or still water over

a sandy bed; the males have a striking spawning eruption. The sticky eggs are laid in three or four batches at intervals of about one week and stick to plants or stones. The development of the embryos takes 6–10 days, depending on how warm the water is. The fry feed on infusoria, rotifers and crustacean larvae on the bottom. As they grow they switch to larger prey and eventually the adult fish feed on caddis-fly and midge larvae and also, to a smaller extent, on vegetable debris.

Economically Gudgeon are of no significance, but are popular as bait and are important as prey species for larger fish.

Size: 10–12 cm, maximum 22 cm
Fin formula: D II–III/7, A II–III/6–7
Fecundity: 1,000–3,000 eggs
Distribution: Europe excepting the southern peninsulas and northwestern Scandinavia, northern Asia as far as the Yenisei, China, the catchment area of the Amur.

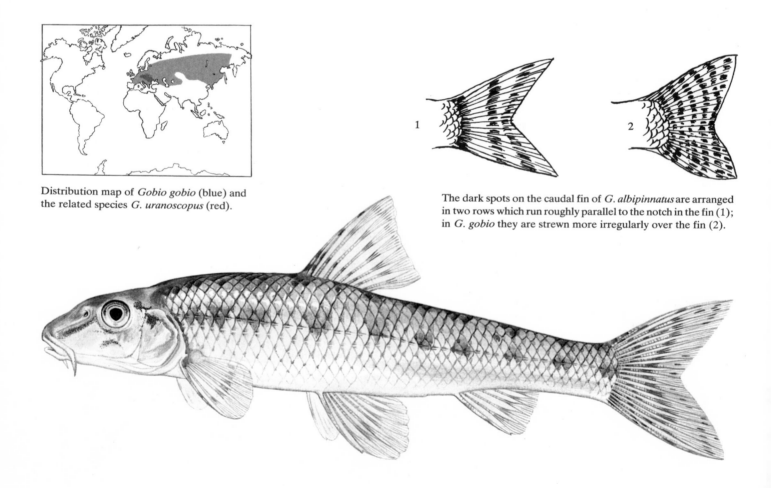

Distribution map of *Gobio gobio* (blue) and the related species *G. uranoscopus* (red).

The dark spots on the caudal fin of *G. albipinnatus* are arranged in two rows which run roughly parallel to the notch in the fin (1); in *G. gobio* they are strewn more irregularly over the fin (2).

Whitefin Gudgeon
Gobio albipinnatus

This fish has a long slender body, two barbels, one at each corner of the mouth, and a bare, scaleless throat like the Gudgeon. It has a lateral line like that of the Riffle Minnow, but the dark spots forming the border are less pronounced; it also has dark spots on its sides and its dorsal and caudal fins. It can be distinguished from the Gudgeon, *G. gobio*, which lives in similar habitats, by its dorsal fins which are colourless. The Whitefin Gudgeon lives in the basins of the Dnepr, the Don, the Volga and the Danube where it frequents the deeper, quieter parts of the rivers. Data on its growth, reproduction and feeding habits are still not available. It is economically unimportant but is a prey species for other larger fishes; sometimes it is used as bait.

This species lives in the upper reaches of rivers, particularly in the grayling and barbel zones, where it can be found in flowing and turbulent stretches of water, where the river bed is stony. Because of its small size and secretive habits it passes unnoticed. Its numbers have declined to the point where it is now classified as an endangered species; in some countries it is protected by law the whole year round.

Also found in the Danube basin is the Danube Longbarbel Gudgeon *G. uranoscopus* — the only European gudgeon with scales on its throat. It has long barbels stretching to its throat. Kessler's Gudgeon (*G. kessleri*) is another that lives in the Danube and Dnestr basins. It is the only one with eight soft rays in its dorsal fin (the other species have seven). It has somewhat shorter barbels than *G. uranoscopus* and a scaleless throat.

Size: 8—10 cm, maximum 13 cm
Fin formula: D II—III/6—7, A II—III/5—6
Distribution:
G. albipinnatus — the Dnestr, Volga, Don and Danube basins
G. uranoscopus — the Danube basin
G. kessleri — the Danube and Dnestr basins.

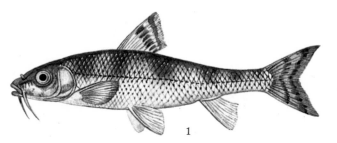
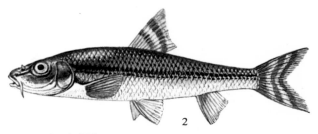

The related species *G. uranoscopus* (1) and *G. kessleri* (2).

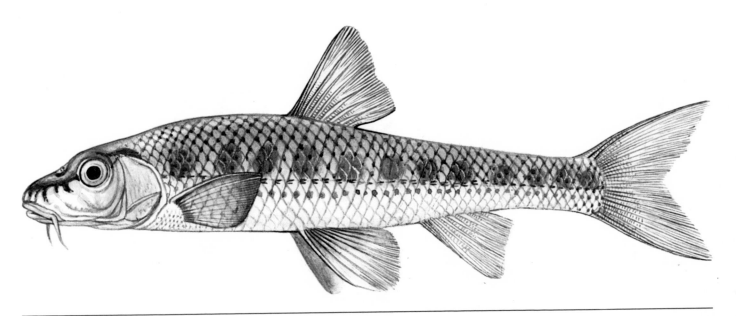

Bitterling
Rhodeus sericeus

A small fish with a relatively deep body and a semi-inferior mouth. It has a body covered with large scales and its lateral line is incomplete, with pores distinguishable only in the first four to seven scales behind its head. For most of the year it has a greyish green back and silvery sides and belly; an opalescent blue-green line stretches along the middle of each side. In the spawning season the colouring of the males is intensified and two islands of spawning tubercles appear above the mouth and eyes, while the sides of the fish turn purple and they have a dark spot behind each operculum.

Bitterling are found mainly in the lower reaches and oxbow lakes of rivers and in lakes, where they often live in inlets with muddy or sandy bottoms. In these creeks live freshwater mussels of the genera *Anodonta* and *Unio*. Reproductive behaviour in the Bitterling is an unusual affair. In the spawning season, which lasts from April to August, the female develops an ovipositor about 6 cm long behind its anal orifice. The males in the spring look for a suitable bivalve and if a sexually mature female approaches the mussel the male attracts it towards the mussel by a complicated ritual. The female eventually inserts her ovipositor into the bivalve's excretory siphon and lays her eggs within the mantle, while the male releases the milt over the inhalant siphon where, together with water, it is sucked into the gill chamber and fertilizes the eggs. The fertilized eggs develop inside the mussel shell and the little bitterlings leave it three to four weeks later. One male will lure several females to the same shell and since the same shell may be used by several pairs, it is by no means uncommon to find over 100 different eggs within it, all at different stages of development. Bitterling have a life span of four to five years and mature sexually when two years old. They feed mainly on plant and animal plankton.

In recent years their once large numbers have started to diminish with increasing pollution and a consequent drop in the number of bivalves.

Size: 6–9 cm
Fin formula: D II–IV/9–10, A II–III/8–10
Fecundity: 40–100 eggs up to 3 mm
Distribution: North of the Alps; absent from Scandinavia, Denmark and the greater part of Great Britain. Extends from the Rhône basin in the west to the Caspian Sea in the east.

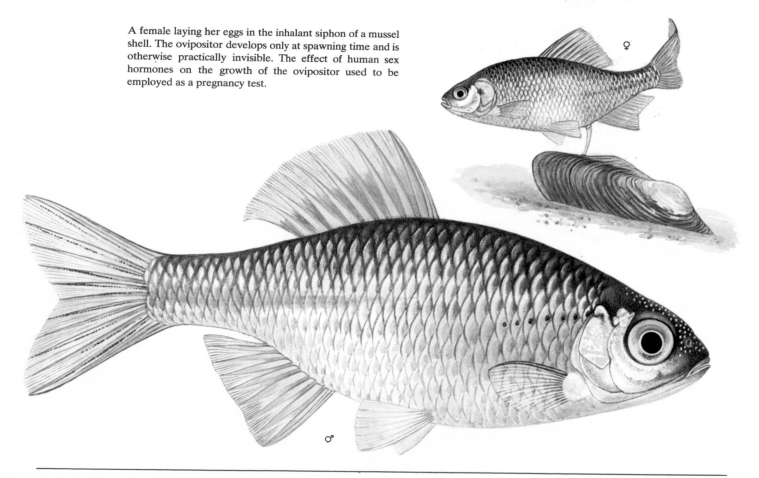

A female laying her eggs in the inhalant siphon of a mussel shell. The ovipositor develops only at spawning time and is otherwise practically invisible. The effect of human sex hormones on the growth of the ovipositor used to be employed as a pregnancy test.

Crucian Carp

Carassius carassius

This fish has a hump-backed look, a look which becomes more pronounced as the fish ages. Like the Carp it has a long dorsal fin. It is golden or greenish gold in colour, darkening on the back. The dorsal and caudal fins are brown while the paired fins are yellowish brown, sometimes with a reddish tinge. In front of the caudal fin younger fishes have a dark spot on the peduncle. There are no barbels round the mouth. The Crucian Carp is much smaller than the Carp and has a tendency to form large populations of stunted individuals with a mean length of only 10−15 cm. They often grow rather slowly, attaining sexual maturity when two to three years old.

Crucian Carp live in enclosed water or, less often, in the lower reaches of rivers, often under extreme conditions; they can hibernate in the presence of a severe lack of oxygen and can go without food for long periods so that the rate of growth depends very much on the space and food available. They feed on zooplankton, benthic animals and plant debris.

Spawning takes place in May and June and the eggs are laid in two or three batches on aquatic plants or submerged parts of marginal plants; development takes between four and seven days.

In some parts of eastern Europe Crucian Carp are of considerable economic significance, particularly in water where they can survive and other species cannot and they are fished both by anglers and on a commercial scale. They have been introduced into many areas of Europe and Britain, often as ornamental fish in fish-ponds.

Size: 20−30 cm, maximum 50 cm
Weight: 0.2−0.5 kg, maximum 1.5 kg
Fin formula: D III−IV/14−21, A II−III/6−8
Fecundity: 30,000−300,000 eggs
Distribution: Originally from rivers flowing into the North, Baltic and Black Seas and into the Arctic Ocean as far as the river Lena. Together with the Carp it has been introduced into parts of Europe and Britain.

The structure of the third hard ray of the dorsal fin is an important character to look for when distinguishing between the Crucian Carp and the Goldfish. In the Crucian Carp (1) the serrations on the ray are roughly the same size, whereas in the Goldfish (2) they become noticeably larger towards the tip of the ray.

Goldfish

Carassius auratus

Goldfish, the most popular fish for small ponds and aquaria, are a variety of *C. auratus*. The native type species has a blackish grey back and its dorsal and caudal fins are blackish grey, it has silvery grey sides with lighter coloured paired and anal fins. In Central and eastern Europe the native form of *C. auratus* occurs in the same places as the Crucian Carp, but it is also found in the Far East and has spread throughout Europe. The decorative form is gold, with a variety of black or white markings. It was originally bred in China from the subspecies *C. auratus gibelio*. Young fish are black. Goldfish can be distinguished from Crucian Carp by the difference in the third hard ray of the dorsal fin. The fish spawn between May and July from the age of two to four years old. Some east European and Asian populations have been found to consist entirely of females. Spawning takes place intermittently and two to four batches of eggs are laid amongst water plants, to which the sticky eggs adhere. The fish feed on zooplankton, floating insects, bottom-living animals and plant debris. They have a life span of eight to twelve years. The type species lives in large stretches of water and can be caught in the main channel of big rivers and lakes. It grows better than the Crucian Carp.

In some places in western Europe the fish compete with Carp for food but in others they are being caught by anglers and fishermen. In many fishponds annual production amounts to 50—100 kg, although the Goldfish may be an unwelcome species in them, if the ponds are intended as breeding areas for other, economically more productive species.

Size: 20—25 cm, maximum 30—45 cm
Weight: 0.2—0.3 kg, maximum 1—2 kg
Fin formula: D III—IV/14—19, A II—III/5—7
Fecundity: 160,000—360,000 eggs
Distribution: Parts of Europe and Asia

The Goldfish, the golden form of *C. auratus* which is kept in ornamental ponds.

Wild Carp
Cyprinus carpio

Wild Carp have robust, cylindrical bodies with golden yellow to brown sides, darker backs and a yellowish white belly. The paired fins and caudal fin are usually tinged with red, while the dorsal fin is greyish blue. The fish has a long dorsal fin, a short anal fin and four fleshy barbels round its mouth; Carp—Crucian Carp hybrids usually have only two barbels. Wild Carp grow more slowly than the artificially bred forms depending on the temperature of the water and the length of the summer. Under central European conditions, at four years old a fish may measure 35 cm and weigh 1 kg, while at 15 years it may measure 60 cm and weigh 4 kg. The fish become sexually mature at four to five years old. They spawn in the water margins of lakes and rivers at the end of May and in June, at temperatures of not less than 15 °C (the optimum temperature is 18 °C); the eggs are attached to aquatic plants. At a water temperature of about 15 °C the young hatch in five days and at 20 °C in three days. The newly hatched larvae measure about 5 mm and remain clinging to the plants until the yolk sac has been digested. The fry feed at first on plankton but soon change to prey they can find on the bottom together with water plants and seeds. Carp live in shoals. They hibernate in deep, muddy spots and do not feed during the winter.

Carp are commercially valuable fishes but the wild form is hardly ever caught today because of the small size of the remaining population. It is important that the wild form is preserved, however, if new genes are to be introduced into the artificially bred forms.

Size: 40—80 cm, maximum 1 m
Weight: 2—4 kg, maximum 30 kg
Fin formula: D III—IV/15—22, A III/5—6
Fecundity: 50,000—1.5 million eggs
Distribution: Originally found in eastern Europe and southern Asia.

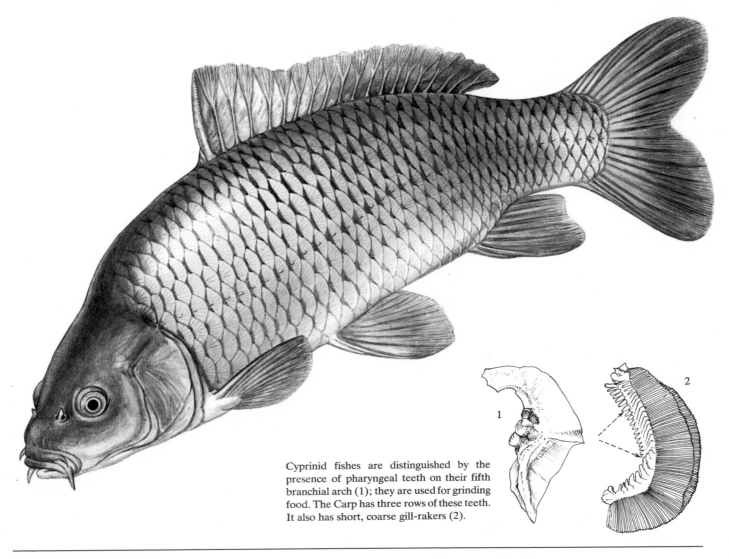

Cyprinid fishes are distinguished by the presence of pharyngeal teeth on their fifth branchial arch (1); they are used for grinding food. The Carp has three rows of these teeth. It also has short, coarse gill-rakers (2).

Pond Carp
Cyprinus carpio

Since Roman times Carp have been bred in artificial ponds for their excellent flesh. With the advent of Christianity the art was passed on to monks, who introduced carp-breeding throughout Europe. By the end of the Middle Ages carp were kept in ponds on all the great estates. Gradually over the years the body form of the artificial carp became deeper until they assumed the form familiar today.

Carp are now distributed all over the world and have become one of the most important freshwater fishes. They are ready for eating between two to four years old when they weigh 1−3 kg. When spawning, the fish are transferred to special ponds which are filled just beforehead. Lately, however, artificial breeding has become increasingly common and the eggs are incubated in special tanks.

During their first year the fry are kept in fingerling (growing) ponds; by the end of the autumn they weigh 20−100 g. In the following autumn when they weigh 0.4−0.8 kg, they are transferred as two-year olds to the main pond and one year later they are caught for the market. Their natural food in the pond is supplemented by waste grain, lupin seeds and molasses, etc. Their rate of growth depends on the temperature of the water as well as on the food supply. Carp grow well at temperatures of over 20 °C, but the fastest growth occurs at temperatures of 25−29 °C. Carp are also bred on a large scale in natural lakes and also in reservoirs where they can be caught by anglers for sport.

In the course of the centuries, selective breeding has produced several forms − a scaly form (1), a scaleless form (2), the Mirror Carp, a form with a few rows of scales (3), the Leather Carp (4) and a partly scaleless form (see the large illustration).

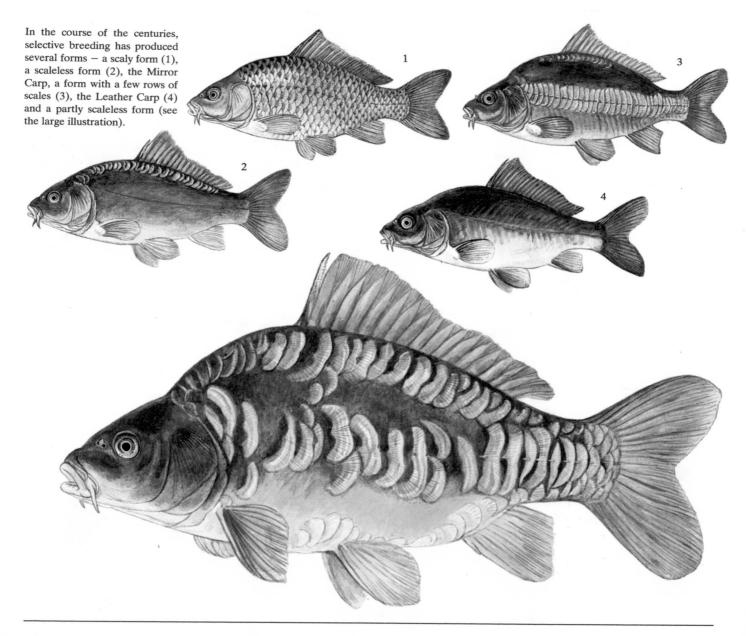

Silver Carp
Hypophthalmichthys molitrix

An atypical carp species with a thick-set, relatively deep body covered with small scales. Its eyes are set strikingly low on its head. It has a greyish green back, silvery sides and belly and grey fins, sometimes with a golden sheen on paired and anal fins.

Originally found in much of China, the Silver Carp has been introduced to various Asian countries and to Europe. It grows quickly and when four or five years old measures 50 cm. It reaches sexual maturity when three years old or later. In its native haunts it swims upstream to spawn; spawning generally takes place on sandbanks at the site of confluent currents, usually in the summer when the water levels are high. The eggs drift for a time, but once the fry have digested the yolk sac they swim to quiet water, where they feed for a short time on zooplankton; once they measure 2 cm however, they change over to a vegetable diet, in particular to unicellular algae. This is a great asset to fish farmers, since the Silver Carp do not compete with other species of carp for food. However, in Europe Silver Carp do not spawn spontaneously and their numbers have to be supplemented every year by artificially bred fry.

Silver Carp are used as a supplementary species in carp ponds and for improving the waters of lakes and reservoirs by ridding them of phytoplankton. They are not of much interest to anglers, however, since they are very difficult to catch with rod and line. Their flesh is of good quality, but the fish have to be gutted very quickly because otherwise the flesh acquires a bitter flavour.

Size: 40—60 cm, maximum 1 m
Weight: 2—4 kg, maximum 10 kg
Fin formula: D II—III/6—7, A II—III/11—14
Fecundity: 60,000—80,000 eggs/kg body weight
Distribution: Found in many parts of China.

The related species *Aristichthys nobilis,* imported into Europe from China, feeds on both animal food and phytoplankton (various algae). It grows very quickly and shows promise as a supplementary fish in carp ponds.

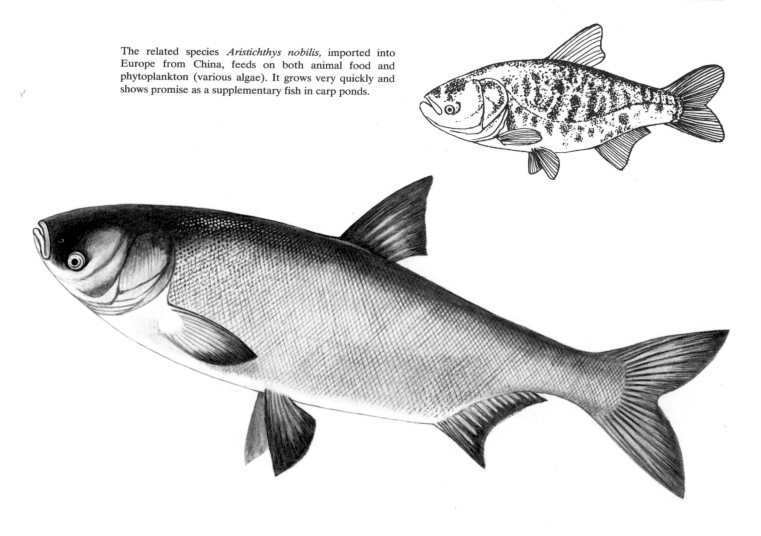

Loaches (Cobitidae) are small freshwater fishes adapted in various ways for a benthic mode of life. They generally have long, rather slender bodies with many barbels around the mouth and no teeth. About 150 species are known from Europe and Asia.

Spined Loach
Cobitis taenia

One of the handsomest members of the family, this fish has a greyish brown back marked with a quantity of dark spots and a pale yellow or orange underside. A row of 12−20 rounded, grey-black spots runs down the middle of the back and two more rows run along the sides; the spots in the upper row are small and long and generally merge, while those in the lower row (also 12−20 in number) are large and separate. There are also two or three transverse rows of small, greyish brown spots on the dorsal and caudal fins. The fish has an elongate, flat-sided body and an inferior mouth surrounded by six barbels. Below each eye there is a large, erectile bony spine with a forked tip, worked by a special muscle, whose prick can prove painful if the fish is handled.

The Spined Loach lives mainly in shallow water with a sandy, (or less often a muddy or stony) bed, in which it frequently buries itself leaving only its head and tail protruding. Its secretive and mainly nocturnal mode of life protects it from predators; it is most likely to be caught by burbots, catfish and eels investigating deposits on the bottom. It feeds mainly on small bottom-dwelling animals. Spined Loaches have a life span of three to five years, growing slowly and spawning near the bottom from April to June. The eggs are laid in batches and the fry hatch in four to six days.

Size: 8−10 cm, occasionally up to 12 cm
Weight: 40−60 g
Fin formula: D 7−9, A 7−9
Distribution: The whole of Europe except Ireland, Scotland, Wales and northern Scandinavia. A number of local races are found in this vast area.

The related *C. caspia* lives in the southern part of the Caspian Sea and in the lower reaches of the Kura and other rivers emptying into the Sea.

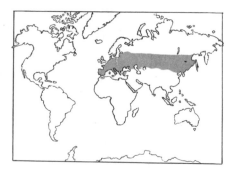

Distribution map for *C. taenia*.

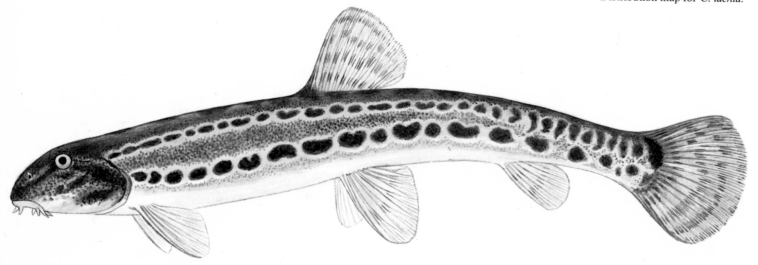

East European Spined Loach
Cobitis aurata

With its long, flat-sided body, this species closely resembles the Spined Loach, but the spine below the eye is thicker and the barbels are longer (the last pair stretches to the back of the eyes whereas in the Spined Loach they reach only to the front of the eyes; the two species are also differently coloured. The East European Spined Loach has only between four and twelve irregular dark brown spots down the middle of its back and one row of 8—15 reddish brown or dark violet spots on its sides. The ground colour of its body is greyish white; its sides and belly are yellowish. At the base of the tail it always has two dark spots which sometimes merge to form a stripe, whereas the Spined Loach has one characteristic black spot close to the upper edge of the tail.

The East European Spined Loach leads a secretive and mainly nocturnal existence like the Spined Loach, but it lives primarily in the upper reaches of rivers and streams with gravelly or stony beds and hides away under stones, not buried in mud. It leaves shelter only when disturbed, but immediately looks for the nearest suitable substitute. At spawning time, in April or May, the females lay a small number of eggs on sand or stones.

Commonest synonym: Sabanejewia aurata
Size: 8—11 cm
Weight: up to 50 g
Fin formula: D 8—11, A 7—9
Fecundity: 1,000—1,500 eggs
Distribution: Relatively rare; occurs in rivers and streams in the basins of the Danube, the Vistula and the Don and in a number of rivers in the Balkans, Asia Minor and the Near East.

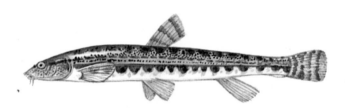

Cobitis elongata is a related species living in the central part of the Balkan peninsula. It grows up to 17 cm long and is most often found in fast flowing water.

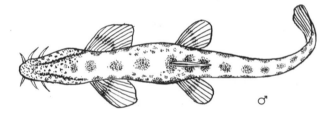

The males of *C. aurata* have a bulge on either side, below the base of the dorsal fin.

Weatherfish

Misgurnus fossilis

A small to moderately large fish with a markedly elongate body mainly cylindrical in cross section, but flat-sided towards the tail and covered with small scales. Of the ten barbels round the mouth, two long pairs are situated on the upper edge of the upper lip, one pair at the corners of the mouth and two very short pairs on the lower lip. The female's pectoral fins are shorter and more rounded than the male's. The colouring of the Weatherfish tends to vary somewhat with the locality; the head is generally brownish to reddish with small spots, the sides and belly are yellow or less often red-tinted and one wide and two narrower dark bands stretch from the head to the base of the tail. The fins are usually yellowish brown and marked with dark spots.

Weatherfish live in muddy ponds, pools and creeks usually at the bottom and sometimes buried in it; they are active mainly at night. In some places with low oxygen concentrations they may be the only fish present, since they obtain oxygen by surfacing and swallowing air and the oxygen is absorbed through the intestines. Weatherfish can sometimes be heard swallowing the air, betraying their presence in what appears to be uninhabited water. They feed on molluscs and other benthic invertebrates and they spawn from April to June. Weatherfish react sensitively to atmospheric changes and when a storm is brewing they become very restless. It is claimed that if the water dries up these fishes can survive for a short time buried in the mud.

Economically they are unimportant, but occasionally individuals are kept in aquaria because of their interesting biology.

Size: 20−25 cm, maximum 35 cm
Weight: 100−150 g
Fin formula: D 8−9, A 7−9
Fecundity: 5,000−30,000 eggs
Distribution: Most of Europe except Great Britain, Scandinavia, the north European part of the USSR, the peninsulas of southern Europe and the Crimea; also found in some parts of Asia.

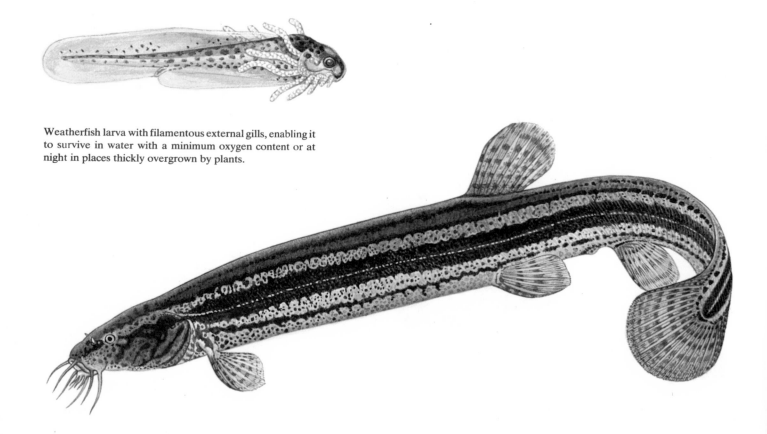

Weatherfish larva with filamentous external gills, enabling it to survive in water with a minimum oxygen content or at night in places thickly overgrown by plants.

Stone Loach
Noemacheilus barbatulus

A small, elongate fish with a rounded head and cylindrical body, which is sometimes mistaken for the Weatherfish. It is distinguished from the Weatherfish by the shape of its caudal fin and the smaller number of barbels round its mouth. There are four around the snout and one at each corner of the mouth. The sides of the fish are covered with tiny, non-overlapping scales but these are absent on its back and belly. Its back is greyish brown or greenish, its sides are yellowish brown with irregular dark marbling and its belly is greyish white to yellowish.

Stone Loaches live in flowing water at the bottom of streams, rivers and ponds where they spend the day hidden under roots and large stones, often in groups of three or five. Unless disturbed they swim very sluggishly or lie immobile on the bottom; they are active in dull weather, after dusk and during the night. They feed on small benthic animals particularly on mosquito larvae and aquatic insect larvae; they pounce on them from their hiding-places and gulp them down. The fish become sexually mature when one year old and live for between five and seven years. At spawning time both sexes have spawning tubercles on their bodies and fins (in males these are present on the inner surfaces of the pectoral and ventral fins). Spawning occurs between April and July; the eggs are laid in two or three batches on the roots of aquatic plants or directly on to the bottom.

Stone Loaches are fairly sensitive to water pollution and have been used as an indicator species; in some localities numbers have declined in recent years. They are an important food fish for trout and anglers sometimes use them as bait. In some places they were regarded as a delicacy at one time and were eaten fried in butter.

Size: 10—15 cm, maximum 18 cm
Weight: 80—150 g, exceptionally up to 200 g
Fin formula: D 9—12, A 7—10
Fecundity: 3,000—25,000 eggs
Distribution: Most of Europe except the Iberian Peninsula, southern Italy and Greece, the north of Scotland and the greater part of Scandinavia; also present over a large part of the USSR.

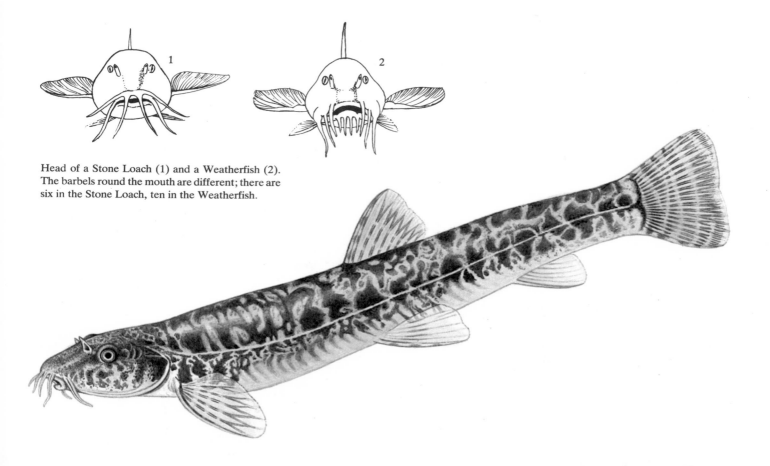

Head of a Stone Loach (1) and a Weatherfish (2). The barbels round the mouth are different; there are six in the Stone Loach, ten in the Weatherfish.

The family Siluridae includes big freshwater catfishes. They have long scaleless bodies, long barbels and long anal fins.

European Catfish, Wels
Silurus glanis

A long-bodied, robustly built fish with a low, wide head, a large snout well equipped with teeth and a pair of long, mobile barbels reinforced with cartilage, one on either side of the mouth; two more pairs of short, immobile barbels are present on the chin. Its back and sides are olive green to bluish grey with light marbled markings on the sides; the belly is cream-coloured or greyish white. White, golden and red-tinged individuals are also known.

European Catfish live in marshes, in the lower reaches of rivers, in lakes and in dams; they are also kept in large fishponds. The fish lie on the bottom in deep water, below weirs or in holes, or hidden by the tangled roots of old trees. They are active after dusk and during the night and spend most of the daytime resting. In the winter they stop feeding and hibernate, retiring to the deepest parts of the water. These fish live for 30–40 years or more and attain sexual maturity when between three and four years old. From May to June they spawn in couples in the evening and at night. The eggs are laid in a primitive nest prepared on the bottom from the remains of plants and the stripped rootlets of willows and alders. The male guards the eggs until the fry hatch out.

The European Catfish has excellent flesh but in specimens weighing over 5–10 kg it tends to be oily; when smoked it is a great delicacy. Some countries breed these economically important fish artificially and some lakes in southern England have been stocked with the fish.

Size: 1–2 m, occasionally 3 m or over
Weight: 50–100 kg, occasionally up to 200 kg
Fin formula: D 3–5, A 77–92
Fecundity: 7,000–25,000 eggs/kg body weight
Distribution: From the basin of the Rhine to the catchment area of the Caspian Sea, with western and southern limits at the Alps, and northern limits in Scandinavia in southern Sweden. It also occurs in inlets of the Baltic, Black and Caspian seas.

European Catfish feed mainly on small cyprinoid fishes but also catch ducklings, small mammals, frogs and newts.

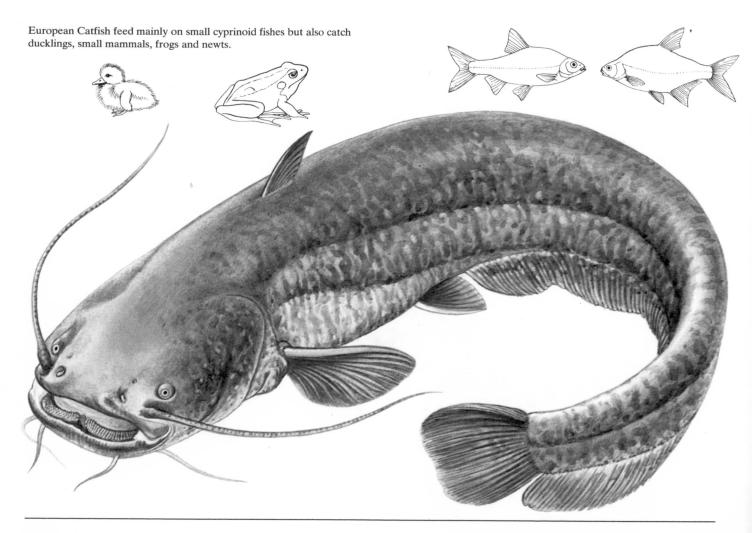

140

In the North American family Ictaluridae are catfishes with an adipose fin between their dorsal and caudal fins.

Horned Pout, American Catfish

Ictalurus nebulosus

This is a heavy thickset fish with a heavy head and eight barbels around its mouth, a feature which can be used to distinguish it from European Catfish. It has an adipose fin on the back and a relatively short anal fin. It is dark brownish green in colour on the back, with lighter marbled sides and a whitish belly, which becomes yellow or orange in the spawning season.

Originally from southeastern Canada and the eastern USA, at the end of last century it was introduced into Europe and bred in ponds where it was assumed that it would eventually grow to weigh one or two kg and would be a profitable fish. The results in central Europe were disappointing but now these fish are being bred again intensively in the USSR, particularly in the south. They have become naturalized in some parts of Europe, occurring in lakes, ponds and in the lower reaches of big rivers but grow more slowly than in their country of origin and become sexually mature when two or three years old. The fish spawn at the end of April and in May, first building a primitive nest on a sandy bed and afterwards guarding the eggs. They are omnivorous in their feeding habits, devouring the eggs and fry of fishes as well as crustaceans, insects and other fishes. They may be unwelcome predators on other more valuable species as well as competing with them for food. They are very resistant to oxygen deficiency and food shortages and can survive under conditions which would be fatal for other fishes.

Size: 15–25 cm, maximum 35 cm
Weight: 0.1–0.3 kg, maximum 0.6 kg
Fin formula: D I/6, A 20–24
Fecundity: 1,000–13,000 eggs
Distribution: Southeastern Canada and the eastern USA; naturalized in Europe.

Horned Pout feed on invertebrates like mosquito larvae and on other fishes like Crucian Carp.

The members of the order *Anguilliformes* have a characteristic snake-like body and no ventral fins. Their dorsal, caudal and anal fins are joined together to form a continuous border. The scales are either minute and inconspicuous or absent altogether. The swim-bladder is connected with the gut and may be reduced. The blood of some species contains toxins, but these are dangerous only if they find their way directly into the blood stream of a warm-blooded animal. The family *Anguillidae* comprises some ten species of eels. Apart from the European Eel, which spends part of its life in fresh water, they are all marine species.

ANGUILLIDAE

European Eel
Anguilla anguilla

This fish has a characteristically long body with small scales embedded in the skin. Immature individuals have a dark brown back and yellowish, sometimes golden sides and belly; as they grow older the back turns almost black and the belly silvery. Before they attain sexual maturity the European Eels live in rivers throughout Europe and in North Africa. In fresh water they grow very quickly and when ten years old the females, for instance, measure 70—90 cm; both sexes reach sexual maturity at between five and ten years old, make their way to the river mouth and then swim together to their spawning grounds, which are assumed to lie in the Sargasso Sea between the Bermudas and the Bahamas. The larvae, known as leptocephali, have deep transparent bodies and bear no resemblance to the adults. They travel to Europe in the surface waters of the Gulf Stream — a journey that takes them three years. On the way their bodies become long and thin and as 'elvers' they enter the rivers and swim upstream to complete their development. European Eels feed mainly on other fishes; they hunt at night and hide under stones or roots during the day. They can survive in mud even if oxygen runs low because they can breathe through the skin.

European Eels are highly prized for the excellent quality and flavour of the moist, boneless flesh. They are caught in trawls and on long lines in the sea and by anglers in fresh water.

Size: up to 2 m, generally 0.5—1.5 m
Weight: up to 4—6 kg, mostly 0.6—2 kg
Fin formula: D 245—275, A 205—235
Distribution: Europe and North Africa.

Development of the larva from hatching (7 mm) to the 25 mm and 75 mm stages. During subsequent development the body grows shorter (70 mm).

In Europe there are two forms of the European Eel — one with a wide head (1) and one with a narrow head (2). From above, the differences are clearly discernible.

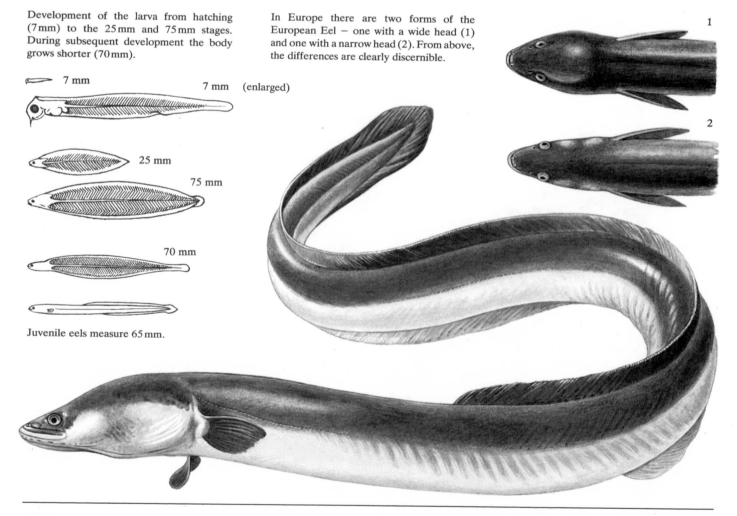

7 mm

7 mm (enlarged)

25 mm

75 mm

70 mm

Juvenile eels measure 65 mm.

1

2

The family Muraenidae comprises about 100 species closely related to the families Anguillidae and Congridae. They have a typical eel-like body with a very long tail and the body is covered with thick, slimy scaleless skin. Their dorsal, caudal and anal fins form a continuous border around the body; ventral and pectoral fins are absent.

Moray Eel
Muraena helena

An easily recognised fish with a dark brown or brownish purple back and sides marked with a quantity of irregular yellow spots of various sizes and with dark marbling; its underside and its head — where the spots are smaller — are lighter. The fish has a relatively deep body, a pointed snout and a large mouth with a single row of long, sharp teeth on each jaw. Its low dorsal fin begins a third of the way along the body, it has a small gill aperture situated roughly in the middle of the rear margin of its head and it has long, tubular nostrils.

The Moray Eel lives in coastal waters, usually with an uneven, stony bottom which provides an abundance of convenient shelters. It is active mainly at night, feeding chiefly on fish and molluscs. Its bite is painful and can be very dangerous; skin divers are the most frequent victims. The blood of the fish is poisonous and tales have been told since the Middle Ages of victims poisoned by fresh Moray Eel blood. Cooking at temperatures of over 75°C destroys the toxicity of the serum, so that in some Mediterranean countries the flesh of the Moray Eel is regarded as a delicacy. It was certainly very popular with the epicures of ancient Rome, who kept Moray Eels in special ponds.

Size: 80—120 cm, maximum 140 cm
Fin formula: D 280—307, A 200—232
Distribution: The Mediterranean and the European and African shores of the eastern Atlantic, but becoming very rare north of the English Channel.

The related species *Gymnothorax moringa* comes from tropical and subtropical coastal waters on both sides of the Atlantic. It usually grows to a length of 30—50 cm but may reach 80 cm. It is hunted for sport with harpoons but its blood is poisonous and must be removed before cooking.

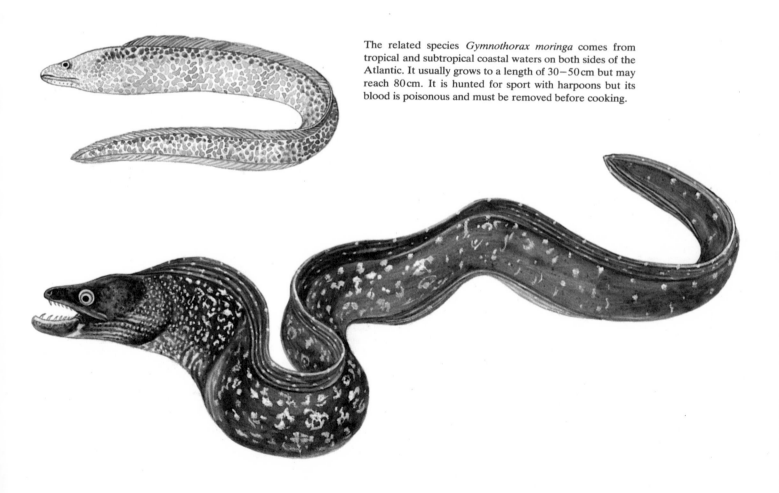

143

Members of the Congridae live in all the oceans except the Arctic. There are over twenty genera in the family. Characteristic features of the family include the position of the dorsal fin which begins above the tips of the pectoral fins; ventral fins are absent. The fish have tubular nostrils.

CONGRIDAE

Conger Eel
Conger conger

A much larger fish than the European Eel with a grey or black body, creamy brown belly and dark-edged unpaired fins and pectoral fins. Young eels live along rocky coasts, where they are usually found in deep pools between the tides and in the offshore area. They feed on fishes such as herrings, rocklings and flatfish and also on large crustaceans like lobsters and crabs. Sexually mature individuals have never been seen but it is assumed that they migrate into the open sea before reaching maturity. They spawn in the eastern part of the Atlantic, between the 30th and 40th latitudes at depths of 3,000 and 4,000 metres.

The Mediterranean populations also reproduce there and quantities of larvae find their way back via the Strait of Gibraltar. The larvae measure up to 160 mm before metamorphosis. In olden times the peculiar larvae of eels (leptocephali) were thought to be a separate genus, usually collected together under the name *Leptocephalus*.

Economically Conger Eels are of little significance. Most of the eels are caught off the southwestern coast of Europe; they are seldom caught in the North Sea. However their flesh is good to eat and they are prized by anglers. The total annual catch amounts to about 11,300 tons.

Size: up to 3 m (the males only to 1.5 m)
Weight: up to 65 kg
Fin formula: D 270–300, A 205–230
Fecundity: 3–8 million eggs
Distribution: Off the European and African shores of the North Atlantic from Iceland in the north to Cape Verde in the south and in the Mediterranean.

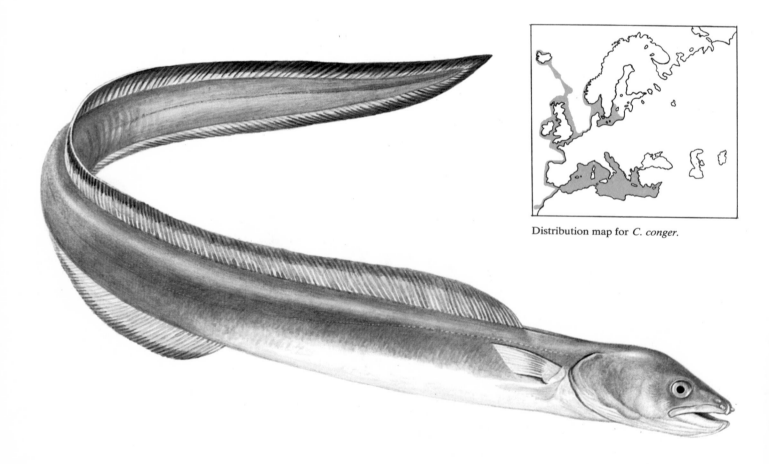

Distribution map for *C. conger.*

The order Cyprinodontiformes, or tooth carps, comprises about 400 species of small fishes occurring on every continent except Australia. The majority are freshwater species but some live in brackish and salt water. They are generally found near the surface of the water where they hunt for food. They either have no lateral line or a poorly developed one. The swim-bladder is not connected with the gut. Members of the family Cyprinodontidae are small egg-laying fishes; the anal fin of the male does not form an organ of copulation.

CYPRINODONTIDAE

Spanish Killifish
Aphanius iberus

This is a tiny fish with a rather flat-sided body and a rounded tail fin. The male is bluish green or bright blue, with an olive green back and light belly. On its sides there are about 15 light blue cross stripes, which may run together. It has a dark brown tail fin with light cross stripes, a light blue-edged dorsal fin and yellowish or brownish ventral fins marked with dark spots. The female is olive brown with brown spots and has colourless fins.

The fish live in shallow water, in a variety of habitats, from ponds and lakes to rivers and also in brackish water and on the coast. They spawn throughout the warm part of the year; eggs adhere to the fine leaves of water plants or to algae and at 24 °C the young hatch in ten days. The fish feed on small planktonic crustaceans, unicellular algae and parts of higher plants. Like various other members of the order they are popular as aquarium fishes and can be kept in normal aquaria as long as the water is hard.

Size: up to 5 cm
Fin formula: D III/9−10, A III/9−10
Distribution: The west coast of the Iberian Peninsula and in fresh and brackish water on the coast of Africa on the opposite side of the Mediterranean.

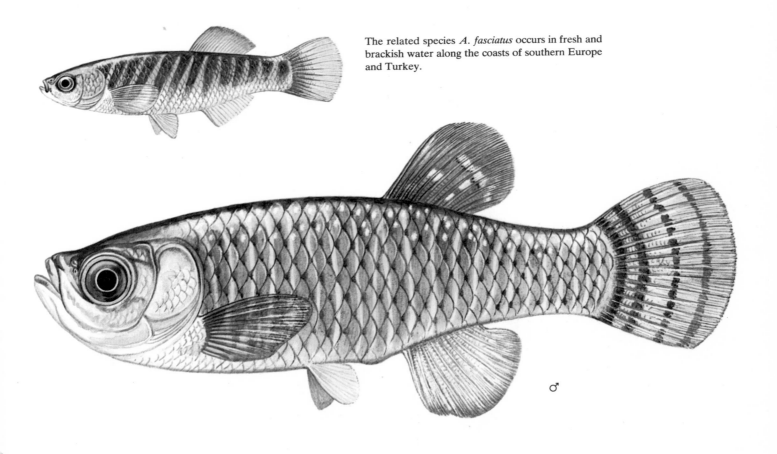

The related species *A. fasciatus* occurs in fresh and brackish water along the coasts of southern Europe and Turkey.

Members of the family Poecilidae are live-bearing tooth carps; in the males the rays of the anal fin have been converted into an organ of copulation.

Mosquito Fish
Gambusia affinis

The only member of the family acclimatized in Europe, this fish tolerates a very wide range of temperatures, from 0 to 30 °C. It is a small fish with a superior mouth and cycloid scales, a greyish brown back, lighter sides and a whitish belly. The fins are colourless, but sometimes have a yellowish tinge; on the dorsal and the caudal fins there are rows of dark spots. Old males are so dark that they sometimes look black. The subspecies *G. a. holbrooki* has a dark spot across its eye.

The fish reach sexual maturity when three to four months old, depending on the temperature of the water and on the rate of their growth. In Europe the females are fertilized for the first time in April and the young are born a month later. Fertilized females have a black spot on the underside in the region of the anal fin, formed from the eyes of the developing embryos showing through the skin. One female can give birth five times in a year and can produce two or three broods without having to be refertilized; the number of young in a brood depends on the size of the female and varies from just a few to several dozen; development of the young in the female's body takes between 20 and 40 days. At birth the young are already active and feed on plankton.

The adult fish feed on mosquito larvae and have been used in many parts of the world to control the *Anopheles* mosquito which carries malaria.

Size: 3.5—7.5 cm
Fin formula: D III/7, A II—III/10—11
Fecundity: 10—30 young
Distribution: Originally the waters of North America from New Jersey as far as Florida. Has been introduced into other continents.

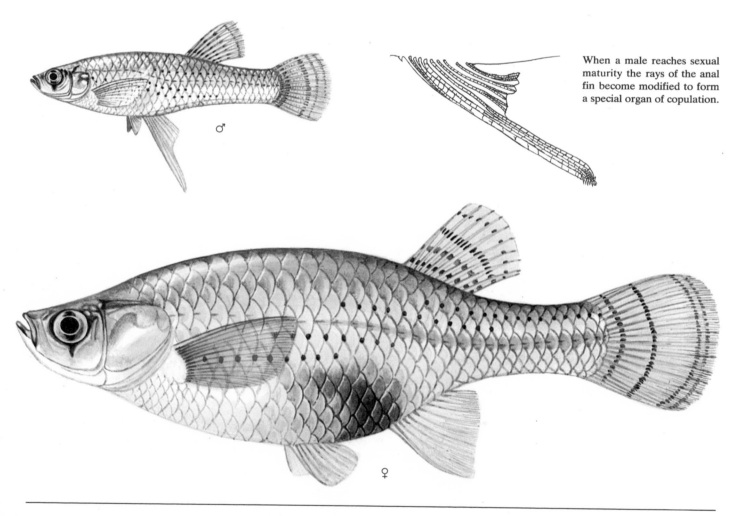

When a male reaches sexual maturity the rays of the anal fin become modified to form a special organ of copulation.

In the order Beloniformes are fishes with elongate bodies covered with cycloid scales. Their dorsal and anal fins are positioned far back on the body, one directly above the other. The front of the straight gut widens to form a stomach; pyloric caeca are absent. The members of this order live in the uppermost layers of warm and temperate seas and occasionally in light, fresh water. They are highly photosensitive. The family Belonidae includes about twenty-five species.

BELONIDAE

Gar Pike
Belone belone

A highly distinctive fish with an extremely elongated body and long jaws with clearly discernible teeth. It has a dark green back and lighter sides with a silvery lustre and yellowish spots. Along each side runs a dark band and the lateral line, which is situated very low down, almost on the belly. Gar Pike are mostly fishes of the open sea, living primarily in the upper layers, but they may also be found in coastal waters. Spawning takes place intermittently from April to October with a peak period from May to August; most females spawn three times in a season. They usually spawn in coastal waters at a depth of 12—18 m and the eggs are attached to algae and floating objects by means of long, filamentous outgrowths. At 20—21 °C development lasts 14 days, but at 12—13 °C four or five weeks. The fry live pelagically like the adult fish. At first they feed on the smallest plankton, later on fish fry and adults take small fish as well. They become sexually mature when between two and four years old when they measure 35—45 cm. Individuals aged between five and nine years old predominate in catches.

Gar Pike are not generally useful economically but annual catches in the Black Sea amount to about 200 tons. The fish's flesh is very tasty, but very bony and because the bones turn green when the fish is cooked some housewives think that it is poisonous.

Size: 30—60 cm, maximum 90 cm
Weight: maximum 1.3 kg
Fin formula: D ii/14—17, A ii/17—21
Fecundity: 10,000—45,000 eggs
Distribution: Atlantic coast of Europe from Portugal to the Baltic and occasionally as far as the southern coast of Iceland and Trondheim in Norway; also present in the Mediterranean and Black Seas.

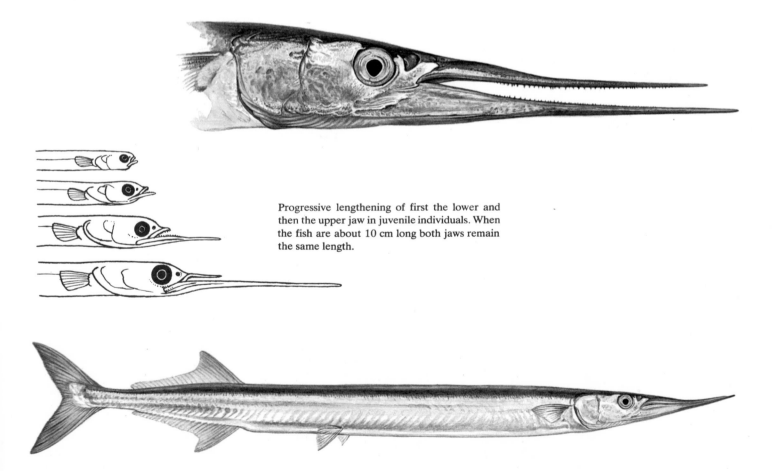

Progressive lengthening of first the lower and then the upper jaw in juvenile individuals. When the fish are about 10 cm long both jaws remain the same length.

Members of the family Scomberesocidae resemble Belonidae species, but have thinner jaws without any large teeth and a row of small fins behind their dorsal and anal fins. They feed mostly on animals of the zooplankton.

Skipper
Scomberesox saurus

This pelagic oceanic fish has very characteristic long fragile beak-like jaws with many small teeth. The fish have a green back, silvery green sides and a yellowish belly. They often live in large shoals in the Atlantic, centred around Madeira and may migrate northwards in the summer in search of food. They live mostly in the uppermost layers of the water.

Skippers spawn in the open sea at considerable distances from the shore; they mature sexually when two years old. The eggs are pelagic, with short outgrowths for flotation. The fish feed mainly on pelagic crustaceans and small fish. In turn, they are important prey species for predatory pelagic species like tunnyfish and when pursued by predators may leap out of the water. Their normal life span is three to four years.

The very tasty flesh of these fish is mostly sold tinned. They are caught with dragnets and with long lines, but also by means of light. First of all a blue light is used to attract the fish to the ship and then red lamps are switched on; the fish assemble below these lamps and all the fishermen have to do is to haul them in. Annual catches amount to upwards of 5,000—10,000 tons.

Size: 25—45 cm, maximum 60 cm
Weight: 0.5—1.6 kg
Fin formula: D ii/9—10 + 5—6 finlets,
A ii/10 + 6—7 finlets
Fecundity: 20,000—30,000 eggs
Distribution: The Atlantic, the North Sea, the Mediterranean and the Black Sea.

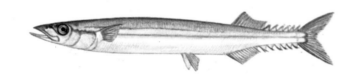

Cololabis saira is a species closely related to *Scomberesox saurus* which lives in the Pacific. It reaches a maximum length of 35 cm, but the fish in catches usually measure 20—30 cm. In recent years the total annual catch has varied from 150,000 to 320,000 tons.

Distribution map of the Skipper.

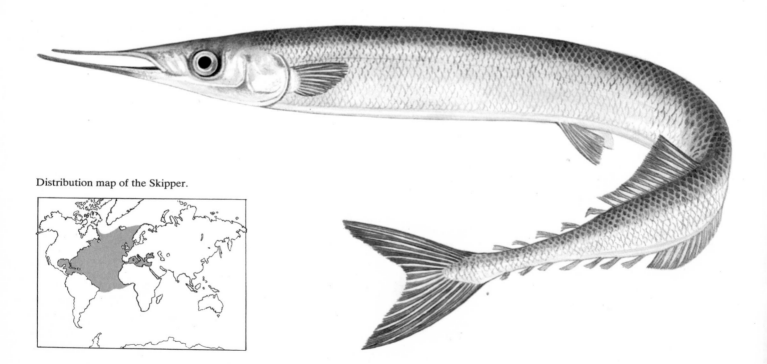

In the family Exocoetidae, known as flying-fishes, are over 60 small, pelagic species, most of which live in the Indian Ocean and in the western part of the Pacific; only 16 species live in the Atlantic. Their distribution is limited by temperature for they cannot survive temperatures of less than 20 °C. They have relatively slender bodies covered with large scales, but their most striking features are the shape and size of their fins. The dorsal and anal fins are relatively small and are situated on the base of the tail, the tail fin has a large lower lobe and the pectoral fins are enormous.

EXOCOETIDAE

Atlantic Flying Fish
Cypselurus heterurus

Like most flying-fishes, this species lives in the upper layers of the water, close to the surface; sometimes a fish 'soars up' out of the water, sometimes even landing on the deck of a boat or on the shore. The flying action is made possible by the quick movement of the caudal fin, which gives the fish impetus. For a time it skims the water energetically flicking its submerged tail. It does not usually leave the water for more than three seconds, during which time it 'flies' between 10 and 25 metres, about one metre above the surface. If there is a strong wind however, it may remain in the air for up to ten seconds and cover approximately 100 m at a height of about five metres. As it skims the water or flies through the air, its long, extensible pectoral and ventral fins act as stabilizers like the wings of a glider, and are not used for active motion. This passive flight provides a form of escape from tunnyfish, swordfish and dolphins.

This flying fish, like most others, has a metallic blue back and silvery sides and belly. They feed mostly on plankton. The fish spawn in the spring and the eggs have capsules with large numbers of filamentous flotation devices.

Size: 10–15 cm, maximum 35 cm
Weight: 0.1–0.3 kg, maximum 1 kg
Fin formula: D 13–14, A 8–10
Distribution: The Atlantic, Pacific and probably the Indian Oceans, also in the Mediterranean Sea.

Members of the genus *Cypselurus* are amongst the best 'fliers'; members of *Oxyporhamphus* (1) and *Fodiator* (2) are poor 'fliers' with much less well developed pectoral fins.

The order Gadiformes contains about 700 species of marine fishes, the only exception being the Burbot (Lota lota) which lives in fresh water. These fishes have only soft rays in their fins and the ventral fins are situated nearer to the head than the pectoral fins. The family Gadidae contains 53 economically important species living mostly in the northern hemisphere. In these fishes the body tapers off sharply towards the tail; it has two or three dorsal fins and one or two anal fins, all of them clearly separate and with space between them. The caudal fin has a wide notch. The fish are distinguished from each other by the shape and spacing of their fins and by the nature of the mouth barbels.

GADIDAE

Polar Cod

Boreogadus saida

Polar Cod live in the region round the North Pole, reaching European waters only to the north of Scandinavia and near Iceland. It is one of the smaller gadid fishes with a greyish to light brown back and lighter sides with a violet or yellow tinge. The entire body is strewn with tiny dark spots and the fins are all dark except the anal fin.

The fish become sexually mature when four years old. They spawn near the coast, chiefly in January and February, under the ice. The females have the biggest roes of all codfishes, but lay the fewest eggs. Fry measuring 5−9 mm can be caught in May; by autumn they measure 2−3 cm and when five years old 21−23 cm, when they weigh 55−65 g. The fish feed on large numbers of animal and phytoplankton species, benthic crustaceans and the eggs of various species of fish. Polar Cod are the main plankton consumers in arctic seas and the only ones in the open sea. They provide food for many marine mammals like seals and whales, for birds like eiders and gulls and, in some regions, for fish like other gadids and polar flounders.

In many places Polar Cod are very abundant and may become more economically important in the future with the decline in other species.

Size: 13−27 cm, maximum 30−40 cm
Weight: 50−150 g, maximum 1 kg
Fin formula: D_1 11−14, D_2 14−17, D_3 18−23, A_1 15−20, A_2 18−22
Fecundity: 9,000−12,000 eggs
Distribution: The Arctic Ocean

Polar Cod feed chiefly on planktonic crustaceans, the shrimp *Euphausia pellucida* being one of the commonest of its food items.

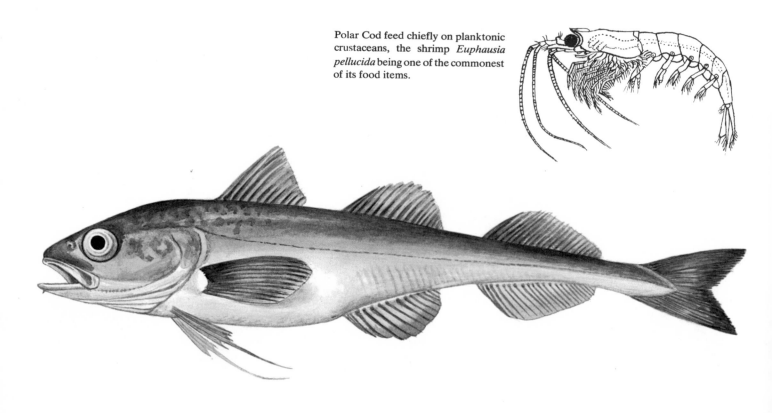

Common Cod
Gadus morhua

The Common Cod has a robust, tapering body, with an upper jaw which projects slightly beyond its lower jaw. It has a conspicuous barbel on its chin, an olive-coloured back and sides marked with large numbers of small yellowish or brownish spots and a dingy white belly. The lateral line is prominent as a lighter band along the middle of the sides. The Common Cod is one of the biggest gadids. It grows fairly quickly and measures 40−50 cm when five years old and 90−100 cm at ten.

The adult fish frequent the deeper waters over the continental shelf, usually between 250 and 300 m and not deeper than 500 m. They are also known to live in sea water diluted by fresh water and to invade rivers. Spawning occurs from the beginning of February to June and reaches a peak in April and May, at depths of 30 to 400 m. One of its most important spawning grounds are the Lofoten Islands, where the fish spawn at a water temperature of 4−7 °C. The larvae, which hatch in about a month, live a pelagic life. After spawning the fish migrate northwards in search of food. They feed mainly on fish, but small individuals also feed on planktonic animals, molluscs and polychaete worms. Cod attain sexual maturity between six and ten years old.

The Common Cod has been economically very important since man began to catch fish in the sea. The average total annual catch today is about 1.5 million tons. They are caught with trawls and seine-nets and also on lines and by anglers. They are sold throughout Europe fresh, frozen, dried or salted. Cod liver oil is an important source of Vitamin D and the fish offal is made into fish meal.

Size: 40−80 cm, maximum 150−180 cm
Weight: 2−4 kg, maximum 40 kg, exceptionally 90 kg
Fin formula: D_1 14−15, D_2 18−22, D_3 17−20, A_1 19−23, A_2 16−19
Fecundity: 0.5−9 million eggs
Distribution: The northern part of the Atlantic, off the coast of Europe as far as the Bay of Biscay in the south and in the White Sea, the Barents Sea, the Baltic and the northern part of the Pacific.

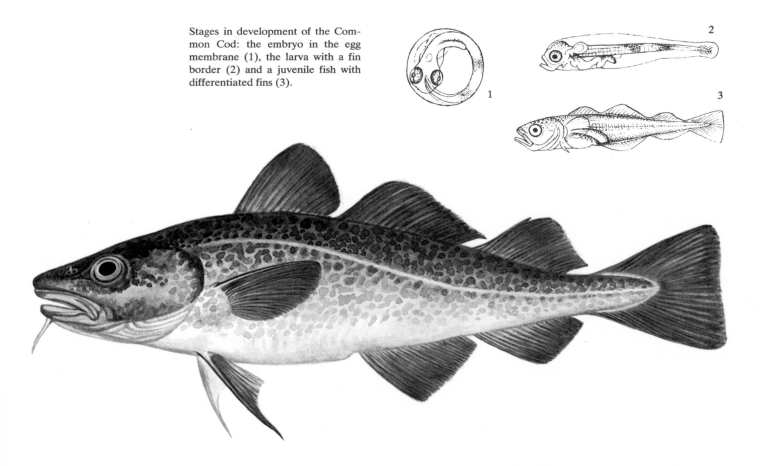

Stages in development of the Common Cod: the embryo in the egg membrane (1), the larva with a fin border (2) and a juvenile fish with differentiated fins (3).

Haddock

Melanogrammus aeglefinus

This big salt water fish has a short first dorsal fin (shorter at its base than the length of the head), relatively large eyes and a short barbel on its chin. It has a dark grey, violet-tinged back, silvery grey sides and a milky white belly. On each side below the first dorsal fin there is a characteristic dark spot and also a conspicuously dark lateral line. Haddock grow slowly, measuring 50 cm when between five and six years old and not reaching 70−80 cm until they are 14−15 years old. In the northern Atlantic they reach sexual maturity when six years old, further south when four to five years old. Haddock undertake regular migrations, frequenting comparatively shallow coastal waters in the summer and moving further out to sea in the winter. Very young fish feed on zooplankton, but from their second year they feed on the bottom, on benthic invertebrates. They are most often found at depths of between 100 and 150 m at a temperature of 1−5 °C.

Spawning takes place from March to June and the larvae hatch in two or three weeks; they are pelagic and drift in the ocean currents far from the spawning sites. The fry are often found in the company of jellyfish. At about two years old they gradually assume a benthic mode of life, swimming in to the coastal shelf waters.

Haddock are economically very important fishes with flesh of better quality than that of Common Cod. The total annual catch is about 500,000 tons. They are caught in various ways, including with trawls, seine-nets and with rods and lines.

Synonym: Gadus aeglefinus
Size: 60−70 cm, maximum 100−110 cm
Weight: 2−4 kg, maximum 17 kg
Fin formula: D_1 14−17, D_2 19−24, D_3 19−22, A_1 21−25, A_2 20−23
Fecundity: 0.5−3 million eggs
Distribution: Along the European shores of the Atlantic from the Bay of Biscay to the Barents Sea; the area round Iceland and Novaya Zemlya.

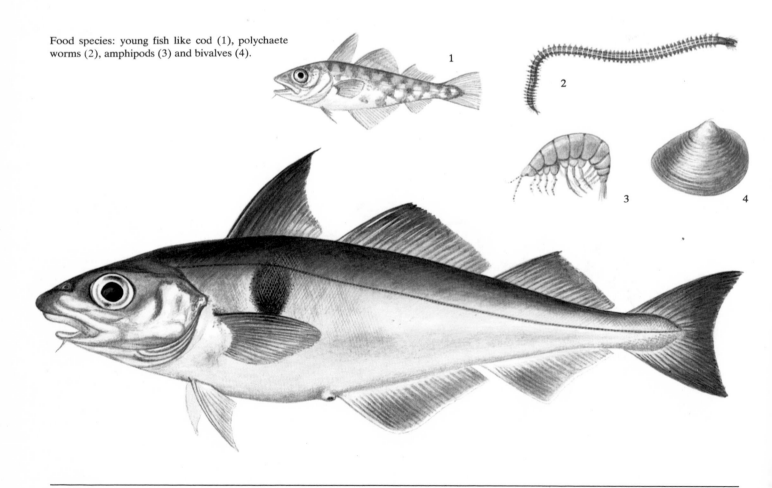

Food species: young fish like cod (1), polychaete worms (2), amphipods (3) and bivalves (4).

Whiting

Merlangius merlangus

An extremely common fish in the North Sea and in parts of the Atlantic Ocean, providing up to 50 % of the catch for the fishing industry. The Whiting has a light greenish blue back, yellowish green sides and a silvery white belly which turns dead white after the fish has died; at the base of each pectoral fin there is a black spot. The three dorsal fins of this fish and the two anal fins follow each other in close succession; the caudal fin has an almost straight edge. Young individuals have a short barbel on the chin. Whiting grow fastest off the coast of Iceland; the smallest specimens come from the Black Sea, in which are found fishes of the subspecies *M. merlangus euxini*, which has longer paired fins.

Whiting are inshore fishes, frequenting coastal waters and rarely venturing into water deeper than 200 m. They spawn throughout the year, but most often between January and July, at a depth of 100—150 m in the winter and at about 80 m down in the summer. The eggs are laid in batches of about four to six at a time; total fecundity can be estimated only approximately. The larvae remain near the shore, down to a depth of 100 m. Later the fry swim further out to sea, often in company with jellyfishes with whom they may seek shelter, only returning shorewards when one year old. From this time on they lead a benthic existence; they attain sexual maturity when between two and four years old. The adult fish feed chiefly on fish like sprats and pilchards, but also on polychaete worms and small crustaceans like *Mysis* and *Gammarus*. They feed mostly during the daylight hours.

About 200,000 tons of Whiting are caught every year (females are most common in the catches, especially among larger individuals).

Synonym: Gadus merlangus
Size: 30—40 cm, maximum 70 cm (in the Black Sea only 20 cm)
Weight: up to 3 kg
Fin formula: D_1 12—15, D_2 18—25, D_3 19—22, A_1 30—35, A_2 21—23
Fecundity: 0.1—1 million eggs
Distribution: European shores from the Barents Sea and Iceland as far as Gibraltar, western part of the Baltic, the Black and Mediterranean Seas.

Distribution map of *M. merlangus.*

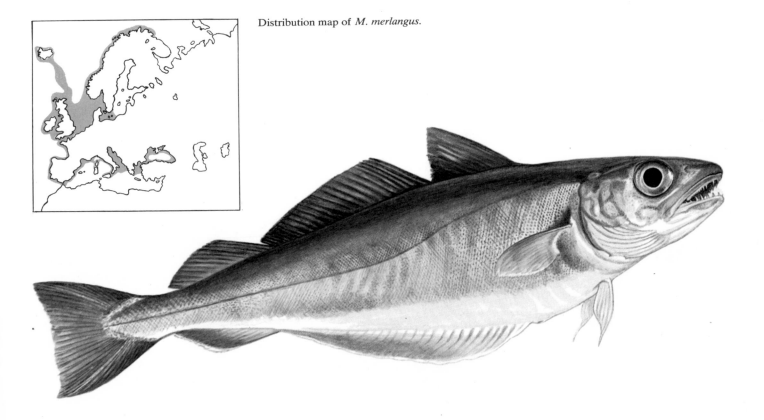

Coley
Pollachius virens

A large, fast-growing fish which may reach 100 cm in length by the time it is 10 years old. It can be distinguished from the similar Pollack by the numbers of its gillrakers, for it has 35—40 while the Pollack has only 26—27. The Coley has a tiny, but clearly discernible barbel on its chin and a concave caudal fin. Its back and head are dark olive green or sometimes dark brown or black, its sides are yellow grey and its belly is silvery white. Coley are common fishes of the North Sea and European Atlantic where they live in small shoals. They spawn throughout the whole of the area, up to Iceland and the Lofoten Islands in the north. Spawning takes place from January or February to May or June in the open sea with a depth of 100—200 m. Coley are highly prolific and may lay up to eight million eggs. Development takes between ten and fifteen days and the newly hatched larvae measure 3—4 mm. They drift in the currents at first, but by midsummer they are living close inshore, often in rocky bays. After a year or two they return further out to sea and lead a pelagic life, feeding on planktonic crustacean larvae and fish eggs. By the time they are six years old they are 60—70 cm long and by ten years old 70—80 cm; they become adult when five or six years old.

Coley regularly migrate long distances northwards to the spawning sites and in the autumn they travel southwards again.

It is at migration time that most of them are caught, in trawls, seine-nets and on long lines. The total annual catch is about 600,000 tons.

Synonym: Gadus virens
Size: 60—90 cm, maximum 130 cm
Weight: 2—5 kg, maximum 12—14 kg
Fin formula: D_1 13—15, D_2 19—24, D_3 19—24, A_1 25—30, A_2 17—24
Fecundity: 5—8 million eggs
Distribution: In the northern part of the Atlantic along the European shores from the Bay of Biscay in the south to the Barents Sea in the north and along the southern coast of Greenland up to the 67th latitude. Also occurs along the western shores of the Atlantic from Hudson Bay to New York.

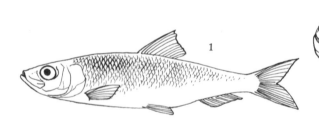
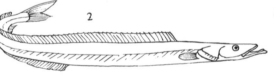

Coley feed mainly on other fishes like herrings (1), Sand Eels (2) and crustaceans such as those of the genus *Euphausia* (3).

Pollack

Pollachius pollachius

Pollack can be distinguished from other codfish by the absence of the barbel on its chin and the striking curve in the lateral line above its pectoral fins. Its lower jaw is longer than its upper jaw and it has very small ventral fins. The first anal fin begins roughly below the middle of the first dorsal fin and the caudal fin is only slightly concave. Its back is coloured dark cinnamon to olive brown, changing to a yellowish green or grey on its sides with an irregular network of russet or yellow spots; it has a light belly and a dark lateral line.

Pollack live in small shoals in coastal waters at the bottom or higher up in the water; large individuals are often found over a hard seabed amongst rocks, small ones over sand. Spawning takes place between January and June at water temperatures between 8 and 10 °C, generally at depths of down to 100 m. The eggs are pelagic, drifting in the sea; the larvae and fry feed on plankton near the shore while the adults feed mainly on small fish like sardines, sprats, mackerel and herrings.

Annual catches of Pollack in recent years have amounted to upwards of 6,000—12,000 tons, most of them caught in Scandinavian, British and Spanish waters. However, these fish are not commercially important, for their flesh is poor in quality. They are good angling fish.

Synonym: Gadus pollachius
Size: 40—80 cm, maximum 130 cm
Weight: 4—8 kg, exceptionally up to 11 kg
Fin formula: D_1 11—14, D_2 11—21, D_3 15—20, A_1 24—34, A_2 16—21
Fecundity: up to 2,800,000 eggs, 1.1—1.2 mm in diameter
Distribution: In the Atlantic Ocean from the coasts of Iceland and northern Norway to North Africa, and in the western part of the Baltic and the Mediterranean.

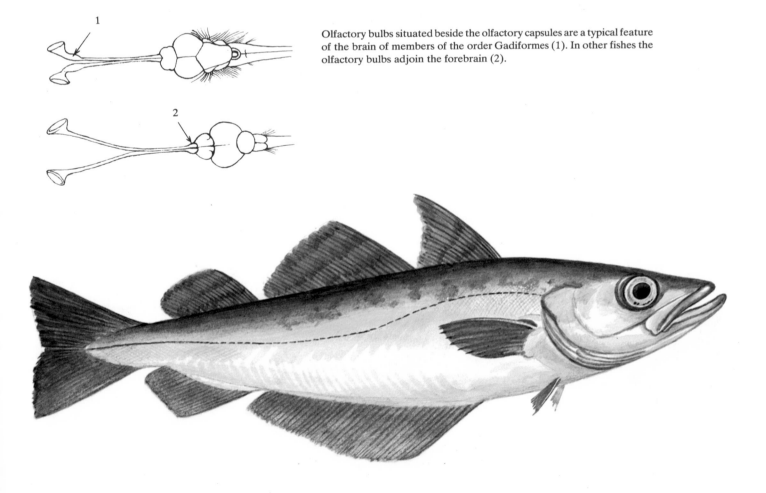

Olfactory bulbs situated beside the olfactory capsules are a typical feature of the brain of members of the order Gadiformes (1). In other fishes the olfactory bulbs adjoin the forebrain (2).

Blue Whiting

Micromestistius poutassou

Blue Whiting are coloured like herrings, with a light bluish grey to grey back and silvery white sides and belly. The dorsal fins are situated wide apart, with the largest space between the second and the third; and the first of the two anal fins is much longer than the second. There is no barbel on the chin and the lower jaw protrudes slightly beyond the upper jaw.

Blue Whiting grow moderately fast and at four years old measure about 30 cm; they reach sexual maturity at a length of 20−30 cm. These Whiting live in enormous shoals in the open sea beyond the bounds of the continental shelf, swimming at depths of 100−300 m in areas where the sea is up to 1,000 m deep; occasionally they are caught near the shore however. They spawn in the early spring in the southern parts of their range, at a water temperature of 8−9 °C in the region of the continental shelf. The larvae and fry live at depths of down to 1,000 m. The adults feed mostly on planktonic crustaceans and occasionally on small fish.

The Blue Whiting is not an economically important fish but it is an important prey species for fish like hake and cod. They are sometimes made into fish meal and the liver contains 50% oil, which is an important source of vitamins A and D.

The larger related *M. australis* lives in the southern Atlantic off the coast of Patagonia; it grows to a length of 50 cm and weighs 1 kg. This species spawns round the Falkland Islands.

Synonym: Gadus poutassou
Size: 30−35 cm, maximum 45 cm
Fin formula: D_1 12−14, D_2 12−15, D_3 23−26, A_1 33−39, A_2 24−27
Distribution: Off the European shores of the Atlantic from the Barents Sea to Gibraltar, off the coasts of Iceland and Greenland, in the region round Newfoundland, in the western part of the Mediterranean.

A diagrammatic front view
to show the large eyes and mouth.

Bib, Whiting Pout

Trisopterus luscus

Although closely related to the Poor Cod, this species has a rather different appearance, with a much deeper body, longer barbel and long ventral fins stretching beyond its anus. Its first anal fin begins roughly below the middle of the first dorsal fin. There are no spaces between the dorsal and the anal fins which are in contact with each other; the caudal fin has an almost straight edge. Because of the height of the body, the lateral line is noticeably more curved than in the Poor Cod. The Bib has a cinnamon brown body with four or five oblique dark stripes, yellow sides and a white belly. At the base of each pectoral fin there is a distinct dark spot.

Bibs form large shoals which swim in inshore waters, particularly in areas with a sandy seabed amongst reefs and large rocks. They spawn in shallow water in March and April; the eggs are pelagic. During their first year the young abound in sandy shallows and may swim into estuaries in the summer. The Bib feed on various invertebrates, like shrimps, small squid and polychaete worms; large individuals will also take fish.

Bib are caught mostly with trawls and purse-seines and annual catches in recent years have been in the region of 15,000 tons. The flesh is quite tasty but does not keep and is used primarily for making fish-meal. Bib may also be caught by anglers.

Commonest synonyms: Gadus luscus, Morhua lusca
Size: 20–30 cm, maximum 40 cm
Weight: up to 2.5 kg
Fin formula: D_1 11–14, D_2 20–24, D_3 18–20, A_1 30–31, A_2 19–22
Fecundity: up to 390,000 eggs
Distribution: Off the European coasts of the Atlantic Ocean from the middle of Norway to Gibraltar, western part of the Mediterranean.

The related species *T. esmarki* (Norway Pout) lives in European waters as far south as the English Channel. It grows to a length of 15–20 cm. It is a more important fish commercially than Bib, with catches reaching up to 400,000 tons, and is an important prey species for larger fishes.

Distribution map of *T. luscus*.

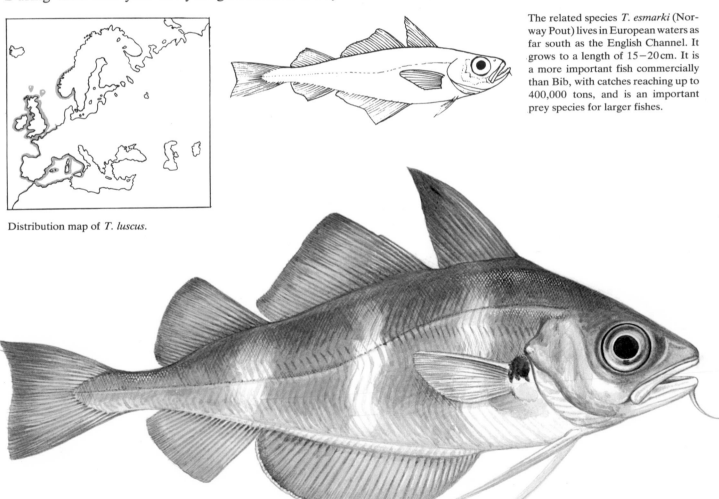

Poor Cod
Trisopterus minutus

Poor Cod are small fishes which live in offshore waters as adults; they are found close inshore only during the first year or so of their lives. As with other cod species, the Poor Cod can be identified by the shape and arrangement of the fins and by the presence of a barbel on the chin. There are three dorsal and two anal fins as is usual in cod but there are no spaces between the dorsal fins and only a small space between the anal fins. The beginning of the first anal fin and the second dorsal fin are in line with each other and the caudal fin has a slightly concave edge. On the chin there is a barbel measuring three quarters of the diameter of the eye or more; eye diameter is equal to the length of the snout. The upper jaw is longer than the lower jaw. The Poor Cod has a yellowish brown back, lighter sides with a coppery sheen and a silvery grey belly. It has a dark spot on the base of the pectoral fin.

Adult Poor Cod feed mainly on crustaceans and molluscs, although large individuals also eat small fish. Spawning occurs in winter in the southern part of its range and in the northern part it occurs in the early spring. The females are relatively highly prolific; the eggs are pelagic. The young fish feed on plankton at first, later switching to benthic organisms which form the diet of the adults.

Because of their small size Poor Cod are economically unimportant, despite their large numbers and the quite good quality of the flesh. However they are used for fish-meal and are an important prey species for larger fishes like cod and whiting.

*Commonest synonyms: Gadus minutus,
Gadus capelanus*
Size: 15–20 cm, occasionally up to 28 cm
Weight: 0.2–0.4 kg
Fin formula: D_1 13, D_2 23–26, D_3 22–24,
A_1 28–29, A_2 23–25
Fecundity: 50,000–350,000 eggs
Distribution: European coast of the Atlantic from the middle of Norway to Gibraltar, off the Moroccan shores, northern part of the Mediterranean, the Adriatic Sea.

Distribution map of *T. minutus*.

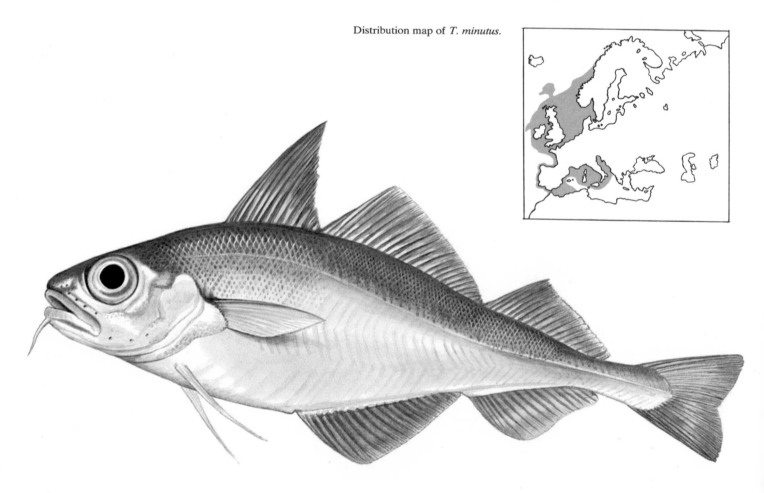

Navaga, Wakhna Cod

Eleginus navaga

Navaga look like Common Cod, but have dorsal fins farther apart from one another; the two anal fins are of roughly equal length and the caudal fin is almost straight-edged. There is a short barbel on the chin. The Navaga has an almost dark brown, grey-tinged back marked with dark spots, lighter sides and a silvery white belly.

Navaga live close to the shore where the water is not very deep. They are adapted to survive low winter temperatures even below freezing point and as soon as the water temperature rises above 10 °C they stop taking food. The fish are often found in brackish water, particularly just before spawning, when they undertake mass migrations, sometimes even into the mouths of large rivers. Spawning begins in December or January under the ice at a depth of about 10 m in fast-moving marine currents over a stony or sandy seabed. The eggs are laid in batches and float in the lower layers of the water. The fish spawn when between two and five years old. They grow slowly and their average length at four years old is about 35 cm. In September, October and March, when their food intake is highest, they feed on fish; when preparing to spawn in November and December and after spawning in February they feed on invertebrates like polychaete worms and crustaceans.

Navaga are of only local economic importance. They are caught chiefly in the autumn and the winter when the flesh has a better flavour.

The northern part of the Pacific Ocean is inhabited by the more robust related species *E. gracilis*.

Synonym: Gadus navaga
Size: 30–35 cm, maximum 45 cm
Weight: 0.5–1 kg
Fin formula: D_1 12–16, D_2 14–21, D_3 20–22, A_1 19–23, A_2 19–26
Fecundity: 6,000–9,000 eggs
Distribution: From the White Sea to the mouth of the River Ob.

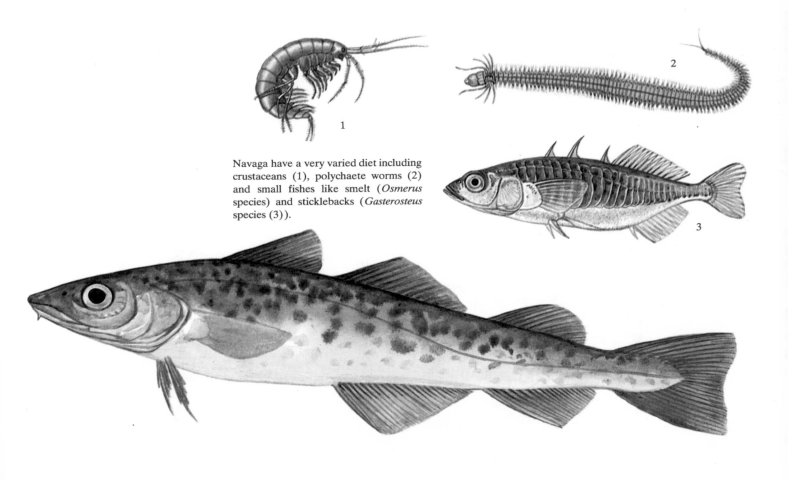

Navaga have a very varied diet including crustaceans (1), polychaete worms (2) and small fishes like smelt (*Osmerus* species) and sticklebacks (*Gasterosteus* species (3)).

Torsk, Tusk

Brosme brosme

Torsk are rather sedentary fishes, living near the bottom in quite deep waters up to 1,000 m deep. They have robust, elongate bodies, and unlike the other cod species described, have a single long dorsal fin and a long anal fin. There is a long barbel on the chin and the lateral line arches over the pectoral fin. The back is greyish brown, the sides are a lighter shade of the same colour and the belly is greyish white. The long dorsal and anal fins both have dark, white-rimmed borders and the ventral fins become darker towards their edges.

These relatively deep-water fish tend to live solitary lives or may form small shoals near a stony bottom. They feed mainly on bottom-living crustaceans and molluscs. Torsk spawn over the whole of their range at a depth of 100—400 m, when the water temperature is between 4 and 9 °C. Near Murmansk they spawn between May and August, further south from April to July. They have large eggs, each with a drop of reddish orange fat. The eggs develop in surface waters and in a year the fry measure 8—10 cm. At five years old the fish measure 34—37 cm. The fish become sexually mature when six years old, when they measure 40—50 cm and they live for a maximum of twenty years.

Torsk are fished primarily off the coasts of Norway, the USSR and Iceland and catches may amount to figures of the order of 10^4 tons. They are mostly salted and dried, but some are sold fresh or frozen.

Size: 40—60 cm, maximum 110 cm
Weight: 1—2 kg, maximum 12 kg
Fin formula: D 85—107, A 62—77
Fecundity: 800—3,000 eggs
Distribution: In the north Atlantic along the coasts of Europe as far south as Denmark, Britain and Ireland, on the eastern coast of southern Greenland and round Labrador in the west.

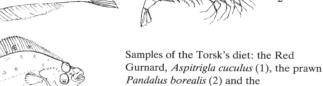
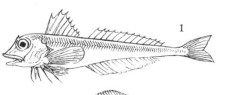

Samples of the Torsk's diet: the Red Gurnard, *Aspitrigla cuculus* (1), the prawn *Pandalus borealis* (2) and the Plaice, *Pleuronectes platessa* (3).

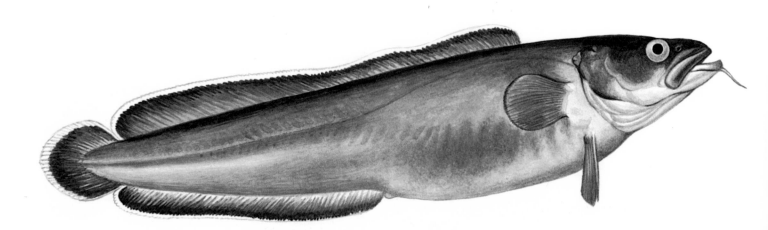

Ling
Molva molva

The ling is a long-bodied sluggish fish which lives in deep water at depths of between 300 and 400 metres, over hard rocky seabeds. Like other members of the genus *Molva,* it has no pores in the lateral line system on the head and it lacks the long, tubular nostrils resembling barbels. Its upper jaw is very slightly longer than its lower jaw and it has a barbel on its chin. It has its two dorsal fins, the first of which is short, the second very long. The ventral fins are short and never extend to the end of the pectoral fins. The eyes are not very large and their width is roughly half the length of the snout. The Ling has a brownish green to grey light-spotted back and a light belly. On the posterior margin of both dorsal fins and the anal fin there is a dark, light-edged spot.

Ling spawn from March to June at a water temperature of 5−10 °C and are highly prolific. The eggs, about one mm in diameter, develop in the surface layers of the sea but once the fry attain a length of 8 cm they retire to the bottom of the sea. There they feed mostly on other fishes like Norway Pout and cod. Both sexes mature when eight to ten years old when they measure 80−100 cm.

Ling are caught chiefly with long lines and hooks and by trawlers; anglers catch them with rods and lines. The total annual catch varies from 50,000 to 60,000 tons. The flesh is very tasty.

Commonest synonym: Gadus molva
Size: 1.2−1.8 m, maximum 2 m
Weight: 30−40 kg
Fin formula: D_1 13−16, D_2 60−70, A 57−66
Fecundity: 5−60 million eggs
Distribution: In the coastal waters of the north Atlantic from Iceland and the Barents Sea in the north to the Bay of Biscay in the south.

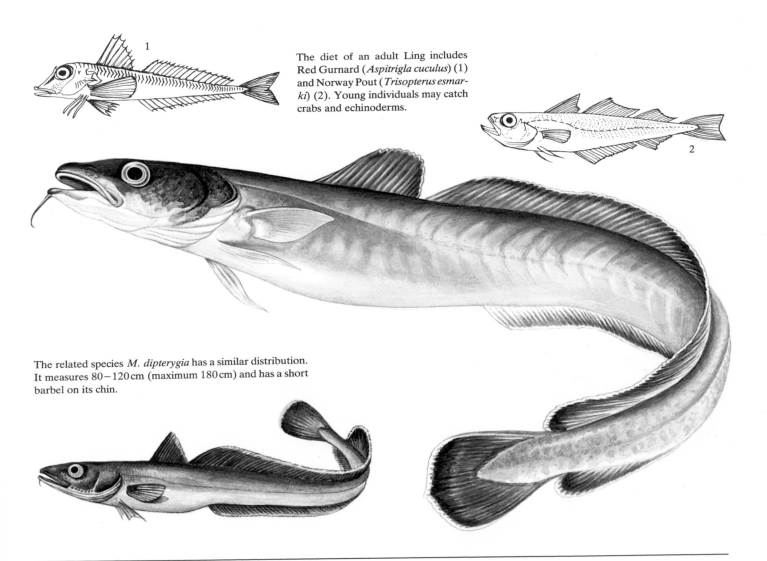

The diet of an adult Ling includes Red Gurnard (*Aspitrigla cuculus*) (1) and Norway Pout (*Trisopterus esmarki*) (2). Young individuals may catch crabs and echinoderms.

The related species *M. dipterygia* has a similar distribution. It measures 80−120 cm (maximum 180 cm) and has a short barbel on its chin.

Spanish Ling
Molva macrophthalma

Molva molva is the largest representative of the genus; the Spanish Ling, *Molva macrophthalma,* is the smallest. It has a narrower, more elongated body than *M. molva* and a short barbel on its chin. Compared with the length of its head however, it has relatively large eyes whose width is approximately the same as the length of the snout. This fish has a smaller number of rays in its first dorsal fin than the Ling (only 10−12), it has a longer lower jaw and long ventral fins which stretch far beyond the end of its pectoral fins. It has a greenish brown back and a silvery white, sometimes yellow-tinged belly. Its dorsal, anal and caudal fins are greyish brown.

Spanish Ling are found mainly in the Mediterranean, in the Bay of Biscay and off Portugal and Morocco in the Atlantic. All other members of the genus *Molva* are found further north in the Atlantic. Spanish Ling live chiefly in the deeper layers of the water close to stony or sandy bottoms, mostly at depths of between 200 and 1,200 metres. They also spawn in deep water on the edge of the continental shelf; the eggs are pelagic. No detailed information on the biology of its reproduction is available. They are predatory fishes which feed primarily on smaller fishes and large invertebrates.

The flesh of the Spanish Ling is of moderately good quality, but it is only of any real economic significance in the Mediterranean region, especially around Spain, where it occurs in the largest numbers. It is caught mostly with trawls drawn along close to the bottom.

Commonest synonyms: Molva elongata, Gadus elongatus
Size: 50−70 cm (maximum 90 cm)
Weight: maximum 7 kg
Fin formula: D_1 10−12, D_2 76−83, A 75−79
Distribution: Occurs south of the coast of England, in the Mediterranean and along the coast of North Africa.

The related Tadpole Fish, *Raniceps raninus,* is found from the middle of Norway in the north to the Bay of Biscay in the south. It measures up to 35 cm and lives near the bottom in inshore waters usually at depths of about 20−30 m.

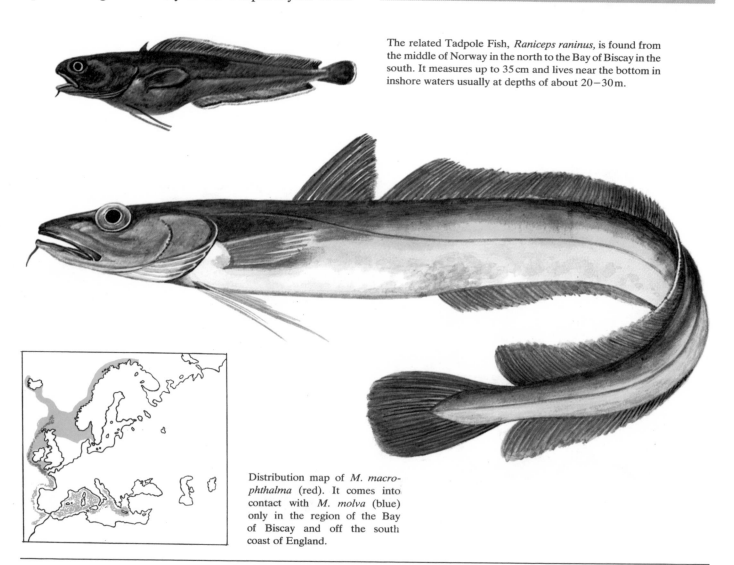

Distribution map of *M. macrophthalma* (red). It comes into contact with *M. molva* (blue) only in the region of the Bay of Biscay and off the south coast of England.

Common Rockling

Gaidropsarus vulgaris

As its name suggests, this fish lives amongst rocks on the seabed and in sandy and stony areas, just beyond the low tide levels around many European coasts. It has a very distinctive first dorsal fin in which the first ray is extremely long, while all the others are short and fine. The second dorsal fin and the anal fin are both very long. The fish has three barbels, one on the chin, the other two in front of the nostrils. It can be distinguished from *G. mediterraneus,* the Shore Rockling, by the pectoral fins which have 20–22 rays, in contrast to those of the Shore Rockling whose pectoral fins have 15–17 rays. Another relative, *G. argentatus,* which has 22–24 rays in its pectoral fins, lives to the north of the Common Rockling's range. The Common Rockling has a pink body like that of a salmon, tinted light brown in places, and its back is marked with dark brown cross bands; it has a light-coloured belly.

In the Atlantic and the Mediterranean, Common Rocklings and Shore Rocklings are found together. Common Rocklings spawn in the winter between December and February. The larvae and fry are at first pelagic and have the characteristic silvery lustre of pelagic organisms. When they measure about 5–6 cm they sink to the bottom and from then on lead a benthic existence in inshore waters. They feed on crustaceans like crabs, prawns and mysids and on small fishes like gobies and wrasse.

Common Rocklings are economically unimportant but are occasionally caught by anglers.

Size: 35–40 cm, maximum 55 cm
Weight: 0.5–1 kg, maximum 2–3 kg
Fin formula: D_1 17+19, D_2 56–64, A 57–60
Distribution: In the North Sea from the coast of Norway to Gibraltar and in the western part of the Mediterranean Sea.

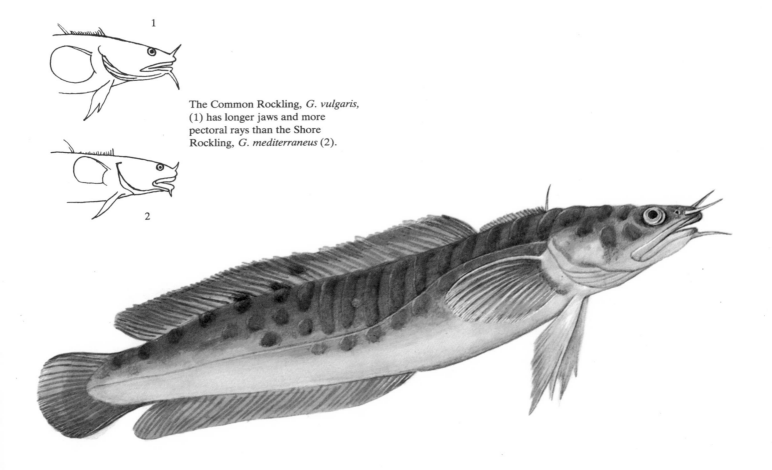

The Common Rockling, *G. vulgaris,* (1) has longer jaws and more pectoral rays than the Shore Rockling, *G. mediterraneus* (2).

Shore Rockling

Gaidropsarus mediterraneus

A similar fish to the Common Rockling with a similar dorsal fin and three barbels. In both fishes the dorsal fin is set in a longitudinal groove. The second dorsal fin and the anal fin are both long and formed of tall rays of equal height. Other characteristic features include a rudimentary swim-bladder, a lower jaw shorter than the upper jaw and a lateral line which curves downwards in front of the anal fin. The fish is very variably coloured. It generally has a more or less dark brown back and sides and a lighter belly. The entire body and fins are marked with numerous light and dark spots of different sizes.

Shore Rocklings are found in rock pools and under seaweeds on rocky shores and in offshore waters on rocks and reefs down to 30 m. At certain times of the year they may be found in large numbers. They swim further out to sea to spawn. Spawning generally occurs in the summer, but the season may last longer into the autumn. The eggs and larvae are pelagic and young individuals mostly remain near the surface. Once they reach about 4−5 cm, when about 3 months old, they migrate shorewards and sink to the bottom. Most stay offshore through their first winter, coming on to the shore itself in the following summer. They feed mainly on small species of fishes, crabs and other crustaceans and worms.

Shore Rocklings are seldom found in catches, but some sea birds.

Commonest synonyms: Onos mediterraneus, Onos tricirratus, Gaidropsarus tricirratus
Size: 30−40 cm, maximum 50 cm
Weight: up to 1 kg
Fin formula: D_1 17−19, D_2 54−60, A 44−49
Fecundity: 100,000−450,000 eggs
Distribution: Atlantic coasts of Europe and North Africa from the middle of Norway as far as Morocco, the Mediterranean and the Black Sea.

Distribution map of *G. mediterraneus*.

Five-barbed Rockling
Ciliata mustela

This species has an elongate, symmetrical body and two dorsal fins, the first of which — as in the other rocklings described — is composed of one strikingly long ray and numerous separate thin rays. Its body is covered with thin scales. It has a relatively short head and at the tip of the snout near the mouth there are five fleshy barbels, two on the anterior margin of the nostrils, two on the upper lip and one on the chin. The lateral line slants downwards at a fairly sharp angle to the middle of its sides above the origin of the anal fin and then runs straight to the root of its tail. The fish's back is dark brown sometimes with a reddish tinge, its belly a light greyish blue. The inside of its mouth and gill chamber is light yellow.

This Rockling lives near the shore in the intertidal zone often hidden amongst seaweeds or in rock pools; they may even be found in pools on sandy shores, where there is shelter from stones or break-waters. Larger individuals are also found in offshore areas on muddy, sandy or hard stony seabeds down to a depth of 5—20 m. They spawn from January to June in shallow water near the shore or in the mouths of rivers. The eggs and larvae are pelagic; the fry, which are silvery with a greenish back, live near the surface until they measure 3—4 cm and then change to a benthic existence. The adults feed chiefly on crustaceans and occasional small fish.

Because of their small size, Five-barbed Rocklings are economically unimportant. The fry however, which occur in large shoals in the upper layers of the water in the spring, form an important food source for some sea — birds.

Synonym: Onos mustela
Size: 20—25 cm, occasionally up to 30 cm
Weight: up to 0.35 kg
Fin formula: D_1 15—18, D_2 45—56, A 40—46
Fecundity: 100,000—400,000 eggs
Distribution: Along the European shores of the Atlantic from north of Norway to southern Portugal.

The related species *Onos cimbrius* occurs in the northeastern part of the Atlantic, as far as the coasts of Norway and England and off the eastern coast of Canada and the USA. It usually measures 30—40 cm, occasionally reaching 50 cm in length, and has only three barbels on its upper jaw. The first ray in its first dorsal fin is strikingly long.

Burbot
Lota lota

The Burbot is the only freshwater member of the cod family. It has a cylindrical body with two dorsal fins, the second of which, like the anal fin, is very long. The ventral fins are sited in front of the pectoral fins and each has a long, filamentous second ray. There is a single barbel on the chin. The fish is greyish brown to greenish with light marbled markings.

The Burbot is a secretive fish living in large rivers, ponds and lakes and sometimes in the brackish waters of the lowest reaches of the rivers. It is fairly common in the Danube and some of its tributaries, where it has been observed hiding among tree roots or driftwood in groups of five or over. It is nowhere near as common in Britain as it once was and is now classified as rare. Burbots spawn in the evening or at night in small shoals in shallow water over sand or gravel, from December to March at water temperatures of 2.8−6 °C. The fertilized eggs drift with the current

and on reaching quiet water sink to the bottom. The young hatch in one or two months depending on the temperature of the water. Burbot are unusual in that their food consumption is highest in cold water in the autumn and winter; in the summer they sometimes fall into a lethargic 'summer sleep'. They are active mainly at night, catching and swallowing fishes only slightly smaller in size than themselves. The flesh and large liver are regarded as delicacies and the liver is rich in Vitamin A, but even so Burbot are not very important economically, primarily because of the difficulty of catching them by night.

Size: 60−70 cm, maximum 120 cm
Weight: 2−5 kg, maximum 24 kg
Fin formula: D_1 9−16, D_2 67−90, A 65−79
Fecundity: 30,000−3,000,000 eggs
Distribution: Rivers of Europe, Asia and America. In Europe absent in the Balkan and Iberian Peninsulas and very rare in Great Britain and Norway.

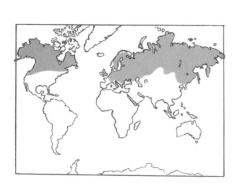

Distribution map of *Lota lota*.

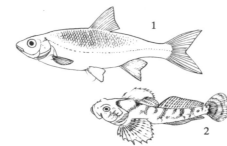

The Dace (1), Miller's Thumb (2) and Minnow (3) all form important sources of food for the Burbot.

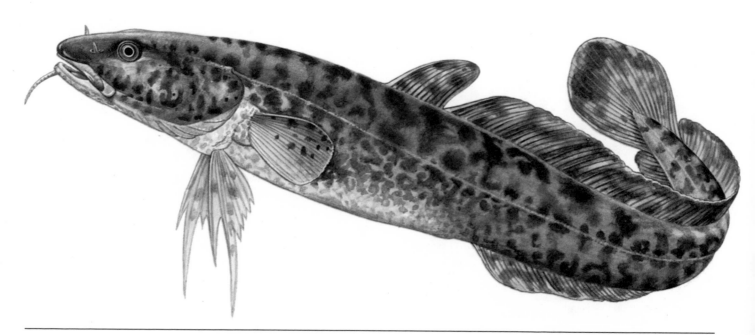

There are about four genera in the family Merlucciidae, with ten species distributed over the temperate and subtropical parts of the Atlantic and Pacific Oceans. They can be distinguished from cods by the absence of barbels and the presence of only two dorsal fins. Sometimes they are classified only as a subfamily of the Gadidae.

MERLUCCIIDAE

Hake

Merluccius merluccius

The only member of the family Merlucciidae in European waters, the Hake has a slender body, a large head and snout and powerful, recurved teeth. In form it resembles a pike and in the Middle Ages was known as *'maris lucius'* or sea pike, which forms the basis for its scientific name *(Merluccius)* and for its vernacular name in many European languages. It has a short triangular first dorsal fin and slightly concave second dorsal and anal fins. It has a greyish blue back and silvery white sides and belly.

Hake live mostly at the edge of the continental shelf at depths of 150−550 m, but in the summer they migrate into shallower water. They remain near the bottom during the day but at night they come to the surface in search of food. They feed chiefly on pelagic fishes like herrings and pilchards. Spawning occurs in the spring in the northern part of their range, generally in water deeper than 200 m and also in summer in shallower water. The eggs and fry are pelagic and depend on the currents to carry them into shallow waters to feed. The males attain sexual maturity when they measure about 40 cm, the females at about 70 cm.

The Hake has very high quality flesh, which is sold fresh or frozen. It is caught mainly with trawls. Total annual catches are usually in the region of 120,000 tons. They used to be larger, but have been severely reduced by overfishing during the last few decades.

Commonest synonyms: Gadus merluccius, Gadus merlus
Size: 1−1.2 m, occasionally up to 1.5 m
Weight: 5−8 kg, maximum 11 kg
Fin formula: D_1 9−11, D_2 36−40, A 36−40
Distribution: Atlantic Ocean from the coast of north-western Africa to Iceland and the Lofoten Islands.

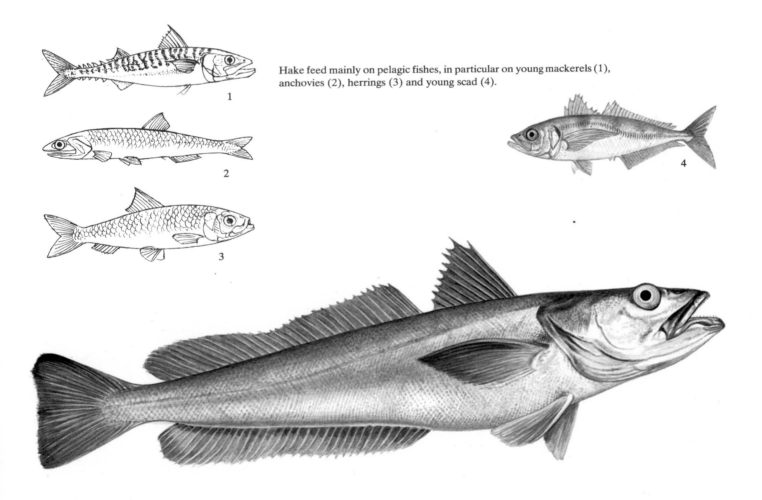

Hake feed mainly on pelagic fishes, in particular on young mackerels (1), anchovies (2), herrings (3) and young scad (4).

The order Gasterosteiformes comprises about 200 species of small fishes with their ventral fins on the thorax or at the beginning of the abdomen. In many cases the body is covered with bony plates. The family Gasterosteidae includes marine and freshwater species inhabiting the northern hemisphere. Marine and brackish water species have well developed bony plates on their sides, freshwater species have only a few plates or none at all. After spawning the males guard the eggs and fry.

GASTEROSTEIDAE

Three-spined Stickleback
Gasterosteus aculeatus

A small fish easily identified by the three spines on its back in front of its dorsal fin. It has a greyish blue, olive green or greyish body and silvery sides and belly. At spawning time, however, the male becomes brightly coloured, the front half of his underside becoming red or orange red, his back a metallic blue and his operculum golden.

The Three-spined Stickleback is a typical euryhaline species, living in the intertidal zone of the sea, in estuaries and brackish lagoons and in completely fresh water. In fresh water the fish usually live in small open ponds or streams and may form very large populations. The male is famed for the care it takes of its offspring. At spawning time, from April to June, the females lay eggs in batches in nests built by the male. The males build the nests from fragments of plants and each lures several females in succession into his nest by a typical 'dance'. After fertilizing the eggs the male actively guards the nest against all intruders whatever their size, and disposes of unfertilized eggs. The growth of the fry depends on the amount of food available; in the sea they usually grow faster. After spawning, a large proportion of the parent generation dies. Sticklebacks become sexually mature when one year old; their average life span is three years. They feed on small crustaceans like amphipods and on fish eggs.

Size: 6.5–7.5 cm, maximum 10–11 cm
Fin formula: D III/8–14, A I/6–11
Fecundity: 60–600 eggs
Distribution: Along the coasts of Europe, the eastern and western parts of North America and eastern Asia. Infiltrates inland up the rivers.

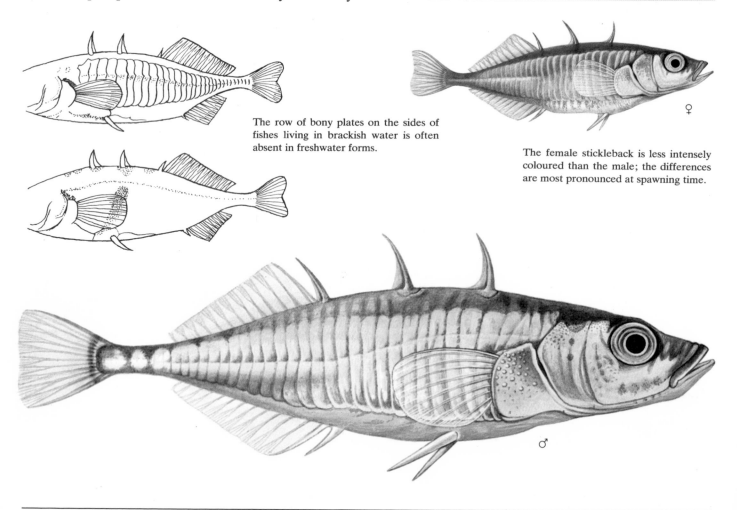

The row of bony plates on the sides of fishes living in brackish water is often absent in freshwater forms.

The female stickleback is less intensely coloured than the male; the differences are most pronounced at spawning time.

Nine-spined Stickleback

Pungitius pungitius

As its name suggests, this fish usually has nine or ten short, separate spines on its back. In fin patterns the spines are generally included in the dorsal fin, the rest of which is composed of soft, branched rays and is roughly the same length as the anal fin. The body is devoid of scales; however, on the sides of the relatively short peduncle, which narrows at the base of the tail, there is a ridge covered with small bony platelets. The back and sides of the fish are olive green, changing to greyish brown; the belly is lighter. The throat of the male and part of its belly are black and the ventral fins, which are composed of one spine and one soft ray, are white or light blue.

These sticklebacks live in fresh and brackish water near the mouths of rivers, in bays and lagoons. Rivers and ponds thickly overgrown by vegetation in the summer are also typical localities, in contrast to the habitats favoured by the Three-spined Sticklebacks, which prefer open water. The male builds a nest amongst dense plants and spawning occurs there, usually between May and August, with one female or with several females in succession. Like other members of the family Gasterosteidae, after spawning the male guards the eggs and protects the fry for a time. During their first year the fry grow to a length of 3.5 cm. The Nine-spined Stickleback has a similar diet to other sticklebacks, but consumes fewer fish eggs and larvae than the Three-spined Stickleback. Sticklebacks are prey for other fishes, like whitefish. They have a maximum life span of three years.

Size: 5—7 cm, maximum 9 cm
Fin formula: D VIII—XI/9—12, A I/8—13
Fecundity: 350—1,000 eggs
Distribution: The catchment area of the Arctic Ocean.

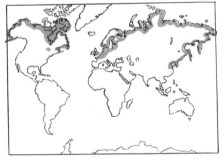

Distribution map of *Pungitius pungitius*.

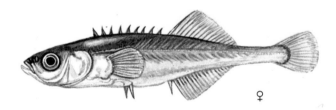

The female is olive green and except at spawning time the males are similarly coloured.

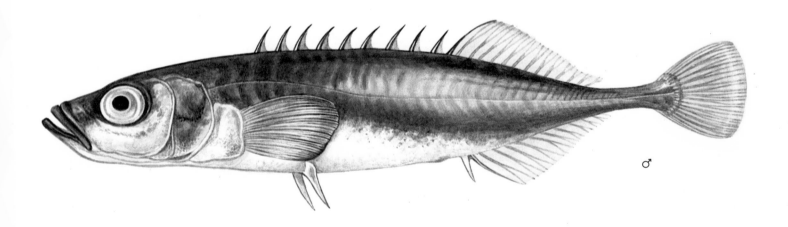

Eastern Stickleback

Pungitius platygaster

A similar species to the preceding one, with between eight and eleven short separate spines on its back, but most often with nine. The dorsal and anal fins are roughly the same length. Unlike the Nine-spined Stickleback however, the sides of the body are covered with between 29 and 32 poorly visible bony platelets and there are no ridges on the sides of the peduncle. Sometimes plates occur only on the front of the body, in which case there are only 6—15 plates present. The body is predominantly greyish green to greyish brown and is marked with irregular dark spots as are the dorsal, caudal and anal fins. Colouring is intensified at spawning time.

This fish has a quite different distribution to the Nine-spined Stickleback since it occurs in brackish coastal areas of the Black Sea, the Caspian Sea and the Sea of Azov and in the lower reaches of the rivers running into them. Spawning takes place from the middle of May to the middle of August. The male builds a nest of fragments of aquatic plants and drives several females into it in succession. The eggs are laid in batches and when spawning is over the male keeps watch first over the eggs and then over the fry. The fish never grow very large. They mature when one year old and do not spawn more than two or three times in their lives. They feed mainly on small crustaceans, insect larvae and the eggs and young of other fishes, while they themselves are eaten by large freshwater and marine fishes.

Size: 4—6 cm, maximum 7 cm
Fin formula: D VIII—XI/7—10, A I/6—9
Fecundity: 300—900 eggs
Distribution: Coastal areas of the Black Sea, the Caspian Sea and the Sea of Azov.

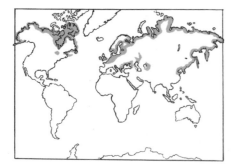

Distribution of the Nine-spined Stickleback (blue) and the Eastern Stickleback (red).

Fifteen-spined Stickleback

Spinachia spinachia

Unlike members of the genera *Pungitius* and *Gasterosteus,* this Stickleback is a solely marine species, never found in fresh water. It has an extremely elongate body with a tapering head and long snout. Its body is pentagonal in cross section owing to the presence of one ridge down the middle of the back and two more on either side along the sides and the belly. The sides are covered with bony plates. There is also one row each of bony plates forming a bony armour on the upper and lower surfaces of the long, thin caudal peduncle. The 15-spined Stickleback has between 14 and 16 (most often 15) separate short spines on its back. It has a brown to greenish brown back and peduncle and a yellow belly. Cinnamon brown spots are present on the anterior part of the triangular dorsal and anal fins.

This stickleback lives in shallows in the intertidal zone as well as in estuaries and does not descend to depths of more than 10 m. It hides amongst growths of seaweeds where at spawning time the male builds a nest roughly the size of a fist, usually not more than one metre from the bottom. The nest is made of algae, plant fragments and small pebbles, which are bound together by a whitish substance secreted by the kidneys, according to some experts, or by glands situated beside the urogenital orifice, according to others. When the nest is ready, the male drives the females into it. Spawning takes place between April and July depending on the temperature of the water, and the male guards the eggs. These sticklebacks feed mainly on invertebrates and occasionally on small fishes. Before winter sets in they leave the shallows for deeper water.

Size: mostly 10−15 cm, maximum 18−20 cm
Fin formula: D XIV−XVII/5−8, A I/5−8
Fecundity: 100−300 eggs
Distribution: Northwestern Atlantic coast of Europe and the Baltic Sea.

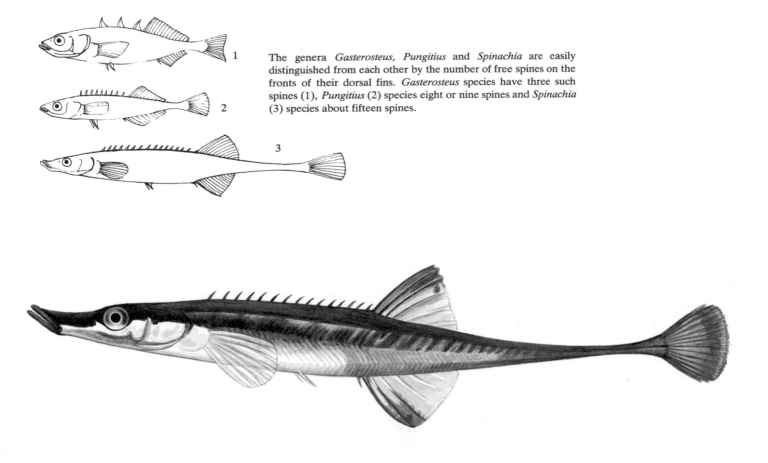

The genera *Gasterosteus, Pungitius* and *Spinachia* are easily distinguished from each other by the number of free spines on the fronts of their dorsal fins. *Gasterosteus* species have three such spines (1), *Pungitius* (2) species eight or nine spines and *Spinachia* (3) species about fifteen spines.

The Syngnathiformes are a rather small order of mostly marine fishes whose jaws form a tubular structure. There are about 10 species in the family Macrorhamphosidae, living mainly in tropical and subtropical seas and characterized by a long, thin snout, a flat-sided body with small fins and a long, barbed spine in the dorsal fin.

MACRORHAMPHOSIDAE

Trumpet-fish

Macrorhamphosus scolopax

A relatively small, deep-bodied fish with a long snout terminating in a small mouth, which appears sporadically off the coast of northwestern Europe as the only species of the family Macrorhamphosidae there. Isolated specimens occasionally stray to the southern coast of Norway and Sweden and rather more are found in the western Mediterranean. The fish has a sharp-pointed spine in its dorsal fin; the longest fin is the anal fin. The body of the fish is covered with rhomboid scales. It has a red back, the colouration paling to pink on the sides, and a much lighter-coloured belly; dead specimens soon lose their colour. The body cavity has a silver lining.

These fish generally live over a sandy seabed at depths of 100−250 m, but are occasionally found in shallower water at 25−50 m or in deeper water at about 600 m. The fish live in small shoals and feed on zooplankton, particularly on crustaceans like crab and lobster larvae and copepods.

Very little is known of their biology and reproduction. They are economically unimportant.

Size: 8−12 cm, maximum 15 cm
Fin formula: D VI−VIII/11−13, A 18−20
Distribution: Coasts of the Atlantic Ocean, the Mediterranean. Also found off the east coast of the USA and probably in the southern Atlantic, western Pacific and Indian Oceans.

Distribution map of *M. scolopax*.

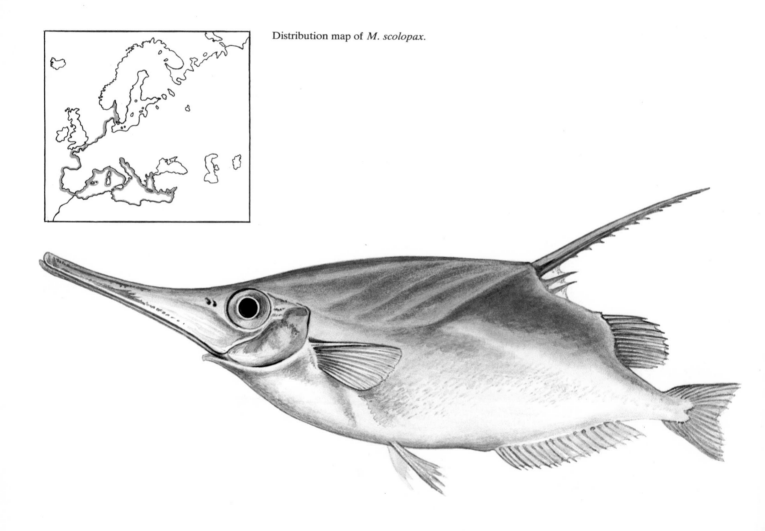

Pipefishes of the family Syngnathidae have characteristic elongate, tapering bodies and long, tubular snouts. Instead of scales their bodies are covered with rings of bone-hard dermal plates or scutes. On the trunk there are seven plates to a ring, on the tail four. The tubular snout terminates in a small, toothless mouth. Ventral fins are absent and the anal fin is either vestigial or is also absent. There are about fifty known species in all the seas.

SYNGNATHIDAE

Great Pipefish
Syngnathus acus

The Great Pipefish has a long thin body, hexagonal in cross section, with a small caudal fin and a vestigial anal fin. It has 19—21 rings of plates on its trunk and 43—46 on its tail. It is very variably coloured from grey to green, light brown and red, occasionally with black and brown stripes.

Pipefish live in shallow coastal waters, generally amongst growths of seaweed but avoiding brackish water. They also occur in the open sea. Spawning occurs between May and August; the females lay eggs in a special brood pouch which can be seen on the ventral surface of the male's tail and which is protected by skin folds and bony plates. During their development in the pouch the eggs are supplied with oxygen from the blood flowing through vessels in the mucus-lined walls of the pouch. The larvae are pelagic and once they have left the brood pouch never return. Great Pipefishes feed on small crustaceans or fish fry, which they suck in with the tubular mouth as if with a pipette.

They have no economic significance, but are sometimes kept in marine aquaria.

Synonym: Syngnathus tenuirostris
Size: 30—40 cm, occasionally up to 45 cm
Fin formula: D 35—42
Fecundity: 100—250 eggs
Distribution: The shores of the Atlantic from the middle of Norway to the north of Spain.

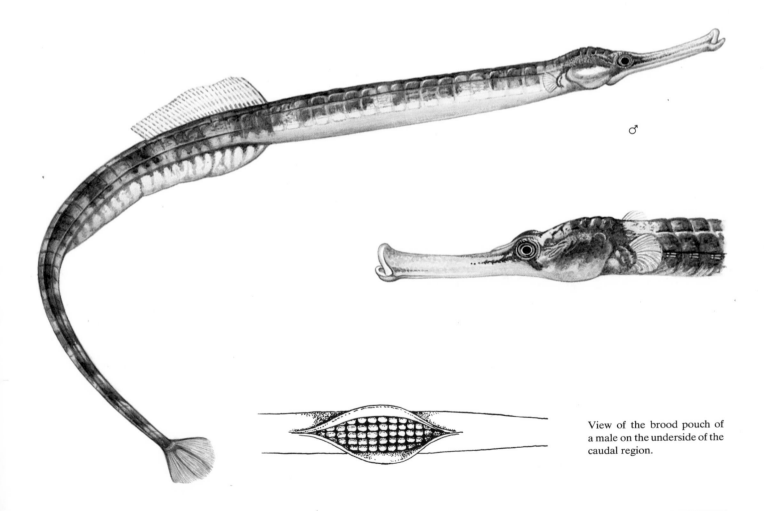

View of the brood pouch of a male on the underside of the caudal region.

Broad-nosed Pipefish

Syngnathus typhle

This pipefish is similar to the Great Pipefish and its body is similarly covered with rings of scutes. It is somewhat shorter however, with only 16–18 body rings and 33–39 caudal rings. It also has a different head. It is very variably coloured, but is generally greenish grey with darker spots.

This pipefish is distributed over a larger area than the Great Pipefish and is also found in brackish water. At one time it was particularly common in beds of eelgrass at depths of 5–20 m on coasts and in estuaries. It is now only locally common due to the disappearance of the eelgrass beds. It spends most of its time suspended in a vertical position. Its habits and breeding biology are very similar to those of the Great Pipefish. The males mature when one year old, when they measure 13 cm or over. The brood pouch is formed on the underside of the caudal part of the body. During spawning, which takes place from May to August, the sexes cling to each other face to face and the female lays 100–200 relatively large eggs in the male's brood pouch; while the eggs are developing, the pouch is sealed to protect them. The larvae hatch some three to four weeks later. Broad-nosed Pipefishes feed on crustaceans like isopods, amphipods and shrimps, also on fishes including several different species of goby.

Broad-nosed Pipefish are economically unimportant, but are sometimes kept by aquarists. They have a life span of only two or three years.

Size: 20–25 cm, exceptionally up to 30 cm
Fin formula: D 28–41
Fecundity: 100–200 eggs
Distribution: Off the European shores of the Atlantic, south of Norway and in the Baltic, the Mediterranean and the Black Seas.

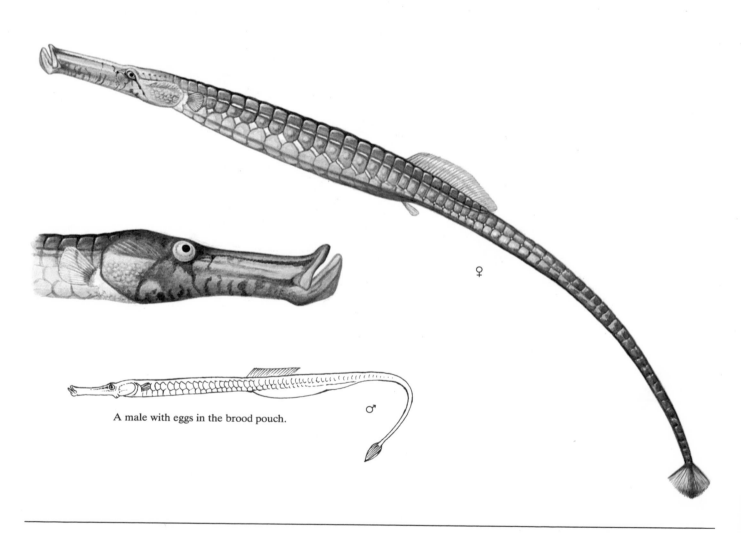

A male with eggs in the brood pouch.

Straight-nosed Pipefish

Nerophis ophidion

The long, thin, serpentine body of this pipefish terminates in a long prehensile tail without a caudal fin; the fish uses its tail to cling to the eelgrass and tubular seaweeds amongst which it lives. It has no pectoral fins. A characteristic feature of this pipefish is the bulge on the top of its snout in front of the eyes. There are 28–32 rings of scutes on the trunk and 68–77 on the tail. The fish is greenish brown in colour with dark stripes and at spawning time the front of the female's body turns blue.

Straight-nosed Pipefishes live in the sea and in brackish water at depths of from one to several dozen metres, but are mostly found in eelgrass beds in shallow water. They spawn in the spring and at the beginning of summer at some distance from the shore. The female sticks the eggs to the ventral surface of the male's body and there they remain until the young hatch. There is no special brood pouch which can be sealed off, as in the genus *Syngnathus*. Straight-nosed Pipefishes feed mainly on planktonic crustacean larvae and have an average life span of three years.

They are economically unimportant, but provide a food source for other fishes. Several other *Nerophis* species live in European waters; a few of them are very prettily coloured, like *N. maculatus,* and are occasionally kept in aquaria. In most cases the females are larger than the males.

Size: ♂ 20–25 cm, ♀ up to 30 cm
Fin formula: D 34–42
Fecundity: 50–300 eggs
Distribution: Coastal waters of the Atlantic Ocean from northern Norway to northwestern Africa, the Baltic, Mediterranean and Black Seas. Also enters the mouths of the rivers flowing into them.

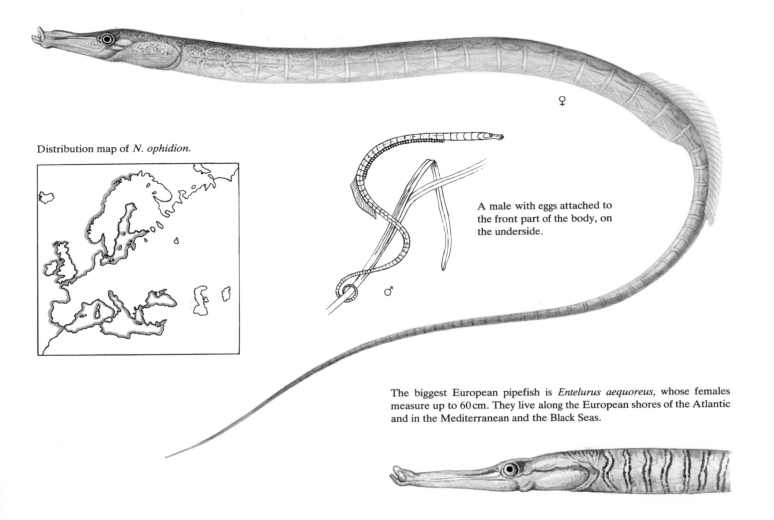

Distribution map of *N. ophidion.*

♀

A male with eggs attached to the front part of the body, on the underside.

♂

The biggest European pipefish is *Entelurus aequoreus,* whose females measure up to 60 cm. They live along the European shores of the Atlantic and in the Mediterranean and the Black Seas.

175

Spotted Sea-horse
Hippocampus guttulatus

Sea-horses are so distinctive that they can be recognised at a glance. They belong to the genus *Hippocampus,* which are all marine fishes with no caudal fin and with the tail twisted round so that it is back to front to the abdomen. The head is held at right angles to the body axis so that the fish looks like a knight in a chess set. Both body and tail are enclosed in bony rings. In all, 25 species of this genus are known in tropical and subtropical seas; only three live in European waters. This species differs from the related *Hippocampus hippocampus* in respect of the larger number of rays in its dorsal and pectoral fin, its longer tubular jaws and the presence of thread-like dermal outgrowths on its head and back. This sea-horse usually has a dark brown, red-tinged body, but may be grey or greyish brown. Its underside is lighter and its sides are marked with large numbers of light spots which sometimes merge to form irregular bands. A pair of bands — a dark one bordered by a light one — can be seen on the dorsal fin. From the spring until well into the summer the sea-horses spawn in the eelgrass beds or amongst seaweeds in relatively shallow water. Spawning is accompanied by a nuptial ritual, during which the female deposits 100—200 eggs in a brood pouch situated at the level of the first 7—8 bony rings on the male's abdomen. Both the eggs and then the larvae develop in the pouch and the young are finally expelled fully formed. Spotted Sea-horses feed mostly on planktonic crustaceans and occasionally on small fishes.

They spend most of their lives in coastal waters in eelgrass beds and anchor themselves to the grass stalks by their coiled prehensile tails; they are seldom found in open water. Sea-horses are sometimes kept in marine aquaria, partly because of their interesting form and swimming action and partly because they create great interest by emitting deep popping sounds, particularly at spawning time.

Synonym: Hippocampus ramulosus
Size: up to 15 cm, usually 10—12 cm
Fin formula: D 18—21
Fecundity: 100—300 eggs
Distribution: Along the European shores of the Atlantic from England to Gibraltar, in the Mediterranean and in the Black Sea.

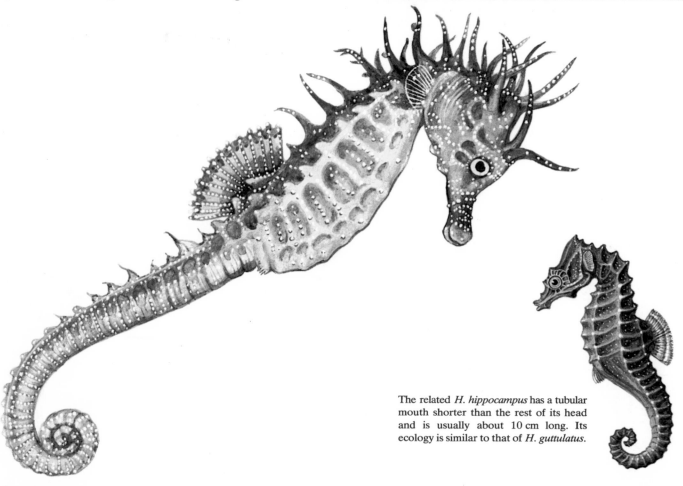

The related *H. hippocampus* has a tubular mouth shorter than the rest of its head and is usually about 10 cm long. Its ecology is similar to that of *H. guttulatus.*

In the order Mugiliformes are marine pelagic fishes with two dorsal fins situated far apart from each other. Many of them are economically important fish. The family Sphyraenidae, the barracudas, contains moderately large to large predatory fishes with long bodies covered with small cycloid scales and with large jaws well armed with teeth. There are roughly twenty species living in subtropical and tropical seas.

SPHYRAENIDAE

Mediterranean Barracuda
Sphyraena sphyraena

Barracudas are rightly regarded as very dangerous fishes, since they have claimed a whole series of human victims. Barracuda wounds can be distinguished from the wounds made by sharks, since they do not have notched edges. Barracudas launch just one attack on a victim, unlike sharks, which will attack several times. The Mediterranean Barracudas attack quickly and their sharp teeth can inflict severe injuries. They are smaller than other barracudas and are less feared by divers, usually attacking only if the divers are carrying harpooned fish, although they keep a constant watch on their underwater activities.

Like other barracudas, this one has a pike-like body; in several languages they are known as sea pikes. They live in coastal waters at depths of up to 100 m, mostly over a sandy seabed. They spawn from April to September and the female lays several batches of pelagic eggs. From the very beginning the fry feed on fish.

The Mediterranean Barracuda has excellent flesh and the total annual catch in European waters, together with *S. barracuda*, amounts to 2,000–3,000 tons. They are also fished for sport.

Size: 30–60 cm, maximum 1 m
Weight: 10 kg, maximum 15 kg
Fin formula: D_1 V, D_2 I/8–9, A I–II/8
Fecundity: 50,000–300,000 eggs
Distribution: In the Mediterranean and the Black Seas, off the Atlantic coast of southern Europe including Spain, Portugal and southern France.

The related *S. guachancho* grows to a maximum length of 1 m and weighs about 5 kg. Its distribution is similar to that of *S. sphyraena*, but it tends to stay closer inshore. It feeds on small fish, crabs and prawns.

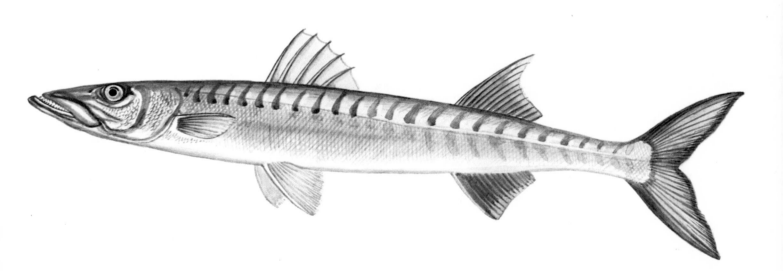

There are about 100 species of fishes in the family Mugilidae, all with a similar build and biology. They differ chiefly as regards their colouring and there are a number of anatomical differences which are often hard to see at first glance.

Golden Grey Mullet
Liza aurata

A typical mullet, with quite a stout body, a short flattened head and a broad terminal mouth. It has the typical mullet colouring, with a grey back and silvery sides, but is distinguished from the others by the presence of a few greyish brown longitudinal stripes on the sides, a large gold-gleaming spot on the operculum and golden shades on the underside of the head and on the sides.

Like other grey mullets, this one lives mainly in inshore waters, bays, river mouths and harbours. The fishes may be seen swimming in tightly knit schools, twisting and turning together. They feed mainly on debris, which they collect from the bottom in the manner described in detail in the description of *Mugil labrosus*. The food is digested in a specially adapted digestive system — the intestine is four and a half times the length of the body. In different localities spawning takes place at different times of year; the eggs are pelagic.

The flesh, which is regarded as something of a delicacy, is generally eaten fresh. In the Black Sea this species may account for up to 80% of the total grey mullet catch, but in northern European waters and round the British Isles it is comparatively rare.

Commonest synonyms: Mugil aurata, Mugil breviceps
Size: 30—40 cm, maximum 52 cm
Weight: 1—2 kg, occasionally up to 2.3 kg
Fin formula: D_1 IV, D_2 I/8—9, A III/9
Fecundity: 150,000—2,000,000 eggs
Distribution: In the Black Sea and the Mediterranean and down the western coast of Europe and Africa from the south of Norway to Angola; rare in the more northerly waters.

A view of the top of the head of two grey mullets. In *Mugil labrosus* (1) the scales continue past the nostrils; they are small and the number of rows is larger. In *Mugil auratus* (2), they extend to the posterior (and sometimes to the anterior) nostril; they are somewhat larger and there are fewer rows.

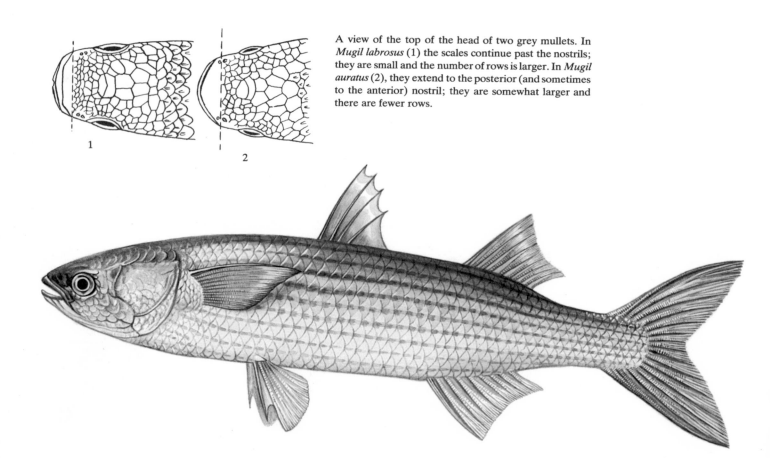

Thin-lipped Grey Mullet
Liza ramada

A typical grey mullet species which can be identified by the thinness of the upper lip, which is free from wart-like papillae. Scales cover the lower jaw and stretch from the middle of the top of the head to the anterior nostrils and very tiny ones extend along the sides of the head beyond the anterior nasal orifices. The pectoral fins are short and do not reach the posterior edge of the eye when bent forwards. This mullet has a bluish green back, metallic silvery opalescent sides marked with longitudinal grey-brown stripes and a light-coloured belly; there are no golden spots on the opercula.

Thin-lipped Grey Mullet live in the sea, but also invade rivers, where they may swim quite a long way upstream and are the commonest grey mullet found in fresh water in southern Europe. During the year they undertake spawning and food migrations and may be found in more northerly waters in the summer, although they are rare in the North Sea. Spawning takes place in the sea in more northerly waters, usually at night. As in other grey mullet spawning shoals, there are more males than females, and they are smaller than the females since they mature one year earlier. The ratio of the sexes in the shoals is 1:3 to 1:5. The spawning season varies with the geographic location and in European waters normally lasts from June to August. The eggs are pelagic and are produced in large quantities. In France and other southern European countries they are salted together with the eggs of other grey mullets and used as a cheap substitute for caviare. The flesh is tasty, but these fishes are often difficult to catch as they are capable of leaping out of the nets.

Commonest synonyms: Mugil ramada, Mugil capito
Size: 30−50 cm, maximum 70 cm
Weight: 1−2 kg, maximum 3 kg
Fin formula: D_1 IV, D_2 I/7−9, A III/8−9
Distribution: In the Atlantic Ocean off the coasts of Europe and Africa, very rarely as far north as southern Norway, to the Cape of Good Hope. Common in the Mediterranean, less so in the Black Sea.

Side and top view of the head, showing the characteristic shapes and arrangements of the scales.

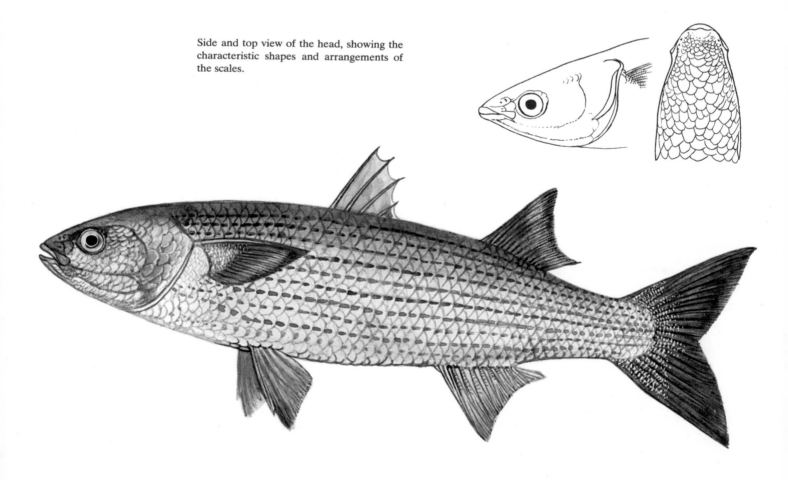

Black Sea Leaping Grey Mullet
Mugil saliens

This fish has the same basic body shape as the other grey mullets, but when seen from above its head is more pointed. The scales on the head extend to the anterior nasal openings and sometimes beyond them to the tip of the snout; the scales in the last 8–10 rows are very small. The lower lip is thin and the lower jaws are covered with scales. This grey mullet has a greyish brown back and sides with longitudinal stripes on a golden background; there are also a few golden spots on the opercula. Spawning and feeding are as described for other grey mullets.

Mullets generally form large shoals which migrate during the year to find food. They are usually caught while migrating, in a variety of ways, but chiefly with seine-nets and dragnets. Particularly good results are obtained with adjustable seine-nets, which allow large sections of the sea to be fenced off. This

technique utilizes the fact that these mullets do not swim under obstacles close to the surface but leap over them. When they arrive at the first nets in their way they try to jump over them and drop into further nets floating on the surface. They may also be caught by anglers although it is very difficult to catch them with rod and line. The practice of breeding these and other grey mullets under semi-artificial conditions in various bays and lagoons is increasing.

Size: 20–30 cm, maximum 40 cm
Weight: 1–1.5 kg
Fin formula: D_1 IV, D_2 I/8–9, A III/8–9
Distribution: In the Atlantic Ocean off the whole coast of western Africa and off European coasts northwards as far as the Bay of Biscay, in the Mediterranean, the Black Sea and the Sea of Azov; also enters fresh water. Together with *Liza aurata* and *M. cephalus* has been introduced to the Caspian Sea where, with *M. aurata*, it is now thoroughly naturalized and actually grows larger than in its original localities.

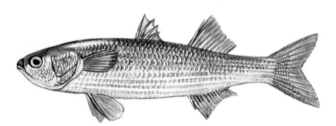

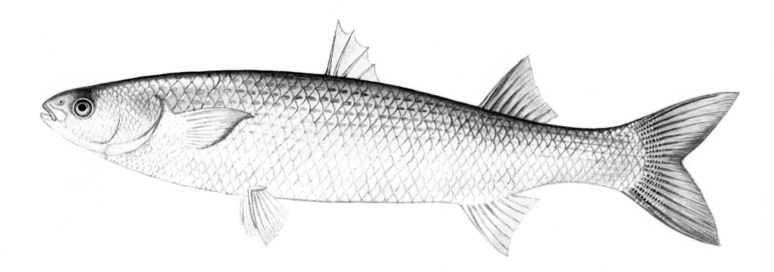

Mugil labeo has a very thick, smooth upper lip and no adipose fold on its eyes. It lives in coastal waters from England to Greece.

Thick-lipped Grey Mullet
Mugil labrosus

As indicated by its common name this grey mullet is identifiable by its strikingly thickened upper lip whose height is more than half the diameter of its eye. The underside of the lip is covered with wart-like papillae; the mouth itself is small and finishes well in front of the anterior edge of the eye. Seen from above, the head is more pointed than in *M. cephalus*. The lower jaws are not covered with scales. This fish has a dark green to blue back and the sides are a lighter blue to silver with seven or eight dark grey stripes running along them.

In the spring these mullet migrate northwards in search of food, returning southwards in the autumn. Like other grey mullets they feed on débris and sediment enriched with the organic remains of plants and animals and on small plants and animals on the bottom. They scrape their food from the seabed, suck it into the mouth together with water and strain it through the dense filter formed by the gill-rakers; the pharyngeal teeth squeeze out any water which may be left and the food is finally digested and processed in the thick-walled stomach and abnormally long intestine. The fish feed both by night and by day. When gathering food the mullets move along head downwards, with their bodies held obliquely at an angle of about 45 degrees to the seabed.

This grey mullet is important to the fishing industry in the Mediterranean and north Europe.

Size: 50−75 cm, maximum 90 cm
Weight: 2−4 kg, maximum up to 8 kg
Fin formula: D_1 IV, D_2 I/8−9, A III/9−10
Distribution: In the Mediterranean and the Atlantic Ocean off the shores of Europe and Africa from Trondheim in Norway in the north to Dakar in the south. Also round Iceland, Madeira, the Azores and the Canary Islands. Their presence in the Black Sea and in fresh water has not been reliably demonstrated.

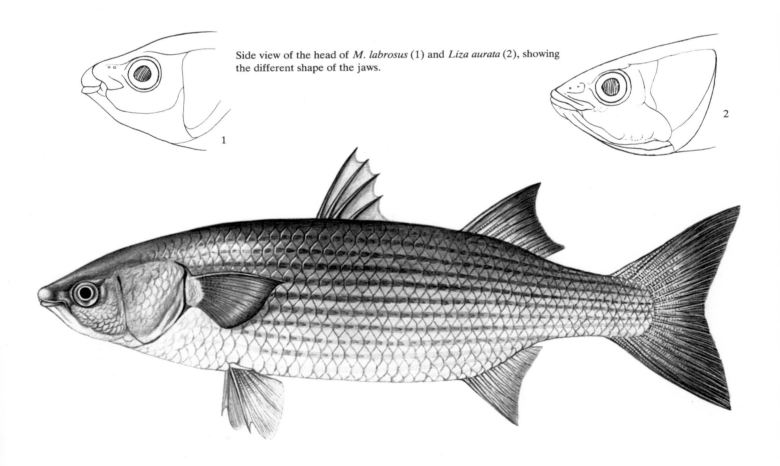

Side view of the head of *M. labrosus* (1) and *Liza aurata* (2), showing the different shape of the jaws.

Common Mullet
Mugil cephalus

This grey mullet is a more important fishery species than any of the others. Its body is shaped exactly like a torpedo and it has a large mouth whose corners extend to the anterior margins of its eyes. It has a thin upper lip and the lower jaws are covered with tiny scales. The eyes of this species are protected by wide adipose lids as far as the pupils, in contrast to those of the others, in which these lids are rudimentary or poorly developed. The back is ashen-grey and along the sides there are usually seven to nine greenish brown stripes with golden or light blue gleaming spaces between them; the opercula are silvery or golden in colour.

This grey mullet is found southwards from the Bay of Biscay along the European shores of the Atlantic and is also present in the Mediterranean, the Black Sea and the Sea of Azov. It also lives in fresh water in the lower reaches of rivers, since, like other grey mullets, it can tolerate changing salinity levels down to only 50 ‰ sea water or less. Although it likes warmth it can tolerate considerable changes of temperature; it has been found at temperatures of only 3.5 °C and has been caught under the ice in frozen inlets. The males become sexually mature when six or seven years old, the females usually a year later. Their reproduction, feeding habits and structure are more or less the same as for other grey mullets and they undertake long spawning and food migrations.

Common Mullet are of considerable economic importance; being a worldwide species they account for a large proportion of the total grey mullet catch, which in recent years has been approximately 120,000 tons. Many people regard their flesh, which is not as oily as that of the others, as the most acceptable of the whole family.

Size: 40–60 cm, maximum 75 cm
Weight: up to 5 kg, exceptionally up to 8 kg
Fin formula: D_1 IV/1, D_2 I/8–9, A III/8
Fecundity: 3–7 million eggs
Distribution: In tropical and warm oceans and seas all over the world.

The blunt-tipped head is covered with scales right to the rostral margin of the snout. Towards the tip of the snout the scales grow smaller and the number of rows increases.

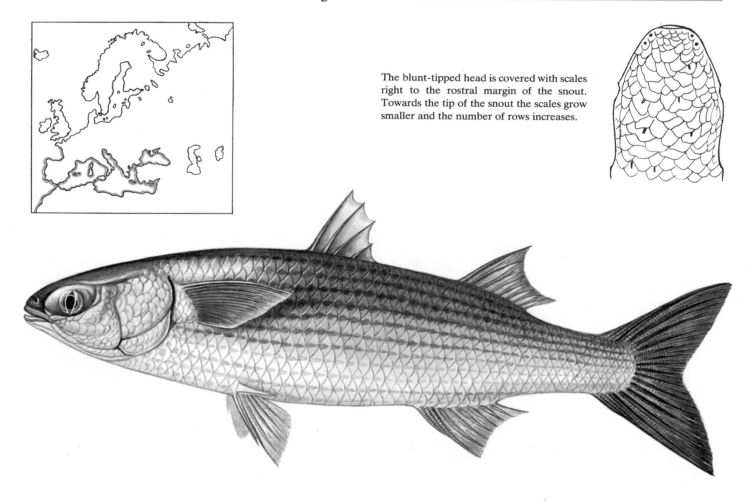

The species belonging to the order Atheriniformes have two dorsal fins set far apart from each other. They have large eggs, which are encased in capsules with tendril-like outgrowths for attachment to aquatic plants. Of the two suborders there are about 150 species in the Atherinoidei. The family Atherinidae contains about 140 species of fish living in salt, brackish and fresh water. They can be recognised by the striking silver band running along the middle of their sides, giving them the name silversides.

ATHERINIDAE

Common Sand Smelt
Atherina presbyter

The commonest representative of the family in northern European waters, the Sand Smelt looks superficially like a small grey mullet, with a long, thin body covered with cycloid scales and two dorsal fins on the back. Its back is green with black-edged scales, it has the distinct silver band running along its sides, typical of the family, and a silvery white belly. Sand Smelts live in large shoals near the shore over a sandy or clayey bottom, in estuaries and harbours and large rock pools down to depths of 20m. They are more common in British waters in summer than in winter, as large numbers migrate northwards in search of food. They feed on small crustaceans and occasionally on fish fry. Spawning occurs very close to the shore from the end of the spring to the end of July. The eggs become entangled in seaweeds by tendril-like filaments; the young fry grow quickly and can often be seen swimming in shoals in rock pools.

Because of their small size they have practically no economic significance but are occasionally caught with seine-nets and used as cattle feed. They also provide food for bigger fishes.

Size: 12–15 cm, maximum 22 cm
Weight: 50–70 g, maximum 110 g
Fin formula: D_1 VII–VIII, D_2 13–15, A I/14–16
Distribution: Off the Atlantic coasts of Europe and northern Africa from northern England to Cape Verde, western part of the Mediterranean.

Distribution map of *A. mochon* (red) and *A. presbyter* (blue).

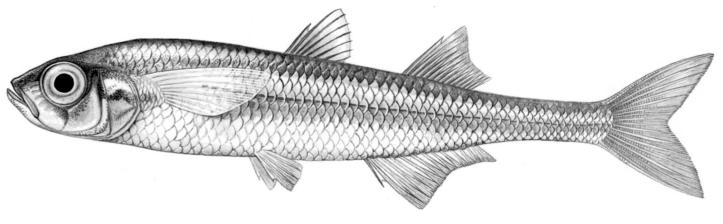

183

Boyer's Sand Smelt
Atherina mochon

This fish is similar to the Sand Smelt, but has somewhat larger eyes and fewer scales in its lateral line. It has a greenish blue to grey back and a silvery belly. Along the middle of its sides runs a silvery stripe the width of one row of scales, but without the pronounced brown spots found in the related species, *Atherina bonapartei*.

It grows slowly; in its first year it measures about 5 cm, in its second 8 cm, in its third about 11 cm and in its fourth 13−15 cm. Both males and females become sexually mature when two years old. The spawning season extends from the end of March to September and eggs are laid intermittently throughout this time. Spawning takes place in coastal waters among dense growths of seaweed, to which the eggs are attached by tendrils. The biggest females arrive first at the spawning sites and the smaller ones follow later. The fry live in large shoals near the shore, moving further out to sea at night but returning the following day. The adults also remain in coastal waters but at somewhat greater depths. The fry feed on the smallest zooplankton; the adults feed on the larger zooplankton species as well as on polychaete worms, barnacles and fish fry.

Although not of any great economic significance they may be caught locally for cattle feed; they also provide an important link in the food chains of predatory fishes.

Size: 10−15 cm, maximum 16 cm
Fin formula: D_1 VII−IX, D_2 10−12, A II/13−15
Fecundity: 50−2,000 eggs
Distribution: The Mediterranean, Black Sea and Sea of Azov and in some places brackish and fresh water near the shore.

The related species *A. hepsetus* occurs in the Black Sea, the Mediterranean and the adjacent part of the Atlantic Ocean. It has small scales and the silver band along its sides is wider than one row of scales.

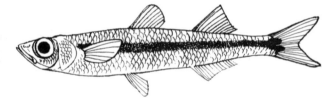

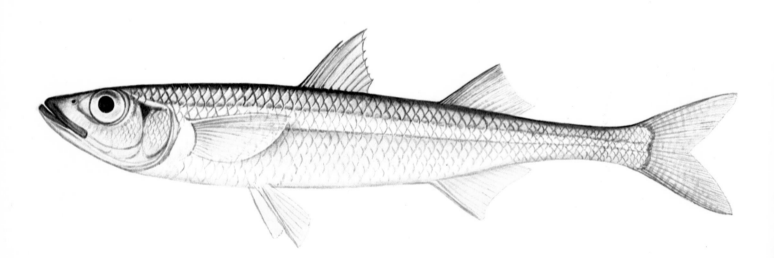

The Zeiformes is a small order of about fifty species of fishes, related to perches. They usually have flat-sided bodies and long ventral fins. All of them live in the sea at the edges of the continental shelves. In the family Caproidae there are some four genera, each with a few species of deep-bodied marine fishes with small, rounded scales. At a cursory glance they resemble another family of the order, the Grammicolepidae, but they have only 21–23 vertebrae in contrast to the Grammicolepidae which have 45–46.

CAPROIDAE

Boar Fish
Capros aper

The Boar Fish is a distinctive fish with a deep body and a relatively small head. It has a long snout and protruding jaws forming a suctorial tube and strikingly large eyes. It has two dorsal fins, the first composed entirely of spines, the second one of soft rays. Its body is covered with small, rounded scales, which are rough to the touch so that the fish feels like sandpaper. These are deep-water fishes which are often associated with coral reefs on the rocky seabeds where they live. But they are also sometimes found in shallower water. The colour of the fish is variable, the deep-water forms being red while the shallow-water fish are brownish yellow in colour and marked with dark transverse bands.

The adult fish spawn from June to August and produce pelagic eggs, each provided with a drop of yellow fat as a flotation device. Boar Fish feed on small zooplankton species, especially on all kinds of crustaceans. These are relatively common fishes in trawler catches but they have no value. Individuals have been found in the stomachs of tunnyfish.

Synonym: Zeus aper
Size: 10–12 cm, maximum 16 cm
Fin formula: D_1 IX, D_2 23, A III/23
Distribution: The Mediterranean, the Atlantic coastal waters of Europe from southern Scandinavia south to the Canary Islands.

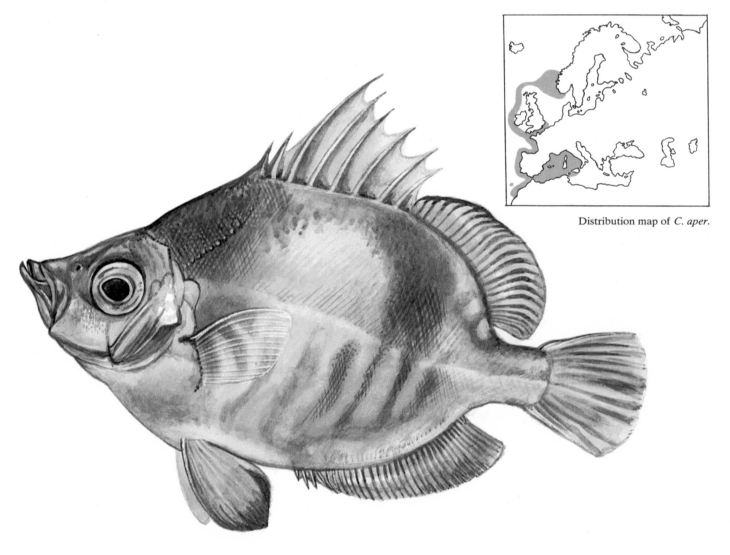

Distribution map of *C. aper*.

The family Zeidae includes fishes with relatively short, deep bodies and compressed sides. In front of the dorsal and anal fins there are 3—5 spines which are sometimes quite separate from the fin itself. The best known of the ten subtropical and tropical genera of this family is Zeus from the eastern Atlantic.

ZEIDAE

John Dory, St. Peter's Fish
Zeus faber

This is a moderately large marine fish with a deep, flat-sided body and high, prominent jaws. It has two distinctive dorsal fins, the first of which is composed of 9—10 thick spines; and two anal fins, the first composed of 3—4 thick spines joined together by webbing and the second entirely of soft rays. On each side, between the ventral and anal fins, along the base of the second dorsal fin and along the bases of both anal fins there are single rows of large scales surmounted by spines; spines are also present in front of and behind the eyes and on the opercula. The fish has a dark brown to brownish yellow back and head, the sides are marked with light yellow bands and the belly is silvery grey; on each side there is also a large reddish brown, yellow-edged spot.

John Dories live in open areas of coastal waters usually at depths of 10—50 m, but they may also sometimes be found as deep as 200 m and sometimes at the surface. They live mainly in small shoals, but are also known to lead solitary lives. The fish swims slowly and when resting on the bottom, occasionally even when swimming, it turns over on to its side. Small shoal-forming fish form the main items of its diet. These fish spawn intermittently from March to June; the eggs are pelagic.

The flavour of its excellent flesh is reminiscent of crab and lobster flesh. It is caught mainly with dragnets and the total annual catch varies from 1,000 to 5,000 tons.

Size: 30—50 cm, females up to 65 cm
Weight: 1—2 kg, maximum 8 kg
Fin formula: D_1 IX—X, D_2 22—24, A_1 III—IV, A_2 20—23
Distribution: In the Atlantic along the coasts of Europe from southern Norway to the Cape of Good Hope, in the Mediterranean and occasionally in the Black Sea.

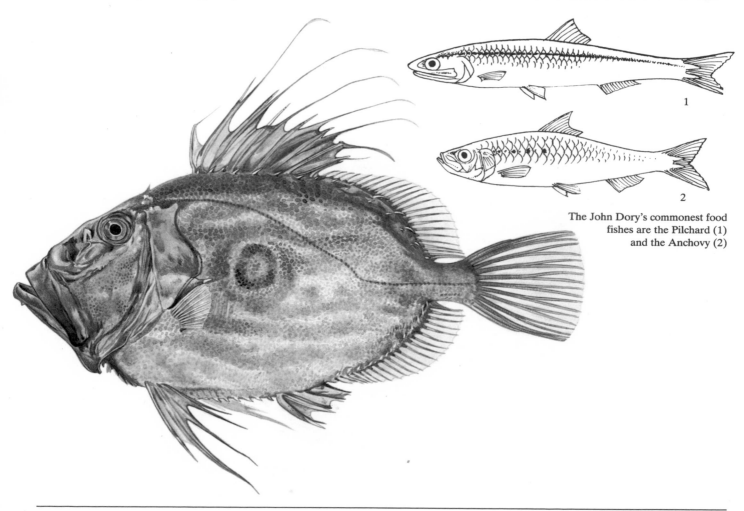

The John Dory's commonest food fishes are the Pilchard (1) and the Anchovy (2)

The order Lampridiformes is a group of marine fishes of uncertain affinities living mostly at considerable depths. The characteristics of the family Lampridae are the same as those described in the species below.

Opah, Kingfish
Lampris guttatus

This is the only known member of the family Lampridae and is unique as regards both its form and its colouring. It has a deep, firm body and its fins are distinctive both in colour and in form — the dorsal fin has a high anterior edge, the anal fin is long and narrow, and the ventral fins are sickle-shaped — none of them have any hard, spiny rays. The lateral line arches high over the base of the pectoral fin and then runs along the middle of the side in a straight line. The jaws are toothless. Because of its colouring this fish cannot be mistaken for any other species. Its back is a steely blue-black or violet which fades on its sides into a finer bluish green with a gold or silvery lustre. Its belly is rusty or purplish silver and all its fins are blood red. Its body is irregularly strewn with numerous round, milky white spots.

These fish live primarily in open water at depths of 100−400 m; they are caught most often in the sea near Madeira, the Canary Islands and the Azores, but generally more by accident than by intention. We do not know much about their biology, but they spawn in the winter months and they feed on shellfish, squids and other fishes.

Like the flesh of salmonid fishes, the tasty, moist flesh of the Opah is highly prized. In rare cases they are caught with rod and line and large individuals in particular are considered special trophies, since they give the angler added prestige. Isolated Opahs are sometimes washed ashore, especially after storms.

Commonest synonyms: Lampris regius, Lampris luna
Size: 80−100 cm, maximum 150−180 cm
Weight: 50−100 kg, occasionally up to 270 kg
Fin formula: D 52−54, A 39−41
Distribution: In tropical and warm oceans and seas all over the world.

Distribution map of *L. guttatus*.

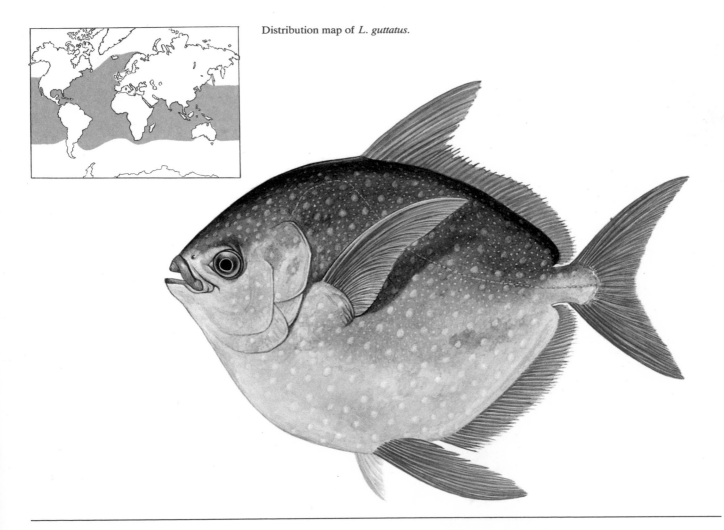

There are just two genera of marine fishes in the family Regalecidae, both distinguished by extremely long, narrow bodies. They are often found in shoals of herrings.

Oar-fish, Ribbon-fish

Regalecus glesne

This is one of the largest deep-sea marine fishes. It has a long, ribbon-like, extremely flat-sided body and in some European countries is also called the 'strap-fish'. Of the 250−300 (according to some sources up to 400) rays in its dorsal fin, the first 10−15 are much longer than the others. They are joined together at the tip by a flat membrane and crown the head like a crest, so that the fish is sometimes also known as the 'King of the Herrings'. It has small pectoral fins and the ventral fins below them are each formed of a single, long, thread-like ray with a wide, fleshy tip. There is no caudal or anal fin and the anal orifice generally lies below the 80th ray of the dorsal fin. The fish is toothless. It has a silvery body marked with irregular short cross stripes and spots and along its sides there are between four and six dark longitudinal stripes studded with numerous small tubercles. The fins are dark red.

This fish is said to live at depths of 300−600 m, but is sometimes carried close to the surface and it is here that occasional individuals are caught. Others are washed up on to beaches by storms. Because of the life that this fish leads little is known about its biology. Small specimens are sometimes found in the stomachs of tunnyfish.

Commonest synonyms: Regalecus gladius, Gymnetrus longiradiatus.
Size: usually 2−4.5 m, maximum 7 m
Distribution: In oceans all over the world.

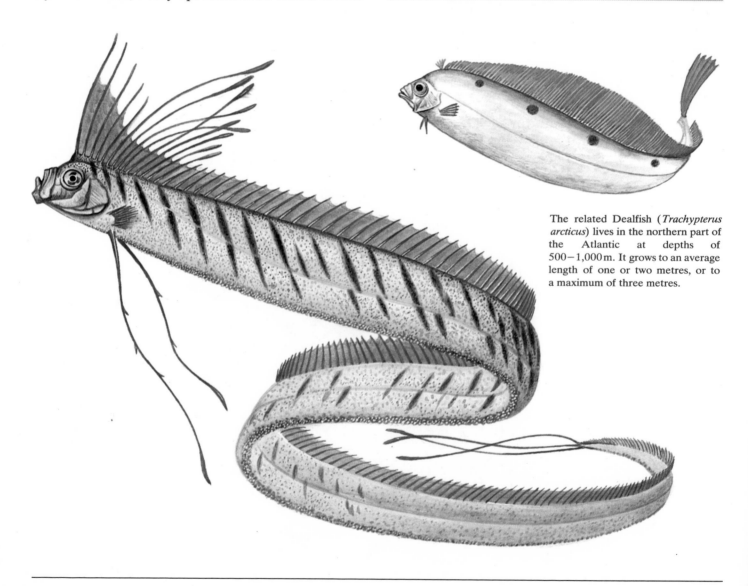

The related Dealfish (*Trachypterus arcticus*) lives in the northern part of the Atlantic at depths of 500−1,000 m. It grows to an average length of one or two metres, or to a maximum of three metres.

The Perciformes, with over 6,000 species, is the largest order of bony fishes; it is divided into up to 20 suborders. Its members are very varied in form, but in all of them the first few rays of the dorsal fin is composed of spines, not soft fin rays. Sometimes these fish are called the Spiny-finned fishes. The family Serranidae contains some 75 genera with about 400 species distributed mostly in tropical and subtropical seas.

SERRANIDAE

Painted Comber
Serranus scriba

This fish has a relatively deep body with compressed sides and a large head with a wide snout. It has two dorsal fins joined together, the first with several strong spines and the second with soft fin rays; the caudal fin is straight-edged or rounded. There are three conspicuous spines on the operculum, of which the middle one is the largest, and the posterior edge of the operculum is also toothed. The colouring of this fish varies with environment. Its back and sides are generally russet or yellowish brown, with five or six, occasionally up to eight, dark cross bands continuing on to its dorsal fin. On the sides of its head there are irregular blue or greenish stripes bordered by dark, usually reddish brown, markings.

Painted Combers live mostly among stones and

rocks over a hard seabed sometimes overgrown with algae, usually at depths of 20–30 m, though in exceptional cases down to 100 m. They often lie in wait among the rocks and then pounce on their prey, which may be relatively large fishes compared with the size of the Comber. They are hermaphrodite – male and female germ cells develop in the body of the same individual. The male and female sex cells sometimes mature at the same time, sometimes at different times, so that eggs may be fertilized by milt from the same individual. Off European coasts the spawning season lasts from May to August.

Painted Combers have very tasty flesh, but are seldom seen in catches.

Commonest synonyms: Perca scriba, Paracentropristis scriba
Size: 20–30 cm
Weight: up to 0.5 kg
Fin formula: D X/14–15, A III/7–8
Fecundity: 17,500–100,000 eggs
Distribution: In the Atlantic Ocean off the coast of Europe and Africa from Britain to Senegal, including the Mediterranean, the Black Sea and the region round the Canary Islands and Madeira.

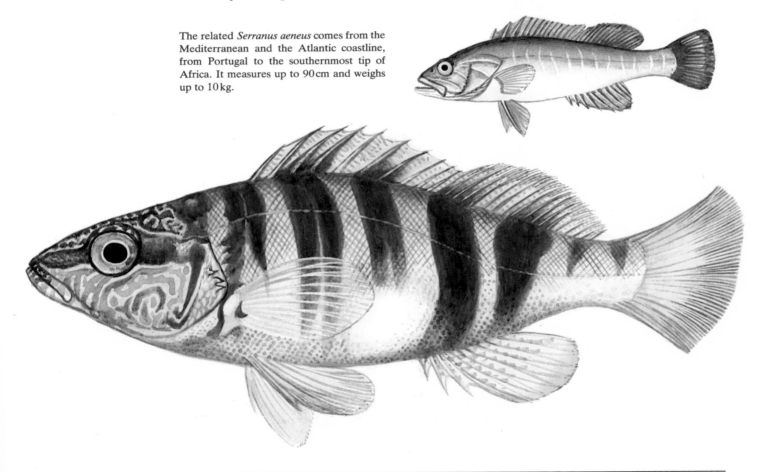

The related *Serranus aeneus* comes from the Mediterranean and the Atlantic coastline, from Portugal to the southernmost tip of Africa. It measures up to 90 cm and weighs up to 10 kg.

Comber

Serranus cabrilla

A close relative of *S. scriba,* but with different colours and with a different tail fin (in *S. scriba* this fin is straight-edged or slightly rounded, while in this species it is slightly concave). The Comber's body is marked relatively regularly with seven to nine red-brown cross stripes of roughly equal width; three, or sometimes only two, yellowish red stripes run lengthwise along its sides to its tail and another three or four similarly coloured stripes lead obliquely over the sides of its head. In males the markings are more pronounced and the colours brighter. The ground colour in both sexes is light brown or grey.

Combers live amongst underwater rocks, wrecked ships and sunken ruins of old buildings. They occur most frequently at depths of 20–60 m, but occasionally may be found down to 100 m. They feed mostly on small fishes. In the Mediterranean Combers spawn intermittently from May to August, while further north reproduction is confined to July and August. Like *S. scriba, S. cabrilla* is an hermaphrodite fish and self-fertilization is possible. The smaller testes lie below the larger ovaries.

Combers have tasty flesh and are relatively popular in the regions bordering the Mediterranean. They are caught chiefly by anglers and do not appear in very large numbers in fishermen's nets.

Commonest synonyms: Perca cabrilla, Paracentropristis cabrilla, Pseudoserranus cabrilla
Size: 25–35 cm, maximum 45 cm
Weight: up to 0.7 kg
Fin formula: D X/13–15, A III/7–8
Fecundity: 20,000–100,000 eggs
Distribution: Off the Atlantic coasts of Europe and Africa from Great Britain to Senegal, the Mediterranean, Black and Red Seas.

Epinephelus alexandrinus lives in the Mediterranean and in the adjoining part of the Atlantic. It measures up to one metre and weighs up to 10 kg.

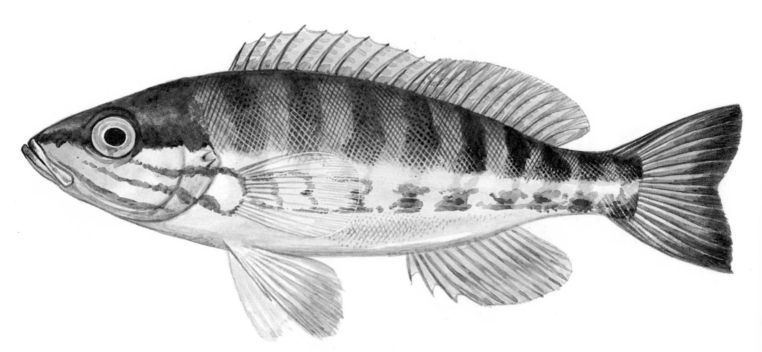

Dusky Perch
Epinephelus guaza

This close relative of the genus *Serranus* used to be included by some zoologists in that genus. Like combers, it has only one dorsal fin, the front section of which has spiny, non-branching rays. It has a similar body, there are three conspicuous spines at the back of its operculum and the posterior edge of its preoperculum is toothed. Some of its systematic characters are different, however, scales are present on the lower jaw and it is much larger and different in colour. Its back and sides are chestnut brown in colour, while its belly and its lower jaw are yellow. It has no longitudinal stripes nor cross bars. Instead, the entire body is covered with irregular light spots of varying sizes and all the fins have light edges.

These sea bass are usually found at depths of 8−150m, chiefly over a stony bottom with an abundance of rock formations, intricate hiding-places and grottos for them to hide in solitary seclusion. Dusky Perch feed mainly on fish and to a lesser extent on large crustaceans and molluscs.

On the whole the flesh is quite tasty, but in old individuals it tends to be stringy and dry. They are caught chiefly with dragnets and long lines and the annual catch in recent years has ranged from 1,000 to 2,000 tons. Anglers also catch them with rods and lines and in the Mediterranean skin divers hunt them with harpoons.

Commonest synonyms: Serranus guaza, Epinephelus gigas
Size: 80−120 cm, maximum 150 cm
Weight: 3−10 kg, occasionally up to 40 kg
Fin formula: D XI/15−16, A III/8−9
Distribution: Along the European and western African shores of the Atlantic, in the Mediterranean and round the Canary Islands. Its northern limits are roughly level with the northern coast of Spain. Very rarely, individuals have been caught further north.

The biggest species of the family is *Promicrops lanceolatus,* which grows to a length of 3.6m and can weigh 350kg. It lives in the Indian Ocean.

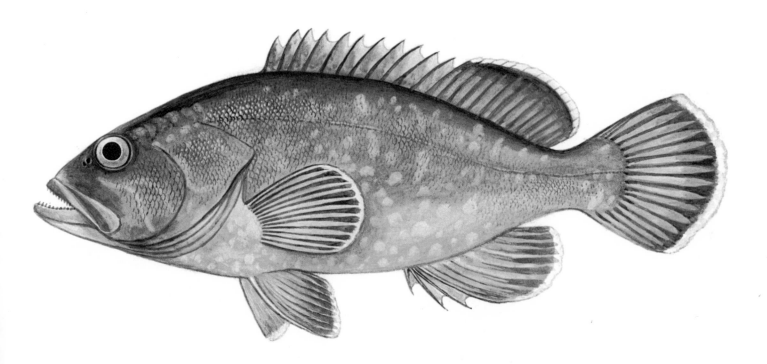

Sea Bass

Dicentrarchus labrax

In some European languages this fish is called the 'Sea Perch', an indication of its similarity to one of the best known European freshwater fishes. It can be distinguished from species of the genus *Serranus* by the presence of two dorsal fins which remain quite distinct from each other, by the position of the ventral fins which lie behind the origin of the pectoral fins and by the presence of teeth on its tongue. This is a flat-sided fish, in which the top and sides of the head are covered with cycloid scales and the operculum has two or more spiny outgrowths. The main colour of the body is silver but the back of the fish is dark grey or olive and in young specimens it is sometimes marked with black spots; in addition there is a dark spot at the back of the operculum.

Sea Bass live in the region of the continental shelf, generally in open water but also near the bottom. They mostly form small shoals which hunt together for food, usually for pilchards, in search of which they migrate during the summer. They have a life span of twenty years and over. Spawning takes place from May to August or from the end of February in the Mediterranean and off the coast of Africa, often in brackish water near river mouths. If the water is relatively fresh the eggs sink to the bottom, but in salty water they float. The larvae hatch in four to seven days; they are extremely voracious, feed rapidly and grow very quickly.

In some countries the flesh of the Sea Bass is regarded as a great delicacy. They are caught with rods and lines, or hunted underwater with harpoons; when caught in nets they form only a very small proportion of the total catch.

Commonest synonyms: Morone labrax, Perca labrax, Labrax lupus, Dicentrarchus lupus
Size: 0.8−1 m
Weight: 10−12 kg
Fin formula: D_1 VIII−X, D_2 I/12−14, A III/10−12
Fecundity: 500,000−2,000,000 eggs
Distribution: In the Atlantic Ocean off the coast of Europe and North Africa, between Tromsö in Norway in the north and Dakar in Senegal in the south; also in the Mediterranean and Black Seas.

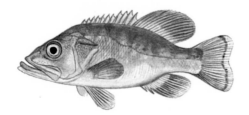

The related Stone Bass (*Polyprion americanum*) occurs from temperate to tropical seas along both shores of the Atlantic. It measures 60−100 cm (maximum 2 m) and weighs up to 40 kg.

In the family Percidae are about 100 species living in fresh and brackish water in the northern hemisphere. The fishes have two dorsal fins (except the Ruffe) and in the anal fin are one or two spiny rays. Their scales are of the ctenoid type.

Pike-perch
Stizostedion lucioperca

The Pike-perch is the biggest freshwater member of the family living in Europe. It is an active predator with a body ideally constructed for fast movement in water, a terminal mouth well supplied with teeth and two strikingly large, sharp dog-teeth in the lower jaw. Distinguishing features include an upper jaw which stretches to the posterior margin of the eye and a lateral line terminating at the base of the caudal fin. The back is greyish green, on the sides there are eight to twelve blackish brown stripes which break up into spots; spots also appear on the caudal fin and both the dorsal fins. The belly is white, although at spawning time it becomes darker, especially in the males.

This species occurs in large deep flowing rivers and lakes and in seawater creeks. It generally lies over a hard stony bed free from mud and plants, but surfaces in the morning and early evening to hunt for food, fishes of all kinds. Spawning usually occurs in April or May. The female lays the eggs on water plants and the male guards them until the young hatch out, fanning them with its fins to keep them clear of mud. The fry feed for a short time on zooplankton but soon begin to hunt the fry of other species. They consort in small shoals remaining at a safe distance from the bank, unlike Pike.

Pike-perch have a life span of 10—15 years and are one of the most valuable of European freshwater fishes, with tasty flesh of very good quality. Since they require plenty of oxygen and clean water they are disappearing from many localities or no longer breed naturally, so that their numbers have to be supplemented by artificial breeding.

Synonym: Lucioperca lucioperca
Size: 40—100 cm, maximum 130 cm
Weight: 2—10 kg, maximum 18 kg
Fin formula: D_1 XIII—XV, D_2 I—III/19—23, A II/10—13
Fecundity: 200,000—1,000,000 eggs
Distribution: Central Europe to southern Scandinavia and part of the Balkan peninsula. Has been introduced into western Europe, and the USA.

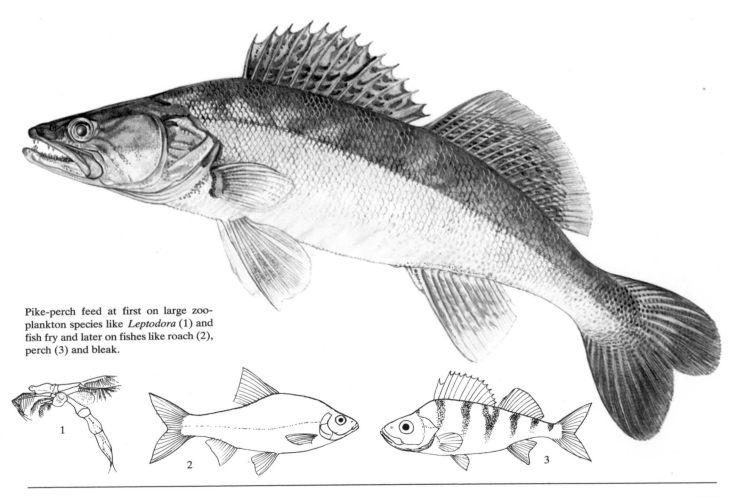

Pike-perch feed at first on large zooplankton species like *Leptodora* (1) and fish fry and later on fishes like roach (2), perch (3) and bleak.

East European Pike-perch

Stizostedion volgense

Although similar in build to the related Pike-perch, this fish is smaller and has a shorter and deeper body. Other distinguishing features include an upper jaw which does not extend beyond the middle of the eye. The scales are somewhat larger so that there are only 70−83 in the lateral line, whereas in the Pike-perch there are 80−95. The two species are very similar in colour, however, except that the East European Pike-perch has only five to seven dark stripes on its sides; they do not break up into spots and they are deeper in colour.

These fishes live in relatively shallow, slow-flowing water over a sandy or stony bed. They are active in the early evening and at night and spend most of the day in hiding-places on the bottom. They are active predators, feeding on small fishes like roach, bleak and perch; they do not hunt large fish because, like the Pike-perch, they have a narrow throat. The fry feed on zooplankton and on the larvae of aquatic insects. They become sexually mature when three to four years old, the females usually a year later than the males. They spawn in April or May in shallow water in quiet creeks and in overgrown river backwaters. Their reproduction biology has not been studied in any detail, but it seems to be similar to that of the Pike-perch.

In most places this is a relatively rare fish and is often mistaken for the Pike-perch. It has very good and tasty flesh.

Synonym: Lucioperca volgense
Size: 35−40 cm, occasionally up to 50 cm
Weight: 0.5−1.5 kg, maximum 2 kg
Fin formula: D_1 XII−XIV, D_2 I−II/20−22, A II/9−10
Distribution: In the northern tributaries of the Caspian Sea and the Black Sea from the Ural to the Danube. Mainly in fresh water, but swims from the mouth of the Volga into the adjacent parts of the Caspian Sea.

Distinguishing features of Pike-perch and European Pike-perch: The Pike-perch (1) has a scaleless preoperculum and dog-teeth, while the preoperculum of the East European Pike-perch (2) is covered with scales and its teeth are all approximately the same size.

Perch
Perca fluviatilis

This is one of the most familiar of the freshwater fishes in Britain. It has a deep, thickset body, with a triangular head and a terminal mouth well supplied with teeth. It has large eyes and two distinctly separate dorsal fins, the first of which is formed entirely of spines and has a characteristic black spot at the back. The body is very distinctively coloured, greyish green to yellowish green with a dark back and five to nine black cross bars on the sides. The belly is lighter and the pectoral, ventral, anal and caudal fins are yellowish orange to red.

Perch live in the most varied localities, in both rivers and lakes, from quiet pools in the upper reaches of rivers and streams to fishponds and reservoirs. They are most often found in places with an abundance of aquatic plants and submerged trees and roots where the shadows match their markings. They spawn in the spring, usually in April and May in fairly large shoals. The fry and young adults form large shoals by day and feed at first on plankton but later on small fish and invertebrates. The shoals break up at night and the perches lie inactive near the bottom. Only big old perches live solitary lives and do not join the shoals. In many localities perch numbers have become much too large and the consequent lack of food has resulted in slower growth in individuals and in stunted populations.

The Perch is a favourite fish with anglers, since its flesh is tasty, firm and white.

Size: 30 cm, occasionally 40 cm, maximum 50 cm
Weight: mostly 0.3−0.5 kg, rarely 1−2 kg, in isolated cases 4−5 kg
Fin formula: D_1 XIII−XVII, D_2 I−III/13−16, A II/8−9
Fecundity: 80,000−250,000 eggs/kg body weight
Distribution: In Europe and parts of Siberia, but absent from Scotland and Norway and from the southeastern European peninsulas.

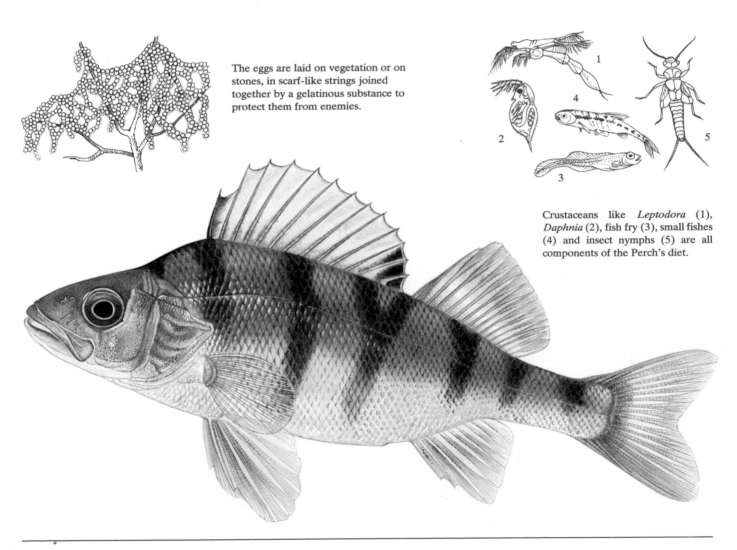

The eggs are laid on vegetation or on stones, in scarf-like strings joined together by a gelatinous substance to protect them from enemies.

Crustaceans like *Leptodora* (1), *Daphnia* (2), fish fry (3), small fishes (4) and insect nymphs (5) are all components of the Perch's diet.

Ruffe, Pope

Gymnocephalus cernua

The Ruffe has a flat-sided body and a weakly arched back with only one dorsal fin, which is, however, divided into two distinct lobes. It has a greyish green dark-spotted back and brownish sides, a yellowish white belly, slightly bluish opercula with a metallic sheen and large numbers of small dark spots on its unpaired fins. It grows very slowly and does not measure 100 mm until it is five to six years old. The males reach sexual maturity by the end of their first year, the females not until their second year. Spawning takes place in April and May and the females lay their eggs on a sandy or stony bed. The fish spawn in shoals of anything from forty to several hundred individuals at a depth of about two metres. The eggs are about one mm in diameter and are not protected by the parents. The larvae hatch in one or two weeks depending on the temperature of the water and feed on the smallest zooplankton; adult Ruffe feed on insect larvae, worms, fish fry and eggs.

These fishes live mostly near the bottom of the lower reaches of rivers, and also in fishponds and reservoirs. In some carp ponds Ruffe may form very large populations which compete with carp and other species for food. They may live in murky water since they are less dependent on vision than the Perch, for instance, when looking for food. Ruffe shun direct light and in the summer descend to greater depths when the water temperature is over 20–25 °C; they spend the winter in the mouths of big rivers, or in the deeper areas of lakes or ponds. The flesh is of very good quality.

Synonym: Acerina cernua
Size: 15–18 cm, maximum 25 cm
Weight: 100–150 g, maximum 200 g
Fin formula: D XI-XVI/11–15, A II/5–6
Fecundity: 1,000–6,000 eggs.
Distribution: In rivers of Europe and Asia from north-eastern France to Kolyma in eastern Siberia. Absent in southern peninsulas of Europe.

Distribution of two related species: *G. cernua* (blue) and *G. schraetzeri* (red).

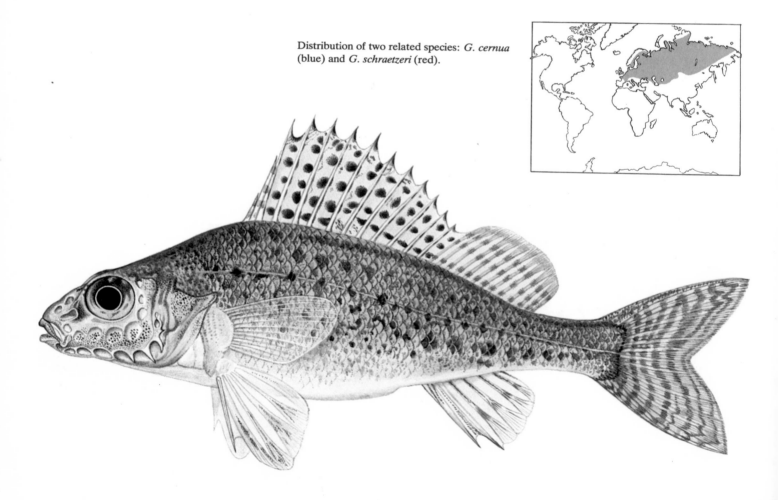

Schraetzer
Gymnocephalus schraetzer

The Schraetzer has a strikingly long, flat-sided snout and a relatively narrower body than the preceding species. It also has smaller scales, so that in the lateral line there are 55−60 scales, half as many again as in the Ruffe. The dorsal fin is longer at its anterior end than in the Ruffe and has more spiny rays; it also has regular rows of dark oval spots running along this part of the fin. The back is olive green and the sides are yellow, with three to four black and sometimes broken longitudinal stripes.

These fish live in the deeper parts of rivers with strong currents and a stony or a sandy bottom. They form small shoals which feed on insect larvae and the fry and eggs of various fishes. However the populations are never so large as to make it a serious competitor of other species, in fishponds for instance. At present no details on its reproduction are available, but its spawning habits are presumably similar in character to those of the Ruffe, except that it probably spawns in parts of the river with a stronger current. This is an economically unimportant fish and is only occasionally caught by anglers.

The related species, *G. acerina,* with a similar body to the Schraetzer, but without any cross bars on it, lives in the rivers flowing into the Black Sea. It lives in strongly flowing water and spawns in early spring; the eggs stick to the river bed. At 14 °C their development takes seven to eight days and the larvae need a further nine to ten days to digest the yolk sac before they begin to feed.

Size: 10−20 cm, maximum 24 cm
Weight: up to 150 g
Fin formula: D XVII−XIX/12−13, A II/6−7
Fecundity: 2,000−10,000 eggs
Distribution: In the Danube basin from Bavaria to the river delta.

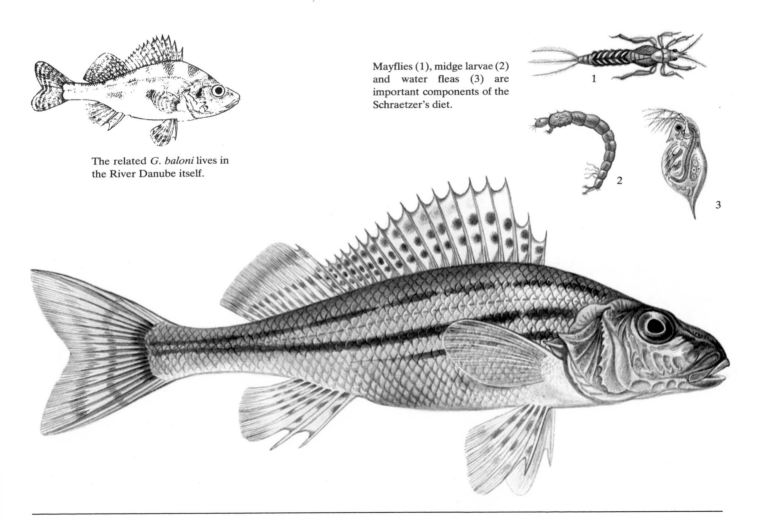

The related *G. baloni* lives in the River Danube itself.

Mayflies (1), midge larvae (2) and water fleas (3) are important components of the Schraetzer's diet.

Streber

Zingel streber

With its fusiform body, this fish closely resembles the larger Zingel, but it is longer and more slender, with a narrow peduncle. The Streber has no scales on the front of the belly, unlike the Zingel, and has fewer rays in its anal and dorsal fins than the Zingel and fewer scales in its lateral line. It is generally yellowish brown or greyish brown in colour, with four or five clearly discernible dark, oblique stripes across its body, but no dark spots.

Relatively little is known of the biology of this fish, but its habits and food are similar to those of the Zingel. However it usually lives in the deeper and faster flowing parts of small foothill rivers, in clean water which is well supplied with oxygen. It grows more slowly than the Zingel and its life span is evidently not more than five years. Spawning occurs in March and April and during that time spawning tubercles appear on the heads, bodies and pectoral fins of the fishes, in greater numbers on the males than on the females.

Zingel streber and *Z. zingel* are endemic to the Danube, but they also live in the Dnestr, the Prut and the Vardar Rivers.

This fish is of little interest to anglers and in any event its numbers are steadily declining. It is unusual amongst European percid fishes in that it lives in fast flowing water. It is found only in a few headstreams of rivers in central Europe and because of its rarity should be fully protected.

Synonym: Aspro streber
Size: 12–17.5 cm
Weight: up to 170 g
Fin formula: D_1 VII–IX, D_2 I–III/10–13, A I/10–11
Fecundity: 600–4,200 eggs
Distribution: In the catchment areas of Danube, Dnester, Vardar and Prut Rivers.

The related *Z. asper* in the Rhône has a shorter peduncle than *Z. streber* and measures about 25 cm.

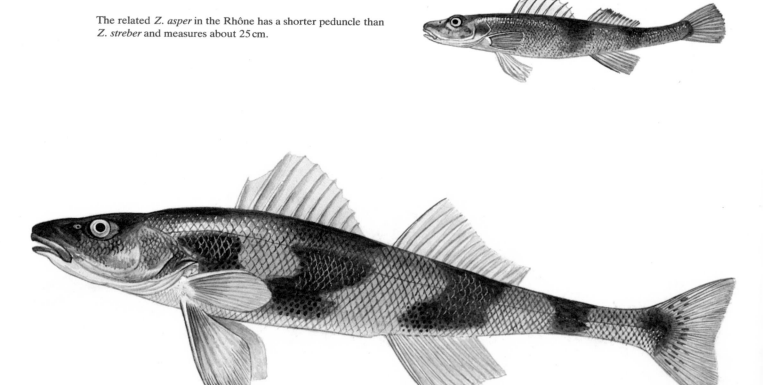

Zingel
Zingel zingel

This perch has an elongate, fusiform body almost circular in cross section, with an inferior mouth and a protruding snout. The body, including part of the head and the front of its belly, is covered with rough ctenoid scales. Its two dorsal fins are relatively far apart and the first is entirely formed of spines. It is yellowish grey in colour, with a brownish tinge on the back and small dark spots over the whole body. There are also four dark cross bars across the sides of the fish but they are often rather indistinct.

These fishes are found only in the main channels of the central European rivers where they live and where there is a strong current and a gravelly or sandy river bed. They seldom approach the bank, but move along the bottom in short 'hops'. During the day they hide away in potholes and under stones and only come out to search for food after dusk, feeding on benthic invertebrates and small fish. At spawning time in April or May, the females lay large, sticky eggs on the gravelly bottom. According to some sources they actually bury the eggs in the same manner as salmonids.

In recent years the numbers of Zingel have diminished, evidently as a result of pollution, and they are now on the list of endangered species. Because of their rarity and their nocturnal habits they are caught only occasionally by anglers. The flesh is said to have a good flavour.

Synonym: Aspro zingel
Size: 30−40 cm, exceptionally up to 45 cm
Weight: up to 1 kg
Fin formula: D_1 XIII−XV, D_2 I/18−20, A I/11−14
Fecundity: 500−5,000 eggs
Distribution: In the basins of the Dnester and the Danube, but not abundant.

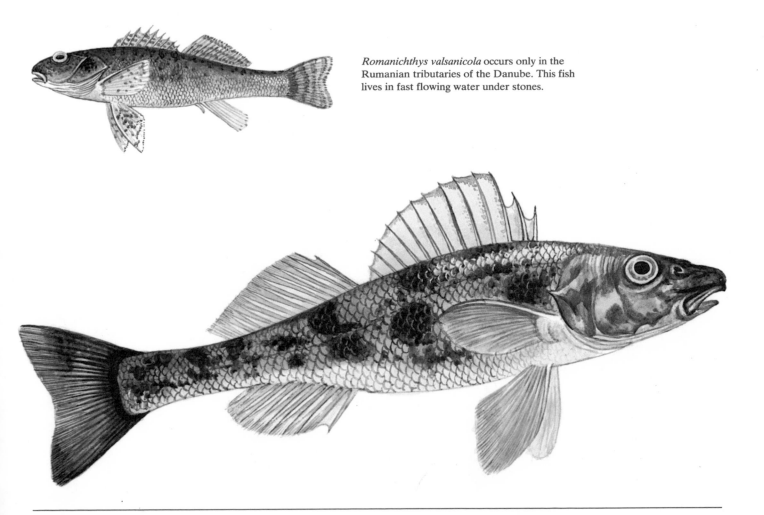

Romanichthys valsanicola occurs only in the Rumanian tributaries of the Danube. This fish lives in fast flowing water under stones.

The thirty-two members of the family Centrarchidae are freshwater fishes, commonly known as sunfishes. They have a single dorsal fin which is narrower at the front than at the back and their scales extend over much of the operculum and cheek. They have high, flat-sided bodies. Although they come originally from North America a number of species have been introduced into Europe. They are all predators and feed on other fishes or invertebrates.

CENTRARCHIDAE

Largemouth Bass
Micropterus salmoides

This species was imported into Europe at the end of the last century from its original home in the Mississippi basin and the Great Lakes of North America. In build it has the appearance of a robust perch. Characteristic features include the form of the dorsal fin, the anterior part of which is distinctly lower than the hind part. This is composed of branched rays and is clearly separated from the front part by a deep cleft. The corners of the large mouth stretch as far as the rear margins of the eyes and the fish has many teeth. Ten rows of rough scales are present on the operculum. The body of the fish is mainly greenish, usually with gleaming gold or silvery green sides and a yellowish white belly. In the adult fish a dark band runs from the eye to the base of the

tail, the body is covered with dark spots and there is always a large black spot at the end of the operculum. However, the colouring is variable.

This species was introduced into lowland rivers of Europe for fishermen, but expectations have not been altogether fulfilled, since the bass does not grow to the same proportions in Europe as it does in North America and what is worse, it competes with native predatory species for food. Under European conditions it matures when three to four years old and generally spawns between May and July. Like the Pike-perch, the male prepares a nest 30—90 cm in diameter in the lake or river bed, lures several females to it and guards the nest until the larvae swim away. In addition to aquatic insects and fish, Largemouth Bass feed on frogs and tadpoles.

Size: 30—35 cm, occasionally up to 50 cm
Weight: 1—2.5 kg (in Europe),
Fin formula: D X—XI/12—13, A III/10—11
Fecundity: 30,000—60,000 eggs/kg body weight
Distribution: In the Danube basin and most of the countries of western Europe; introduced into Great Britain in 1934.

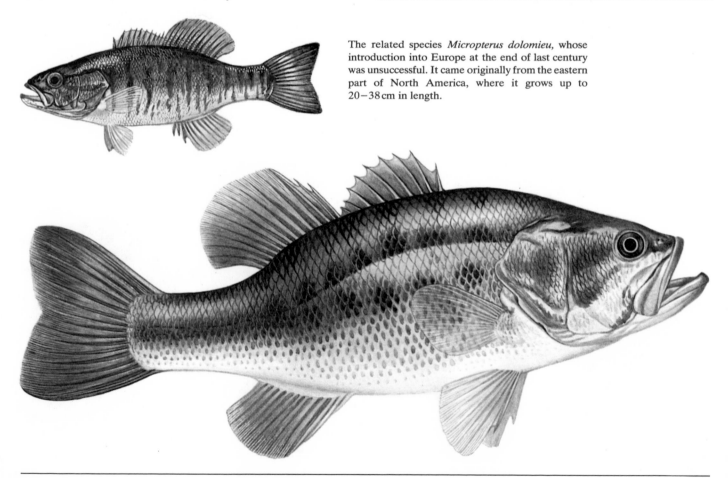

The related species *Micropterus dolomieu,* whose introduction into Europe at the end of last century was unsuccessful. It came originally from the eastern part of North America, where it grows up to 20—38 cm in length.

Pumpkin-seed Sunfish
Lepomis gibbosus

Manifestly the most brightly coloured freshwater fish living in Europe, the Pumpkin-seed Sunfish keeps its colouring the whole year round. It has a deep but rounded body with a long dorsal fin, flattened sides and large scales. Its back is usually olive green in colour and its sides are bluish, with round orange or reddish brown spots. Luminous blue to bluish green undulating longitudinal stripes are present on its opercula, each of which has a long, posteriorly directed process marked with a very conspicuous red, dark-bordered spot. Its belly is pink to orange.

These sunfish are found chiefly in shallow, overgrown areas of rivers and lakes, with still clean or gently flowing water. They feed on plankton, benthic invertebrates and fish fry. The fish become sexually mature when three to four years old and spawn in May and June. After first clearing the bottom of rubbish the male excavates a shallow nest some 20–40 cm in diameter. The nests often form small, loosely connected colonies. While building the nest and for some time after, the male energetically drives away all other fishes, including females of its own kind. After a time the attacks on the females grow milder until finally the males begin to drive the females towards the nests instead of away from them. During spawning the female lies in the nest on her side under the male, and with vibrating bodies the fish release eggs and milt at short intervals. Spawning usually takes 15–30 minutes and when it is over the male again drives the female away and guards the nest until the young are hatched.

Size: 15–20 cm, maximum 25 cm
Weight: 0.2–0.3 kg, maximum 0.5 kg
Fin formula: D X/10–13, A III/10–12
Fecundity: 500–5,000 eggs
Distribution: Originally from the eastern part of North America. Because of their attractive colouring these sunfish were imported into Europe for ornamental ponds and aquaria at the end of the last century. They have found their way into open water and now occur locally throughout much of Europe, including the British Isles.

The related species *Amploplites rupestris,* also introduced into Europe, comes originally from the eastern part of North America, where it grows up to 30 cm long and weighs up to 0.5 kg. Like the rest of the family the male builds a nest at spawning time.

Members of the family Bramidae are fishes with deep bodies and long dorsal and anal fins. There are no spines on these fins but the anterior few rays may be unbranched. There are about ten species frequenting the open sea; they are known as Dolphin Breams.

Ray's Bream

Brama brama

This fish has a deep, flat-sided body, long dorsal and anal fins and a deeply concave tail fin. It has a greyish blue back with greyish green sides and its belly has a silvery blue lustre. The pectoral fins and the eyes are both gold-bordered; the dorsal and anal fins are dark. These bream live mostly in the upper and middle layers of the open sea at depths of 100–300m, deeper in northern waters. Spawning occurs at a temperature of about 20 °C; fry have been found at depths of up to 2,700m in both the Mediterranean and the middle of the Atlantic. The bream feed chiefly on small shoal-forming fishes. In western Europe dead specimens are sometimes found washed up on the shore by the autumn tides and individuals occasionally appear in the catches of North Sea trawlers; in the Mediterranean they are seen more frequently.

The flesh of this bream is often attacked by parasitic worms, which reduce its commercial value. At the end of the winter and the beginning of the spring, a special hunt for dolphin bream is organized off the western coast of the Iberian Peninsula, when hundreds of small boats lay out long lines with hooks going down to depths of 90–110m. The hauls are sometimes very good, with catches of up to 60–70 bream per 100 hooks.

Synonym: Brama rayi
Size: 65–70 cm, maximum 80 cm
Weight: 2–4 kg, maximum 6 kg
Fin formula: D iii–v/30–33, A ii–iii/27–30
Distribution: In the Mediterranean, in the northeastern Atlantic from Scandinavia to Madeira and in the seas around Iceland.

Main components of the diet of this bream: Shad (1), Herring (2), Mackerel (3).

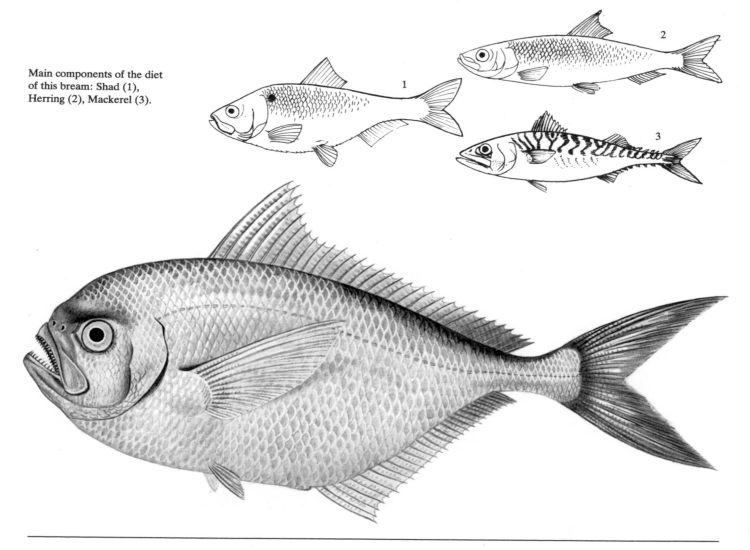

The family Centracanthidae contains two genera with a total of seven species distributed along the eastern shores of the Atlantic. They have elongate bodies with slightly compressed sides.

Caramel
Spicara alcedo

This is a small perch-like fish with a narrow elongate body. It has a greyish brown to blue-grey back and its sides are marked with lighter-coloured wide cross bars, especially at spawning time in the females. In the males the silvery blue spots and stripes on the sides of the body and head are accentuated at this time. There is a striking dark spot on each side above the end of the pectoral fin.

This fish is found in coastal waters, usually amongst growths of seaweed and eelgrass on a sandy or muddy sea bed. Spawning occurs in daylight hours from April to July; the males excavate dish-like nests in the bottom with their caudal fins and the fertilized eggs adhere to the sand or mud. Like all members of this genus, *S. alcedo* changes its sex during the course of its lifetime. Practically all the fry develop at first as females which become sexually mature by the end of their first year. By the time they are three years old, when they measure 13—15 cm, they have changed sex, so that fish measuring more than 16 cm in length are virtually all males.

This species provides the best eating of all the family and consequently it is fished extensively in the Mediterranean and also in the Black Sea, along with other *Spicara* species; it is only of minor economic importance, however.

Commonest synonym: Maena smaris
Size: 14—16 cm (females), up to 20 cm (males)
Weight: 50—120 g
Fecundity: 2,500—12,000 eggs
Fin formula: D X—XII/9—12, A III/8—10
Distribution: In the Mediterranean and the Black Sea and in the Atlantic off the coasts of Spain and Portugal.

The related species *S. maena* from the Black Sea, the Mediterranean and the adjacent part of the Atlantic. It has a conspicuously deep body and grows to a length of 25 cm. At spawning time the males excavate nests up to half a metre in diameter in a sandy seabed.

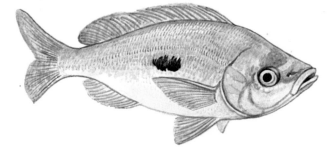

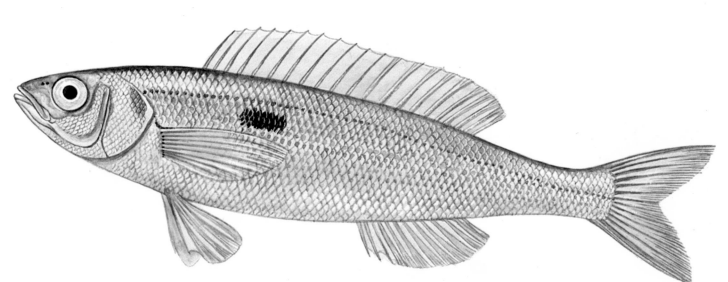

Deep-bodied Pickerel

Spicara smaris

In form and habits this fish is very similar to *S. alcedo,* but there are differences in colouring. The back of this fish is greyish brown to dark yellowish brown, while its sides are lighter and yellowish in shade, with longitudinal blue stripes. On each side, above the end of the pectoral fin, there is a conspicuous dark spot and sometimes a few faintly discernible cross bars; blue spots are present on the dorsal and anal fins. The colouring is intensified at spawning time.

This fish lives in coastal waters in similar localities to *S. alcedo,* but it also lives in estuaries. The reproduction biology of the two species is similar, but this species undertakes spawning and food migrations during the year, mostly in the spring and autumn. The fishes spend the winter in deeper water, so that once the temperature of the water falls below 10 °C they are no longer found near the shore. They feed on animals of the zooplankton, mainly on copepods and also on small benthic animals.

The question of synonyms in the genus *Spicara* is very complicated, since in the past sex-related and seasonal colour differences were often taken to indicate specific differences and consequently the same species were described by different authors under different names. The situation was further complicated by the sex change from female fish to functional male which occurs part way through the lifespan before scientists realized that this process was happening.

Commonest synonyms: Spicara flexuosa, Maena chryselis
Size: 13–16 cm (females), 15–20 cm (males)
Weight: 50–100 g
Fin formula: D X–XII/10–12, A III/8–10
Fecundity: 1,000–10,500 eggs (according to other sources 6,000–63,000)
Distribution: In the Mediterranean, the Black Sea and the Sea of Azov, in the Atlantic Ocean in the area off the west coast of the Iberian Peninsula.

The most widespread of the *Spicara* species is *S. smaris* (distribution in blue). Two others are found only in the western end of the Black Sea (distribution shown in red).

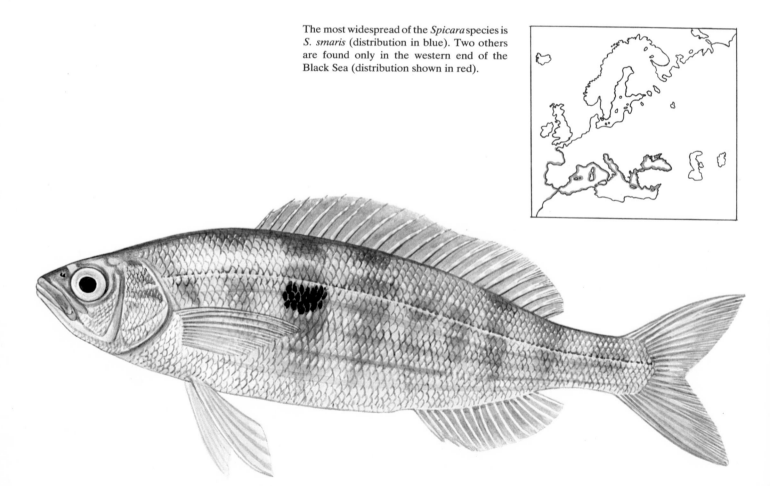

The members of the family Carangidae have a distinctive fin pattern with a short first dorsal fin and long second dorsal and anal fins. There are a total of about 200 marine species in the family, mostly living in tropical waters.

Scad, Horse Mackerel
Trachurus trachurus

A slender, flat-sided fish with a large head and a distinctive curving lateral line bordered by bony plates, a feature characteristic of horse mackerels. These become heavier towards the posterior end of the body where they are surmounted by sharp recurved spines. The Scad is one of six horse mackerel species found off the European coast. It is predominantly greyish blue in colour, tinged with yellow on the head, pectoral fins and caudal fin.

This is a pelagic species, living mainly in open water over the continental shelf, where it forms large shoals and undertakes long migrations. At the beginning of the summer Scad migrate northwards in search of food and when the temperatures drop later in the year they move southwards again. Young fish feed primarily on planktonic crustaceans and fish eggs, but after the first year the diet changes to small fish like cod and pilchards, larger crustaceans and squid. In the temperate belt they spawn in the summer, in tropical waters intermittently throughout the year. Scad are commercially important fishes and in recent years the total annual catch has varied from 120,000 to 250,000 tons. They have tasty flesh.

Commonest synonyms: Scomber trachurus, Caranx trachurus
Size: mostly 25–30 cm, in exceptional cases up to 50 cm
Weight: up to 1.5 kg
Fin formula: D_1 VIII, D_2 I/28, A II/23–29
Fecundity: 30,000–130,000 eggs
Distribution: In the eastern part of the Atlantic from Trondheim in Norway in the north, south to South Africa, in the Mediterranean and the Black Seas and in the western part of the Atlantic along the Argentinian and Brazilian coasts.

The related species *T. capensis* is sometimes regarded as only a subspecies of *T. trachurus*. It lives off the coast of Africa from the equator in the west to Mozambique in the east. It usually grows up to 25–35 cm in length, reaching a maximum of 50 cm.

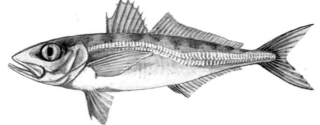

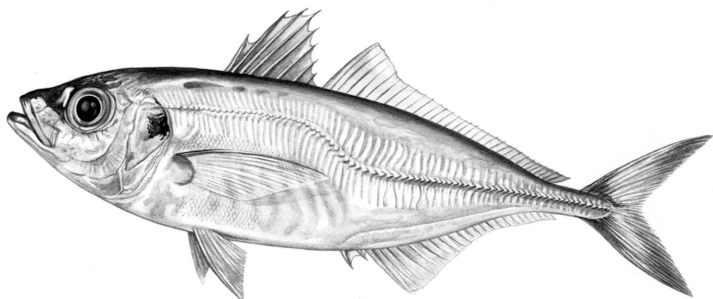

Mediterranean Scad
Trachurus mediterraneus

The Mediterranean Scad resembles the Scad in colouring, shape and size, but the bony scutes covering its curving lateral line are much smaller and there are between 78 and 92 present, in contrast to the Scad where there are only 70−80 scutes present. Like the Scad, Mediterranean Scad undertake long seasonal migrations in search of food. When young they feed on zooplankton, when adult chiefly on small fishes. In the Black Sea for instance, young anchovies and gobies are amongst the most frequent prey species.

Mediterranean Scad become sexually mature when two years old and in the Mediterranean and Black Sea spawning goes on intermittently from May to August, usually during the evening. Young fish up to one year old often take shelter in large numbers under the 'umbrellas' of medusae (in particular of the species *Rhizostoma pulmo*), where they are safe from enemies. In the Black Sea there are two races of Mediterranean Scad (one small, the other larger), which live in separate shoals and also differ in respect of their fecundity and longevity (the members of the smaller race usually live between seven and eight years and those of the larger race 13−14 years). The fry and small individuals are a favourite prey of piscivorous birds like seagulls.

Size: 30−40 cm, occasionally up to 55 cm
Weight: 1−2 kg
Fin formula: D_1 VIII, D_2 I/26−34, A II/21−31
Fecundity: 100,000−200,000 eggs in the small race; 100,000−2,000,000 eggs in the large race
Distribution: In the Mediterranean and the Black Sea, off the coast of western Europe and in the North Sea.

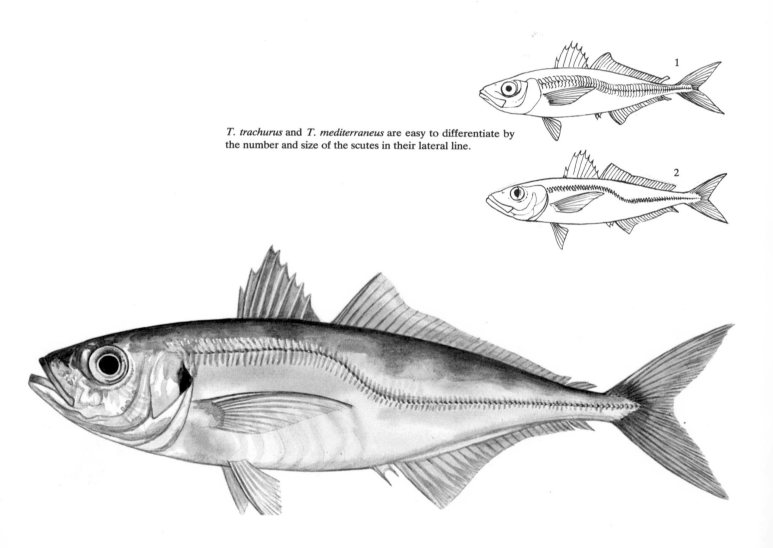

T. trachurus and *T. mediterraneus* are easy to differentiate by the number and size of the scutes in their lateral line.

Pilot-fish
Naucrates ductor

Pilot-fish live in all the warm oceans, also in the Mediterranean and Black Seas but seldom stray into colder waters, venturing only as far north as the British Isles. They go on long migrations and their small shoals may accompany sharks, whales and ships over long distances, giving the fish their name. This habit has been explained in various ways. The prevailing view is that the fish feed on the remains of the sharks' prey or on garbage from the ships, but this theory seems to be disproved by the fact that the stomachs of netted pilot-fish mostly contain small fish. Other experts have suggested a commensal role for the Pilot-fish — they keep the sharks clear of parasites and avoid attack by their agility. Yet another explanation is that sharks, whales and ships act as carriers for the eggs of the Pilot-fish, which they attach to them by sticky processes. Spawning occurs in the summer.

The larvae and fry look completely different from the adult fish and have on occasion mistakenly been described as an altogether separate species. They are frequently found in association with seaweeds or jellyfish.

An adult Pilot-fish has a torpedo-shaped body rounded in cross section. The sides of the head are covered with scales. It can be immediately recognised by its colouring — the body is basically greyish blue with a silvery underside and there are between five and seven dark cross bars banding the fish. There are two short spines in front of the anal fin and four similar spines in front of the dorsal.

Synonym: Gasterosteus ductor
Size: 30—50 cm, maximum 70 cm
Weight: 0.5—1.5 kg, occasionally up to 2.5 kg
Fin formula: D III—V + I—II/26—28, A II + I/16—18
Distribution: Cosmopolitan.

Naucrates ductor derives its common name from its habit of accompanying sharks and other large fish in shoals.

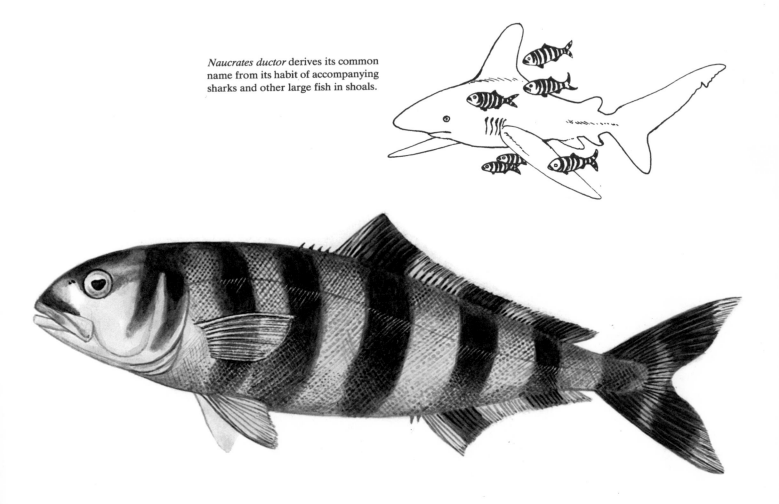

The Bluefish is placed in a genus and family of its own, the Pomatomidae. It is thought to be related to members of the families Carangidae and Serranidae.

Bluefish
Pomatomus saltatrix

This predatory pelagic fish is over one metre long when adult. The body and the sides of its head are covered with tiny cycloid scales; the jaws and palate are armed with strong, sharp teeth. The first dorsal fin is shorter and narrower than the second and is formed of hard spines. The Bluefish has a greenish to greenish grey back and silvery sides and belly below the lateral line. At the base of each pectoral fin there is a dark spot.

Bluefish live mostly in large shoals in the open sea where they pursue the various pelagic fishes which are the main source of their food. In some years they also appear in large numbers near the shore. The shoals go on relatively long food migrations appearing to migrate northwards in the summer and to return to lower latitudes in the autumn. Spawning occurs in the spring and summer, probably in the open sea; the eggs are pelagic. The fry at first remain in deep water feeding on crustaceans and molluscan larvae, but when they measure about 10 cm they swim closer inshore and from then on begin to feed on the fry of other fishes.

Bluefish are quite important to the fishing industry, especially along the Atlantic coast of America, where they are caught with dragnets. The total annual catch varies from 30,000 to 40,000 tons. They are also caught by anglers and skin divers with rods and lines and with harpoons.

Commonest synonyms: Perca saltatrix, Temnodon saltator
Size: 60—90 cm, maximum 120 cm
Weight: up to 12—15 kg, occasionally 25 kg
Fecundity: 100,000—200,000 eggs (according to some sources up to 1,200,000 eggs)
Distribution: In tropical and subtropical waters of the Atlantic, Pacific and Indian Oceans.

Distribution map of *P. saltatrix*

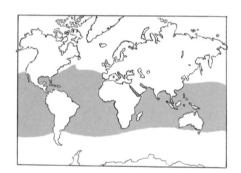

The family Sciaenidae or drum-fishes contains mainly perch-like fishes, all with long dorsal fins divided by a deep notch into two parts; the front part of this fin is short, high and triangular while the hind part is somewhat lower and much longer. A characteristic feature shared by these fishes is the deep booming sounds they produce from the vibrations of special muscles connected with the swim-bladder. The sounds are effectively amplified by the swim-bladder and are so loud that they can be heard above the surface. The 150 members of the family are all marine fishes living in tropical and temperate seas, although some of them may be found in the mouths of large rivers.

SCIAENIDAE

Brown Meagre
Sciaena umbra

The Brown Meagre is a relatively large fish, with a characteristically arched body and flat belly. It is mainly dark grey to yellowish green in colour with a lighter belly. The first rays of its otherwise dark ventral and anal fins are white. This fish lives in coastal waters usually at depths of between two and ten metres, but occasionally deeper, hiding amongst seaweeds growing over stony sea beds. It feeds on crabs, molluscs and small fishes and spawns during the summer.

The economic importance of this fish is virtually nil and although its flesh is quite tasty it is not as popular as the flesh of other related species. The Brown Meagre is popular with harpoon fishermen, however, since when hit it puts up a brave fight.

Synonym: Johnius umbra
Size: 30–50 cm, maximum 70 cm
Weight: 1–2 kg, exceptionally up to 4 kg
Fin formula: D X–XI/22–25, A II/6–8
Distribution: Along the west coasts of Europe and Africa from the Bay of Biscay to the equator, in the Mediterranean and the Black Sea.

The related species *S. hololepidotus* measures 70–150 cm and has a maximum weight of 50 kg. It lives in the Mediterranean Sea and in the Atlantic Ocean along the coast of Africa as far south as Angola.

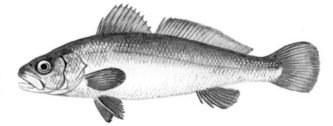

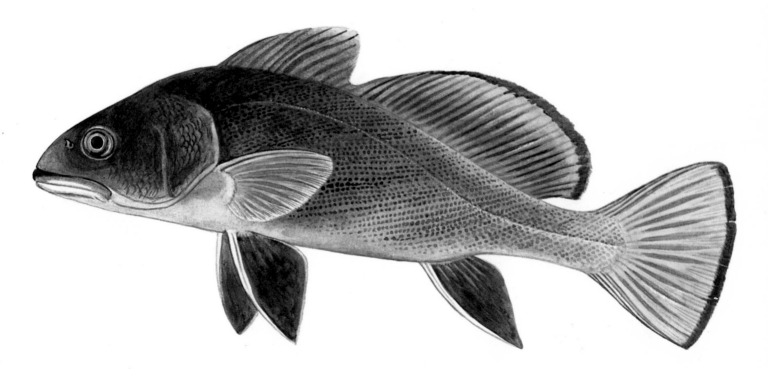

Drumfish
Sciaena cirrosa

This fish has a similar form to the Brown Meagre, but is quite differently coloured, since its greyish blue body is marked with characteristic golden orange stripes leading obliquely downwards and forwards. The fins also have a golden orange tinge. There is a short, thick barbel on the lower jaw, another characteristic feature.

This species lives in coastal waters; adults are found over a soft, muddy or sandy seabed overgrown by aquatic vegetation, down to depth of about 100 m, whereas juveniles are frequently found in brackish water in the mouths of rivers. It feeds chiefly on molluscs and small fishes. Spawning takes place in the summer months, sometimes continuing into the autumn; when the temperature falls the fish retire to deeper water.

These fish are occasionally caught commercially or for sport with rods and lines or harpoons, but they are not economically important; they are generally caught at depths of about 150 m. The related South American species *Sciaena canosai* is a commercially important fish in Argentina.

Synonym: Umbrina cirrosa
Size: 30–70 cm, maximum over 1 m
Weight: 1–4 kg, maximum over 20 kg
Fin formula: D_1 X–XI, D_2 II/21–23, A II/7
Distribution: In the Mediterranean, Black and Red Seas, European and African coasts of the Atlantic Ocean from the Bay of Biscay to Guinea.

Distribution map of *S. umbra* (red) and *S. cirrosa* (blue).

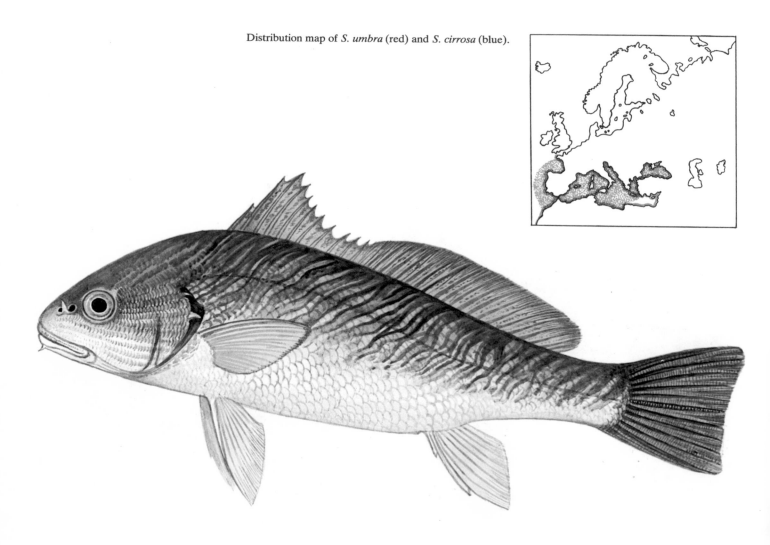

The family Sparidae contains mostly tropical and subtropical species, the largest number occurring in the eastern part of the Atlantic. These 'sea breams' all live on the continental shelf and they range in size from 15 cm to 1.5 m. All have a single long dorsal fin with a front portion composed of several strong spines and the anal fin always has three strong spines at the front. Some species are of considerable economic significance.

Common Dentex
Dentex dentex

There are about fifteen species of moderately large to large fish in the genus *Dentex*. The Common Dentex is a robustly built fish with a large head and a large mouth with four to six large pointed teeth in front and small, similar-shaped teeth behind. Mature males have a large hump behind the eyes and, apart from the forehead, the head is completely covered with small ctenoid scales. The fish has a greyish blue back with silvery, blue-spotted sides and a light-coloured belly. The dorsal fin is light bluish yellow and the pectoral fins have a reddish tinge. Adults have a large yellow spot on the operculum.

Little is known of the biology of these large fish, which grow to a length of over one metre. They live in smallish shoals over rocky sea beds at depths of about 200 m. In the spring they swim shorewards to shallower water, returning seawards in the winter months. They are predators and actively hunt other fishes. The flesh is very tasty, but the fish are seldom seen in fishmarkets owing to the comparative rarity of this species.

Synonym: Dentex vulgaris
Size: up to 1 m, maximum 1.4 m
Weight: up to 10 kg
Fin formula: D XI/11, A III/8
Distribution: In the Mediterranean and the Black Sea and in the Atlantic from Cape Verde to Brittany.

The smaller related species *D. macrophthalmus* lives in the same area as *D. dentex*. It measures up to 25 cm (maximum 40 cm) and has strikingly large eyes and small scales.

Ringed Sea Bream
Diplodus annularis

One of the smaller Sea Bream, this fish has a robust, relatively deep body with an arched back which slants down steeply towards its snout. The single dorsal fin runs along more than half its back, but the anal fin is much shorter. There are eight sharp cutting teeth in both jaws, together with large, rounded teeth behind for crushing. The sides of the fish are a light yellowish brown with a silvery sheen; the back is darker with a golden lustre. On either side of the peduncle there is a large black spot.

As in many other members of the family Sparidae, the gonads contain both male and female germ cells. In some individuals the male germ cells mature first, the female cells later. The greater part of the population is unisexual, however. Spawning takes place intermittently from June to September on warm evenings in coastal waters. The eggs are pelagic and the larvae remain in the surface layers of the water at a depth of between 10−12 metres. The fry descend deeper, to the sea bed, where they can find sand or empty mollusc shells; by October they measure 30−50mm. Adult fish feed on algae, diatoms, sponges, polychaete worms and shrimps.

Diplodus annularis is a fish of coastal waters, living close inshore in summer and swimming out to deeper water in the winter. They often hide amongst seaweeds. Its economic significance is very small, but individuals may be caught locally by anglers.

Synonyms: Sparus annularis, Sargus annularis
Size: 7−14cm, maximum 35 cm
Fin formula: D X−XI/11−12, A III/10−11
Distribution: In the Atlantic Ocean from southern France to Cape Verde, the Mediterranean and the Black Sea.

The distribution of all three *Diplodus* species is very similar. In the Black Sea *D. annularis* is the most widespread; the other two are found only occasionally in its western part.

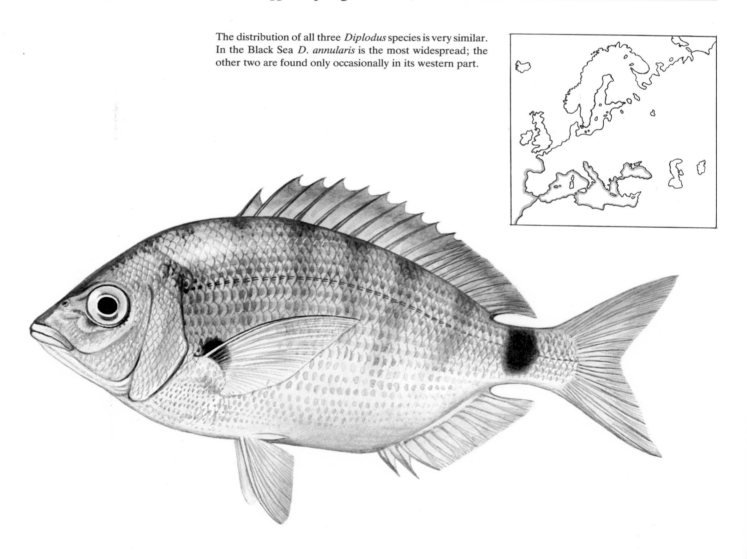

White Sea Bream

Diplodus sargus

A deeper-bodied fish than *D. annularis*, with more scales in its lateral line, over 60 compared with less than 55, and more rays in its dorsal and anal fins than the previous species. Its teeth are similar to those of *D. annularis*. It has silvery grey or sometimes golden sides with eight or nine dark cross bars, a dark-bordered caudal fin and grey ventral fins. There is a large dark spot on the back of the peduncle which extends down on to either side.

These sea bream live at depths of between two and twenty metres in inshore brackish waters along the European and African Atlantic coasts. They feed on algae, shrimps, molluscs and other fishes. They are hermaphrodite, developing first as males and later as females. The fish spawn from April to June on a rocky sea bed, especially where there is a dense growth of seaweed. The fry form small shoals, living in brackish waters and lagoons in the spring and summer, returning to the sea in the autumn; old fish live solitary lives.

Economically they are unimportant, but they are occasionally caught by anglers or may appear in fishermens' nets.

Size: 20–30 cm, maximum 45 cm
Weight: maximum 2 kg
Fin formula: D XI–XII/12–15, A III/12–14
Distribution: Along the European and African shores of the Atlantic Ocean, from southern France in the north to Angola in the south, in the Mediterranean Sea and the Black Sea.

The related species *D. vulgaris* grows to a length of 30 cm and is distinguished by two wide, dark cross bars — one at operculum level and the other at the base of the tail. It lives in shallow inshore waters, where it feeds on bottom-living animals and also on algae.

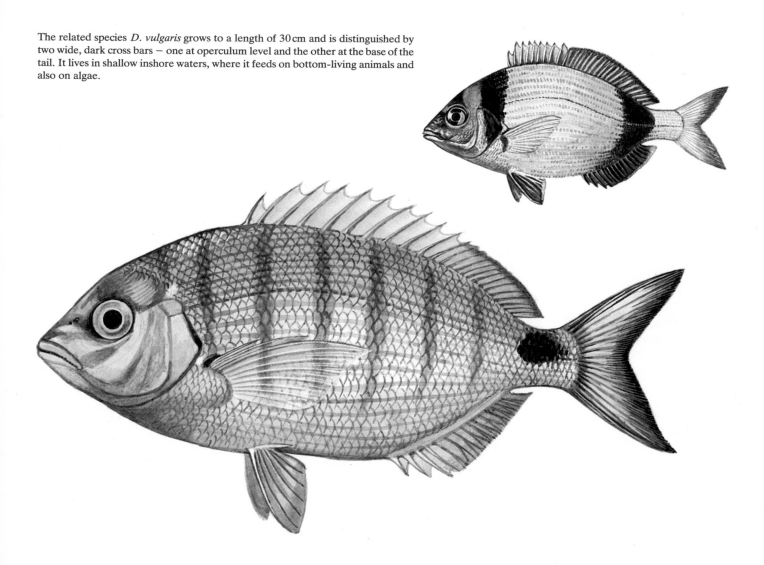

Bogue
Boops boops

The Bogue has an elongate body with rounded sides. It has strikingly large eyes and characteristic teeth which are notched like a saw. The related *Sarpa salpa* has a deeper flatter-sided body, smaller eyes and only 11 spiny rays in its dorsal fin (*B. boops* has over 13). The Bogue has an olive yellow, sometimes greenish back, lighter yellowish sides with a silvery sheen, a silvery white belly and three or four golden gleaming bands on the sides below the lateral line.

These sea bream live along the European shores of the Atlantic as far north as Britain and northern Scandinavia, along the west coast of Africa to Cape Verde and Angola; they also live in the Mediterranean, the Black Sea and the North Sea. They are most common in the Mediterranean, where they live in shoals of upwards of 100 individuals which remain near the shore, in water down to 150 m deep, where there is a sandy sea bed. In the North Sea and the Black Sea they are rare. In the Mediterranean spawning occurs in April; sexually mature individuals measure 12–15 cm. The gonads contain both male and female sections, but only one part develops to maturity. In the Black Sea eggs can still be found in July, August and September. The fish feed on algae, encrusting sponges and crustaceans.

These fishes are of economic significance only in the Mediterranean.

Synonym: Box boops, Sparus boops
Size: 20–30 cm, maximum 60 cm
Fin formula: D XIII–XIV/14–17, A III/16–17
Distribution: The European and African shores of the Atlantic Ocean.

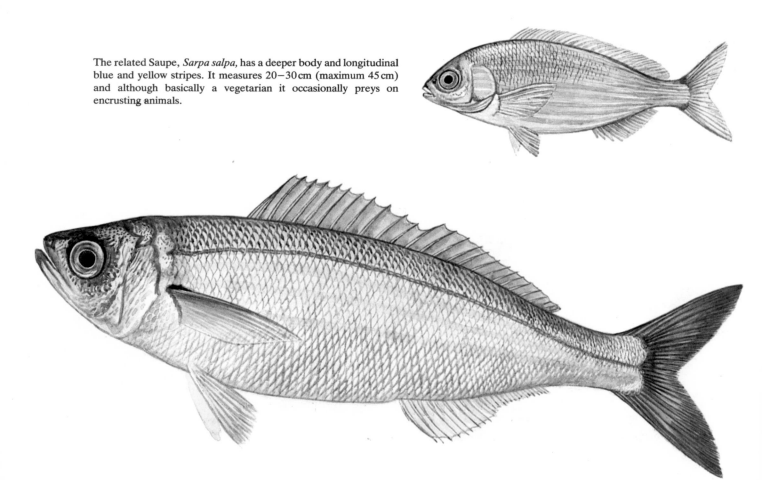

The related Saupe, *Sarpa salpa,* has a deeper body and longitudinal blue and yellow stripes. It measures 20–30 cm (maximum 45 cm) and although basically a vegetarian it occasionally preys on encrusting animals.

Common Pandora
Pagellus erythrinus

In form, this species closely resembles the related Spanish Bream, *P. bogaraveo,* but it has a larger, somewhat more slanting head and smaller eyes, two to five soft rays fewer in its anal fin and longer pectoral fins, the rays of which stretch as far as or slightly beyond the origin of the anal fin. The teeth at the front of the mouth are pointed, but in the angles of the jaw there are a few molar-like teeth. The scales on the head extend to the anterior edge of the eyes. The upper half of the body is red, the lower half silvery pink and here and there on the back and on the upper half of the sides there are flashing bluish green spots. The inside of the mouth is black.

This species is common in the coastal waters of the Mediterranean and Black Seas and also in the Bay of Biscay, from which it migrates northwards in the summer. It occurs in the vicinity of the British Isles and has occasionally been found off the southern coast of Norway. In the south it extends along the coast of Africa as far as Angola. At present little is known of its biology. In European waters it generally keeps well out to sea in the winter and swims shorewards in the spring. It is found most often over a sandy or clay sea bed at depths of 10–120 m, but has also been seen over rocks. It is a hermaphrodite; during the first years of its life it functions as a female and later as a male. In the Mediterranean it spawns from the spring to the end of the summer, with a peak period in July and August. The fry collect together in shoals in shallow water. These fish feed mainly on crustaceans, molluscs and bottom-dwelling fishes.

Common Pandora are fished off the coast of Africa and on a smaller scale in the Mediterranean, mainly with dragnets. The flesh is of moderately good quality and the total annual catch is in the region of 25,000–30,000 tons.

Commonest synonyms: *Sparus erythrinus, Pagellus bellotti*
Size: 20–30 cm, maximum 55–60 cm
Weight: 1–2 kg, occasionally up to 5 kg
Fin formula: D XII/9–11, A III/8–10
Distribution: Off the European and African shores of the Atlantic, in the Black Sea and the Mediterranean.

The related species *P. mormyrus* is found in coastal waters between the Bay of Biscay and Angola and also occurs in the Mediterranean and the Black Sea. It grows to a length of 20–40 cm (maximum 50 cm) and is strikingly striped. It is often described under the generic name *Lithognathus*.

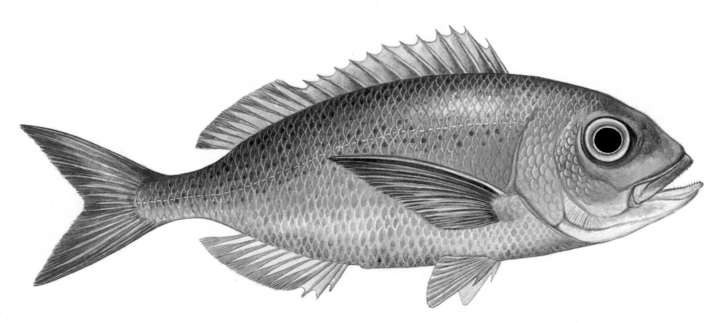

Spanish Bream
Pagellus bogaraveo

This sea bream has a relatively small head but large eyes whose diameter is greater than the length of its snout. Scales cover the top of the head as far as the middle of the eyes. Its pectoral fins are long, but do not reach the origin of the anal fin as they do in the Pandora, *P. erythrinus*. They have similar teeth however, curved front teeth which are sharp and not very long and two or three rows of small, rounded teeth on the sides of the jaws. The back and fins of the fish are pink to reddish orange in colour, the sides are lighter and the belly is silvery, sometimes with a trace of blue. At the origin of the pectoral fin and the upper edge of the operculum there is a small dark spot, especially in old individuals; the roots of the rays of the deeply cleft tail fin are dark. Young fish are lighter in colour than older ones.

The fry can be seen and caught in inshore waters, swimming close to a stony sea bed, at depths of about 30−40 m. The adult fish live further from the shore, at depths of 100−300 m, either pelagically or near the bottom. They feed on crustaceans when young, or on various species of fish when older. Little is known of their reproduction or of their mode of life in general. In the seas south of England they spawn at the end of the summer, in the southern parts of their range somewhat earlier.

In the Bay of Biscay and the Mediterranean, Spanish Bream may form a substantial part of dragnet catches; they are also caught with rods and lines. The fish has white and very tasty flesh.

Commonest synonym: Sparus bogaraveo
Size: 30−35 cm, maximum 50 cm
Weight: 1−2 kg, occasionally up to 4.5 kg
Fin formula: D XII−XIII/11−12, A III/11−12
Distribution: Coasts of the Atlantic Ocean from southern Norway to Dakar in Africa, the Mediterranean.

Distribution map of *P. bogaraveo*.

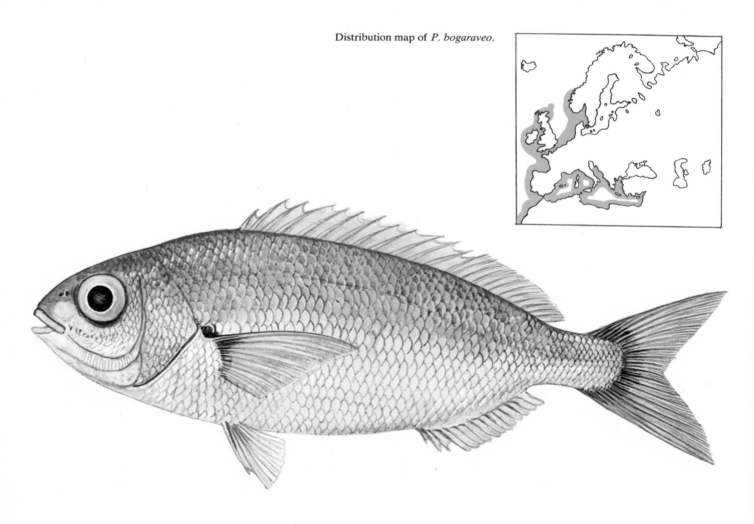

Red Sea Bream
Pagellus centrodontus

In its biology and form this species resembles the other members of the genus *Pagellus*, but it has a somewhat deeper and more thickset body than *P. bogaraveo*. The two are similar in colour, but the Red Sea Bream has a conspicuously large dark spot above the base of the pectoral fins at the beginning of the lateral line. The latter is clearly discernible with the dark openings in the scales and runs along the upper third of the body. The back of the fish is brownish red to brick red and it has silvery white sides and belly, with red or orange red fins.

These sea bream live in coastal waters mostly at depths of 100–300 m, but young individuals often live in shallower waters close inshore. The spawning season varies with geographical locality and lasts from spring to the late autumn, with a peak period in July and August. The eggs are pelagic like those of the other members of the genus. The young fish feed on algae and small invertebrates, older individuals also feed on larvae and small fish.

These sea bream are caught mainly with dragnets off the coast of Ireland, in the Bay of Biscay and off the Atlantic and Mediterranean coasts of Spain. The total annual catch in recent years has amounted to 12,000–15,000 tons, most fish being caught by the Spanish fishing fleet. The flesh is white and tasty.

Commonest synonyms: Sparus centrodontus, Pagellus cantabricus
Size: 30–40 cm, maximum 60 cm
Weight: 1–2 kg, occasionally up to 5 kg
Fin formula: D XII/10–13, A II/12
Distribution: Along the eastern shores of the Atlantic from southern Norway to Morocco, in the Mediterranean and the Black Sea. More abundant in the southern part of its range.

The related Bronze Bream *(P. acarne)* has a similar range but is absent from the Black Sea. It has no dark spot at the beginning of its lateral line and its caudal fin is darker. It measures up to 30 cm.

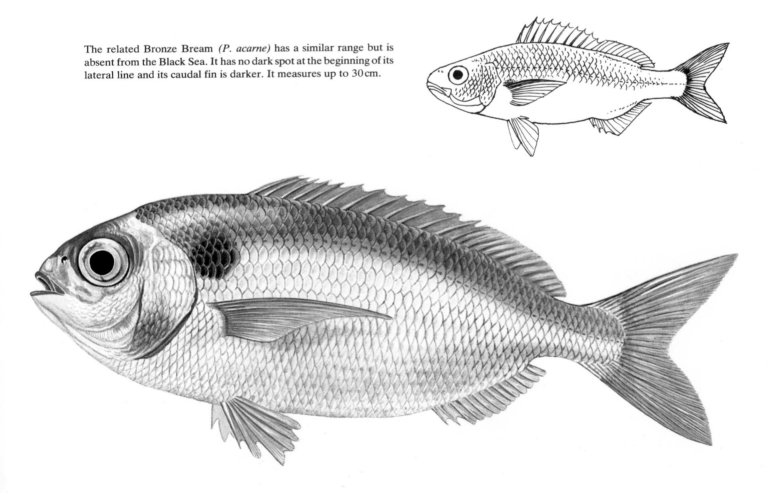

Common Sea Bream
Pagrus pagrus

This species is similar to the Golden Sea Bream, *P. aurata,* but has fewer soft branching rays in the dorsal and anal fins. The top of its head is extremely convex. In the mouth there are between four and six large, sharp teeth at the front of the jaws and two rows of flat teeth capable of crushing shells at the back. Its main difference from *P. aurata* is in its colouring, which is predominantly rosy red with a silvery lustre on the sides. The back is darker and the fins are red.

These Bream live mostly over a sandy or clayey sea bed at depths of 20–50 m, but in exceptional cases may be found 150 m deep or more. They often frequent parts of the sea bed overgrown with algae and sea-grass. They feed partly on fish but mainly on molluscs and crabs, crushing their shells with their strong teeth. Like *P. aurata* this Bream is an hermaphrodite but the data on its reproduction biology are very meagre. The fish spawn at the end of the summer and in the autumn and the eggs are pelagic. The larvae and fry live in shallower water than the adult fish, which retire to deep water when the winter comes.

These fish have white and very tasty flesh and are caught mainly with dragnets, chiefly off the coast of Mauretania and Senegal, where the total annual catch comes to 10,000–12,000 tons; annual catches in the Mediterranean are 1,000–2,000 tons. The Common Bream is also popular with anglers.

Commonest synonyms: Sparus pagrus, Pagrus vulgaris
Size: 40–50 cm, exceptionally up to 75 cm
Weight: 1–3 kg, maximum 6–7 kg
Fin formula: D XII/9–11, A III/8–9
Distribution: In the Atlantic Ocean off the coast of Europe and Africa, approximately from the Bay of Biscay to Angola, and in the Mediterranean, especially the western area.

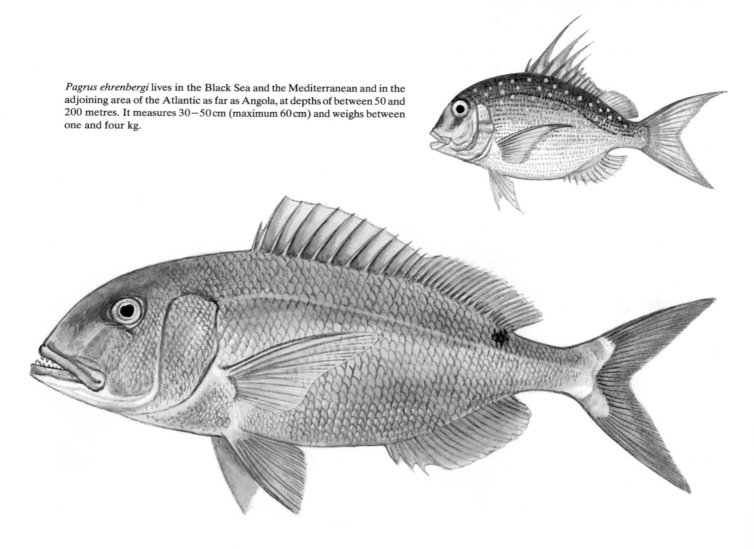

Pagrus ehrenbergi lives in the Black Sea and the Mediterranean and in the adjoining area of the Atlantic as far as Angola, at depths of between 50 and 200 metres. It measures 30–50 cm (maximum 60 cm) and weighs between one and four kg.

Golden Sea Bream
Pagrus aurata

This fish has a deep body with a long dorsal fin, an arched back and a high head with a sharply sloping top. In the front of each jaw there are six strong, sharp-pointed, wide-based teeth considerably larger than the three rows of flat, strong crushing teeth behind them. The body and fins are greyish blue with a silvery sheen, especially on the belly and sides. There are two dark spots above the origin of the pectoral fins beside the upper edge of each operculum, while on the front of the head between the eyes there is a golden band. Although conspicuous in the living fish the two spots quickly fade once the fish is dead.

These sea bream live in areas of the sea with a stony or rocky seabed, generally at depths of about 30 m. They usually form shoals which migrate shorewards in the spring and out to sea again with the advent of winter and are also found in river mouths and lagoons, where the water is brackish. They feed on fishes, crustaceans and molluscs and may wreak havoc in oyster beds, since not even oyster shells are proof against their powerful teeth. Spawning occurs at considerable depths in the open sea from October to December. The fish are hermaphrodite; the upper front section of each gonad develops as a testis and the rest as an ovary, the testes developing earlier in the life of the fish than the ovary. These bream have tasty flesh and the annual catch is in the region of 2,000–5,000 tons. Attempts are being made to breed them semi-artificially in some of the inlets of the Adriatic.

Commonest synonyms: Sparus aurata, Chrysophrys aurata
Size: 25–35 cm, maximum 60–70 cm
Weight: 0.5–3 kg, maximum 6 kg
Fin formula: D XI/12–14, A III/11–12
Distribution: In the Atlantic Ocean along the coasts of Europe and Africa, from the southern coast of the British Isles in the north to the Gulf of Guinea in the south. Golden Sea Bream is commonest in the western part of the Mediterranean Sea and is much less abundant in the Black Sea.

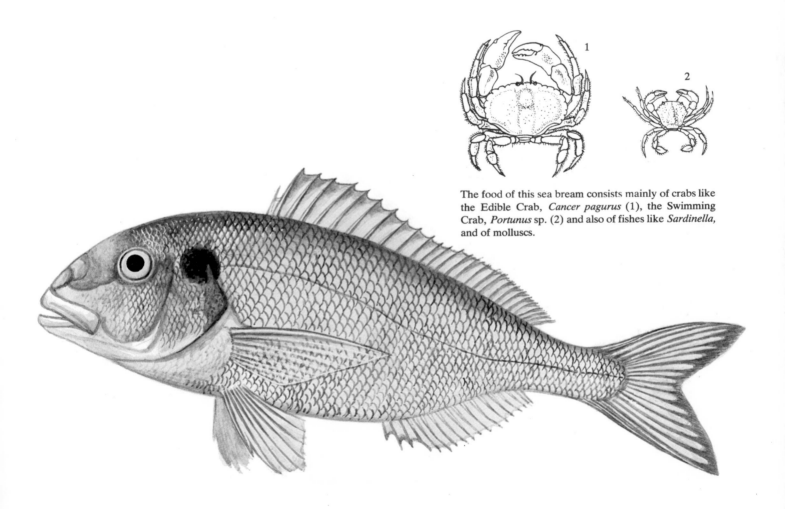

The food of this sea bream consists mainly of crabs like the Edible Crab, *Cancer pagurus* (1), the Swimming Crab, *Portunus* sp. (2) and also of fishes like *Sardinella*, and of molluscs.

Black Sea Bream

Spondyliosoma cantharus

A deep-bodied species with jaws that stretch to the anterior corner of its eyes. The teeth are rather different to those of the other sea bream, for they are all roughly the same size, relatively small, sharp and slightly recurved; only the front teeth are somewhat larger and they are used for nibbling algae. The body is grey in colour with a darker tone on the back and a lighter grey with a golden sheen on the sides; its forehead is dark red to brown. Below the lateral line there are three or four longitudinal gold stripes; the dorsal and anal fins are dark, with two or three rows of darker spots, the edge of the caudal fin has a dark border and the paired fins are grey.

This sea bream lives in the Atlantic Ocean and in the North Sea, in deep water in the winter but swimming northwards into inshore areas in the summer months. It is most often found on rocky shores, but also appears on sandbanks among growths of seaweed. It is one of the few members of this family whose males make a nest prior to spawning, usually a shallow depression in a sandy seabed. When spawning is over the male guards the eggs and the newly hatched young, which remain for several weeks in the vicinity of the nest before finally dispersing. Spawning takes place between February and May, depending on the temperature of the water. The young fish feed on zooplankton, the adults nibble seaweed and also eat the animals which live in it, like crustaceans and small fishes.

In some regions Black Sea Bream are caught with rods and lines and occasionally with nets, but their numbers are too small for them to have any great economic significance.

Commonest synonyms: Sparus cantharus,
Cantharus vulgaris
Size: 30–40 cm, maximum 50 cm
Fin formula: D XI–XII/10–13, A III/9–10
Distribution: Atlantic coastal waters from Norway to the Canary Islands, Mediterranean Sea.

Distribution map of *S. cantharus.*

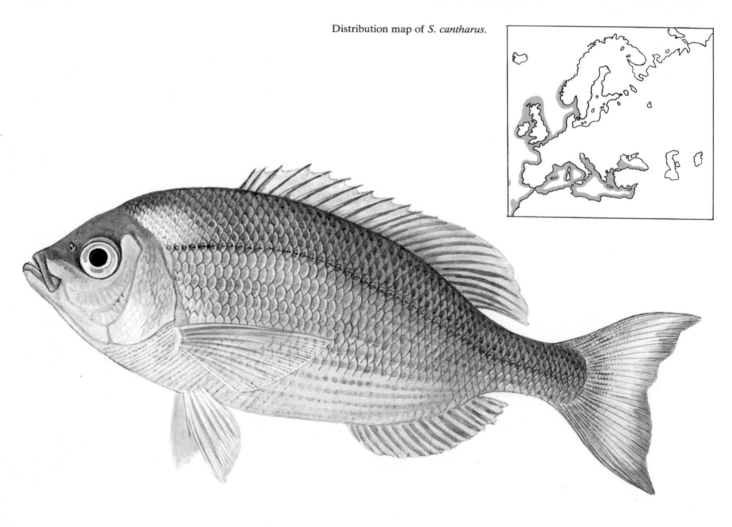

In the family Mullidae there are about sixty species of small marine fishes living chiefly in the coastal waters of tropical and subtropical seas. The fish have flat-sided bodies covered with large, thin scales and a characteristic head with a steeply curving profile and a pair of long barbels on the lower lip. The first of the two dorsal fins has spines, the ventral fins are situated ahead of the pectoral fins and the fish have no swim-bladders.

Red Mullet
Mullus barbatus

Red Mullet are purplish red to brownish red in colour, tinged yellow or silvery on the sides and with a lighter belly. The fins are usually reddish to golden yellow. The colouring is very variable, however, and depends on the depth, the time of day and the type of environment in which the fish are found.

They usually live in small shoals close to the shore, over a sandy or a muddy seabed, mostly at depths of between two and twenty metres. Spawning takes place from May to September; the fish spawn during the night and the eggs are laid in batches. The larvae and fry live pelagically, but once they grow to between 3.5−5 cm they embark on a benthic mode of life. They feed on various bottom-dwelling invertebrates, in particular on molluscs, worms and small crustaceans. The tactile barbels on the underside of the jaw are used in the search for food.

The Red Mullet has very tasty flesh and is an important commercial fish. Together with the Surmullet (*M. surmuletus*) there is a total annual catch of 30,000 to 40,000 tons. These species were both highly prized by the ancient Greeks and Romans, who often served them live so that guests could watch their handsome colours fade as they died.

Size: 20−30 cm, maximum 40 cm (females)
Weight: up to 1−1.5 kg
Fin formula: D_1 VII−VIII, D_2 I/7−8, A II/6−7
Fecundity: 4,000−90,000 eggs, according to some sources up to 1,000,000
Distribution: In the Mediterranean, the Black Sea and the Sea of Azov.

The two species of the genus *Mullus* can be distinguished from each other by the length of their barbels, the slope of their forehead and the colour of their dorsal fins. *M. barbatus* (1), *M. surmuletus* (2).

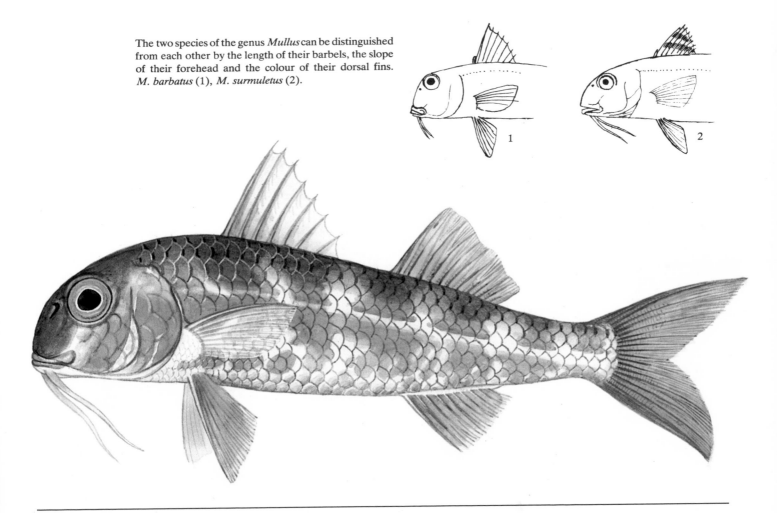

Surmullet
Mullus surmuletus

This close relative of the Red Mullet can be distinguished from it by its colouring and the less steeply angled front of its head, which forms an angle of 40—52 degrees with the long axis of the body. In the Red Mullet the angle is 44—58 degrees. There are also other differences in the relative lengths of their barbels and in the number of small scales below the eyes — two in *M. surmuletus,* three in *M. barbatus.* Otherwise the two species are very similar in both form and habits. The Surmullet has a reddish brown body with three or four yellow stripes running along its sides from the eyes to the caudal fin and there is also a dark red and yellow stripe running along the upper edge of the first dorsal fin. The colouring is very variable however, and changes with locality, depth and time of year.

Surmullet live in small shoals, mainly on sandy sea beds at depths of 3—100 m. With their long tactile barbels they explore the bottom for food and may tear up the sea bed looking for prey. They feed chiefly on small benthic animals, including the fry of fishes, molluscs, polychaete worms and crustaceans. They spawn during the summer at depths of 10—160 m and the eggs are pelagic. The fry begin life at the surface and only later descend to a benthic existence. They have bluish backs and silvery sides.

The fish has very tasty flesh, which in ancient times was considered to be a delicacy — the Romans kept them in lagoons, since they can survive in brackish water. Today they are caught in the Mediterranean and in the Bay of Biscay with dragnets and by anglers.

Size: 25—35 cm, maximum 50 cm
Weight: 0.5—1 kg, very rarely up to 1.5 kg
Fin formula: D$_1$ VII—VIII, D$_2$ I/7, A II/5—6
Distribution: Off the Atlantic shores of Europe and Africa from southern Norway south to Senegal, and in the Mediterranean Sea.

Distribution map of *M. surmuletus.*

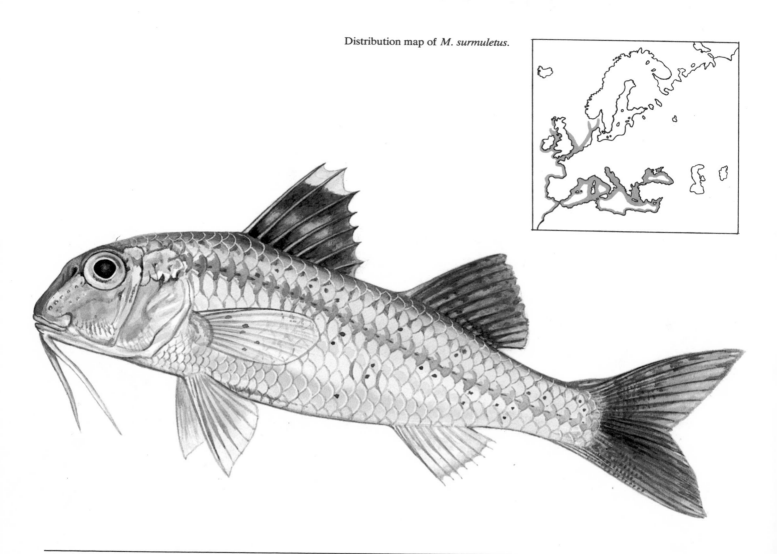

There are two genera in the family Cepolidae with five or six species of marine fishes frequenting open water in the coastal waters of the sea. They have elongated, flat-sided bodies without caudal fins, these being replaced by joined dorsal and anal fins. They live in the Pacific and Atlantic Oceans.

Red Bandfish
Cepola rubescens

This fish has a long eel-like body with long dorsal and anal fins, in each of which there are over 60 rays. Its large eyes account for one third of the length of the head. Its scales are very small. It has a red back and lighter red sides with a silvery sheen and its belly is orange or yellow. The dorsal fin is also yellow, the pectoral fins are pink and the fin that runs around the tail is reddish in colour.

Spawning occurs in June in littoral waters; the eggs are planktonic and each has a tiny oil droplet as a flotation device. Adult fish burrow into the muddy bottom of the seabed at depths of 20–200 m. They are active mainly at night when they leave their burrows to search for food, mainly small crustaceans and arrow worms.

Red Bandfish are economically unimportant fishes, although they are caught from time to time by anglers and sometimes are found in large numbers, especially after storms which may have disturbed the burrows. They form part of the diet of other fishes. Related species caught off the coast of Japan are sold there in fishmarkets.

Size: 30–50 cm, maximum 70 cm
Fin formula: D 67–74, A 60–70
Distribution: In the Mediterranean and the adjoining part of the Atlantic, from Britain in the north to Cape Verde in the south.

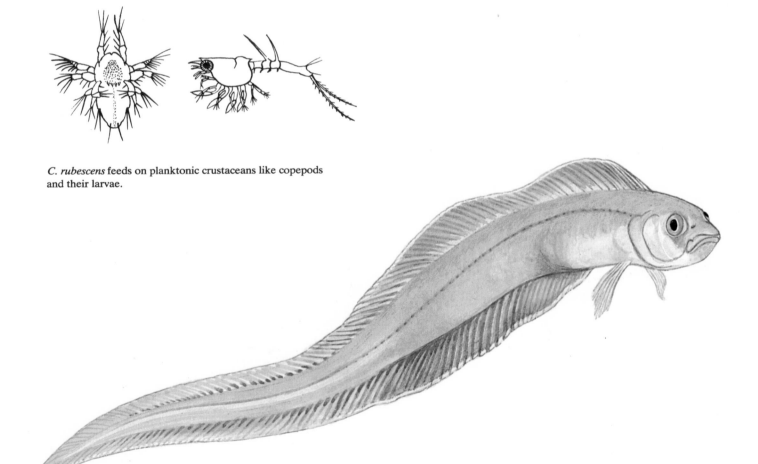

C. rubescens feeds on planktonic crustaceans like copepods and their larvae.

The family Echeneidae (the remoras) is a small group of about ten marine fishes in which the first dorsal fin has been converted to a powerful sucker on the flattened top of the head and behind it.

Shark-sucker
Echeneis naucrates

This is a moderately large greyish brown marine fish with a slender, elongate body. It can be immediately recognised by the presence of an oval suctorial disc across the crown of its head and the anterior part of its back, formed as a modification of the first dorsal fin. The converted fin rays are seen on the disc as between 21 and 28 cross folds resembling the slats of a Venetian blind. Like other remoras this fish attaches itself firmly by its sucker to the bodies of sharks, rays, other large fish, turtles, whales and ships and is then carried around the oceans. The sucker creates a vacuum when it is pressed against a fish and is then very difficult to loosen. Suction or release of the individual folds of the disc is regulated by pressure changes in the cavity below the sucker, which are influenced by the lateral line system. Shark-suckers may free their hosts of parasites by feeding on them; they also feed on the remains of their hosts' food and on invertebrates and smaller fish. When close to prey the Shark-sucker quickly relaxes its hold on its host and pounces. Little is known of its reproductive biology except that its eggs are pelagic.

Nowadays few people eat its rather oily flesh, but in the Middle Ages it was very popular. Remoras were supposed to influence the course of ships and the death of the Roman Emperor Caligula was attributed to his ship being delayed by these fish. Native fishermen in the Caribbean and in Australian waters sometimes use remoras to catch turtles. They tie a rope to the fish's tail and let it down over the side of the boat; when a turtle comes along the fish attaches itself to the shell and both are hauled in together.

Synonyms: Echeneis remora
Size: 30−40 cm, maximum 70 cm
Weight: 1−2 kg
Fin formula: D_2 35−42, A 35−37
Distribution: In all tropical and subtropical seas, occasionally in the Mediterranean and in the Atlantic as far as the southern coast of Britain.

The related species *Remora remora* has only 16−20 lamellae on its suctorial disc, (in contrast to *E. naucrates,* which has 21−28), rounded pectoral fins and a notched caudal fin. It measures 20−40 cm and lives in the same regions as *E. naucrates.*

The Labridae or wrasses are a large family of marine fishes with about 600 species. They include tiny fishes only 6−7 cm long and giants measuring up to 3 metres and weighing over 100 kg. They have large cycloid scales and protrusible jaws like cyprinid fishes, with fleshy lips. Most of them are brightly coloured. They have a single dorsal fin, the anterior portion of which is spiny. They are mostly found in coastal waters where they hide in growths of seaweed and defend their domains against all intruders.

LABRIDAE

Corkwing
Crenilabrus melops

A smallish deep-bodied fish, the young of which may be seen in rock pools in the lower tide levels during August and September around northern European coasts. The adults also live in pools and below the intertidal zone, down to a depth of about 30 m. The colouring of the fish is very variable and depends on locality, age, sex and time of year, but basically it is mottled greenish or greenish brown in colour, some-times tinged with red. Behind each eye and on the peduncle there is a dark spot.

Spawning occurs at the end of the spring and the beginning of the summer. Like other members of the family, the male builds a nest among rocks and seaweeds and defends it until the young are hatched; they are pelagic at first but soon swim shorewards to the intertidal zone. These wrasse feed chiefly on molluscs and small crustaceans. They are of no interest to anglers, but are often caught.

Synonym: Symphodus melops
Size: 15−20 cm, maximum 25 cm
Weight: up to 0.4 kg
Fin formula: D XIV−XVII/8−10, A III/9−10
Distribution: European and African coasts of the Atlantic Ocean from Scandinavia to Morocco, shores of England and Ireland, western parts of the Mediterranean and the Baltic Sea.

Distribution map of *C. melops.*

The related species *C. ocellatus,* which occurs in the Mediterranean, the adjacent part of the Atlantic and in the Black Sea. There is a large dark spot on each operculum in both sexes.

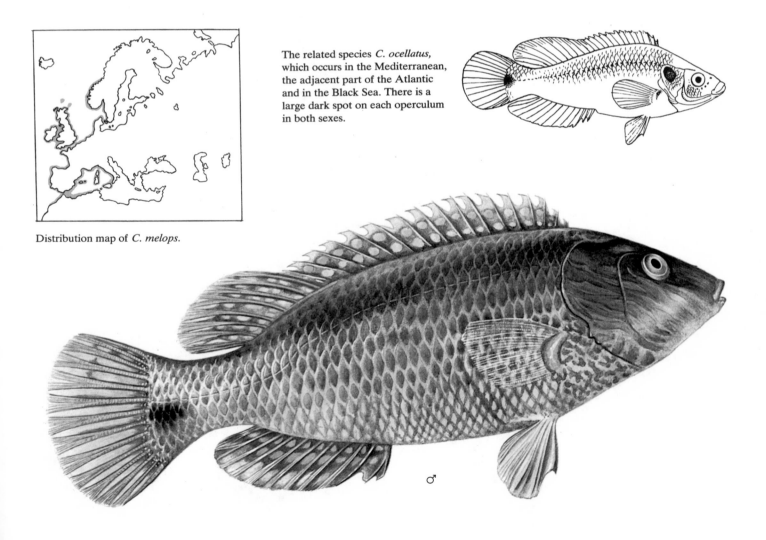

♂

225

Five-spot Wrasse
Crenilabrus quinquemaculatus

A smallish deep-bodied wrasse. There are fine serrations on the posterior and lower edges of the preoperculum, as in the preceding species. Male fish are green in colour, females brownish grey and there are five cross rows of brown to dark brown spots and a similar spot on the operculum. There are also two large black spots in the middle of the dorsal fin and two small lighter spots on the anal fin.

These wrasses live on the coast, amongst seaweeds on rocky shores. They spawn between March and May; the male builds a nest from aquatic plants in a sandy seabed or among stones at depths between 15 cm and two metres and provides it with a crescent-shaped wall reinforced with small stones and algae. Spawning is probably intermittent and at a temperature of 16–18 °C hatching occurs after about five days. The fry measure about 40–65 cm by June.

Economically these are unimportant fishes, but because of the structure of the nest, its care of the young and its colouring and size it is a suitable fish for marine aquaria.

Synonym: *Symphodus roissali*
Size: up to 21 cm
Fin formula: D XIV–XV/8–10, A III/8–10
Fecundity: 5,000–40,000 eggs
Distribution: In the Black Sea, the Mediterranean and the adjacent part of the Atlantic coast.

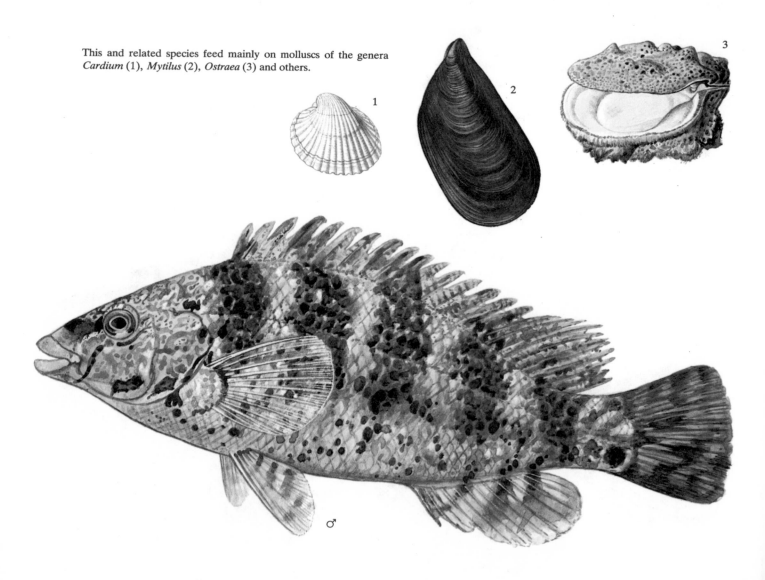

This and related species feed mainly on molluscs of the genera *Cardium* (1), *Mytilus* (2), *Ostraea* (3) and others.

Thrush Wrasse

Crenilabrus tinca

This fish is similar in form to the other members of the family, but there are no dark spots on its dorsal fin and the spots on its body form two longitudinal bands running along its sides. Its colouring is very variable. Basically it is greenish in colour, darker on the back and lighter or greyish on the belly. Along their sides the males have two rows of red spots interspersed with a few smaller light blue spots; in the females the spots form brown bands. At the origin of the tail the males have a reddish brown spot, the females a brown spot. In the males the dorsal and anal fins are bordered by a row of small red spots and still smaller light blue spots; they also have red spots on their head. The pectoral fins are yellow, lighter in the females, while the ventral fins are light blue with red spots in the males and light green with brown spots in the females.

This is a littoral species living a solitary life amongst seaweeds and rocks, often throughout the year but sometimes retiring into somewhat deeper water in winter. Unlike other members of the family which hide away, Thrush Wrasse often swim about in open water. These fish feed on benthic invertebrates, mostly small molluscs but also on crustaceans and polychaete worms. Spawning occurs from April to May or June. The eggs are laid in a nest in three or four batches. The larvae hatch after five to nine days in the Black Sea, but after only four days in the Mediterranean. For the first few months the larvae lead a pelagic life.

Thrush Wrasse are economically unimportant but are occasionally caught by tourists or anglers.

Synonym: Symphodus tinca
Size: 10−15 cm, maximum 25−30 cm
Weight: up to 0.3 kg
Fin formula: D XIV−XV/10−12, A III/9−11
Fecundity: 12,000−58,000 eggs
Distribution: In the Black Sea, the Mediterranean and the adjoining part of the Atlantic coastline from the Iberian Peninsula in Europe, south to Morocco in North Africa.

As in most members of the Labridae, there are marked differences in the colouring of the sexes of *C. tinca*. The females are less gaudily coloured and their fins lack the blue borders and the small red spots.

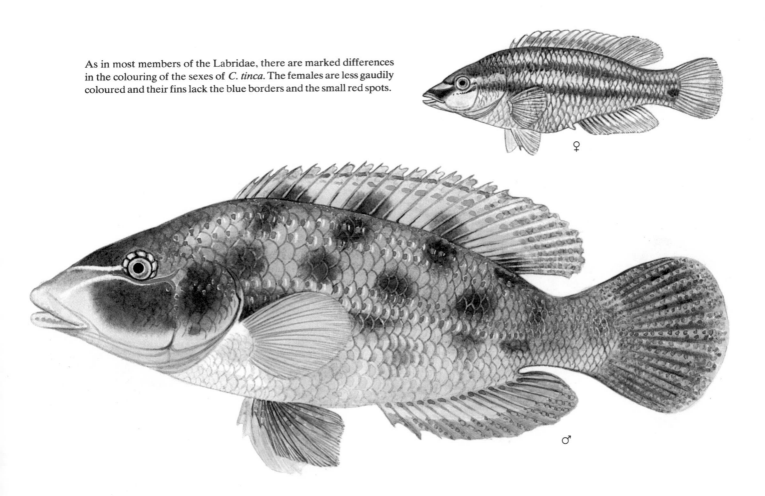

Goldsinny
Ctenolabrus rupestris

The Goldsinny can be easily distinguished from other members of the family by the several rows of teeth present in the mouth; the others have only one row of teeth. It is a smallish elongate fish, distinctively coloured with a brown or reddish orange body, sometimes tinged with gold, a darker back and reddish fins. There are two black spots present, one at the beginning of the dorsal fin and another near the base of the caudal fin. On the sides of the fish there are sometimes a few dark vertical bars or a lighter band of colour.

This is one of the commonest members of the family in northern Europe, but it is only locally common, usually only present in areas where the coast plunges immediately into deep water. The fish can be found amongst rocks and seaweeds at depths of 10–50 m, and on rocky coasts are also present in shallower water. They feed on molluscs and crustaceans. In the winter they appear to swim out to deeper water and may sometimes form small shoals. Spawning occurs from the spring until late in the summer. The eggs are found in the littoral zone and in the open sea. In the summer the larvae develop very quickly, virtually in two days.

Economically these fishes are unimportant.

Size: up to 10–12 cm, maximum 18 cm
Fin formula: D XVI–XVIII/8–10, A III/7–8
Distribution: European coasts of the Atlantic Ocean from Gibraltar to the Lofoten Islands, western part of the Baltic Sea, the Mediterranean and the Black Sea.

Distribution map of *C. rupestris*.

Commonest articles of diet include mussels *Mytilus* (1) and also decapod crustaceans of the genus *Pandalina* (2).

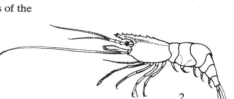

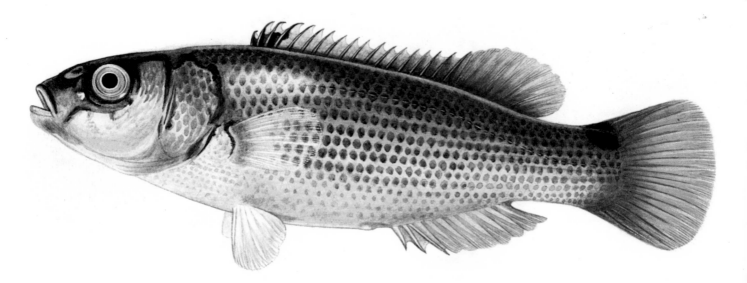

Cuckoo Wrasse
Labrus mixtus

This species is very similar in form and habits to the Ballan Wrasse, *L. bergylta,* but it has a more tapering head and a larger mouth which stretches almost to the anterior margin of the eyes. It also has a different number of rays in its long dorsal fin (16–18 spines, 11–14 soft rays) and has distinctive colouration with marked colour difference between the sexes. Mature males have irregular blue spots and longitudinal stripes on the head and sides, whereas females and sexually immature males have yellowish blue heads and reddish orange or red bodies with blue markings and with three dark spots on the back.

These fishes live over hard rocky sea beds at depths of 10–100 m or occasionally down to 180 m. Small individuals and fry are also found in tidal zones, but with the advent of winter the fish tend to retire to deeper water. At spawning time the male builds a nest in a depression in the sea bed to which it lures females while chasing other males away. The eggs and larvae are pelagic. These fish feed mainly on molluscs and on crustaceans like squat lobsters and crabs; they are often found in lobster pots, apparently searching for food. They grow slowly and in the north may live up to seventeen years.

The flesh is edible, but Cuckoo Wrasse have no economic significance. They are sometimes kept in aquaria because of their handsome colouring, but their aggressiveness creates problems.

Commonest synonyms: Labrus bimaculatus, Labrus ossifagus, Labrus lineatus
Size: 20–35 cm, males up to 40 cm
Weight: up to 1 kg
Fin formula: D XVI–XVIII/11–14, A III/10–12
Distribution: In the coastal waters of the Mediterranean and the Atlantic coast of Europe and Africa from the middle of the Norwegian coast to Dakar, rare off the coast of Madeira, the Azores and the Canary Islands.

A female with markedly different colouring from the sexually mature male. The colouring is less striking and there are three dark spots on the posterior part of the back.

Ballan Wrasse
Labrus bergylta

A deep-bodied wrasse with a green or greenish brown back and sides and a light yellowish green belly. On the sides of the fish there are several irregular dark cross bars and an irregular pattern formed of short red stripes which is continued on to the underside of the head; the scales on the belly and on the lower part of the sides are red-edged. The colouring is very variable however, depending on the age and sex of the fish and the habitat in which it is living. The fin rays of the dorsal fin are an important diagnostic feature for fishes of the genus *Labrus*. In this species there are 19–20 spines and 9–11 soft fin rays. The mouth is small and does not extend to the anterior edge of the eyes.

This wrasse lives chiefly over rocky seabeds densely covered with seaweeds, mostly below the low tide level at depths of 2–30 m. The male builds a nest made of algae on the bottom, in which the female lays her eggs; spawning occurs between May and August. For a short time the larvae and fry live pelagically in shoals but they soon return to inshore waters where they form smaller shoals or live solitary lives near the bottom. They feed mostly on molluscs and small crabs, crushing the shells with their strong teeth. These wrasse seem to be particularly susceptible to cold, and dead fish may be seen in considerable numbers washed up on the shore after very cold weather. They are good angling fish and may be caught with rods and lines on rocky shores; they have quite high quality, tasty flesh.

Commonest synonym: Labrus maculatus
Size: 30–40 cm, maximum 60 cm (males)
Weight: 1–2 kg, maximum 3.5 kg
Fin formula: D XIX–XXI/9–11, A III/8–10
Distribution: In the northeastern Atlantic from the middle of the Norwegian coast to southern Morocco and in the greater part of the Mediterranean.

The related *Labrus turdus* occurs in the Atlantic south of the Bay of Biscay and in the Mediterranean; it is the only member of the genus *Labrus* in the Black Sea. It is brightly, but very variably coloured and grows up to 45 cm in length (in the Black Sea it only reaches a maximum of 35 cm).

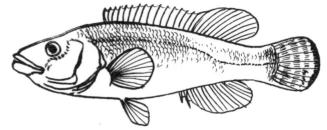

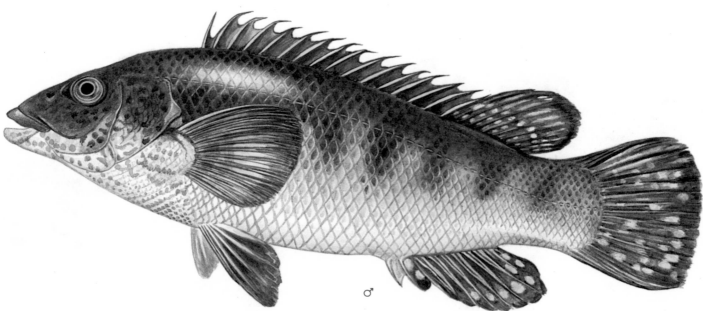

Brown Wrasse
Labrus merula

In form, habits and behaviour this wrasse largely resembles the other members of the same genus. It is easy to distinguish from related species living in the same localities (*L. bergylta, L. mixtus, L. turdus*) by its colouring, for it has a light grey to light olive green back and sides with faint, irregular mottling; its belly is usually lighter in colour. Its small mouth is heavily armed with teeth but does not extend to the anterior edge of the eyes.

This is a common species especially in the Mediterranean, where it may occur in small shoals, or lead a solitary life in coastal waters over sandy or stony sea beds overgrown with seaweeds. Spawning occurs at the end of the spring and during the summer. The male, which is larger than the female, makes the nest beforehand from seaweeds in a depression in the sea bed, or in a space between rocks. When the work is

completed he drives sexually mature females towards and over the nest, where they lay the eggs. For a time the larvae and fry lead a pelagic existencè, but when they measure about 4 cm they assume a benthic mode of life. The fish are active during the day; at night they sleep hidden away between stones or in clumps of algae. They are very timid and the slightest disturbance immediately sends them into hiding even during the daytime. Although occasionally found in fishermen's catches, these wrasse are not of any practical significance chiefly because of their small size.

Size: 15—25 cm, maximum 30 cm
Weight: 0.5—0.8 kg
Fin formula: D XVIII—XIX/11—13, A III/9—10
Distribution: In the Mediterranean and along the European and African shores of the Atlantic, from the south of the British Isles to the coast of Mauritania.

The Brown Wrasse has strong teeth which are used for crushing the shells of the marine animals on which it feeds, including barnacles (1), chitons (2) and small shrimp-like crustaceans (3).

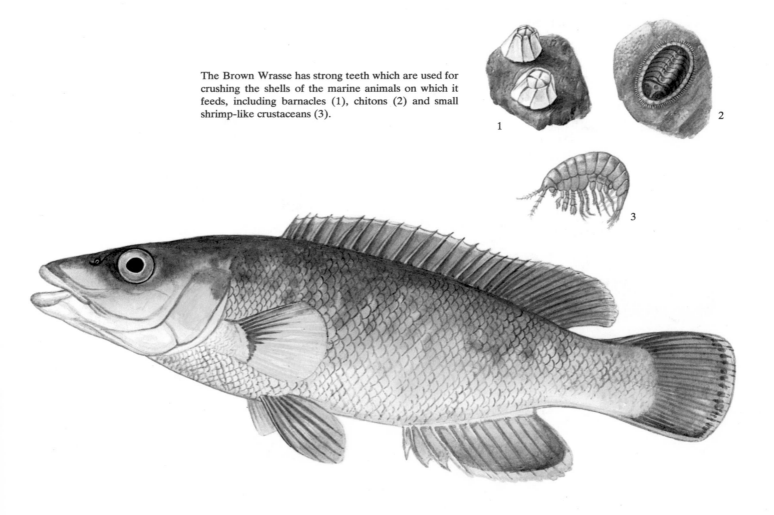

Rainbow Wrasse

Coris julis

This wrasse has an elongate body with a single long dorsal fin which can be used to distinguish it from other genera of the family, for it has only nine or ten thin flexible spines. In all there are ten species of the genus *Coris* living in tropical and subtropical seas. The first three hard rays of the dorsal fin are longer in males than in females. The teeth are characteristic; those in the outer row are sharp and conical and the two front teeth (together with the first two in the next row to a lesser extent) protrude like small tusks. The colouring of the fish is very variable and depends on sex, age and depth. Adult males generally have a bluish green back, a wide orange-yellow band on each side leading from the eye to the caudal fin, with a shorter and narrower dark stripe below it and a silvery white belly. The edge of the operculum has a bright, light blue spot and at the beginning of the dorsal fin there is a large, oval, black or grey spot which is absent in the females. Females have brown backs and golden bands on their flanks. The males are larger than the females and the sexes are so different

that they were formerly described as separate species – the males as *C. julis* and the females as *C. giofredi*. The position is further complicated by the fact that these fish develop first of all as females, but later in life the ovaries degenerate, the testes develop and the fish function as males. Individuals up to 8 cm in length are all females, those over 15 cm are all males; about two thirds of the individuals measuring between 8 cm and 15 cm are males. Some males retain the female colouring. Spawning takes place throughout April and the eggs are pelagic. The fish feed on crustaceans and on molluscs. They occur at depths of 3–120 m, where they live amongst seaweeds growing on rocks and are active during the daytime.

These fishes are economically unimportant, but they are very voracious and will take anglers' bait.

Size: up to 25 cm
Fin formula: D IX/12, A III/12
Distribution: In the Mediterranean and the adjoining parts of the Atlantic coast of Europe; occasionally found in the Black Sea.

Some *Coris* species are particularly brightly coloured and may be kept in marine aquaria. One such species is *C. gaimard* which grows up to 35–40 cm; it is found in the tropical parts of the Pacific and Indian Oceans.

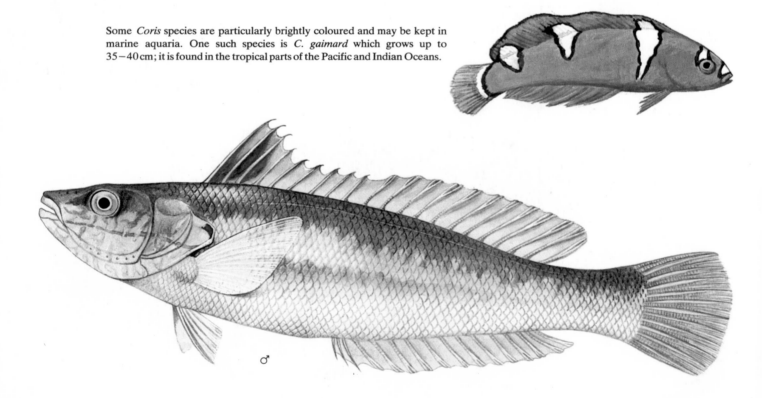

Members of the family Pomacentridae are deep-bodied fishes with strikingly large eyes and small jaws. Their lower pharyngeal teeth are fused to form a single plate and on either side of the head there is only one nasal orifice instead of two. There are about ten genera of coastal marine fishes in the family. These are the coral fishes living in coral reefs in tropical and subtropical waters.

POMACENTRIDAE

Blue Damselfish
Chromis chromis

This fish is the only European representative of the family. It is a small fish with a deep, oval body, compressed sides and a deeply forked caudal fin. Its long dorsal fin is composed largely of spines and its entire body, the head and the bases of its fins are all covered with scales; those on its sides are relatively large and their posterior edges have black borders. It has a small terminal mouth. Its lateral line, while unbroken over most of the body, takes the form of separate pores on the peduncle. The fish is black-brown with a silvery violet sheen on its sides.

These fishes live in shallow coastal waters where they usually form small shoals either in open water or close to a stony bottom. They spawn between June and August at depths of one to six metres. The male chooses a suitable spot, and cleans the surface of a stone or a piece of rock with his lips. He then tempts a sexually mature female to the site by 'dancing' actions and invites her to spawn. The ovoid eggs are attached to the substrate by thread-like tendrils and are guarded for a long time by the male, who keeps them clean by fanning them with his pectoral fins and also drives away intruders. The fry and the adult fish feed on algae and zooplankton. They swim into deeper water before the onset of the winter, since they cannot tolerate temperatures of below 5−6 °C.

These fish are economically uninteresting.

Size: 8−10 cm, maximum 16 cm
Fin formula: D XIV/9−11, A II/9−11
Distribution: In the Black Sea, the Mediterranean and the Atlantic off the southwestern coast of the Iberian Peninsula and the coast of northwestern Africa as far as Dakar, in the vicinity of Madeira, the Canary Islands and the Azores.

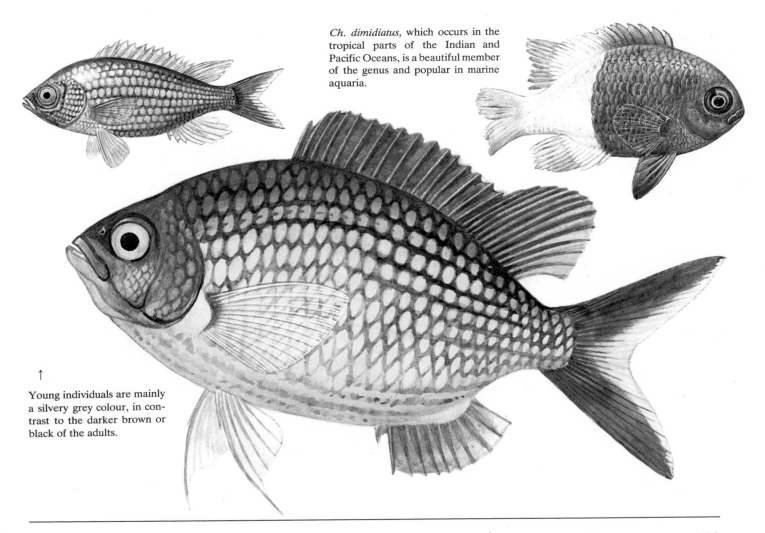

Ch. dimidiatus, which occurs in the tropical parts of the Indian and Pacific Oceans, is a beautiful member of the genus and popular in marine aquaria.

↑
Young individuals are mainly a silvery grey colour, in contrast to the darker brown or black of the adults.

TRACHINIDAE

Greater Weever, Dragon Weever

Trachinus draco

This fish has an elongate, flat-sided body with strikingly long second dorsal and anal fins. There are venom glands at the base of the spiny pectoral fins and the first dorsal fin and on the spiny processes of the opercula, all of which secrete highly toxic poisons. Great care should be taken when handling live and freshly dead fish, for wounds from the spines with the venom glands are painful and can be dangerous. The Greater Weever also has two characteristic small spines on the upper surface of the head in front of the eyes; these are absent in the three remaining *Trachinus* species. The colouring of the fish is grey-brown with a large number of narrow, oblique dark stripes on the sides, leading downwards and backwards to the lighter yellowish belly. There is a dark spot on the spiny dorsal fin.

These fish spend the greater part of the day buried in sandbanks, usually with only their eyes protruding, and are more active at night when they come closer to the surface of the water. In the summer they live in shallow coastal waters but in autumn they descend to greater depths and are sometimes found as deep as 100 m. They feed on small fish, shrimps and other crustaceans. Spawning occurs between June and August and the eggs are pelagic.

Weevers are quite popular for their tasty flesh, which is eaten fresh or smoked particularly in the Mediterranean countries, but the fish do have to be handled with care.

Size: 20–39 cm, maximum 45 cm
Weight: 300–800 g
Fin formula: D_1 V–VII, D_2 29–33, A II/30–35
Distribution: Shelves of the Atlantic Ocean from the middle of Norway to the south of Africa, the Mediterranean and the Black Seas.

Distribution map of *T. draco*.

234

Lesser Weever
Trachinus vipera

This species is similar in form to the Greater Weever, but it is stouter and shorter, its pectoral fins are rounded and it has no small spines in front of its eyes. In both species the first dorsal fin is almost black, but they are differently shaped and the rays are of different lengths. In this species the caudal fin has a black border.

Unlike its relatives, the Lesser Weever remains permanently buried in clean sand in shallow water, where it be very common and is a common cause of injury to unwary feet. Its venom glands are situated at the base of the first dorsal fin and the spiny processes on its opercula. The poison has a very powerful effect and the Lesser Weever is one of the most venomous fish in Europe (according to some authors it is one of the most venomous species in existence). Injury requires immediate first aid, cut-ting open the wound and squeezing out the blood and venom, followed by prompt medical attention.

Lesser Weevers feed on small bottom-dwelling crustaceans, bivalves and fishes, probably being most active at night. They spawn between May and September; the eggs are pelagic and the larvae develop in the open sea.

Occasionally they are netted by fishermen, but they are economically unimportant. They may present a danger to shrimp fishermen, shrimp trawling over a sandy bottom, who have to sort their catch with great care.

Size: 8–15 cm, maximum 20 cm
Weight: up to 300 g
Fin formula: D_1 VI–VII, D_2 21–25, A I/24–26
Distribution: On the continental shelf of the Atlantic from the south of Sweden to South Africa, less abundant in the Mediterranean.

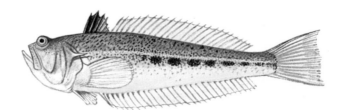

Among related species, *T. araneus* is supposed to have the tastiest flesh. This is also the biggest species (up to 50 cm) and is found mostly in the Mediterranean. It has six or seven characteristic dark spots on its sides.

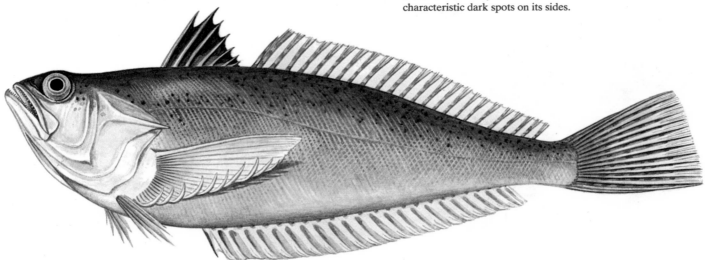

235

The members of the family Uranoscopidae resemble weevers; some of them have electric organs on their heads which can emit discharges of up to 50 V. There are about thirty-six species all of which live in the sea.

Star-gazer
Uranoscopus scaber

This close relative of the weevers has much shorter second dorsal and anal fins, a massive head and no venom glands below the spiny rays of the first, black dorsal fin, although it does have venom glands in the large spines on the opercula. The prick of these spines is very painful, but far less dangerous than the wounds produced by weevers' spines. Its eyes are situated on the top of its flattened head and it has a superior mouth. It has a characteristic fleshy outgrowth on its lower jaw which is normally concealed in the oral cavity, but which can be extruded and employed as a lure for catching prey; it measures up to one third of the length of the head. The fish is mainly greyish brown in colour with irregular light spots.

Star-gazers live in shallow coastal waters, usually buried in a sandy or muddy substrate, with only the tops of their heads, eyes and lures showing. Their food consists mainly of small fish, crabs and other bottom-dwelling invertebrates. Spawning occurs during the summer and the eggs are pelagic. Although Star-gazers are economically unimportant they sometimes form part of fishermen's catches. The flesh of the fish is quite good and is usually eaten in the form of fish soup.

Size: 15—25 cm, maximum 30—35 cm
Weight: up to 0.8 kg
Fin formula: D_1 IV, D_2 13—15, A 13—14
Fecundity: 18,000—125,000 eggs
Distribution: In the Mediterranean and the Black Seas and along practically the whole west coast of Africa.

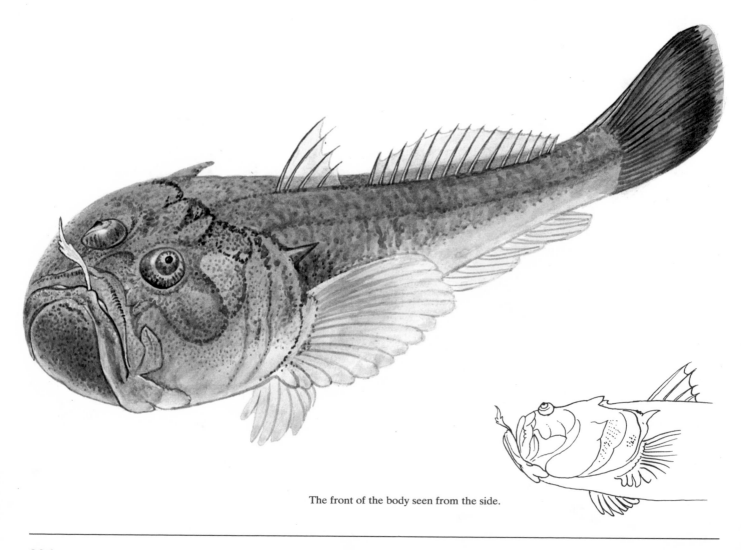

The front of the body seen from the side.

There are over 400 species of small fish in the family Blenniidae, living in the coastal waters and intertidal zones of warm and temperate seas. They have one long dorsal fin with spines anteriorly and soft rays posteriorly. Their scaleless bodies are protected from desiccation by a thick layer of slime. When the tide goes out on rocky shores they may commonly be found in rock pools.

BLENNIIDAE

Shanny, Smooth Blenny
Blennius pholis

These widespread fishes live under stones and in rock pools in the intertidal zone off rocky coasts, but may also be encountered on sandy beaches in shallow bays, as long as there is shelter in the form of scattered rocks and pools. They also live in the sublittoral zone at depths of down to 30 m.

This is the only blenny without fleshy outgrowths above the eyes and it has instead a smoothly rounded forehead. Its dorsal fin is the same height throughout, except for a notch where the spines are succeeded by soft rays. There are 15–24 teeth in the jaws. The colouring of these fishes is very variable and depends partly on the habitat. The back is usually dark brown to green and the sides and belly are lighter. The whole of the body is mottled with light and dark spots.

Spawning occurs in the spring and summer and the eggs are attached to the undersides of stones or to the upper surface of small cavities in the rocks. The male guards the eggs and keeps them supplied with fresh water by fanning them with his large pectoral fins. The fry feed mainly on crustaceans like water fleas and copepods, the adult fish on small crabs, worms and molluscs.

These small fishes are economically unimportant although they are prey for other fishes.

Size: 10–15 cm, maximum up to 18 cm
Fin formula: D XII/17–19, A I/17–19
Distribution: Off the west and southwest coasts of Europe, including the most westerly part of the Mediterranean and the Atlantic coast of North Africa.

The related species *B. pavo* lives in the Black Sea, the Mediterranean and the adjoining part of the Atlantic. The males have a striking fleshy crest on the head. The fish grow up to 13 cm in length and are often kept in marine aquaria.

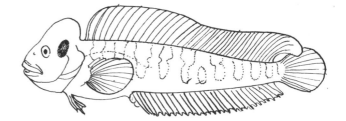

237

River Blenny
Blennius fluviatilis

A typical blenny which can be identified by the very small excrescences above the eyes and the additional longitudinal fleshy fold on the head. There is no notch in the dorsal fin and the spiny section is joined directly to the soft-rayed section. The back and sides of this fish are olive green, the belly is yellowish white and the entire body is speckled with large brownish green blotches.

This blenny lives in small lakes, slow-moving rivers and small streams. The fish need shallow, but clean water. Adult individuals live solitary lives amongst boulders and under roots but the fry frequent the river banks in small shoals. They feed at first on zooplankton, but when bigger their prey consists of caddis-fly, mayfly and stone-fly larvae and the larvae of other bottom-dwelling creatures.

At spawning time all suitable sites under stones, roots and banks are occupied and defended by the now deep brownish black males which, after building their nests, lure females heavy with eggs into them. The female attaches the eggs to the upper wall of the nest, where they are then fertilized by the male, which actively guards them until the young are hatched. He fans the eggs with his pectoral fins to ensure that they are continuously supplied with fresh water rich in oxygen and he also removes unfertilized and damaged eggs. At 20 °C the fry hatch in 14 days, during the whole of which time the male goes without food. The female does not participate in the care of the young fishes.

This is an economically unimportant species.

Size: 10–12 cm, maximum 15 cm
Fin formula: D XII/17–18, A II/16–18
Distribution: In fresh water in the Mediterranean region from the south of Spain to Asia Minor and in Morocco and Algeria.

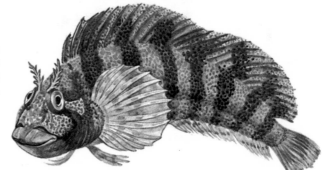

The related Tompot Blenny, *B. gattorugine* is relatively abundant off the Atlantic coast of Spain and Portugal, in the Bay of Biscay and around the western coasts of the British Isles as well as in the Mediterranean. It grows up to 20 cm in length. It has striking dendritic processes above its eyes, a distinctive dorsal fin and distinctive colouring.

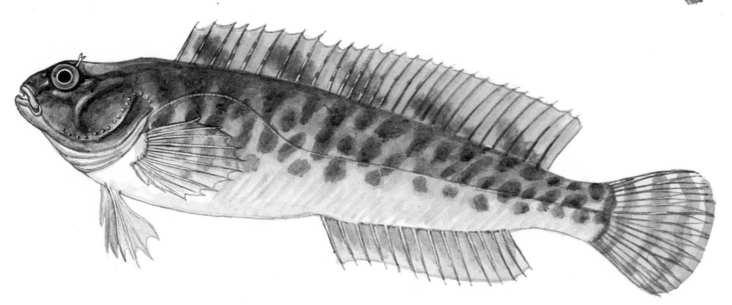

Butterfly Blenny
Blennius ocellaris

A very distinctive blenny with a long spiny ray at the front of the first dorsal fin, a deep body and a fleshy protuberance above each eye. The colouring of the fish is also very recognisable. There is a large dark, white-bordered spot on the first dorsal fin, together with several dark vertical cross bars. Other dark bars run obliquely across the second dorsal fin. The back of the fish is greenish brown with five to seven dark cross bars, its sides are lighter in colour and its belly is dingy white.

In the Mediterranean these fishes spawn at the end of the winter; further north spawning occurs at the end of the spring and in the summer. The eggs are laid in hiding-places like those of other blennies and the male keeps watch over them. The larvae and fry live in open water but after a few weeks they assume a bottom-dwelling mode of life. At first they feed on the larvae and young of crustaceans; later their diet consists of small crustaceans, worms, algae and small fishes. This is the only blenny species that lives throughout a large variety of depths from 10 to 100 m. They are most often found in places where there are broken shells and dense seaweed growth, but they may also occur on sandy seabeds where they can find shelter below stones, in empty shells, in tin cans and in other types of litter found nowadays in coves and creeks.

Size: 12–15 cm, maximum 20 cm
Fin formula: D XI/14–15, A II/15–16
Distribution: In the Mediterranean and along the adjoining shores of the Atlantic to the southern coast of England; occasionally found in the Black Sea.

The related *B. sphinx* is found in the coastal waters of the Mediterranean and the Black Seas. It grows up to 8 cm long and can be distinguished from the Butterfly Blenny by its different colouring, its different dorsal fin and its unbranched protuberances above the eyes.

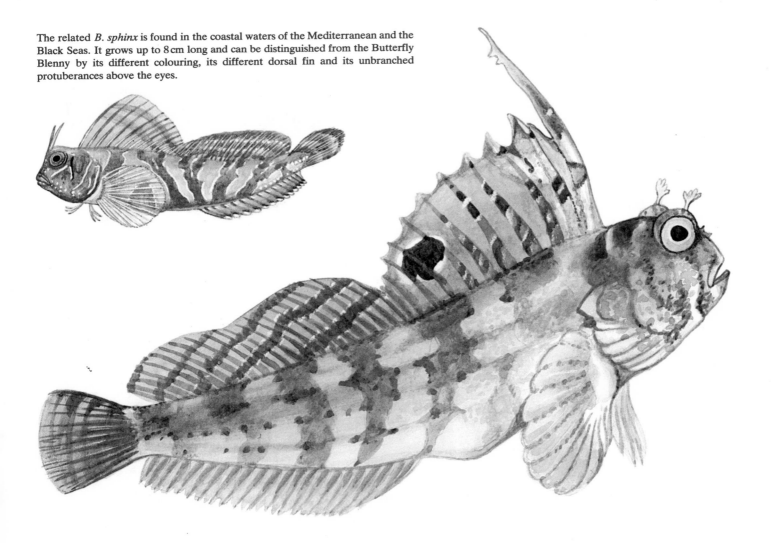

Bloodthirsty Blenny
Blennius sanguinolentus

This blenny has an elongated and thickset body with between four and seven branched processes behind the eyes but these are small, shorter than the diameter of the eye. On the posterior edge of the nostril there is another outgrowth with between two and five small branches at its tip. Other distinguishing features include the form of the dorsal fin — the spines and soft rays are not separated by a notch and the dorsal fin is not connected with the tail fin. There are 31—44 teeth in each jaw. The colour of this fish is green or greyish yellow to olive with a yellowish belly and dark spots on the back and sides. The dorsal fin is the same colour as the back, the anal fin is yellowish, sometimes with a reddish tinge and small spots. The caudal, ventral and pectoral fins are also yellowish, while the pectoral fins also have four or five rows of small red spots.

Bloodthirsty Blennies live amongst rocks in the coastal areas of the sea, at greater depths than other species, and they start spawning sooner. The eggs are laid on the undersides of stones or in empty mollusc shells near the shore. Development takes 15—20 days, the male guards the eggs and does not feed during this time. There are usually about 50 eggs per square centimetre and a total of 3,000—12,000 are produced by one female, of which not more than 200 are fertilized. Like those of other species, the females lay the eggs in three batches. The fry at first live pelagic lives and when they measure 2—2.5 cm they can still be caught 25—30 km from the shore. These blennies feed mainly on algae and molluscs.

These are economically unimportant fishes but they do provide food for other fish species.

Size: 15—20 cm, maximum 25 cm
Fin formula: D XII—XIII/20—22, A II/20—21
Fecundity: 3,000—12,000 eggs
Distribution: In the Black Sea, the Mediterranean and the adjoining part of the Atlantic.

The related *B. nigriceps* is a small blenny growing to a maximum length of 4 cm; it is considered to be the most beautifully coloured member of the genus. At spawning time the usually plain black head becomes brilliantly marked, often with lemon-yellow cheeks.

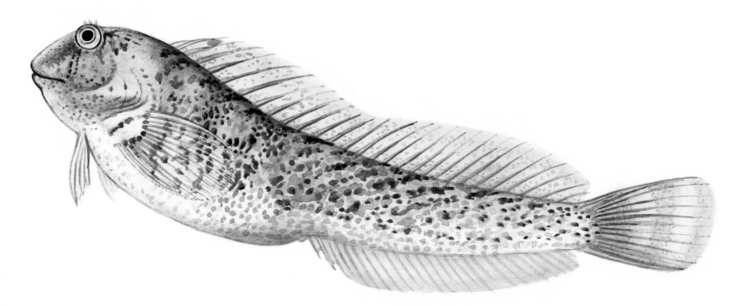

Capuchin Blenny
Coryphoblennius galerita

An unmistakable blenny for the nape of its neck bears a longitudinal crest, which commences with a large and usually triangular hump and proceeds towards the dorsal fin with between three and nine filamentous and sometimes branching tentacles. At the back of the nostril there is a short process with a branched tip and a similar but even shorter one at the front. The spiny and soft-rayed sections of the dorsal fin are separated by a deep notch; the spines are shorter than the soft rays. The pectoral fins stretch as far as the anal fin and in young individuals may stretch as far as the 11th or 12th ray of the anal fin. There are 55−65 teeth in the upper and 35−45 in the lower jaw, with a strong canine tooth in each lower jaw. The colour of this fish is greyish yellow and there are two rows of transverse brown spots, in groups of two or three, along the upper and undersides of the body. The crest on the head is blue and there are also bluish-coloured spots on the body.

Spawning takes place from April to July. The male makes a nest in a small cavity in the rocks and then tempts several individual females into the cavity in succession, so that one nest contains eggs from a variety of females. When a female approaches, the male comes partly out of the nest, wriggling his whole body and touching the female with the tip of his snout. If the female fails to show interest the male comes right out of the nest and tries to lure the female into it. Once in the nest the female turns over and attaches the eggs to the underside of the rock. They are then fertilized by the male which protects them until the young hatch. The young are pelagic and can be caught as far as 150 km from the shore.

This blenny feeds on barnacles, on planktonic crustaceans and on their larvae. It lives in coastal waters near the shore and can often be seen out of the water on rocky coastlines or on wave-washed harbour installations.

Commonest synonym: Blennius galerita
Size: 6−8 cm, maximum 9 cm
Fin formula: D XII−XIII/16−18, A II/18−19
Distribution: Off the western coast of Europe from the southwest of England, in the Mediterranean and the Black Sea.

The related *C. tentacularis* has a similar distribution. It grows up to 15 cm long, is differently coloured to *C. galerita* and has a dorsal fin which is of equal height throughout and has no notches. Above its eyes it has two long somewhat branched processes whose length, in some individuals may be up to three times the diameter of the eye.

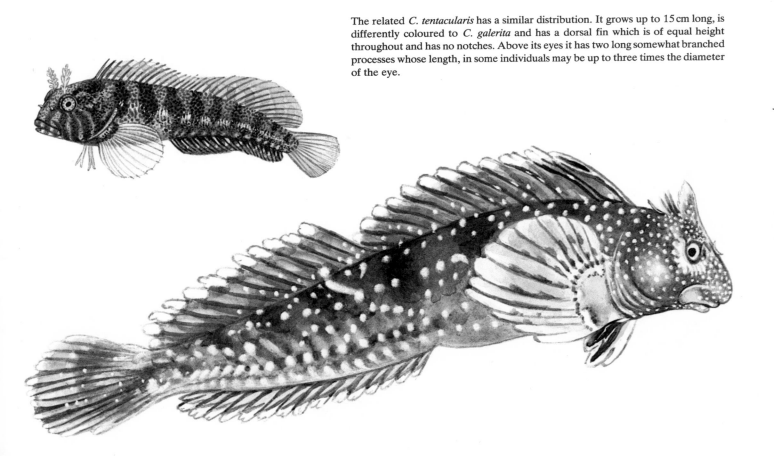

The Pholidae is a small family of little fishes with long, extremely flat-sided bodies which live in coastal shallows in the northern part of the Atlantic and Pacific Oceans.

Butterfish, Gunnel
Pholis gunnellus

The Butterfish is a long slimy fish with a short head and a small mouth pointing obliquely upwards. Its distinctive dorsal fin, which is composed of short, spiny rays, runs along practically the whole length of its long back. The anal fin is about half the length of the dorsal fin, the pectoral fins are small and the ventral fins are rudimentary. There is no lateral line. This fish is yellowish brown to greyish green in colour, with irregular cross bars forming a curious reticular pattern on the sides. Along the base of the dorsal fin there are between nine and fifteen black eye-spots with white borders and a black stripe leads from the eye to the mouth.

Butterfish are quite common in the lowermost zone of the intertidal area and also in the sublittoral zone, at depths of not more than 80—100 m. They hide amongst rocks and seaweeds and when the tide goes out may often be found under stones and seaweed in rock pools. The fish is very difficult to catch since it is so slimy, hence the name Butterfish. Spawning occurs between November and February. The female lays her eggs amongst stones or in empty mollusc shells and guards them either herself or together with the male. The larvae, which hatch in one or two months, are at first pelagic but once they grow to about 35 mm their lifestyle changes to one near the bottom. Adult fishes feed on various worms, molluscs, fish eggs and small crustaceans.

Size: 15—20 cm, maximum 25 cm
Weight: up to 0.25 kg
Fin formula: D 75—82, A II/39—45
Fecundity: 100—200 eggs
Distribution: Atlantic coasts of Europe from the Barents Sea to northern France, along the coasts of Iceland, southern Greenland and off the Atlantic coast of North America.

The related *P. laeta* lives near the seabed in coastal waters in the eastern Pacific at depths of 50—70 m. It grows up to 25 cm long.

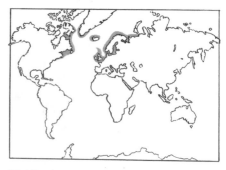

Distribution map of *P. gunnellus*.

The family Anarrhichadidae includes a group of five moderately large marine fishes notable for their numerous large teeth and powerful jaws. Three species live in the northern part of the Atlantic, the other two in the northern Pacific.

ANARRHICHADIDAE

Common Wolf-fish, Common Catfish

Anarrhichas lupus

The Common Wolf-fish is the most widespread in European waters. It is most frequently found in deep water on sandy seabeds among stones or in holes in rocks, sometimes at depths of over 200 m. It has an elongate body with a long dorsal fin stretching from the back of its head almost to its separate caudal fin. Like other wolf-fishes, it has no ventral fins and only rudimentary scales. Its characteristic feature is its wide mouth with large, bluntly conical teeth. Most of its body is dark yellowish green in colour, with a few vertical stripes; its belly is pale yellow.

Common Wolf-fishes swim with undulating movements of their whole bodies, rather like eels. They are known to undertake migrations, but it is not entirely clear where they go; it has been claimed that the fish swim eastwards in the spring and westwards again in the autumn. Spawning probably occurs during the second half of the winter at considerable depths. The eggs are large, 5.5—6 mm in diameter, and sink to the bottom in clumps. The fry live at the bottom at first, gradually moving into the middle layers of the sea as they grow larger, where they feed on fish eggs and planktonic organisms. As they grow larger still they descend to the sea bottom again and feed on echinoderms and molluscs.

In the northern areas of the Atlantic Ocean, Common Wolf-fish are often caught by cod trawlers; they are sold as rock salmon or rockfish and in Scandinavia the liver is regarded as a delicacy. Wallets, handbags, light ladies' footwear and book-covers are made from its strong, firm skin.

Size: 80—100 cm, occasionally up to 120 cm
Weight: 4—10 kg, maximum 21 kg
Fin formula: D 69—79, A 42—48
Fecundity: 10,000—25,000 eggs (acc. to Erenbaum, after Nikolsky up to 40,000)
Distribution: From the coast of Greenland to Novaya Zemlya, southwards as far as the coast of France.

The Common Wolf-fish feeds mainly on marine molluscs, crustaceans and echinoderms like cockles (1), whelks (2) and hermit crabs (3), crushing their hard shells with its strong, conical teeth.

A wolf-fish scale showing the characteristic incremental zones of close and more widely spaced rings, from which age and the growth rates are determined.

243

Spotted Wolf-fish, Spotted Catfish

Anarrhichas minor

This species has a similar distribution to the Common Wolf-fish, but descends to even greater depths of 450 m and usually lives over sandy or muddy sea beds. It grows faster and is bigger, but its teeth are distinctly smaller and it feeds on thin-shelled molluscs and echinoderms. These fishes take their name from the somewhat remote resemblance of their teeth to a wolf's fangs. Every year the old worn teeth are shed and new ones immediately begin to grow in their place, but while the new teeth are growing the wolf-fish feed on soft foods or go hungry. The Spotted Wolf-fish is greenish to greyish brown in colour and the whole of the body and dorsal fin are thickly sprinkled with dark spots which seldom appear on the other fins. The larvae and the fry have dark stripes however, like those of the Common Wolf-fish. Spotted Wolf-fishes spawn at the end of the winter in similar situations to those used by the Common Wolf-fish.

It has good quality, tasty flesh, which can be prepared in a variety of ways and its skin is used like that of the Common Wolf-fish to make wallets and shoes etc. In recent years the average annual catch of Spotted Wolf-fish has been about 12,000 tons.

Skin of the Pacific species *A. orientalis* is inserted by Eskimoes into the seams of their waterproof clothing and footwear because on contact with water it swells up and keeps the water out.

Size: 1.0—1.8 m, exceptionally up to 2 m
Weight: 3—17 kg, maximum 45 kg
Fin formula: D 74—80, A 45—47
Fecundity: 15,000—50,000 eggs
Distribution: The northern part of the Atlantic.

The related species *A. latifrons* is also found in the northern parts of the Atlantic Ocean where it lives at depths of about 800 m. It grows up to 80—120 cm long usually, occasionally reaching 180 cm. Its mushy flesh, which contains up to 92 % water, is of poor quality and is used only for fish meal.

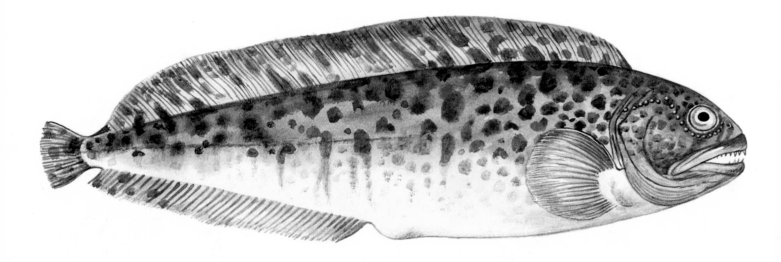

Members of the family Zoarcidae have elongate bodies covered with small cycloid scales. Some of them are oviparous (they produce eggs) while others are viviparous (they bear their young alive). There are about 200 mostly benthic species. Their taxonomic position is not clear; sometimes they are classified as relatives of the cods and sometimes of the gobies.

ZOARCIDAE

Eelpout, Mother of Eels
Zoarces viviparus

A distinctive slimy fish with a tapering body and a slightly flattened head. Its dorsal, caudal and anal fins are all united to form a coherent fin border running all round the body of the fish. The dorsal fin is unusual in being composed mostly of soft rays with a few spines near the tail. The small ventral fins are situated on the throat ahead of the pectoral fins. The Eelpout is very variably coloured but is usually predominantly greyish green marked with a series of irregular light blotches.

It is common in coastal waters in both intertidal and sublittoral zones and may also be found in brackish waters near river mouths. Because of a certain similarity to eels and their habit of lying buried in mud, these fishes were at one time thought to be 'mothers of eels.' They feed on bottom-dwelling crustaceans and also on occasional molluscs and small fishes. Breeding occurs in August or September, the eggs are fertilized internally after mating and after developing for four months in the female's ovaries the young are born alive, as tiny fishes measuring 4–5 mm, which remain for a time near the bottom. It is assumed that during their prenatal development the larvae are nourished by a substance secreted by the walls of the ovaries. Eelpouts become sexually mature when two years old.

The annual catch amounts to about 8,000 tons. The fish's flesh is greasy and is best smoked.

Commonest synonym: Blennius viviparus
Size: average 25–30 cm, exceptionally up to 50 cm
Weight: 1–1.5 kg
Fin formula: D+C 72–85 + 0–XVII + 16–24, A 80–95
Fecundity: 20–400 larvae
Distribution: In the coastal waters of the Atlantic from the White Sea to the Bay of Biscay. They spend the summer close to the shore, swimming to deeper water in the winter.

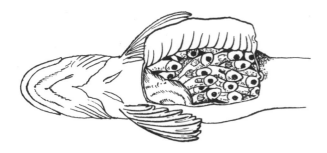

View of the abdominal cavity of a female with young.

The related *Gymnalis viridis* lives in the Arctic Ocean and in the northern part of the Atlantic. It has an average length of 10–20 cm, growing to a maximum of 30 cm. It has no ventral fins.

Esmark's Eelpout

Lycodes esmarkii

This fish is similar in form to the previous eelpout, with an elongated body, a combined dorsal-caudal-anal fin border, a very wide head, large pectoral fins and small ventral fins situated on its throat. It has thick, fleshy lips and its whole body is covered with scales, deeply embedded in the skin. Scales even cover the unpaired fins and the base of the pectoral fins; on the inner surface of the latter they continue along the first third of the fins. This species has a double lateral line, the upper part of which runs roughly along the middle of the sides to the root of the tail, while the lower part curves downwards behind the pectoral fins and continues along the underside to about two thirds of the way along the tail. Most of the body is dark greenish brown in colour, but the belly is yellowish white. On the back there are six to eight double oblique yellow stripes shaped like inverted letter Y's, especially in young fishes.

Together with *L. vahlii* and one or two others, this species is classified as a cold-water fish, since it occurs chiefly at temperatures of 2−5 °C. It is a deep-water fish found comparatively rarely over muddy substrates at depths of 250−500 m. It spawns in the autumn and feeds mainly on echinoderms, in particular on sea urchins, starfish and brittle stars. It is occasionally taken by trawlers.

Size: 50−65 cm, maximum 75 cm
Weight: 2−3 kg
Fin formula: D + 1/2 C 113−118, A + 1/2 C 97−102
Fecundity: up to 1,200 eggs, 6 mm in diameter
Distribution: Off the coasts of Europe and America in the northern part of the Atlantic, north as far as the 73rd line of latitude.

The related *L. vahlii* is found in similar areas to *L. esmarkii*. It lives near the bottom of the sea at depths of down to 500 m and usually grows to a length of 20−35 cm, reaching a maximum of 50 cm. It is a source of food for various cods.

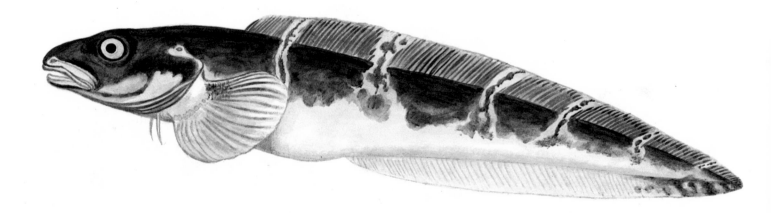

Members of the family Ammodytidae are small marine species living for the most part in the northern hemisphere. They have elongate bodies covered with cycloid scales, no swim-bladder and usually no ventral fins. The lower jaw protrudes noticeably. There are about six genera living in the Atlantic, the Indian and the Pacific Oceans; these form very important prey species for a variety of predators.

AMMODYTIDAE

Lesser Sand Eel, Lesser Sand Lance

Ammodytes tobianus

This species has an elongate body, long dorsal and anal fins, and a movable, protrusible upper jaw. It has a yellow to bluish grey back and its sides and belly are silvery white.

These are common inshore fishes, living in the intertidal zone of sandy beaches and also into the sublittoral zone down to a depth of about 30 m. They lie buried in the sand or remain near the bottom. In some parts of their range, including the Baltic populations, there are two races, spawning either in spring or autumn. However, the more northerly race of the Atlantic spawns only in spring. Spawning occurs at depths of about 20 m on a sandy seabed and the eggs are buried in the sand. The fish feed on zooplankton and on the larvae of other fishes including herrings and their own kind.

Sand Eels form an important component of the prey of mackerels, herrings, cods and piscivorous sea birds. This and other species are caught in large quantities off the coasts of Japan, Korea and China as well as off the coasts of western Europe; the greater part of the catch goes to making fish meal. Another species, *A. marinus,* which lives off the coasts of northern Europe and Greenland, has more vertebrae (68−73) than *A. tobianus* (60−65) and more rays (59−64) in its dorsal fin.

Size: 13−18 cm, maximum 20 cm
Fin formula: D 50−57, A 25−31
Distribution: Off the coasts of Europe from the Bay of Biscay to Murmansk, including the coasts of Britain, Iceland and Scandinavia; in the Baltic and the Gulf of Finland.

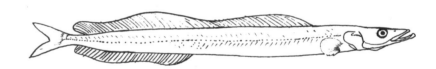

The species *A. cicerelus* has a different distribution; it lives in the Mediterranean and Black Seas and in the Atlantic Ocean together with *A. tobianus* as far as the south of Norway. It grows to a length of 18 cm.

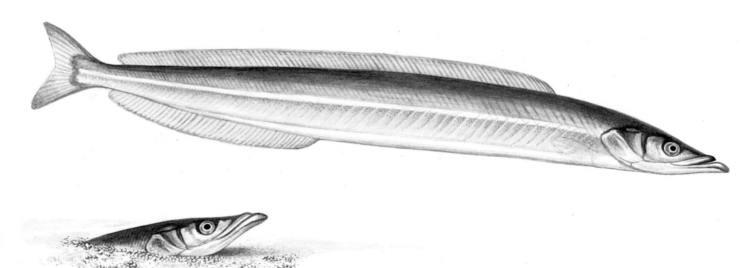

247

Greater Sand Eel, Greater Sand Lance

Hyperoplus lanceolatus

An elongate fish, similar in form to the previous species but about twice as large and without a protrusible upper jaw. There are two large tooth-like structures just inside the mouth, on the roof of the mouth. The back and the upper part of the sides are bluish green, the underside and the belly silvery white. On either side of the front of the head there is a conspicuous black spot.

Greater Sand Eels live in inshore areas with sandy bottoms like the Lesser Sand Eels, but they are much less common and may be present in much deeper water, down to depths of 150 m. Spawning takes place at the end of spring and in summer at depths of 20–100 m. The eggs are laid in the sand and the larvae and fry are pelagic. At first they feed on small planktonic organisms and on the eggs and larvae of other fishes, but later they feed on larger crustaceans and other fishes including Lesser Sand Eels.

This species is of little economic significance if only because of its small numbers.

Commonest synonym: Ammodytes lanceolatus
Size: 20–30 cm, maximum 35 cm
Weight: maximum 120 g
Fin formula: D 52–61, A 28–33
Fecundity: 15,000–30,000 eggs
Distribution: Off the Atlantic coasts of Europe from the Bay of Biscay to the North and Baltic Seas, around the coast of Iceland.

Distribution map showing the association of this species with the shallow water of the coastal shelf.

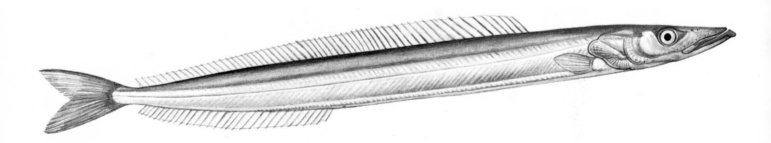

About forty species of pelagic marine fishes belong to the family Scombridae, all of them fast swimmers. They have a fusiform body which is rounded in cross-section, a characteristically narrow peduncle with a lateral flange and a deeply forked tail. They are easily identified by the small fins (finlets) between the dorsal and caudal fin above and between the anal and caudal fin below. The pectoral fin is held characteristically high on the body. They are important both economically and to sport fishermen.

SCOMBRIDAE

Atlantic Bonito
Sarda sarda

The Atlantic Bonito is closely related to mackerels and tunnyfishes; it has a similar body and a number of finlets along the upper and lower edges of its peduncle. At one time it was classified in a separate family, the Cybiidae, but it is now included in the family Scombridae, together with the tunnyfishes and mackerel, as they are obviously related.

At present there are six known bonito species, only two of which live in the Atlantic; economically the Atlantic Bonito is the most important. It can be distinguished from the others by the seven to nine oblique dark stripes on the dorsal half of the body. It is a very efficient, fast swimmer, like all members of the family, and from the age of two or three months feeds on fishes, like anchovies, pilchards and mack-

erels. It grows very quickly; at only three months old some individuals may measure up to 35 cm long and weigh about 0.5 kg. The spawning season begins in April, but the majority of fish do not spawn until June when the shoals break up and the fish swim closer inshore. Spawning does not occur in the north Atlantic but does occur in the Mediterranean and European waters. In the winter the fish remain out in the open sea.

The Atlantic Bonito has very tasty, relatively oily flesh, which is mostly eaten smoked or tinned. It is caught chiefly with seine-nets and dragnets and in recent years the total annual catch has ranged from 35,000 to 60,000 tons, much of it from European waters of the Atlantic.

Size: 40−50 cm, maximum 85 cm
Weight: 1−3 kg, exceptionally up to 7 kg
Fin formula: D_1 XXI−XXIV, D_2 II/13−16, A II/11−13
Fecundity: 400,000−500,000 eggs
Distribution: The eastern and western shores of the Atlantic in waters with temperatures of more than 15 °C. In European waters this fish is present in the North Sea and common in the Mediterranean; in some years large populations occur in the Black Sea.

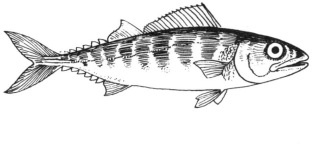

A young Bonito showing the strikingly different colouring. The stripes on its sides are vertical, not oblique.

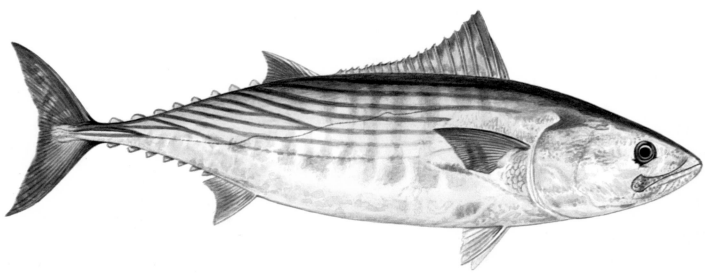

Mackerel
Scomber scombrus

A familiar fish, bluish-green in colour with characteristic zigzag stripes on the back. It has a large number of finlets behind the second dorsal and anal fins, a long, strong tail and a deeply forked tail fin. The dorsal fins are rather far apart and the first one has more than nine rays.

Mackerels are gregarious fishes whose large shoals are found mostly in coastal waters; they seldom swim out beyond the edge of the continental shelf. They generally live close to the surface but the absence of a swim-bladder allows them to descend quickly to depths of 300 m. In the course of the year these fishes undertake long spawning and food migrations. They feed on zooplankton and small fishes, especially on pilchards and anchovies. Mackerel become sexually mature when three or four years old and spawn between May and July; the eggs are pelagic and have large oil globules as flotation devices. Large numbers of eggs are produced and fry are abundant in coastal waters in the summer. After spawning the adults usually migrate northwards in search of food; with the advent of winter they retire southwards to warmer and deeper waters.

The economic importance of Mackerel is considerable and for years this has been one of the ten most valuable fish species in the world. The average annual catch is usually in the region of one million tons, but in recent years it has been necessary to fix quotas to ensure maintenance of its numbers. It has very tasty, oily and juicy flesh and is eaten fresh, smoked and tinned. It is also a frequent source of food for other predatory fishes.

Size: 30–40 cm, maximum 60 cm
Weight: 1–1.6 kg
Fin formula: D_1 X–XV, D_2 II/10–12, A II/8–13
Fecundity: 200,000–500,000 eggs
Distribution: In the northern part of the Atlantic from the coast of North America to the coast of Europe as far as the northern coast of Norway; also in the Mediterranean and Black Seas.

Larval stages measuring 8 mm and 19 mm and a juvenile individual. Larval stages have unbroken dorsal and anal fins stretching to the origin of the caudal fin; incipient differentiation of the finlets on the base of the tail can be seen in the juvenile individual. Such stages are likely to be present together in the summer, since spawning extends over three months.

8 mm

19 mm

70 mm

Chub Mackerel

Scomber japonicus

In form and habits this species closely resembles a Mackerel but it has a swim-bladder, larger eyes, fewer than nine rays in its first dorsal fin and substantially larger scales in the area between its operculum and its pectoral and ventral fins. Its colouring is also different — it has dark, grey-blue spots below its lateral line and on its belly and the dark, zigzag stripes on its back are less pronounced than in the Mackerel.

This is a cosmopolitan fish living in all the temperate and warm oceans, but its range does not extend as far north as that of the Mackerel. It becomes sexually mature when three or four years old and the fishes usually spawn intermittently in February and March. Spawning generally takes place at night and is often preceded by a shoreward migration, sometimes over a considerable distance. In the summer the fish migrate in search of food, mainly zooplankton and fishes like pilchards and anchovies; during these migrations they may cover over 30 km a day and the shoals are accompanied by flocks of seagulls. When cold weather sets in the fishes descend to greater depths, usually to 100 m or more.

The economic importance of the Chub Mackerel is enormous and during the past ten years this has been the fifth most important species in the world. The fish are caught with dragnets and seine-nets and annual catches average two million tons; catches are particularly large off the coasts of Japan and China. This mackerel has very tasty flesh.

Synonyms: Pneumatophorus japonicus, Scomber colias
Size: 30−50 cm, maximum 60 cm
Weight: up to 1.5 to 1.7 kg
Fin formula: D_1 IX−X, D_2 II/9−10, A I−II/9−10
Fecundity: 350,000−2,500,000 eggs
Distribution: Cosmopolitan.

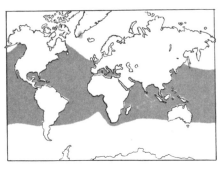

Distribution map of *S. japonicus*.

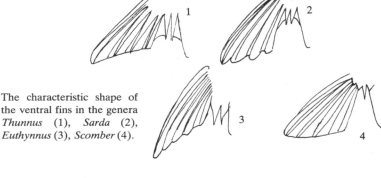

The characteristic shape of the ventral fins in the genera *Thunnus* (1), *Sarda* (2), *Euthynnus* (3), *Scomber* (4).

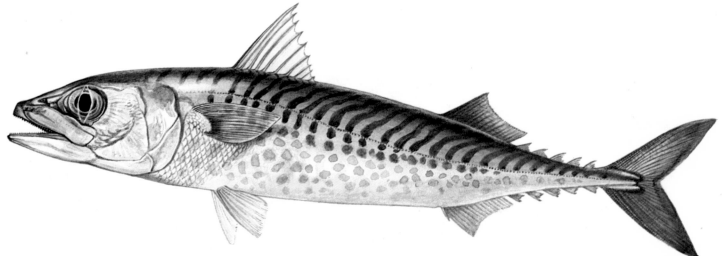

Tunny, Blue-fin Tuna

Thunnus thynnus

There are thirteen tunnyfish species in four genera, of which the Tunny is probably the best known. It is also the biggest and grows the fastest, so that when three years old some individuals are already a metre long. Like all tunnyfish this fish is an outstandingly good swimmer and virtually never stops moving throughout its life, since a continuous flow of water through the open mouth into the gill chamber is essential to maintain its oxygen supply. The faster the fish swim, the greater is the oxygen consumption, but at the same time stale water in the gill chamber is also exchanged more rapidly for fresh. The gills have a very large respiratory surface and the blood contains proportionally more haemoglobin (respiratory pigment) than that of any other fish, so that their respiration is highly efficient. The lowest speed measured for the Tunny is 8 km an hour, but for short periods it can develop a speed of 60–80 km an hour (according to some sources 90 km an hour). Its streamlined hydrodynamic shape is ideal for fast and enduring swimming. When swimming the dorsal and anal fins are retracted into grooves and at high speed the pectoral fins are also held close to the body.

Tunnyfishes undertake long migrations sometimes right across the ocean. For instance examination of tagged individuals has shown that some had travelled from Mexican waters to the coast of Japan or from Florida to the Bay of Biscay. Vertical migration also takes place to the deeper layers of water during the daytime and back to the surface at night. In the spring Tunny swim shorewards, where they spawn between April and August, depending on the temperature of the water. They feed mainly on shoal-forming fishes, like mackerel, herring and sand-eels.

Tunny are important fishes economically and are caught in a variety of ways. The total annual catch in recent years has ranged from 50,000 to 70,000 tons but the catch is variable and the fish are susceptible to overfishing, when numbers may drop dramatically.

Commonest synonym: Scomber thynnus
Size: 2–3 m, occasionally up to 5 m
Weight: 300–500 kg, occasionally up to 900 kg
Fin formula: D_1 XII–XIII, D_2 I–II/13–15 + 7–9, A II/11–13 + 6–8
Distribution: In all the oceans. The fishes prefer warm water with a temperature of about 30 °C, but may be found in water as cold as 5 °C.

The related *Euthynnus pelamis* lives in the warmer areas of the great oceans. In Europe it may be found as far north as the south coast of England. It usually reaches a length of 60–70 cm and weighs up to 25 kg. With an annual catch of up to 600,000 tons it is economically the most valuable of the tunnyfish.

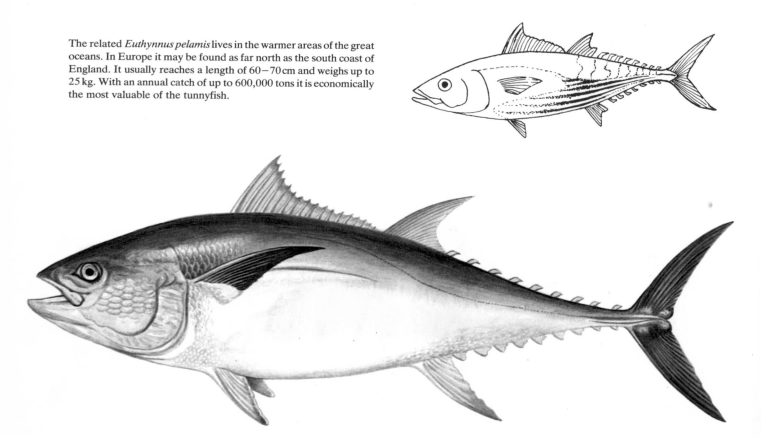

Long-fin Tunny
Thunnus alalunga

As its name suggests, this fish is notable for its long, falciform pectoral fins which stretch beyond the end of its second dorsal fin. Otherwise it is similar in form to the Tunny. It has a large swim-bladder and, unlike other tunnyfishes which have red flesh, it has white flesh — a fact which makes it highly prized. It is found in warmer waters than the Tunny, usually where the water temperature is 15 °C or more, so that it is rarely seen north of the 40th latitude. Consequently, in European waters it only ventures north of the Bay of Biscay very occasionally. At the edges of its range, young, sexually immature individuals are most common, mostly swimming close to the surface. The adult fish remain largely in tropical waters at depths of 150—200 m.

An excellent swimmer, this tunnyfish undertakes long migrations during which time the shoals travel at considerable speeds, often covering 28—30 km in a day. The muscles on its sides, which are used most in swimming, are supplied with oxygen and nutrients by a special, richly branching vascular system. This blood system also plays an important role in maintaining body temperature; when the fish puts on speed the system raises the body temperature until it is as much as 10—12 °C higher than the temperature of the water — a unique phenomenon among cold-blooded animals — and excess body heat is lost as a result.

According to world fishery statistics this species takes second or third place among the tunnyfish for the size of its catches, which amount to some 200,000 tons a year.

Commonest synonyms: Germo alalunga, Scomber germo
Size: usually 60—100 cm, exceptionally up to 130 cm
Weight: 4—15 kg, occasionally up to 45 kg
Fin formula: D_1 XIV—XV, D_2 12—16 + 8—9,
A 12—15 + 7—9
Distribution: Relatively abundant in the tropical and subtropical areas of all the oceans.

The related *Thunnus albacares* also lives in the warmer areas of the great oceans. It measures 100—150 cm but may reach 250 cm in length and weighs 30—40 kg (maximum 200 kg). Annual catches in recent years have ranged from 250,000 to 350,000 tons, the greater part of which comes from the Pacific.

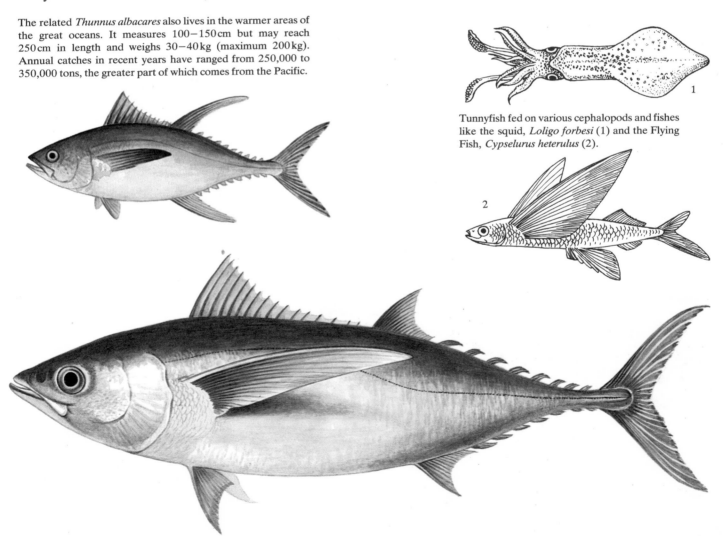

Tunnyfish fed on various cephalopods and fishes like the squid, *Loligo forbesi* (1) and the Flying Fish, *Cypselurus heterulus* (2).

The family Xiphiidae has only one recent species, the Swordfish, which lives in open water in the tropical, subtropical and temperate areas of all the big oceans. Occasionally it penetrates into the Black Sea from the Mediterranean, but is otherwise seldom encountered in coastal waters. The Swordfish is very closely related to the tropical Istiophoridae (sailfishes and marlins), the species of both having elongate upper jaws and snouts, forming a 'sword'.

XIPHIIDAE

Swordfish
Xiphias gladius

This fish takes both its scientific and common names from its exceedingly long, tapering, flattened upper jaw which is shaped like a sword and accounts for one third of its total length. It is no mere ornament, but is used chiefly for slaughtering prey and also acts as a stabilizer. Swordfish have no ventral fins or scales and the adults have no teeth. Adult fishes have deep blue backs; the upper part of their sides has a metallic blue sheen, while the lower half is lighter in colour. Swordfishes are excellent swimmers and undertake long, solitary migrations in search of food. With their torpedo-shaped bodies and large, crescent-shaped caudal fins they can develop speeds of 70 km an hour over short distances. They feed mainly on fishes like mackerel and herring and on squid. Spawning occurs during the summer in tropical and subtropical waters and the young grow rapidly.

Swordfish play a strange role in the mythology of the sea and have been known to ram wooden ships and boats with their swords. Most stories are probably exaggerated, but harpooned fish may attack the boats as they are drawn in. Because of their tasty flesh and their size, swordfish are valuable food fishes and are caught both by anglers and commercial fishermen alike. The total annual catch in recent years has amounted to about 34,000 tons.

Size: 4−5 m, occasionally more
Weight: 400−500 kg (the record is 537 kg)
Fin formula: D_1 III/5−30, D_2 4, A_1 9−11, A_2 3−5
Fecundity: up to 16,000,000 eggs
Distribution: Cosmopolitan

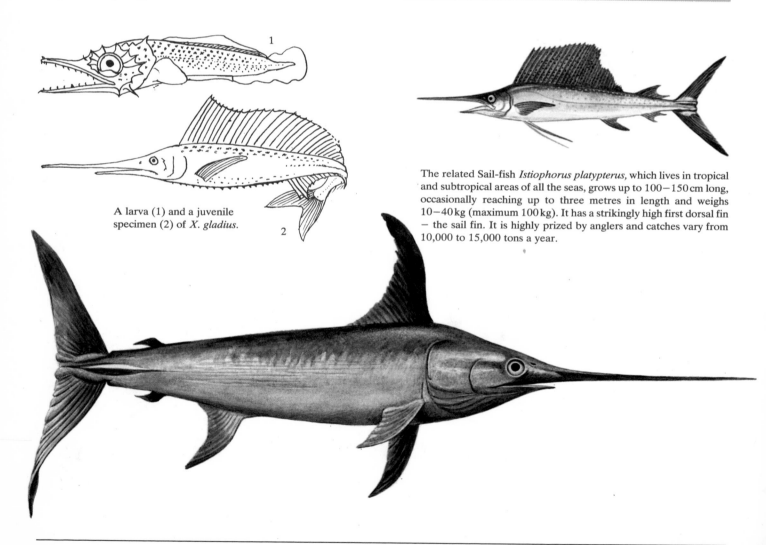

A larva (1) and a juvenile specimen (2) of *X. gladius.*

The related Sail-fish *Istiophorus platypterus,* which lives in tropical and subtropical areas of all the seas, grows up to 100−150 cm long, occasionally reaching up to three metres in length and weighs 10−40 kg (maximum 100 kg). It has a strikingly high first dorsal fin − the sail fin. It is highly prized by anglers and catches vary from 10,000 to 15,000 tons a year.

Members of the family Gobiidae are small fishes whose ventral fins are fused together to form a weak suction disc with which the fishes cling to rocks. The lips are very thick, the eyes prominent and often protrude dorsally. Most of them live in the sea, but members of the genus Proterorhinus are permanently freshwater species. Before spawning they build nests and afterwards the eggs are guarded, generally by the males.

GOBIIDAE

River Goby
Gobius fluviatilis

A typical goby in shape, a small fish with a large head and longish body, narrowing towards the tail. The eyes are large and protuberant. There are two dorsal fins, the first short and the second longer. The back and sides of the fish are a dark brownish or yellowish grey with an indistinct mosaic of dark, confluent spots; on the sides there are 10—12 large separate spots and there are small dark spots on the fins. The colour of the males changes at spawning time, when they become almost completely black with yellow-bordered unpaired fins. Spawning takes place from April to June and the male builds a nest in sand dotted with smallish stones; the eggs are attached to the underside of the stone by the females. Several females lay their eggs in one nest, which is then guarded actively by the male for the entire incubation period. River Gobies become sexually mature when two years old, when they measure about 10 cm. They feed mainly on crustaceans, but also on worms, midge larvae and molluscs, and are preyed upon by Pike-perch and sturgeons. They are fished in the Black Sea, where the annual catch amounts to about 30,000 tons.

Size: 14—16 cm, maximum 20 cm
Fin formula: D_1 VI, D_2 I/15—18, A I/13—16
Fecundity: 400—3,000 eggs
Distribution: In the Black and Caspian Seas, the Sea of Azov and their tributaries.

Distribution of *G. fluviatilis* (red) and *G. ophiocephalus* (blue).

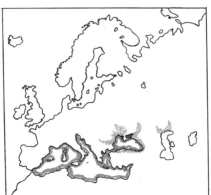

♀

255

Black-spotted Goby

Gobius melanostomus

This goby can be recognised by the large black spot at the posterior end of its first dorsal fin. It has a dark greyish or yellowish brown body with irregular confluent spots and further dark spots along the lateral line. In young individuals the large, elongate black spot at the end of the first dorsal fin has a white border. In males the colour changes at spawning time, they become very dark and their enlarged unpaired fins become white at the edges.

Spawning begins in the spring, as soon as the temperature of the water rises to 6 °C, and is at its most intense at the end of April and during May. The nests are built in the intertidal zone of the Black Sea and the Sea of Azov and the eggs are laid in the littoral brackish waters of both seas on the undersides of stones, in cracks and gaps in the rocks, on projecting parts of the seabed and on objects which have fallen into the water. When spawning is over the females swim into deeper water. The nest is guarded by the male, which fans it with his pectoral fins to assure a constant supply of fresh water rich in oxygen flowing over the eggs. Since the eggs in one nest are of different ages the larvae hatch at different times. The fish attain sexual maturity in their second year, when they grow to 5 cm and over. These fishes do not feed during the winter, only beginning again in the spring, when the temperature of the water reaches about 8 °C; they feed mostly in the summer. The adults feed primarily on molluscs and worms and to a lesser extent on crustaceans, the fry on zooplankton. While spawning and guarding the nest the males do not feed and rapidly lose weight, so that many of them die. *G. melanostomus* is the commonest goby in the Black Sea. They are fished intensively, annual catches reaching up to 50,000 tons, and are usually sold tinned in tomato sauce.

Size: 11−17 cm, maximum 25 cm
Fin formula: D_1 VI, D_2 I/12−17, A I/10−14
Fecundity: 200−4,000 eggs
Distribution: Along the shores of the Black Sea, the Sea of Azov and in their tributary rivers.

The related *G. batrachocephalus* is the largest member of the genus in the Black Sea. It grows to a length of 25−30 cm or occasionally up to 35 cm. It also lives in the Sea of Azov and the Dardanelles, but unlike *G. melanostomus* it mostly remains in the sea and seldom enters fresh water.

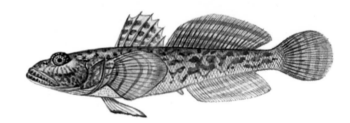

♀

Black Goby
Gobius niger

One of the most widespread of the gobies, this is also one of the darkest in colour. Its body is dark brown with a greyish tinge and it has lighter patches irregularly distributed along its sides. It has characteristically large scales, of which there are fewer than 45 in the lateral line, in contrast to other *Gobius* species which have more than 45.

This goby lives in sandy and clayey areas, especially in estuaries and sheltered coastal bays; it is often associated with eel-grass beds and is usually found at depths of 2–80 m. It is a marine species, never found in fresh water, although it does live in the brackish waters of the Baltic and the Sea of Azov. Spawning occurs intermittently from May to August, usually in four instalments, and since the eggs are very small the average fecundity of the females is high. As in other *Gobius* species, the eggs are laid in nests on the undersides of stones, in gaps in the rocks and even in large mollusc shells. While guarding the nest the males stop feeding and many of them die. Unusually in gobies, the larvae are pelagic at first and feed on zooplankton. The adult fish feed on molluscs, prawns, small crabs, polychaete worms and fish fry.

These are economically unimportant fishes, since nowhere do they form populations large enough to make it worthwhile catching them. They form part of the food of bigger fishes.

Size: 8–12 cm, maximum 15 cm
Fin formula: D_1 VI, D_2 I/11–13, A I/9–13
Fecundity: 15,000–20,000 eggs
Distribution: From the middle of the coast of Norway to Cape Verde on the coast of West Africa and in the Baltic, the Mediterranean and the Black Seas.

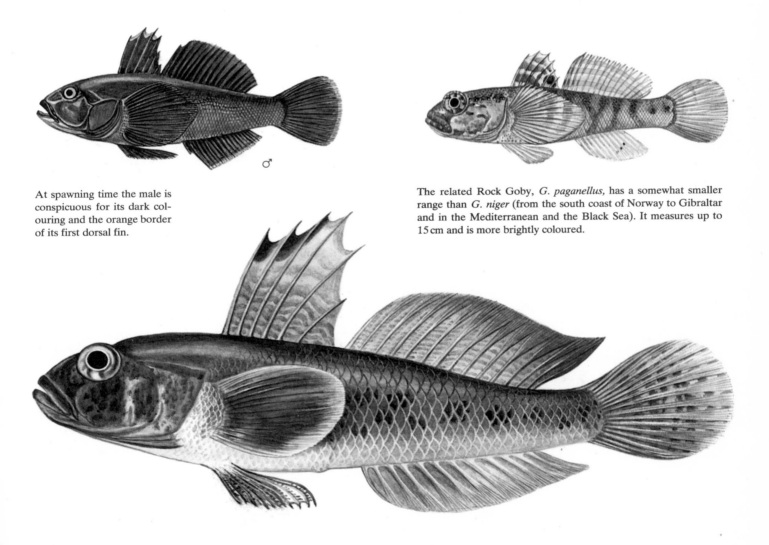

At spawning time the male is conspicuous for its dark colouring and the orange border of its first dorsal fin.

The related Rock Goby, *G. paganellus,* has a somewhat smaller range than *G. niger* (from the south coast of Norway to Gibraltar and in the Mediterranean and the Black Sea). It measures up to 15 cm and is more brightly coloured.

257

Snakehead Goby

Gobius ophiocephalus

One of the larger species of the family, this goby has a flat-sided body and high dorsal fins, the height of the second one increasing towards the tail. The top and back of its head, its throat and the base of its pectoral fins are covered with cycloid scales. It has a greenish brown body, strikingly mottled as a result of the confluence of many single dark brown spots, while on the dorsal, caudal and pectoral fins there are longitudinal stripes also produced by the union of dark brown spots.

These gobies live in the Black Sea off the shores of the Crimea, the Caucasus, Bulgaria and Rumania, in the Sea of Azov, the Mediterranean and in the adjoining parts of the Atlantic. They also live in the deltas of the big rivers flowing into these seas, mostly amongst seaweeds. The fish spawn from March to June, depending on the temperature of the water, from the age of two years onwards. Before spawning starts the male builds a nest of seaweed in which five to ten females lay their eggs. The fry and young fish feed chiefly on plankton; the adult fish are predatory and hunt small fishes like other small gobies and sand smelts, crustaceans and small molluscs.

This species has practically no economic significance and is caught only incidentally with other more valuable species, in places where it forms large populations.

Size: 20—25 cm
Fin formula: D_1 VI, D_2 I/13—16, A I—II/11—16
Fecundity: 7,000—22,000 eggs
Distribution: In the Black Sea, the Sea of Azov and the Mediterranean, also found in the adjoining part of the Atlantic Ocean.

The related Giant Goby *G. cobitis* lives in the Black Sea, the Mediterranean and the coastal waters of the eastern part of the Atlantic from the Bay of Biscay to Morocco. It usually grows up to 15—20 cm, occasionally 28 cm, and is not found in fresh water.

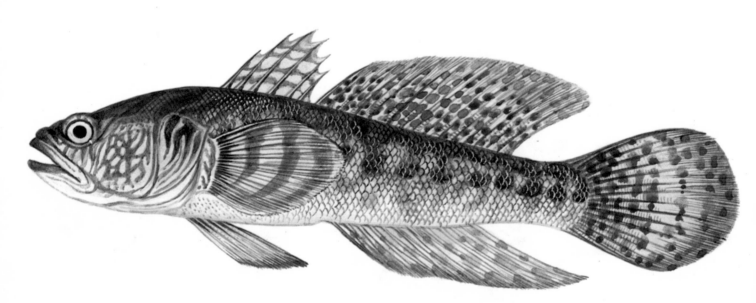

Common Goby
Pomatoschistus microps

This is the goby most likely to be found in estuaries, in intertidal pools and in salt marshes on all the European coasts. It is abundant in all these places and is also found in brackish or almost fresh water. They are usually dark grey in colour but may be yellowish or light grey, the body is marked with an irregular network of speckles and there are light saddle-spots on its back and dark smudges on its sides. The males are a little differently coloured from the females; they have dark cross bars on their sides and a dark spot on the posterior edge of the first dorsal fin.

A characteristic feature is the absence of scales on the top of the head and on the throat; the lateral line scales are large and there are between 43 and 50 scales present in the lateral line.

Spawning occurs from April to August, but mostly in May or June; the females lay the eggs in empty bivalve shells and the males subsequently guard both the eggs and the larvae.

Common Gobies feed on small crustaceans like amphipods, copepods, isopods and small shrimps. They are important prey species of fishes like eels and flounders as well as being eaten by birds (gulls and waders). They thus play an important part in the food chain in sandy and marshy areas of the coast where they are abundant, down to depths of 40 m. They are sometimes kept in marine aquaria.

Commonest synonym: Gobius leopardinus
Size: 3–5 cm, occasionally up to 8 cm
Fin formula: D_1 VI, D_2 I/8–10, A I/8–10
Fecundity: 500–1,000 eggs
Distribution: Along the European shores of the Atlantic south of the Arctic Circle and in the Baltic, the Mediterranean, the Black Sea and the Sea of Azov.

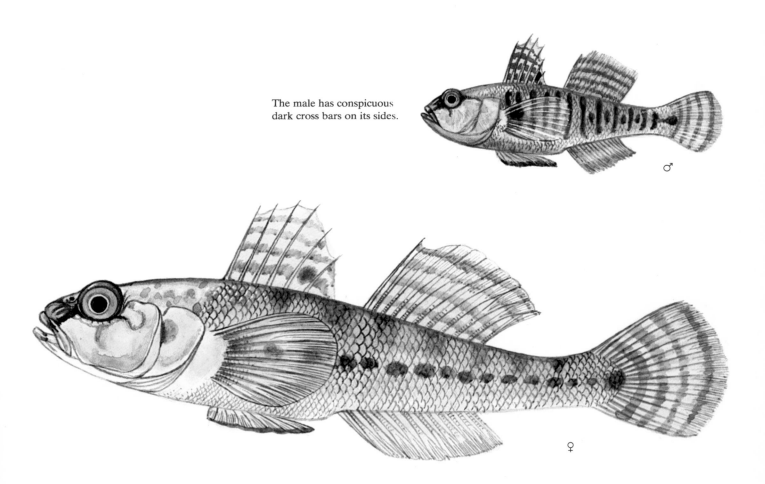

The male has conspicuous dark cross bars on its sides.

♂

♀

Sand Goby
Pomatoschistus minutus

A small goby, similar in form to the previous species, but with much smaller scales, between 58 and 70 in the lateral line, and with scales on the head and throat. The suction disc has short finger-like processes on its anterior edge. The usually sandy brown body is mottled with dark speckles and saddle-spots on the back. A row of large dark spots runs along the middle of the sides and on both dorsal fins there are four narrow, oblique dark-coloured bands. At spawning time in particular, the males have a dark violet or black light-bordered spot at the back edge of their first dorsal fin.

Sand Gobies live over sandy seabeds in the sublittoral zones of the European coasts, rarely in intertidal or estuarine areas. They are most common at depths of 5−12 m and at distances of up to 100 m from the shore. They are usually found in small shoals close to the seabed and in the winter they descend to greater depths. Spawning takes place from March to July at depths of down to 40 m. The females lay the eggs on stones or algae but also in mollusc shells, generally in three or four instalments. The males keep watch over the eggs and the larvae. The latter live in open water until they grow to about 17 mm in length. The fish become sexually mature when a year old, and only have life spans of two or three years. They feed chiefly on small crustaceans like amphipods, copepods, isopods and small shrimps, and are themselves prey for larger species of fishes like flatfishes, sculpins, codling and bass and they make good bait for these species.

Commonest synonym: Gobius minutus
Size: 6−8 cm, exceptionally up to 10 cm
Fin formula: D_1 VI, D_2 I/9−11, A I/9−11
Distribution: The Atlantic coasts of Europe from the north coast of Norway as far south as Gibraltar, the Mediterranean and the Black Seas.

Distribution map of *P. minutus*.

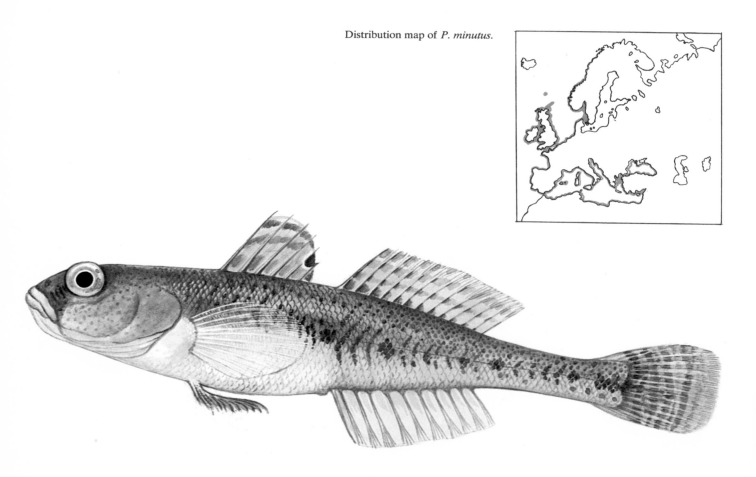

Painted Goby
Pomatoschistus pictus

Another typical small goby with a relatively robust body and a well developed suction disc with a smooth anterior edge. Its body is covered with large scales, the number in the lateral line being 35—41. The colour of the fish varies from brown to light yellow and it is irregularly marked with small dark spots. The scales have dark edges and there are four or five clusters of large dark spots on its sides, the first one below the pectoral fins. There are also two rows of dark spots on both the dorsal fins and an orange stripe along their upper edges. Male Painted Gobies are more brightly and more distinctively coloured than the female Painted Gobies.

These gobies live in the sublittoral zone from the low water mark to a depth of 50 m or more, most often on coarse sand or gravelly seabeds or in beds of eelgrass. Unlike Common Gobies, they are never found in estuaries or in the intertidal zone. Spawning occurs from April to July and the females, like those of the Common and Sand Gobies, lay their eggs in mollusc shells where they are guarded by the males until the larvae hatch. The newly hatched larvae live pelagic lives until they grow to 12 mm in length, when they assume a benthic mode of life. Like other members of the genus *Pomatoschistus*, this species is short-lived with a life span of only one or two years. The fish are economically unimportant themselves, but provide a source of food for other fishes.

Commonest synonym: Gobius pictus
Size: 5—7 cm, maximum 9.5 cm
Fin formula: D_1 VI, D_2 I/8—10, A I/10
Fecundity: 500—1.000 eggs
Distribution: The Atlantic coasts of Europe south from Trondheim to the Bay of Biscay.

Distribution map of *P. pictus*.

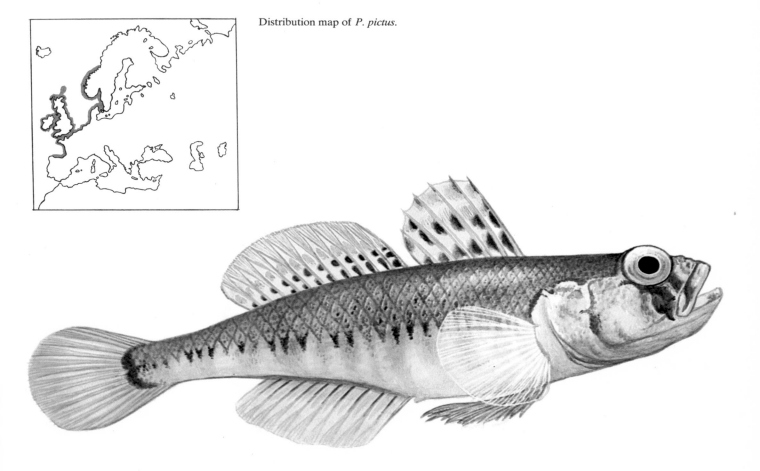

Mottled Black Sea Goby

Proterorhinus marmoratus

This is a small fish with a wide head and a fusiform, flat-sided body covered with tiny, rough scales. It has characteristic tubular, antenniform anterior nostrils and a suction disc below its wide, spoon-shaped pectoral fins. It has no lateral line. This goby is generally yellowish grey to greyish brown in colour, with a few irregular, dark transverse spots and a black spot at the base of the caudal fin. If disturbed or taken out of the water, the colouring often fades.

The fish are active at night and spend the daytime hidden under stones, mostly in the intertidal zone of the sea and along the edges of rivers, but also in thickly overgrown swamps, irrigation canals and muddy flood waters. They are poor swimmers and propel themselves over the bottom with curious jerking movements. When disturbed they dash into hiding like a shot. They feed on small insect larvae, worms and molluscs.

This species has a maximum life span of five years, but both sexes often die after they first spawn when two or three years old. Spawning takes place from March to May in shallow water. The females lay the eggs in special nests on the seabed, often on shells or stones. The males may fight at spawning time and after spawning one of the parents is said to guard the eggs. The sexes can be differentiated by the shape of the urogenital tubercle, which is longer, thinner and pointed in the males. Except at spawning time, however, sexual differences in small individuals are almost indistinguishable.

These gobies are of no practical significance except that they do act as prey species for larger fishes. They are sometimes used as bait by fishermen and are occasionally kept in aquaria.

Size: 8–10 cm, exceptionally up to 12 cm
Fin formula: D_1 VI–VII, D_2 I/14–17, A I/11–16
Fecundity: up to 2,500 eggs
Distribution: In the intertidal zone of the Black Sea, the Sea of Azov and the Caspian Sea and in their tributary rivers, sometimes in the foothills of the mountains.

View of the anterior part of the underside of a goby, showing the characteristic suction disc formed by fusion of the ventral fins.

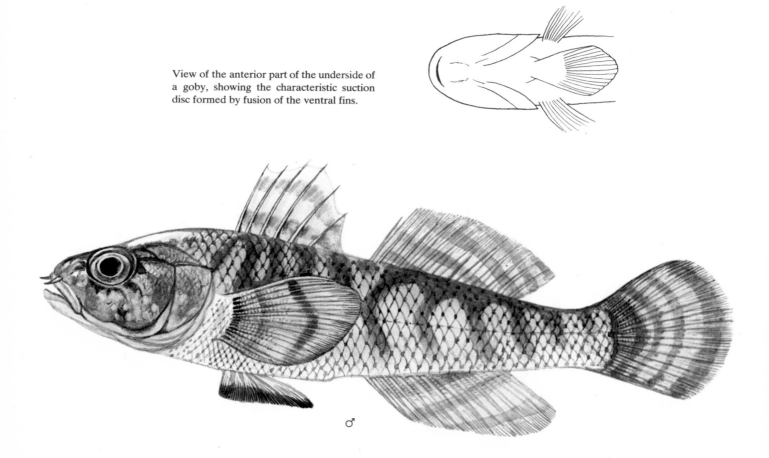

♂

The Callionymidae are a small family comprising marine coastal fishes with scaleless bodies, large eyes situated on the top of the head and a small, protrusible mouth. On the preopercula there are two to four sharp bony processes. There are nine genera in the family and a total of about forty-five species, all living in temperate and subtropical seas.

CALLIONYMIDAE

Spotted Dragonet

Callionymus maculatus

A distinctive small fish, with an elongated body and 'sail-like' dorsal fins. In both sexes these fins are spotted but the spots are more striking in adult males, which have four rows of dark-centred spots between the very elongated spines. There are four bony spines on the preopercula, three pointing upwards and the fourth basal one forwards. Young individuals have a yellowish brown back and a quantity of small, bright brown spots arranged so as to form two stripes on their sides, which are further speckled with blue spots. Adult males are very variably coloured.

This species usually lives at greater depths than the Common Dragonet, *C. lyra,* but also in shallower areas, mostly in water between 90 and 300 metres deep, and it is also less common than the other species. It is most often found swimming above sandy sea beds. The fish spawn from April to June and the eggs and fry are pelagic. Nothing is known of its growth or diet. Its economic significance is nil.

Size: 8–12 cm, maximum 16 cm (males)
Fin formula: D_1 IV, D_2 9, A 8–9
Distribution: In the Atlantic Ocean from the coasts of northern Norway and Iceland to Gibraltar and in the Mediterranean.

Callionymus bairdi occurs in the Caribbean region. It lives amongst seaweeds, on sandbanks and on coral reefs and is often kept in aquaria.

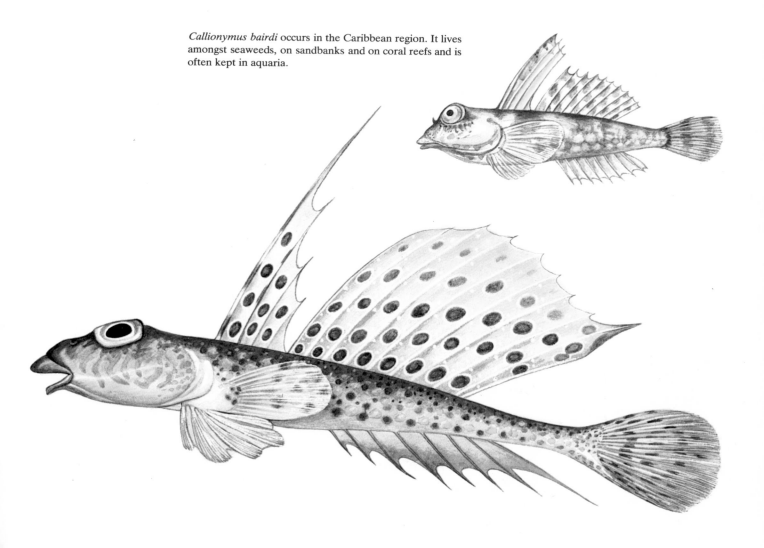

Common Dragonet

Callionymus lyra

The most common and the largest dragonet in European waters, it can be easily distinguished from the previous species by the four bony spines on the preopercula, two of which point upwards, one backwards and the fourth forwards beneath the skin. Adult males have enormously elongate first dorsal fins, orange in colour with red or mauve bands; on the second dorsal fin there are four light blue stripes. The anal fin has dark edges and the caudal fin has a bluish tinge. They have yellow, red-tinted backs with light blue or mauve spots and an orange stripe bordered above and below by a blue stripe, on their sides. The females are brownish, with lighter sides and a dingy white belly.

These fish live in shallow coastal waters of 50 m or less, off the coast of Norway. The fish spawn in November and December, in Danish waters from April to August and in the English Channel from January to June; at spawning time the males are gorgeously coloured. The sexes swim vertically together towards the surface, the male embracing the female with his pectoral fins. The eggs, released by the female and fertilized by the male, rise to the surface. The fry lead a pelagic existence at first but when they measure about 10 mm they sink to the bottom. Males have a life span of between four and six years, females of six to eight years. The males grow somewhat faster than the females; when four years old they measure about 20 cm, the females only about 15 cm. They feed on crustaceans, polychaete worms and molluscs.

Of no economic importance themselves, these fish are food for other larger species.

Size: 15—20 cm, maximum 30 cm (males)
Fin formula: D IV/9, A 9
Distribution: In the Black Sea, the Mediterranean and the adjoining parts of the Atlantic, from the middle of Norway and the coast of Iceland to Cape Verde on the west coast of Africa.

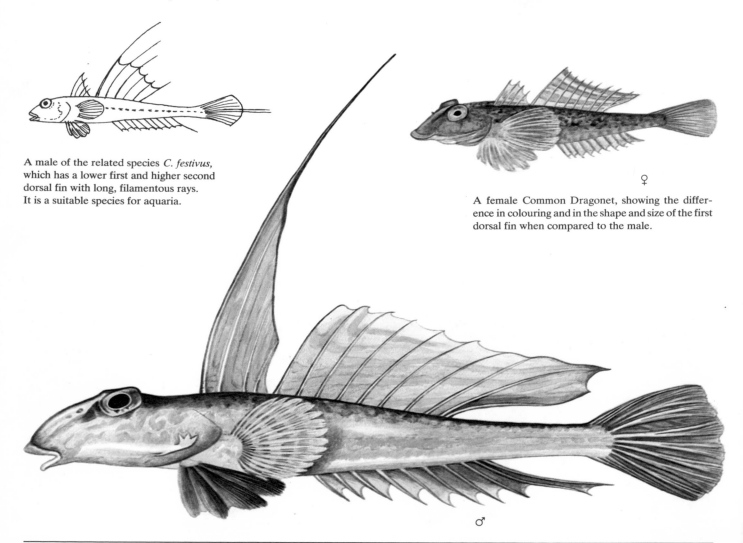

A male of the related species *C. festivus,* which has a lower first and higher second dorsal fin with long, filamentous rays. It is a suitable species for aquaria.

♀

A female Common Dragonet, showing the difference in colouring and in the shape and size of the first dorsal fin when compared to the male.

♂

In the order Scorpaeniformes are over 1,000 species of mostly benthic fishes usually with large heads and wide pectoral fins. In the family Scorpaenidae there are some 350 marine species, most of which live in the Pacific and Indian Oceans and only about 60 are known from the Atlantic. They are large fishes rather like perches in form and sometimes called sea-perches or red perches from their bright red colouring. They include a number of venomous species. Spines on the head and the spiny rays of the dorsal fin, which are connected with venom glands, can cause painful injuries which take a long time to heal and in some cases may lead to paralysis, of the fingers for instance.

SCORPAENIDAE

Redfish, Norway Haddock

Sebastes marinus

Most of the members of the genus *Sebastes* live in the northern part of the Pacific, but the Redfish is one of four species inhabiting the Atlantic. It is a deep water fish, widely distributed in the North Atlantic and found mostly at depths of 100−600 m or less often at 700−900 m, in water at a temperature of 2−6 °C; young individuals tend to be commoner in shallower water, older ones in deeper water. Redfish grow slowly and have life spans of 30 years or more. The red colour of the fish is deepest on the back and fades to yellowish red on the belly.

Redfish bear their young alive, mating in August or September and the females give birth in May and June of the following year to numerous larvae which drift northwards in the currents, remaining in the surface layers of the water. Redfish feed on other fish like herring and capelin and form an important prey species for sperm whales.

These are economically important fishes with tasty flesh. They are caught mainly with dragnets and the total annual catch in recent years has been about 500,000 tons.

Commonest synonyms: *Perca marina, Sebastes norvegicus, Perca norvegica*
Size: usually 40−60 cm, maximum 80−100 cm
Weight: up to 15 kg
Fin formula: D XIV−XVI/14−16, A III−IV/7−9
Fecundity: 30,000−350,000 larvae
Distribution: Throughout much of the north Atlantic.

Up to a length of 30−35 cm Redfish feed mainly on pelagic invertebrates and on the fry of cods and herrings, larger individuals mostly on fish. Prawns of the genus *Pandalus* (1) and young herrings (2) are often found in their alimentary tracts.

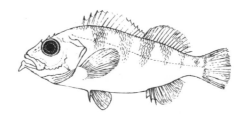

The related Redfish (*Sebastes mentela*) occurs in cold and subarctic waters in the northern part of the Atlantic. It grows to a length of 30−50 cm or to a maximum of 70 cm.

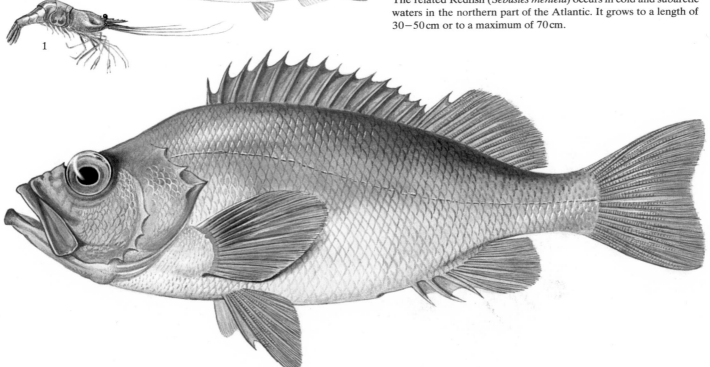

Lesser Scorpion Fish
Scorpaena porcus

A rather small scorpion-fish with a relatively large head. On both head and body, especially below the dorsal fin and above the lateral line, this fish has a quantity of dermal excrescences, the largest and most conspicuous of which are above the eyes. There are none on the lower jaws. At the bases of the spines of the dorsal fin and on the spines on the opercula are venom glands, poison from which trickles into wounds made by the spines and causes painful inflammation. The fish is grey in colour and marked with dark speckles and spots which are sometimes arranged in two or three indistinct, irregular dark cross stripes; the dark spots on the fins also sometimes form longitudinal or cross stripes.

These fishes live near the shore and in the intertidal zone, usually at depths of 20−50 m but occasionally down to 100 m or more. They remain hidden among stones or amongst seaweeds and sometimes partly buried in the sand. Spawning occurs intermittently between May and September; the eggs, larvae and fry are pelagic, but once the fry reach 12−15 mm in length, they then retire to the seabed. The fish reach sexual maturity when three years old, some of the males when just over two years. When young they feed on small invertebrates, but adults feed on crabs, prawns and other small fishes. They are particularly active in the evening.

The moderately good flesh is eaten in some of the countries of southern Europe but these are not economically important fishes.

Size: 15−25 cm, maximum 30 cm
Weight: 0.3−0.7 kg
Fin formula: D XI−XII/8−10, A III/5
Fecundity: 2,500−180,000 eggs
Distribution: In the Atlantic southwards from the Bay of Biscay along the coast of Africa, abundant in the Mediterranean and the Black Sea.

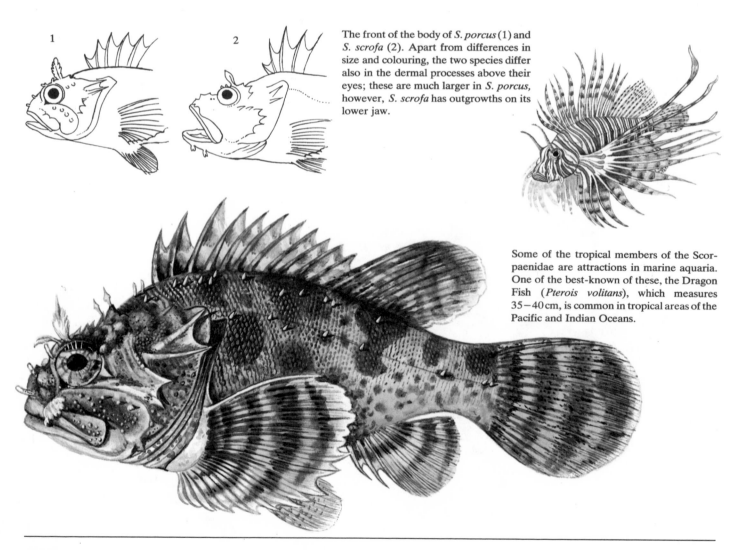

The front of the body of *S. porcus* (1) and *S. scrofa* (2). Apart from differences in size and colouring, the two species differ also in the dermal processes above their eyes; these are much larger in *S. porcus,* however, *S. scrofa* has outgrowths on its lower jaw.

Some of the tropical members of the Scorpaenidae are attractions in marine aquaria. One of the best-known of these, the Dragon Fish (*Pterois volitans*), which measures 35−40 cm, is common in tropical areas of the Pacific and Indian Oceans.

Red Scorpion Fish

Scorpaena scrofa

This species is larger than the Lesser Scorpion Fish, with different colours and many dermal processes on its lower jaw and chin. Large excrescences above its eyes are less striking than in the previous species. Practically the whole of the body is dark reddish brown with dark mottling, and only the belly is lighter. The colouring is very variable, however, depending on the habitat in which the fish is living. These fishes live on stony or sandy seabeds overgrown with seaweeds, at depths of 20−100 m or occasionally down to 200 m or more. They generally hide amongst plants or stones or sometimes partly bury themselves in the sand, from whence they ambush their prey. They feed mainly on fishes, crabs and prawns and the wide mouth allows a Scorpion Fish to swallow prey over half its size.

Spawning is intermittent and takes place from May to August; the eggs are pelagic. Both *S. porcus* and *S. scrofa* have the biological peculiarity of regularly shedding their upper layer of skin, somewhat in the manner of snakes. The skin is shed on an average once every 28 days, though sometimes twice a month, according to the food intake and resultant growth. The spines of its dorsal and anal fins and some of the spines on the head are connected to venom glands, whose poison is less venomous than that of weevers, but can nevertheless cause painful inflammation. Fishermen are the most frequent victims; bathers are virtually never injured.

The annual catch amounts to 2,000−4,000 tons; the flesh is of moderately good quality.

Size: 25−30 cm, maximum 50 cm
Weight: up to 1.5 kg
Fin formula: D XI−XII/8−10, A III/5−6
Fecundity: 10,000−200,000 eggs
Distribution: Off the south coast of England and in the Bay of Biscay, abundant off the northwestern coast of Africa and in the western part of the Mediterranean, absent from the Black Sea.

Scorpaena ustulata has a similar distribution; it measures 15−20 cm and lives mostly at depths of 50−300 m. As in *S. scrofa*, the spines on its dorsal fin and some of the spines on its head are connected to venom glands, the poison from which causes painful inflammation.

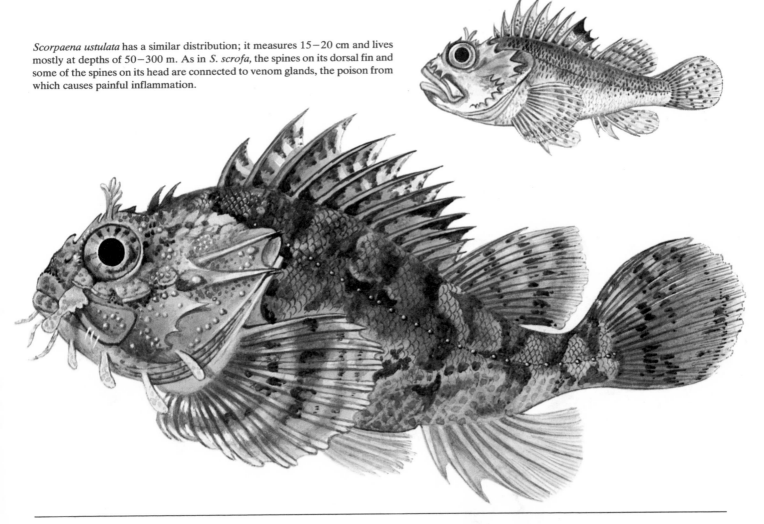

The family Triglidae comprises some eighty-five species of marine fishes adapted to living on mud in the intertidal zones of the sea. Their bodies are covered with ctenoid scales or with bony plates which are surmounted by a quantity of sharp outgrowths, especially on the head. The first three rays of the pectoral fins are free and thicker than the others; they carry sensory cells for the reception of chemical stimuli and are used for stirring up the top layer of the mud in search of food as well as for locomotion. Gurnards can make sounds by using special muscles on the swim-bladder, while the bladder itself amplifies the sounds. These sounds keep the shoal together especially at spawning time. Some experts include the flying gurnards (Dactylopteridae), whose best known representative in European water is the Flying Gurnard, Dactylopterus volitans, in the gurnard family.

TRIGLIDAE

Red Gurnard

Aspitrigla cuculus

This is one of the smallest gurnards in European waters. It is dark red in colour on the head, back and sides, but the belly is lighter and pinkish grey. The whole body is covered with small scales, but those in the lateral line are noticeably larger. Distinguishing features include the first dorsal fin, which is short and high, the second one low and long; the pectoral fins stretch only as far as the anal orifice.

Red Gurnards are relatively common in shallow inshore waters at depths of 20–150 m, over a wide variety of sea beds. They spawn in the summer and the fry grow up to 10 cm in the first year, up to 15 cm in the second and in the third up to about 20 cm. Adults become sexually mature when three or four years old, the males sooner than the females. The larvae feed on crustacean larvae and copepods, the adult fish mostly on crustaceans like shrimps and crabs, but also on small fishes and squid.

These fishes are not abundant, but occasionally a few individuals appear in trawler catches and they are sometimes caught by anglers.

Size: 20–30 cm, maximum 40 cm
Weight: up to 1 kg
Fin formula: D_1 IX–X, D_2 18, A 16–17
Distribution: Off the coasts of Europe from the north of Denmark and England to Cape Verde in Africa, and in the Mediterranean except at the eastern end.

The head and front of the body of *Aspitrigla cuculus* (1) and the related *Aspitrigla obscura* (2), which has a strikingly long second ray in its dorsal fin and differently shaped scales in its lateral line. *Aspitrigla obscura* measures up to 30 cm.

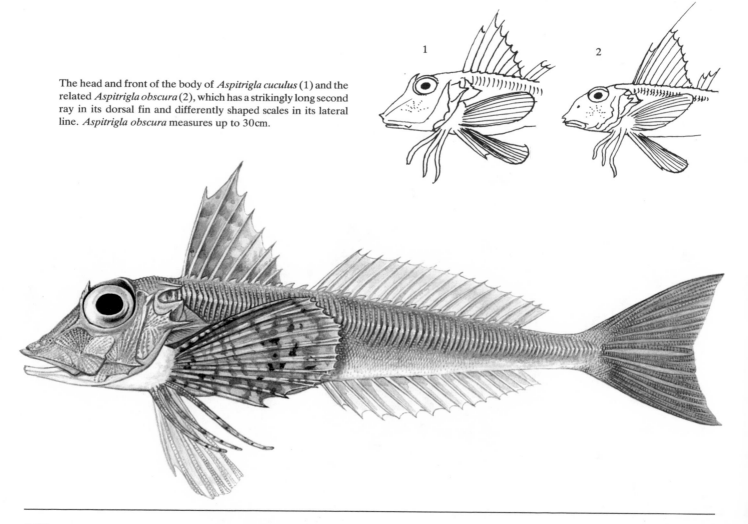

Grey Gurnard
Eutrigla gurnardus

The most common gurnard of British waters, this fish is abundant in inshore areas from the low water mark to a depth of 140 m, most often over a sandy seabed. In the spring the fish migrate closer inshore and with the approach of autumn and the colder weather move further out to sea again.

It has characteristic rough, silvery luminescent scales which have bony outgrowths along the lateral line. The body is somewhat variably coloured, with greyish green tones predominant, a white-spotted back and a white belly. The males attain sexual maturity in their third year, when they measure 18 cm, and the females in their fourth year, at a length of about 24 cm. Females are far commoner in the population than males.

Spawning occurs intermittently throughout the summer and the eggs and larvae are pelagic; the young fish switch to a benthic mode of life on the bottom when they measure 3 cm in length. They feed mostly on crustaceans, including animals like shrimps and crabs, but also on small fishes.

Annual catches of Grey Gurnards in recent years have varied from 4,000 to 6,000 tons, a large proportion of which goes to the making of fish meal. They do not make particularly good eating for their flesh is rather bony.

Commonest synonyms: Trigla milvus, Trigla gurnardus
Size: 25−40 cm, exceptionally up to 55 cm
Weight: up to 1 kg
Fin formula: D_1 VII−IX, D_2 18−20, A 17−20
Fecundity: 200,000−300,000 eggs
Distribution: Found on the continental shelf from Murmansk in the USSR, south to the southernmost point of Morocco and also in the Mediterranean and the Black Seas.

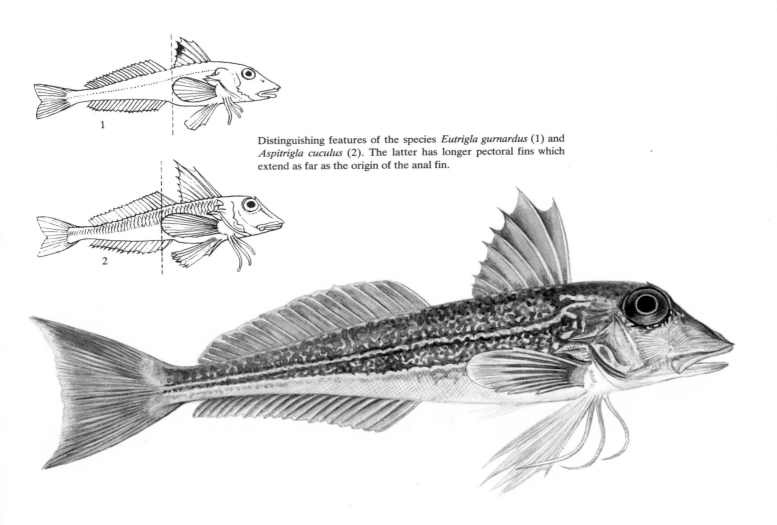

Distinguishing features of the species *Eutrigla gurnardus* (1) and *Aspitrigla cuculus* (2). The latter has longer pectoral fins which extend as far as the origin of the anal fin.

Yellow Gurnard, Tub Gurnard

Trigla lucerna

This is the largest member of the family Triglidae, attaining a length of 75 cm and an immediately recognisable fish from its brightly coloured long pectoral fins. These are variably coloured in black, blue and red, with many white or blue spots and they extend as far back as the first rays of the second dorsal fin. The body is very variably coloured, the predominant shade being brownish red or orange with a lighter yellowish belly.

This species is most common at depths of 5–200 m, where it lives on the rocky and sandy seabeds of the continental shelf, 'sitting' propped up on the free rays of its pectoral fins. It is a more sedentary species than the others and feeds on molluscs as well as on crustaceans and small fishes. Spawning occurs inter-mittently from May to July in European waters, but off the coast of Africa it continues through the winter. The eggs and larvae are pelagic, but the fry live on the seabed like the adults.

This relatively abundant species has tasty flesh and forms the greater part of gurnard catches in Europe. These amount to about 13,000 tons a year, coming mainly from the coast of Spain.

Commonest synonyms: Trigla hirundo, Trigla hyrax, Trigla corax
Size: 30–60 cm, exceptionally up to 75 cm
Weight: 700–900 g, occasionally up to 1,500 g
Fin formula: D_1 IX–X, D_2 15–18, A 14–17
Fecundity: up to 150,000 eggs
Distribution: In the Black Sea, the Mediterranean and the Atlantic Ocean from the middle of the Norwegian coast to equatorial Africa.

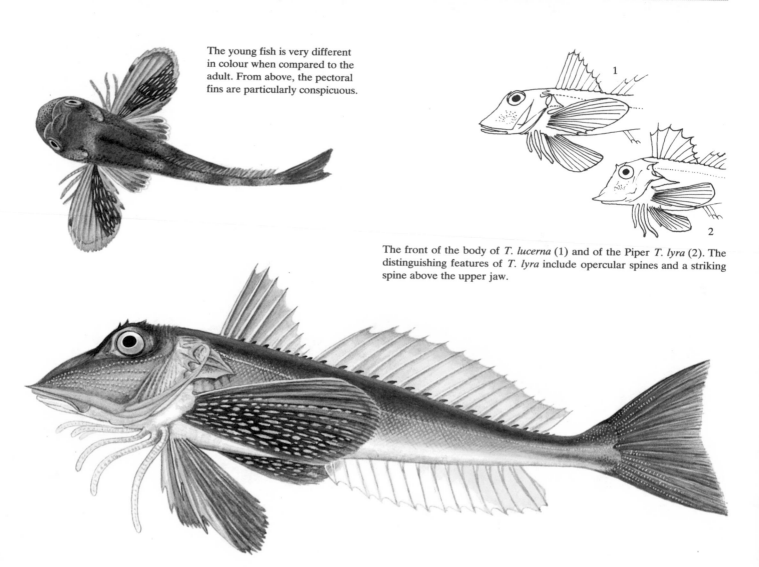

The young fish is very different in colour when compared to the adult. From above, the pectoral fins are particularly conspicuous.

The front of the body of *T. lucerna* (1) and of the Piper *T. lyra* (2). The distinguishing features of *T. lyra* include opercular spines and a striking spine above the upper jaw.

In the family Cottidae are about 200 species of marine and freshwater fishes mostly with dorsoventrally flattened bodies and thick, scaleless skin. The majority live in the northern part of the Pacific but five species live in fresh water in many parts of Europe, Asia and North America.

Miller's Thumb, Bullhead

Cottus gobio

The Miller's Thumb is a small fish with a fusiform body, a large, dorsoventrally flattened head and smooth, scaleless skin. Its body is predominatly grey or light brown with irregular darker mottling and four indistinct, dark cross bars; the fins are generally irregularly grey and spotted. The male has a larger head and wider mouth than the female and a longer, tubular urogenital tubercle.

These fishes live in the shallower parts of rivers with uneven stony river beds, where they usually hide under stones in the daytime, becoming active mostly in the evening and at night. They leave their shelters only when disturbed and make for the nearest fresh hiding-place by means of short hops, for they do not possess a swim-bladder and are very poor swimmers. They live for up to eight years. Spawning takes place from March to May. The comparatively few eggs are usually laid on the undersides of stones and are guarded during incubation by the male.

It used to be thought that Miller's Thumbs devoured trout eggs and that they competed with trout and other salmonoid fishes for food, but their status as a pest now seems to have been largely overestimated and in fact they form an important food source for these fishes. They themselves feed on aquatic insect nymphs and bottom-dwelling crustaceans like *Gammarus,* but rarely on eggs. Anglers occasionally use them as bait.

Size: 12—14 cm, maximum 16 cm
Fin formula: D_1 V—IX, D_2 13—19, A 10—15
Fecundity: 100—1,300 eggs
Distribution: In the greater part of Europe.

Comparison of the distributions of *C. gobio* (blue) and *C. poecilopus* (red).

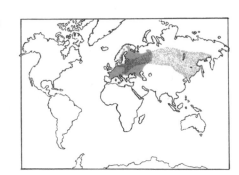

Alpine Bullhead
Cottus poecilopus

The Alpine Bullhead closely resembles the Miller's Thumb, but it has a wider mouth, its lateral line is generally incomplete and its longer ventral fins stretch to or beyond the anal orifice. Its first dorsal fin has a striking orange border, especially in the male, which also has a larger, wider head than the female, longer fins and darker colouring. In both sexes the back is brown to olive green and is marked with small brown spots, the belly is white or yellowish and there are usually four or five dark spots on the sides.

This Bullhead lives chiefly in mountain rivers and streams at higher altitudes than the Miller's Thumb and may be found as far up as the sources of the streams. The two occur together at the transition from lowlands to foothills. Their habits, the places they frequent and their food are similar, but the Alpine Bullhead population is smaller and the fishes need a higher oxygen content and cleaner water. If threatened, the fish opens its opercula, erects its spines and turns to face the enemy with open mouth and spread pectoral fins. If the enemy is determined it hops away into shelter under a stone.

These Bullheads attain sexual maturity in their second year and spawning takes place between March and May in a depression made by the male under a stone. He then protects the eggs until the larvae hatch. They live for a maximum life-span of five or six years.

Size: 15 cm, maximum 20 cm
Fin formula: D_1 VIII−IX, D_2 16−20, A 12−15
Fecundity: 200−800 eggs
Distribution: Northern Europe and Asia but absent from British Isles, France and Scandinavia.

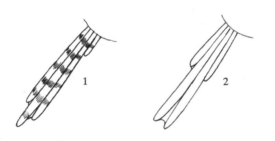

The Alpine Bullhead (*C. poecilopus*) (1) can be distinguished from the Miller's Thumb (*C. gobio*) (2) by its pectoral fins which are marked with regular cross stripes in the former species.

Sea Scorpion, Long-spined Bullhead

Taurulus bubalis

Two *Taurulus* species are known in the Atlantic off the coast of Europe, the Sea Scorpion and the Norwegian Bullhead, *T. lilljeborgi*. On its operculum *T. bubalis* has a large backwardly directed spine which is at least equal to the diameter of the eye in length. The spine of *T. lilljeborgi* is always shorter than the diameter of the eye. The ventral fins are composed of three rays in *T. bubalis*, two in *T. lilljeborgi*. Male Sea Scorpions can be distinguished from females by the crest on the back of the neck, longer fins and a longer urogenital tubercle. The fish have reddish brown bodies with dark cross stripes, but at spawning time the males have orange red bellies marked with white and light blue spots.

They live in inshore and intertidal waters, down to a depth of 30 m, always amongst rocks and seaweeds;

in the winter they retire to deeper water. Spawning takes place early in the spring in March and April. The female attaches the eggs to stones or to algae, but they are not protected by the male. The embryos take six to seven weeks to develop and the newly hatched larvae are pelagic, returning shorewards again when they measure 13–14 mm. The fish feed on crustaceans such as shrimps, prawns and crabs, on small fishes like gobies and occasionally on brittle stars and molluscs. *T. lilljeborgi* lives at greater depths (50–80 m) and also spawns there.

Neither species is economically important.

> *Synonym: Cottus bubalis*
> *Size:* 12–15 cm, maximum 20 cm
> *Fin formula:* D_1 VII–X, D_2 10–14, A 8–10
> *Distribution:* Atlantic coasts of Europe from the Bay of Biscay to northern Norway, shores of Britain, Ireland and Iceland, the Baltic Sea.

T. lilljeborgi has only two soft rays in its fins *(T. bubalis* has three); it has the same distribution as *T. bubalis*.

Distribution map of *T. bubalis*.

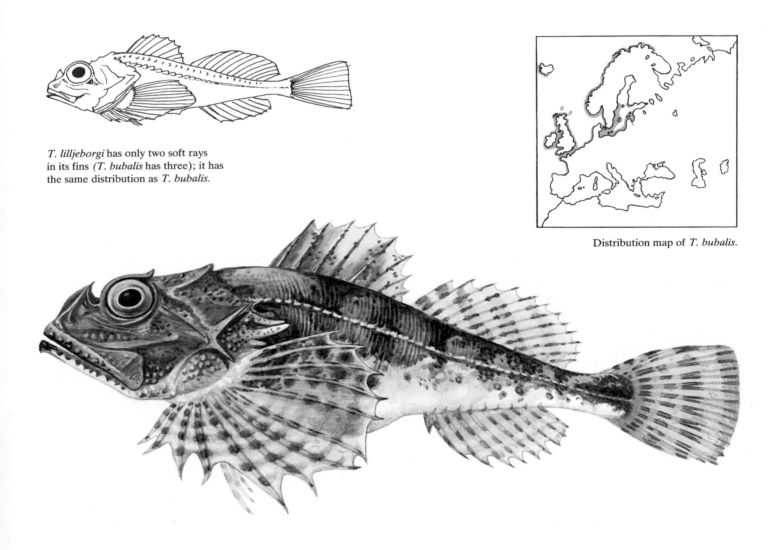

Two-horn Sculpin

Icelus bicornis

This small, characteristically shaped fish has a large head armed with large, bony spines and with further spines on the preopercula. On its sides there are two rows of large scales with small spines on their posterior edges, so that the fish looks as if it has two lateral lines. The males have a strikingly large urogenital tubercle, projecting up to one cm beyond the surface of the body. The fish are yellowish brown in colour, with dark brown spots and lighter sides.

This species is distributed almost in a circle around the north pole, being absent only from the area between Novaya Zemlya and the New Siberian Islands, where it is replaced by *Icelus spatula*. The majority of *Icelus* species are found in the northern Pacific however. In Europe *I. bicornis* occurs along the Atlantic shores of Scandinavia as far as the south of Norway. It is found in depths varying from a few metres to 600m, the younger individuals usually preferring shallow water while adult fish are found mostly at depths of 40–180m. These fishes are only found in cold water with a temperature in the region of 0 °C or less to the point where the sea freezes; the maximum temperature they can tolerate is 7–9 °C. They live only in salt water, being intolerant of even a small amount of fresh water mixed with the salt, but live over a wide range of sea beds. Spawning occurs from August to October and the females lay small numbers of relatively large eggs up to 3mm in diameter. They feed on bottom-dwelling polychaete worms and on crustaceans.

Economically these are unimportant fishes.

Size: up to 12 cm
Fin formula: D VII–X/17–23, A 12–17
Fecundity: 150–300 eggs
Distribution: The Arctic Ocean and the northern part of the Atlantic.

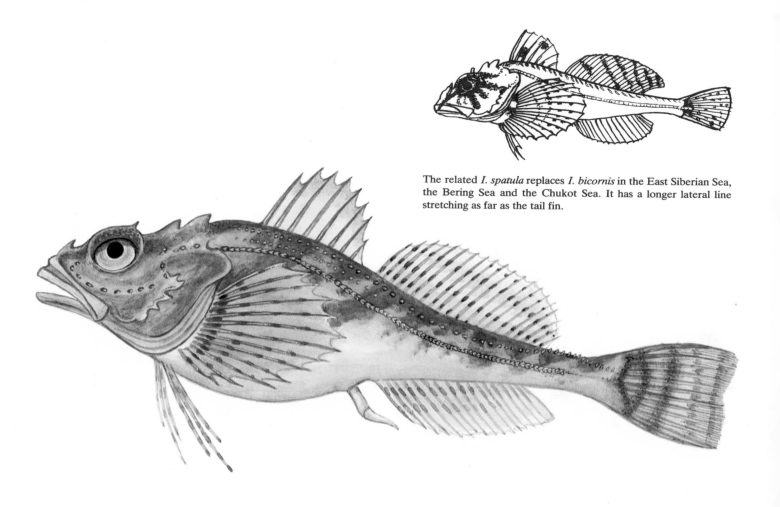

The related *I. spatula* replaces *I. bicornis* in the East Siberian Sea, the Bering Sea and the Chukot Sea. It has a longer lateral line stretching as far as the tail fin.

Four-horn Sculpin

Myoxocephalus quadricornis

The form of this fish is clear evidence of its kinship with the freshwater bullheads of the genus *Cottus*. It has a wide head and its opercula are equipped with four horny protuberances from which it takes its name. When viewed from the side and from above, other striking protuberances, usually wider at the top, can be seen behind the eyes and on the back of the neck; those on the neck are usually larger but the size is very variable. The second dorsal fin is very long, especially in males, and when folded lengthwise it stretches to the origin of the caudal fin; its rays are generally covered with spine-like teeth, a unique feature unknown in the other members of the genus. The adult fish are greenish brown to brownish grey in colour, without any pronounced spots, and have a lighter, usually yellowish white belly.

They are found amongst rocks overgrown with algae and other aquatic plants, where they live hidden away among stones, in both fresh and coastal waters.

The fry are often found in river mouths. Spawning takes place at the end of the autumn and in the winter and the eggs are laid on the bottom; the pelagic larvae appear in the spring and by August they measure 20—22 mm. These fishes feed mainly on crustaceans and other small fish.

This species is economically unimportant as catches are not very large, but its flesh is white and quite tasty.

Commonest synonym: Cottus quadricornis
Size: 20—30 cm, females occasionally up to 35 cm
Weight: 150—200 g, occasionally up to 0.5 kg
Fin formula: D_1 VII—IX, D_2 13—16, A 13—16
Fecundity: 2,000—6,200 eggs
Distribution: Circumpolar in the Arctic Oceans, the White Sea, the Barents Sea and the Baltic, in Scandinavian and Karelian Lakes (including Lakes Onega and Ladoga) and in the Great Lakes of North America, where they are relics of the last glacial period, as they are in the Baltic.

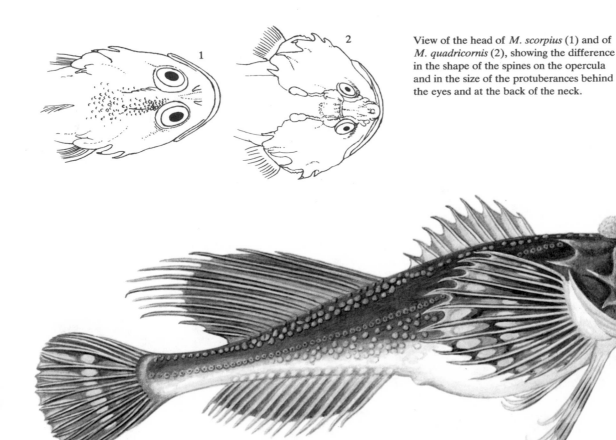

View of the head of *M. scorpius* (1) and of *M. quadricornis* (2), showing the difference in the shape of the spines on the opercula and in the size of the protuberances behind the eyes and at the back of the neck.

Bull Rout

Myoxocephalus scorpius

This is the largest Sea Scorpion found on British coastlines. Its head is less wide than that of *M. quadricornis* and the protuberances behind the eyes and at the back of the neck are less strongly developed, but the spines on the opercula are larger and their prick is more painful. On the sides there are bony spiny plates protruding from the skin above and below the lateral line. In the males the number of these plates is larger and they are better armed, whereas in the females they are usually thinner and fewer and are sometimes absent altogether. The back of the fish is greenish brown to grey with a few dark spots. The belly is usually cerise red in the males and more orange in the females and in both sexes it is marked with large spots which also appear on the sides; the colouring is very variable, however.

These fishes live mainly in inshore waters and in the intertidal zones, in rock pools, estuaries and in sandy areas, down to depths of 25 m. In harbours they can often be caught around the submerged concrete foundations of piers and other installations, but are less likely to be found on the shore in the southern parts of their range. Bull Routs become sexually mature when three or four years old and spawn from December to March. The females lay their eggs among stones on the seabed and the males stand guard over them. They feed mainly on fishes and to a smaller extent on large crustaceans and worms.

They are economically unimportant but are eaten in some of the northern parts of their range after skinning.

Commonest synonym: Cottus scorpius
Size: 25–30 cm, in Arctic waters up to 60 cm
Weight: 0.3–0.5 kg, occasionally 1 kg or over
Fin formula: D_1 VII–XI, D_2 14–17, A 10–15
Fecundity: 2,000–3,000 eggs
Distribution: In all the seas around northern Europe as far as the Bay of Biscay and in the Baltic. Also occurs off the Atlantic coast of North America.

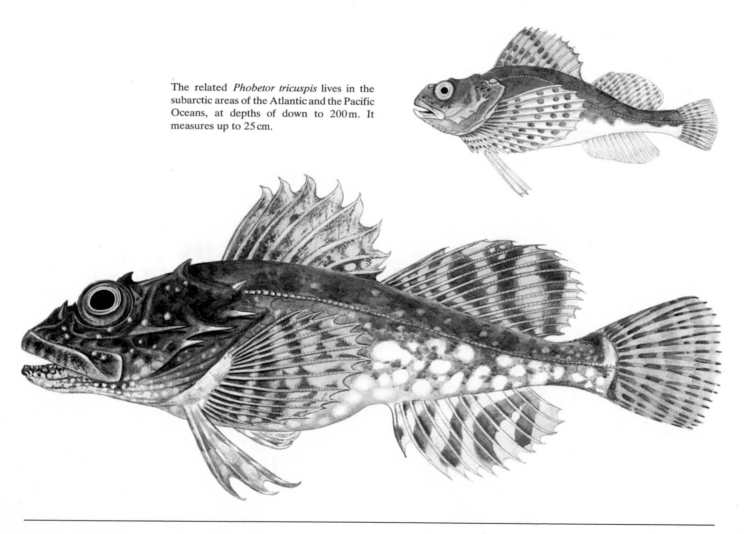

The related *Phobetor tricuspis* lives in the subarctic areas of the Atlantic and the Pacific Oceans, at depths of down to 200 m. It measures up to 25 cm.

The Agonidae are a small family with about fifty species of fishes whose bodies are protected by bony armour. They have broad heads but the body and tail are very narrow. They are small benthic fishes living for the most part in the northern parts of the Pacific and Atlantic oceans. The majority live in the Pacific; only two species occur in the European Atlantic.

Pogge, Armed Bullhead

Agonius cataphractus

A distinctive fish, completely covered with bony armour plates. It has a flattened head and a long snout with two pairs of large, bony spines; similar spines are present on the opercula. On the underside of the head there are many short barbels. The back and sides of the fish are dark brown, with four often indistinct dark bands; the light-coloured belly is sometimes marked with dark spots and the fins are yellowish with dark spots or bands.

These are common inshore fishes, particularly in estuaries and in water from 20–70 m deep. Southern populations migrate inshore in winter but northern populations seem to live in the same place throughout the year. They are found mostly over sandy sea beds, but also occur over stony areas. Spawning takes place from February to May and the female lays the relatively large eggs on brown algae. The yellowish or orange eggs are protected by strong egg capsules and incubation probably takes a year. The larvae live pelagic lives, but when they measure about 20 mm they sink to the bottom and take up a benthic mode of life. At one year old they measure 6–7 cm and at two years old 10–11 cm; they become sexually mature when three or four years old. The fry feed at first on zooplankton, the adults on benthic crustaceans, polychaete worms, molluscs and brittle stars.

These are economically unimportant fishes, but are sometimes caught in prawn trawls.

Size: 10–15 cm, maximum 22 cm
Fin formula: D_1 IV–VI, D_2 6–8, A 5–7
Fecundity: 500–2,500 eggs
Distribution: Along the coast of northwestern Europe as far as Murmansk, in the western part of the Baltic.

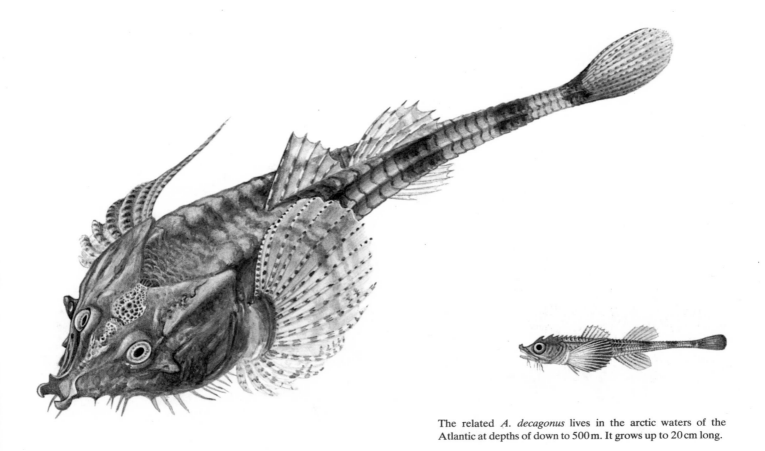

The related *A. decagonus* lives in the arctic waters of the Atlantic at depths of down to 500 m. It grows up to 20 cm long.

In most of the representatives of the family Cyclopteridae the ventral fins have been modified to form a circular suction disc. There are about twenty-five species, living in the Pacific and Atlantic Oceans.

Lumpsucker
Cyclopterus lumpus

The Lumpsucker is a very easily recognisable fish, with a heavy, rounded body covered with bony denticles arranged in seven rows (one row on the back, two on each side and two on the belly). Adult Lumpsuckers have only one dorsal fin — the second. The first dorsal fin is present only in juveniles. Adults have dark bluish grey backs and sides, with dark spots on the sides, and at spawning time the males have brick-red bellies and fins and almost black backs. The fry and young fish are yellowish olive in colour with a silver stripe on the head.

Lumpsuckers spend most of their lives near the sea bed far from the shore, at depths of 50–200 m. The adult fish attach themselves firmly to rocks or to the seabed by means of their suction discs, so that they are sometimes found in nets still clinging to stones.

They swim shorewards only to spawn, a process which occurs from February to May. Spawning occurs on a stony substrate and the eggs are laid in batches, at a temperature of 5–8 °C. Once it is over the females return to deeper water, while the males remain to guard the eggs throughout the whole two months of development. For many of them it means death, for they may be left high and dry by strong ebb tides or fall prey to piscivorous birds. Lumpsuckers feed chiefly on small crustaceans, polychaete worms and fry of other fishes; large ones also catch fish.

At one time the flesh of the males was smoked and eaten in some European countries and the eggs are still sold, after being dyed and potted as a kind of substitute for true caviare.

Size: 25–30 cm (males), 30–40 cm (females), maximum 60 cm
Weight: 1–5 kg
Fin formula: D_2 10–11, A I/10–12
Fecundity: 80,000–200,000 eggs
Distribution: In the northern part of the Atlantic Ocean as far south as Portugal, in the Baltic Sea as far as the Gulf of Finland.

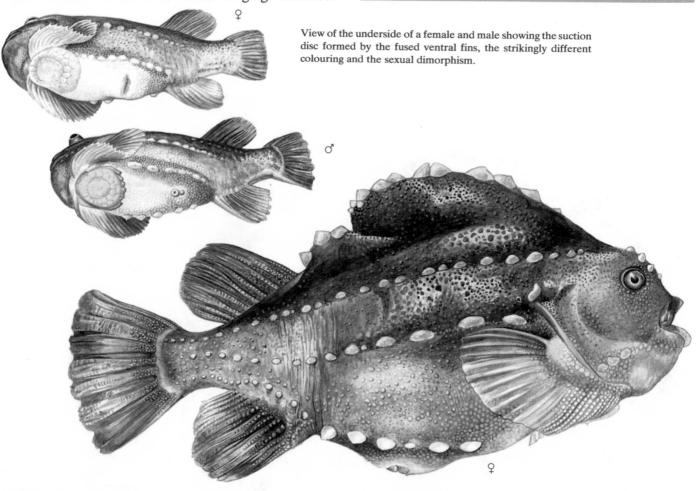

View of the underside of a female and male showing the suction disc formed by the fused ventral fins, the strikingly different colouring and the sexual dimorphism.

In the family Liparidae are about 120 species of marine fishes, about 75 % of which live in the northern Pacific Ocean. They have wide heads and thin and sometimes transparent skin. The ventral fins form a suction disc, similar to that found in the preceding family, the Cyclopteridae.

Common Sea Snail
Liparis liparis

A small plump, rather slimy fish with a rounded belly and a relatively wide head, but with a flat-sided body and tail. It has long dorsal and anal fins virtually joined to the caudal fin, large rounded pectoral fins which extend on to the throat of the fish and ventral fins which have been converted into a large round suction disc. The skin is loose and folded and covered with small prickles. The fish has a dark brown back and sides with large numbers of dark spots and a light-coloured belly; there are also dark spots and stripes on the unpaired fins.

Common Sea Snails live mostly on the seabed near the shore, at depths of 5–100 m, but appear very rarely in the intertidal zone where another Sea Snail, Montagu's Sea Snail *(L. montagui)* is found. They spawn between January and March near the bottom and females lay their eggs on stones and plants, particularly amongst sea anemones. At first the larvae live a pelagic life and only assume a benthic mode of existence when they measure over 2 cm. They feed mainly on worms and crustaceans but large individuals may also take small fish; shrimps and crabs are favoured prey items and these fishes can become pests when living on shrimping grounds.

Although fairly common in some places, sea snails are economically unimportant since they have watery tasteless flesh.

Commonest synonym: Cyclopterus liparis
Size: 10–15 cm, maximum 20 cm
Fin formula: D 35–43, A 29–30
Fecundity: 500–800 eggs
Distribution: In the northern part of the Atlantic and the coastal subarctic waters of the Arctic Ocean.

The related species *L. callyodon* lives along the Pacific coast of North America. In the front of its dorsal fin there is a triangular notch. It measures up to 12 cm.

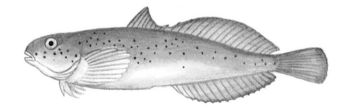

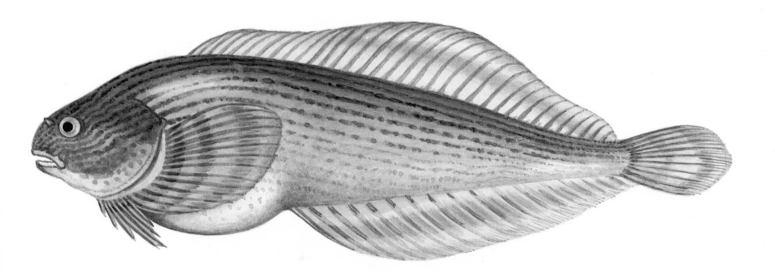

The order Dactylopteriformes contains a single family, the Dactylopteridae, with two genera and a few species of subtropical and tropical marine fishes. At first glance these are reminiscent of gurnards, with which they are often associated, but they have bony scutes on their heads, large eyes and strikingly large pectoral fins which look like 'wings'.

Flying Gurnard

Dactylopterus volitans

Fairly small fishes, with rather massive bodies and enormous pectoral fins. These fins are divided into two very different sections, which have quite separate functions. The lower part is formed of a few free stout rays, on which the fish can 'walk' over the seabed. The upper part forms what looks like an enormous wing. These fishes cannot really fly, for their bodies are too heavy and the most they can produce is a somersault or two. The fins are used, however, to deter predators, for when spread out fully the pectoral fins make the fish look very much larger than they actually are.

The fish are grey or brownish in colour and are often marked with light and dark spots. The ventral fins are tinged with red and the pectoral fins are brown, with regular rows of light blue spots.

The fish live in open water near to the coast, at depths of 10–30 m over a sandy or clayey sea bed. They feed on small bottom-dwelling animals. They spawn in the summer, in shallow inshore waters; the fry live a pelagic existence, but do not move very far from the shore and often fall prey to pelagic fishes like tunnyfish or mackerel.

Flying gurnards are economically unimportant in Europe, but in some countries, like Japan, for instance, they are cooked and eaten.

Size: 20–30 cm, maximum 45 cm
Fin formula: D_1 V–VI (with two free rays in front of it), D_2 7–9
Distribution: In the Mediterranean, the eastern and western part of the Atlantic Ocean from the British Isles as far south as the coast of Angola and from Florida to Rio de Janeiro.

The related *D. orientalis* is fairly common in the Indian Ocean and the southwestern part of the Pacific. It is slightly larger than *D. volitans* and its pectoral fins are generally more gaily coloured, but according to some authors it is only a subspecies of that fish.

Distribution map of *D. volitans.*

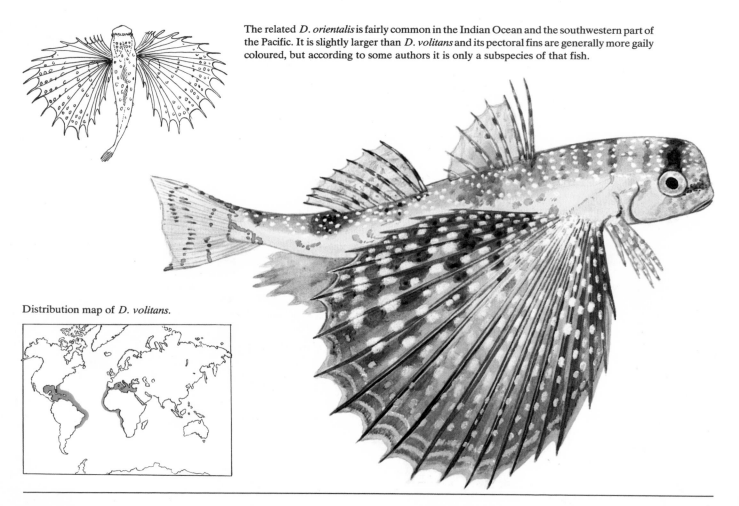

The order Pleuronectiformes comprises about 500 species of marine coastal fishes which every now and again invade fresh water. They have asymmetrical bodies with compressed sides and lie on one of their sides, so that the other one forms the back. They range in size from 10 cm to giants measuring 4.5 m and weighing 330 kg. Flatfish larvae are typical fish larvae, transparent and completely symmetrical and it is only later that they lose their symmetry, metamorphose (see p. 284) and take up a life on the bottom of the sea. Many flatfishes are economically important, with high quality tasty flesh. The Bothidae is a large family with 200 species whose eyes are on the left side of the body; their pelagic eggs are provided with a single drop of fat. The dorsal fin begins on the head behind the eyes and all the rays in it are soft. About thirty-eight genera live in tropical and temperate seas.

BOTHIDAE

Scaldfish, Smooth Sole
Arnoglossus laterna

The Scaldfish has a thick body for a flatfish and a small head with the eyes on the left side. The ventral fin on the side where the eyes are (the upper side of the fish) is much larger than the one on the blind side or lower surface of the fish. The fish is sometimes

yellow in colour, sometimes brown or grey, with darker markings and a row of darker spots running along on each side of the fins.

Scaldfishes live off European coasts in large numbers, mostly over sandy seabeds at depths of 10−60 m but sometimes down to 200 m. They spawn from May to July on a sandy seabed and the larvae live in the open sea for a considerable time. When they measure 15−30 mm they sink to the bottom and metamorphose into adults. Larvae feed on plankton but adults feed on benthic crustaceans and small fish like gobies.

These are economically unimportant fishes, never being big enough or common enough to provide good catches, but they do get caught in seine-nets and trawls with other species.

Size: 12−15 cm, maximum 25 cm
Fin formula: D 83−95, A 60−74
Distribution: Along the coasts of Europe from the North Sea to the Mediterranean.

The related *A. imperialis* has a similar distribution, but does not occur in the eastern part of the Mediterranean or in the Black Sea. It measures 12−18 cm, reaching a maximum of 25 cm, and can be distinguished from the Scaldfish by the strikingly long first rays of its dorsal fin and its generally lighter colouring.

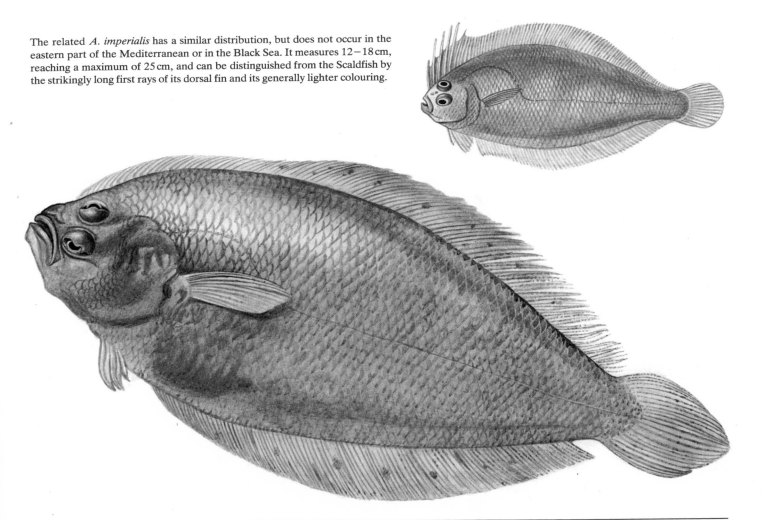

The members of the small family Scophthalmidae are flatfishes with eyes on the left side of the body. Their ventral fins are both the same size, not larger on the left side as in the Bothidae.

Brill

Scophthalmus rhombus

The Brill resembles the related Turbot, but can be distinguished from that fish by examining the first rays of the long dorsal fin, which are branched and devoid of webbing for half their length in the Brill, and by the absence of bony tubercles on its sides. Problems of identification may arise if hybrids between the Brill and the Turbot are examined. These occur in nature and have features intermediate between the parents. They usually have tubercles. The Brill is covered with small cycloid scales, which are embedded deep in the skin on the underside of the body. The upper surface is greenish or greyish brown and is mottled with large dark and small light spots. The underside is creamy white.

Brill live mostly on the sea bed at depths of 5—70 m.

The adult fish usually stay in one place where colour adaptation makes them virtually indistinguishable from the background. Sometimes they partly bury themselves in the substrate, which is usually sandy but may be gravel or mud. In the Mediterranean they spawn from March to June, further north from May to August. The eggs and larvae are pelagic, only metamorphosing and assuming a benthic existence when they measure 2—3.5 cm. The fry feed mainly on crustaceans and other small invertebrates, the adult fish chiefly on small fish and fish larvae.

The total annual catch of this species is now only 1,000—2,000 tons, largely as a result of excessive fishing in the recent past. To ensure an increase in the size of its populations, a minimum protective length of 30 cm has been introduced.

Commonest synonym: Rhombus rhombus
Size: 40—50 cm, exceptionally up to 75 cm
Weight: 1.5—4 kg, occasionally up to 7.5 kg
Fin formula: D 70—84, A 54—63
Fecundity: 1,000,000—10,000,000 eggs
Distribution: Off the European shores of the Atlantic Ocean from Norway southwards as far as the coast of Morocco; also in the Baltic, the Mediterranean and the Black Seas.

The related Norwegian Topknot (*S. norvegicus*) lives in the northeastern part of the Atlantic. It is smaller than the Scaldfish and catches usually contain individuals measuring only 12—15 cm long (maximum 20 cm).

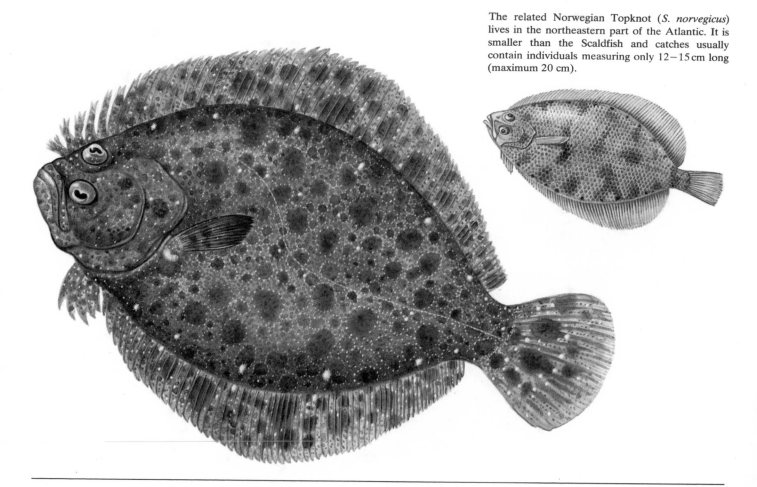

Turbot

Scophthalmus maximus

The Turbot has a relatively robust body, so rounded as to be almost spherical and a large head. Its dorsal fin begins on its head, just in front of its eyes, and has simple unbranched first rays which are webbed for more than two thirds of their length, a feature which can be used to distinguish it from Brill. The body is scaleless, but instead its upper surface is irregularly studded with small, sharp, bony tubercles. The lateral line describes a bulging arc above the pectoral fins. The colouring of this fish is very variable, depending on the seabed, for it changes to match the background, so ensuring perfect camouflage. The upper (left) side is usually greyish or olive brown, with large numbers of dark spots which continue on the fins. The under side is light and unpigmented.

Turbot live on the bottom in shallow coastal waters, at depths of not more than 80−100 m. They become sexually mature when five years old and spawn between April and August at depths of 10−40 m, not very far from the shore. The number of eggs is enormous. The larvae are at first pelagic and symmetrical and possess a swim-bladder. When they measure 2.5−3 cm they metamorphose and take up their adult life on the bottom. The fry remain in shallow water close to the shore and feed on planktonic crustaceans; young fish often live in the intertidal zone but older larger individuals live in deeper water and feed almost exclusively on other fishes, like sand-eels, whiting and sprats.

Turbot are caught mostly with nets and with baited lines and the total annual catch may amount to 8,000−10,000 tons. Although not particularly large this catch is economically significant, as Turbot are considered to be one of the best flavoured sea fish.

Commonest synonyms: Rhombus maximus, Psetta maxima
Size: 50−80 cm, maximum 1 m
Weight: 5−12 kg, maximum 25 kg
Fin formula: D 57−72, A 42−56
Fecundity: 1−10 million eggs, maximum 15 million
Distribution: In the Atlantic Ocean from the middle of Norway to Gibraltar, in the Baltic, the Mediterranean and the Black Seas.

Adult turbots are active predators feeding almost exclusively on other fishes like young cods (1) and on the sand eels of the genus *Ammodytes* (2) and crabs (3).

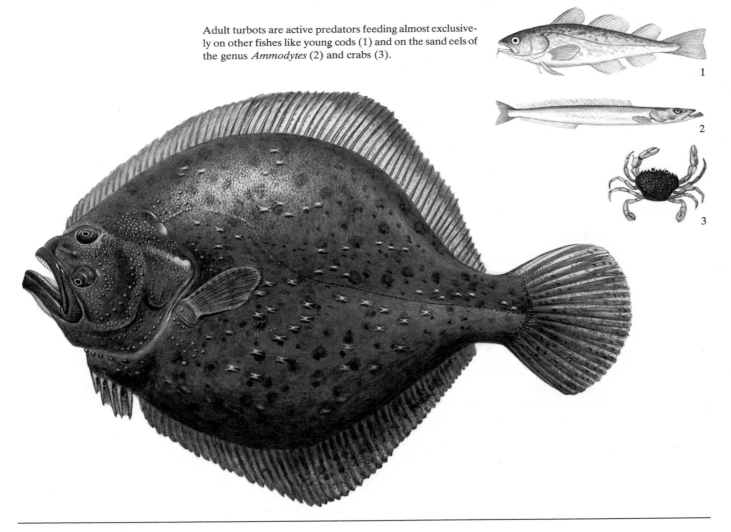

Megrim

Lepidorhombus whiffiagonis

Like other members of the family Scophthalmidae, the Megrim has both eyes situated on the left uppermost side of the body as an adult. It has an elongate, not rounded or spherical body however, and has more rays in its dorsal and anal fins than the others. Its caudal fin is vaguely rhomboid in form. It has a light yellowish brown upper surface with darker spots and an almost dead white underside, sometimes with red spots.

Megrims are deep water flatfish, living at depths of 50–300 m, often on the edge of the continental shelf where they lie buried in soft, sandy or clayey sea beds. Spawning takes place between March and June at considerable depths; the eggs and larvae are pelagic. The larvae like those of all flatfishes, are at first bilaterally symmetrical, have a swim-bladder, are the same colour on both sides and swim perfectly normally. When they reach a certain size (in this species about 20 mm), they begin to metamorphose,

the body begins to flatten sideways, the swim-bladder shrinks, the skull begins to develop unequally and one eye begins to shift to the crown of the head closer to the other eye. In some flatfishes the viscera, jaws and paired fins also develop unequally. The dark colouring on the side from which the migrating eye has come generally fades and the fish lie with that side facing downwards; they remain in this position for the rest of their lives. Like other flatfishes, Megrim feed on small fish and benthic invertebrates.

They are caught mainly with trawls and the average annual catch is about 20,000 tons. They have pleasantly flavoured, rather dry flesh.

Commonest synonym: Rhombus megastoma
Size: 30–45 cm, maximum 60 cm
Weight: 1–2 kg, maximum 5 kg
Fin formula: D 85–91, A 67–75
Distribution: In the western parts of the Mediterranean, the Atlantic coasts of Europe and Africa from Iceland and northern Norway to Morocco.

Lepidorhombus boscii usually grows to a length of 30–35 cm (maximum 40 cm). It lives at greater depths (down to 1,000 m) than *L. whiffiagonis;* a striking characteristic is the presence of two round black spots at the rear of its dorsal and anal fins.

Distribution map of the related species *L. whiffiagonis* (red) and *L. boscii* (blue).

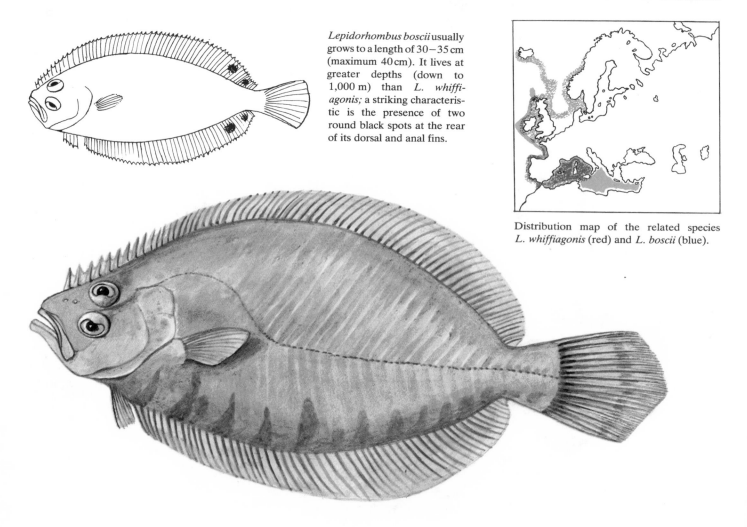

The Pleuronectidae are a large family in which the eyes are situated on the right side of the body of the fishes (although there are individual exceptions in which the eyes are on the left side).

PLEURONECTIDAE

Halibut
Hippoglossus hippoglossus

The Halibut is the largest of the flatfishes (individuals weighing 130 kg have been landed at British ports in recent years) and has a thick but narrow, elongate body. The upper surface of the body is greenish brown or sometimes dark brown or black, but the underside is dingy white. Halibut grow fairly quickly, so that at 10 years old the males measure about one metre and weigh 16 kg, while the females measure up to 130 cm and weigh 30 kg. Nowadays females have a life span of up to 30 years, but when the Halibut were fished less intensively than they are today, they were known to live for up to 50 years. Spawning takes place at the end of the winter and early in the spring in deep water at depths of 300−700 m. Males attain sexual maturity when seven or eight years old, the females when ten to eleven years old; development takes two to three weeks. The larvae are pelagic, but once they measure about 4 cm they migrate to the bottom, where they metamorphose and assume

a bottom-dwelling mode of life. Young individuals between two and four years old live close to the shore, but as they age they move to deeper water (100−1,500 m). After spawning both sexes migrate northwards in search of food. Young individuals feed on crustaceans like crabs and prawns, but once the fish reach 30−35 cm in length their diet includes more fish like herring, cod, flatfishes, and skate. Halibut live over sandy or stony sea beds, but also hunt for fish in open water.

They are very valuable marine species, but the total annual catch has declined from a former 13,000−17,000 tons to 7,000 tons. They are very vulnerable to overfishing because they become sexually mature so late and whole populations have been fished out in many localities. They have very tasty flesh and are generally sold smoked.

Size: 150−180 cm (males), maximum 470 cm; 200−230 cm (females)
Weight: 15−20 kg, maximum 350 kg
Fin formula: D 96−108, A 72−83,
Fecundity: 1.3−1.5 million eggs
Distribution: In the northern part of the Atlantic and adjoining areas of the Arctic Ocean.

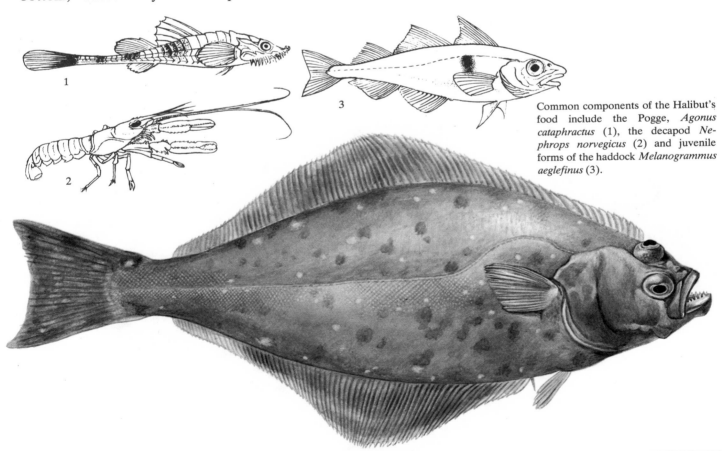

Common components of the Halibut's food include the Pogge, *Agonus cataphractus* (1), the decapod *Nephrops norvegicus* (2) and juvenile forms of the haddock *Melanogrammus aeglefinus* (3).

Dab
Limanda limanda

One of the most common and familiar flatfishes on sandy shores on all the European coasts, this little fish is very similar to the Plaice, but it can be identified by the pronounced arc in the lateral line above its pectoral fins. Its body is covered with small, overlapping scales. Those on the upper surface are toothed, making the fish feel rough to the touch, but on the lower left side only the edges of the body are rough. The upper surface of the body and fins is usually brown or greyish brown, marked with irregular darker spots. The underside of the body is white and the unpaired fins are grey from below.

Dabs live on sandy sea beds in coastal waters, mostly at depths of 20–50 m, but young fish tend to prefer shallow water from 2 to 25 m, while large individuals also live at depths of 150–200 m, especially in the winter. In the southern part of their range males attain sexual maturity when two or three years old and females when three or four, but in the north maturity comes a year or two later. The average life span is 10–12 years. They spawn in the spring and summer, most frequently at depths of 25–50 m; the eggs, larvae and fry live in open water. When they measure 13–18 mm the fry move to the bottom and assume a benthic existence although they have not yet completed metamorphosis.

Dabs are caught chiefly with trawls and seine-nets; despite their small size they are popular with anglers, since they live near the shore and rise well to bait. The total annual catch varies from 15,000 to 18,000 tons and comes largely from the North Sea, where Dabs are particularly abundant. They are delicious.

Commonest synonym: Pleuronectes limanda
Size: 20–30 cm, maximum 45 cm
Weight: 0.5–1 kg, occasionally up to 1.5 kg
Fin formula: D 68–80, A 50–61
Fecundity: 50,000–150,000 eggs
Distribution: In the Atlantic Ocean from the White Sea as far south as the Bay of Biscay, the North Sea and the western part of the Baltic Sea.

Distribution map of *L. limanda*.

Like other flatfishes, *Limanda limanda* feeds on various bottom-dwelling invertebrates like polychaete worms of the genus *Amphitrite* (1), brittle stars (2), molluscs (3) and small fish.

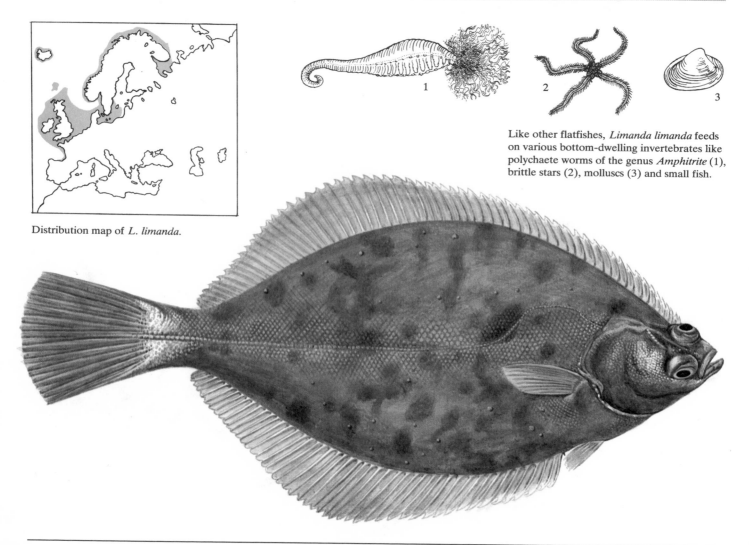

Lemon Sole

Microstomus kitt

This fish can be readily distinguished from related species of the genera *Pleuronectes, Limanda* and *Liopsetta* and from several other *Microstomus* species by its almost elliptical body and very short peduncle. It has a relatively thick, fleshy body and a small head with the eyes on the right side, a very small mouth and pouting lips. The lateral line arches slightly above the pectoral fins; the body is covered with smooth-edged scales. On its upper surface the fish is usually brown or reddish brown, usually with irregular dark spots, and the under surface is white. As in other flatfishes, the colour camouflages the fish so that it matches its background exactly and it can change colour relatively quickly.

Lemon Soles are abundant only in some parts of their range, mostly on sandy or stony seabeds at depths of 30−200 m. The males reach sexual maturity when three or four years old, the females when four to six years old; both have a life span of about 17 years. Spawning occurs throughout spring and summer, with a small peak in May and June. The symmetrical pelagic larvae metamorphose and become bottom-dwellers when they measure about 3 cm. Lemon Soles feed mainly on polychaete worms with some molluscs and crustaceans, but they are more specialized in their feeding than many other flatfishes, because their small mouth sets a limit on the size of their prey.

This is an economically important species and the total annual catch varies from 8,000 to 10,000 tons, more than half of which is caught by British fishermen. However, with the decline in the size of catches in recent years, a minimum permissible size of 25 cm has been introduced for its protection.

Synonyms: Pleuronectes kitt, Pleuronectes microcephalus, Microstomus microcephalus
Size: 30−40 cm, maximum 65 cm
Weight: 1−2 kg, maximum 2.5 kg
Fin formula: D 85−98, A 69−97
Distribution: In the Atlantic Ocean from the White Sea to the Bay of Biscay, the North Sea.

Distribution map of *M. kitt.*

Microstomus pacificus differs in both form and colouring from *M. kitt.* It is a very valuable species which occurs along the Pacific coasts of Canada and the USA and reaches a length of 25−50 cm or a maximum of 70 cm.

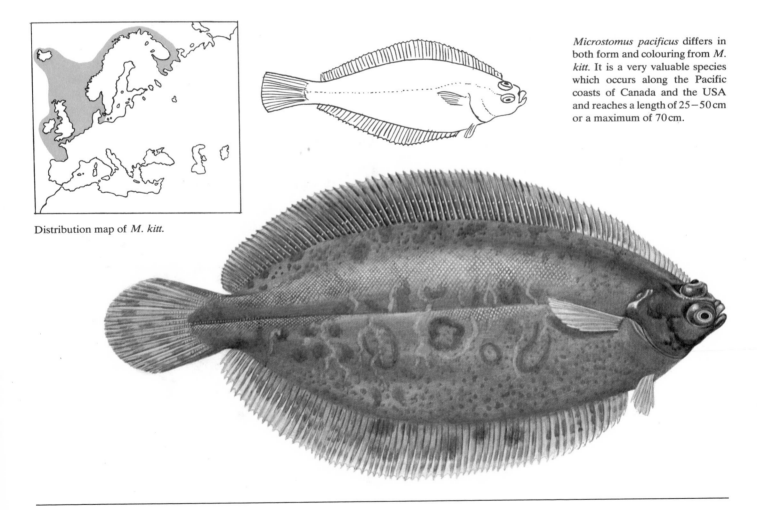

Polar Flounder

Liopsetta glacialis

This is the only representative of the genus *Liopsetta* in European waters; other species live in the northern part of the Pacific. This fish has a rounded body with a small head and eyes on the right side of the head; the dorsal fin begins roughly above their mid-point. It has an almost straight lateral line arching only slightly above the pectoral fins. The males usually have ctenoid scales, the females cycloid scales. The upper surface of the body is brown or dark olive in colour, with a large number of dark, confluent rounded spots which continue on the unpaired fins. The underside of the body is white, but occasional individuals have dark spots on it.

This species lives in cold water and tolerates water temperatures close to freezing very well. The fishes live in shallows close to shore and also in the brackish waters of river mouths, usually over a clayey seabed. They feed on polychaete worms, molluscs, crustaceans and small fish, lying in wait buried in mud or sand for their prey. By wriggling its body the fish stirs up the substrate, covering itself up so thoroughly that even on close inspection the only thing that can be seen are the bumps of the eyes. Like other flatfishes, flounders can turn their eyes in all directions and can also move them separately. These fish become sexually mature when four or five years old and usually spawn between January and March in the cold waters under the ice.

The flesh is white and tasty, but the total size of the catch is unknown. Catches are composed mainly of five to six year old fish.

Commonest synonym: Pleuronectes glacialis
Size: 25−30 cm, maximum 35 cm
Weight: 0.5−1 kg, maximum 1.5 kg
Fin formula: D 50−62, A 33−44, P 8−12
Fecundity: 50,000−200,000 eggs
Distribution: In Arctic waters from the Barents Sea in the west to the Chukot Sea in the east.

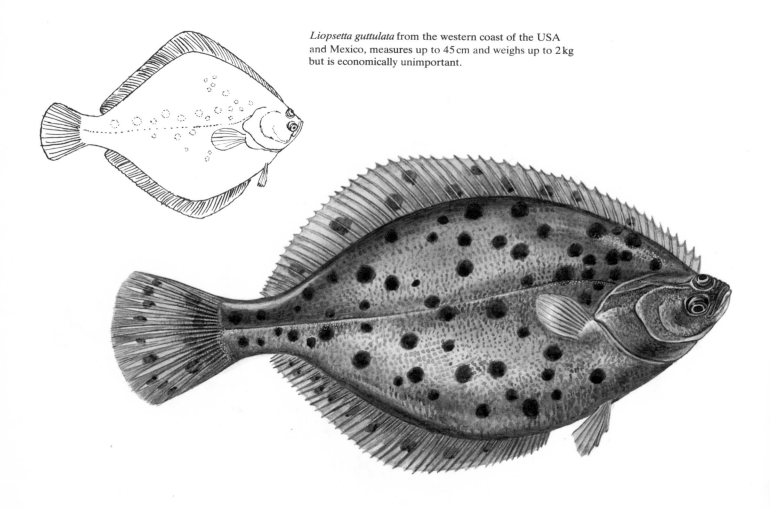

Liopsetta guttulata from the western coast of the USA and Mexico, measures up to 45 cm and weighs up to 2 kg but is economically unimportant.

Flounder
Platichthys flesus

While closely resembling the Plaice in both form and colouring, this species has no knobbly ridge on its head, but does have a row of small, sharp teeth, easily detected by touch, along the base of its dorsal and anal fin. Both sides of the body are covered with cycloid scales embedded deeply in the skin. There are a few spiny bony plates on the upper surface of the head and along the lateral line, which runs almost straight down the middle of the fish. The position of the eyes in *P. flesus* is the least constant of any flatfish; they are generally situated on the right side, but many individuals have eyes on the left.

Flounders become much more common in the northern part of their range than in the south. In the Black Sea, for instance, they account for 2.5 % of the flatfishes caught, but in the Barents Sea for 40—50 %. They are the only flatfishes found in fresh water and are common in the brackish waters of estuaries, especially in the summer. They live on a sandy or clayey seabed from the intertidal zone to a depth of 60 m and are particularly active at night,

spending the days buried in sand on the bottom. Tidal migrations occur, the fish swimming shorewards with the incoming tide in search of food and back to deeper water again as the tide recedes. Flounders feed on polychaete worms and on many kinds of molluscs and can be a pest in cockle beds; in fresh or brackish water they may feed on midge larvae. Spawning occurs from January to June or even longer, often in the same localities as the Plaice, *P. platessa*, so that hybrids are not uncommon. The eggs, larvae and fry are pelagic.

In some regions this is an important species economically; in the Baltic Sea for example, flounders are caught in large numbers.

> *Commonest synonym: Pleuronectes flesus*
> *Size:* 25—35 cm, maximum 50 cm
> *Weight:* 0.5—2 kg. maximum 3 kg
> *Fin formula:* D 50—68, A 33—48
> *Fecundity:* 80,000—2,750,000 eggs
> *Distribution:* Along the coast of Europe from the Barents Sea to Gibraltar, in the Mediterranean, the Black Sea and the Sea of Azov.

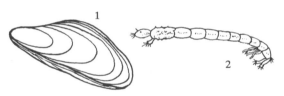

Flounders feed on benthic animals like molluscs (1) and polychaete worms in the sea and on midge larvae (2) when in brackish or fresh water.

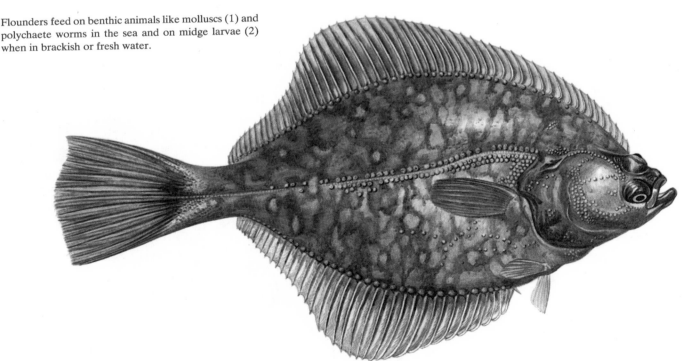

Plaice

Pleuronectes platessa

The Plaice is caught on a larger scale than any other flatfish both in European waters and on a worldwide basis. It is closely related to the members of the genera *Limanda* and *Liopsetta* and, like them, is primarily a right-sided species. However, in a small percentage of individuals the eyes move to the left side of the body at metamorphosis. Behind the eyes the Plaice has a bony ridge, divided into four to eight knobbly protuberances, a feature which can be used in identifying the species. Both surfaces of the body are covered with small cycloid scales. Plaice are easy to recognise from their colouring — on the upper surface the fish are rich brown or greenish brown marked with irregularly distributed bright red or orange spots. The underside is white.

These fishes are found on sandy seabeds at depths of 1—250 m, most frequently at 10—15 m. Young individuals are found in very shallow water and may also invade the brackish water of estuaries, but Plaice are not as tolerant of fresh water as Flounders. They usually spawn between January and May. The eggs and larvae float at first in the surface layers of the water, but by the time they measure 13—17 mm the fry have metamorphosed and assumed a life on the bottom. In the south the males become sexually mature when three to six years old, the females when four to seven years old, whereas further north they mature between eight to ten and nine to twelve years old respectively. They have an average life span of 25—30 years. Molluscs form the most common items in their diet and they crush the shells of these animals with strong pharyngeal teeth, but they also catch bottom-dwelling fishes.

The total annual Plaice catch averages 150,000—170,000 tons, mostly of individuals aged between six and twelve years old.

Commonest synonym: Platessa platessa
Size: 40—60 cm, maximum 90—100 cm
Weight: usually 1—3 kg, maximum 7 kg
Fin formula: D 67—84, A 45—61
Fecundity: 100,000—600,000 eggs
Distribution: In the greater part of the Mediterranean, in the Baltic Sea and in the Atlantic from Gibraltar to the Barents Sea. Also around Iceland and off the south coast of Greenland.

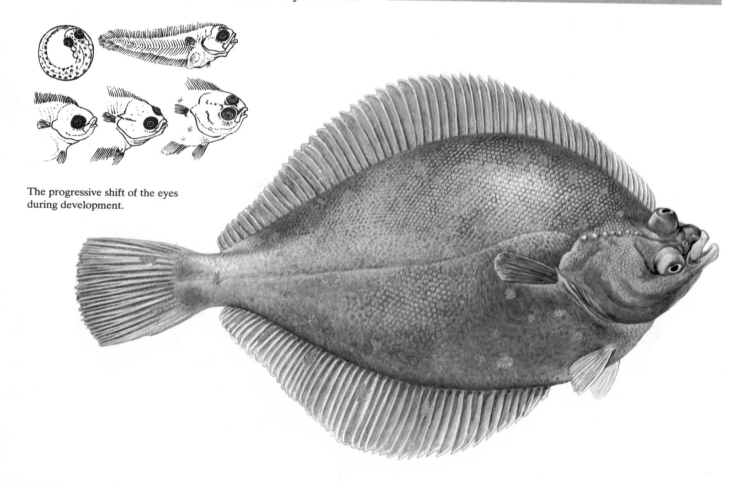

The progressive shift of the eyes during development.

Greenland Halibut
Reinhardtius hippoglossoides

This is the only representative of the genus *Reinhardtius*. It has eyes on the right side of its body, the upper eye right on the top of the head with the dorsal fin beginning behind it. The lateral line follows a practically straight course from the end of the head to the caudal fin, which is straight-edged. The colouring of the upper surface of the body varies from brown to greyish and greenish brown; in adults the underside is also pigmented and is only a little lighter in colour than the upper surface.

This fish is found mostly at the edge of the continental shelf at depths of 200—2,000m, in cold northern waters at a temperature of near freezing. Unlike most flatfishes it does not remain on the bottom, but swims more normally with its back upwards and not with its side upwards like the majority of flatfishes. It is more symmetrical in form than most of its relatives and is coloured on both sides, features related to its different mode of life. It feeds on a variety of different fishes like capelin, redfish and cod. The males become sexually mature when nine or ten years old, the females usually two years later. Spawning takes place between May and July at depths of 700—1,500m; the eggs, larvae and fry are pelagic. Metamorphosis begins when the fry reach 6—8.5cm; the underside of the body grows paler and they retire to shallower water to live on the bottom. Later when they measure 16—20cm, the underside begins to grow darker again and they take to swimming more often in the open sea.

Greenland Halibut catches take second place among the flatfishes and the total annual catch in recent years has varied from 70,000 to 130,000 tons. The flesh of the fish is white and very tasty especially when smoked.

Commonest synonyms: Hippoglossus groenlandiensis, Pleuronectes hippoglossoides
Size: 80—100cm, maximum 120cm
Weight: 10—25kg, occasionally up to 45kg
Fin formula: D 90—103, A 66—79
Fecundity: up to 300,000 eggs 4—4.5mm in diameter
Distribution: In the northern part of the Atlantic from the Barents Sea to the North American coast.

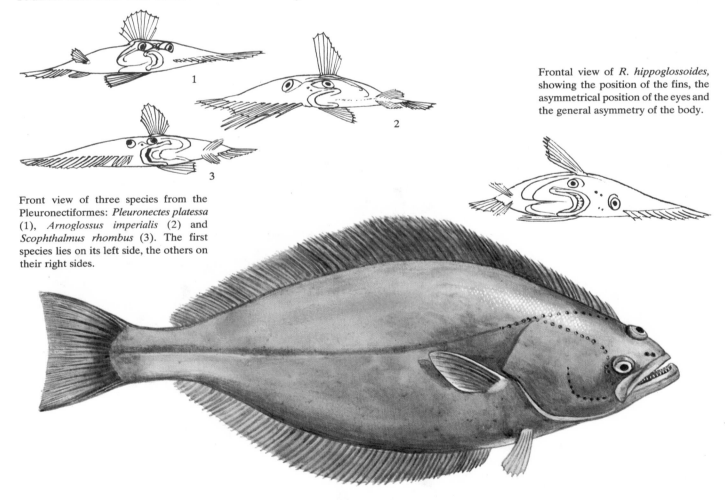

1   2   3

Front view of three species from the Pleuronectiformes: *Pleuronectes platessa* (1), *Arnoglossus imperialis* (2) and *Scophthalmus rhombus* (3). The first species lies on its left side, the others on their right sides.

Frontal view of *R. hippoglossoides*, showing the position of the fins, the asymmetrical position of the eyes and the general asymmetry of the body.

In the family Soleidae are about thirty genera of marine fishes with eyes on the right side of their bodies. They obtain food by churning up the seabed to look for worms, molluscs and small crustaceans. Many species live off the coast of South Africa, but there are also several European species.

Dover Sole
Solea solea

Known as a sole since it resembles the sole of a shoe in shape, this familiar food fish has a small rounded head, a crooked mouth and small eyes. As in all the soles, the head projects forward of the mouth, so that the mouth is on the side of the head, not at the end as in members of the Pleuronectidae. On the underside of the head are small tubular nostrils and close to the mouth are short dermal papillae. The upper surface of the body is brown with irregular light and dark spots, with a black spot at the end of each pectoral fin. Its underside is creamy white.

Dover Soles live mostly on sandy seabeds at depths of 10–100 m or occasionally as far down as 200 m and are particularly common in the North Sea and the Bay of Biscay. They migrate inshore to spawn between April and August at depths of 40–50 m. The larvae at first live a pelagic life but when they measure 12–15 mm the left eye begins to shift to the right side of the head and, as metamorphosis progresses, they adopt a benthic mode of life. The adult fish usually spend the daytime buried in the sand or mud, becoming active at night when they can sometimes be detected near the surface. They feed on worms and molluscs and have a life span of up to 20 years.

This is the most common species of the family Soleidae caught by commercial fishermen, with an annual catch of 35,000–45,000 tons. The flesh of the fish is white and tasty.

Synonym: Pleuronectes solea
Size: 30–45 cm, maximum 60 cm
Weight: 1–2 kg, maximum 3 kg
Fin formula: D 70–87, A 54–74
Fecundity: 10,000–150,000 eggs
Distribution: The Atlantic coasts of Europe and Africa, the Mediterranean Sea, the southern parts of the North Sea and the western parts of the Baltic Sea.

Distribution map of *S. solea.*

Front of view of *S. solea,* showing the position of the fins and the asymmetry of the body.

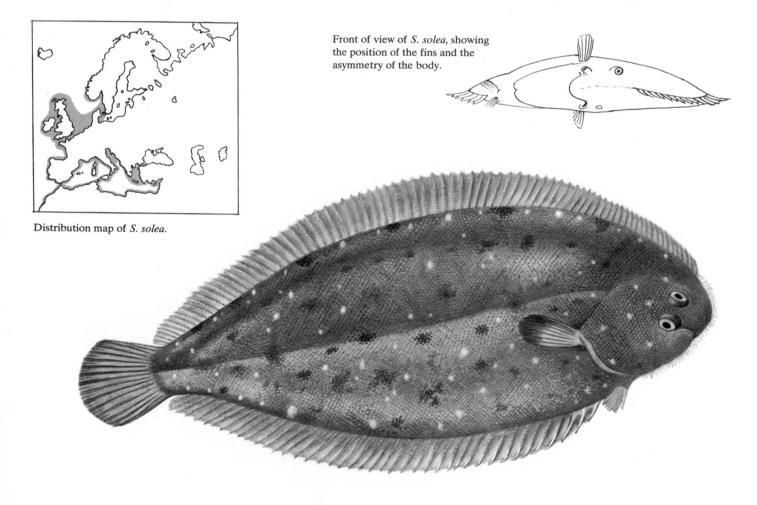

Sand Sole
Pegusa lascaris

At first glance the Sand Sole is very similar to the much commoner Dover Sole. The tip of its head is rounded, its dorsal fin commences in front of its eyes and is joined by narrow webbing to the base of the caudal fin, together with the anal fin. The first nostril opening on the underside of the head, however, is quite distinctive and forms a large rosette nearly as large as an eye. The Sand Sole is also rather different in colouration, the upper surface being light brown to greyish brown with large dark spots and small white spots; in the centre of each pectoral fin there is a round black spot.

Sand Soles live on sandy or clayey seabeds on the continental shelf at depths of 30−250 m, migrating into shallower water in the summer. They have a long spawning season depending on locality, spawning in April in some places and in others at the end of September. Eggs and larvae are found in various layers of the water, often at considerable distances from the shore. Adult Sand Soles feed mainly on polychaete worms and molluscs and also on the fry of bottom-dwelling fishes.

They have relatively tasty flesh, but are not as popular as other types of sole. The small size of the catches makes them economically unimportant.

Synonyms: Solea lascaris, Pleuronectes lascaris
Size: 20−35 cm, maximum 45 cm
Weight: 0.5−1.5 kg, maximum 2 kg
Fin formula: D 67−76, A 53−65
Distribution: In the Mediterranean and the Black Sea and off the coast of Europe and Africa, from Ireland as far south as Angola.

The front of the left, 'blind' side of the head of *S. lascaris*. The anterior nostril, which is roughly the same size as an eye, has a very wide, rounded and branched tip, giving it the appearance of a rosette. There are also numerous small dermal papillae in its vicinity.

The related *Monochirus luteus* is present in the Mediterranean and in the Atlantic from the south of Norway as far as Dakar. It grows to a length of about 15 cm.

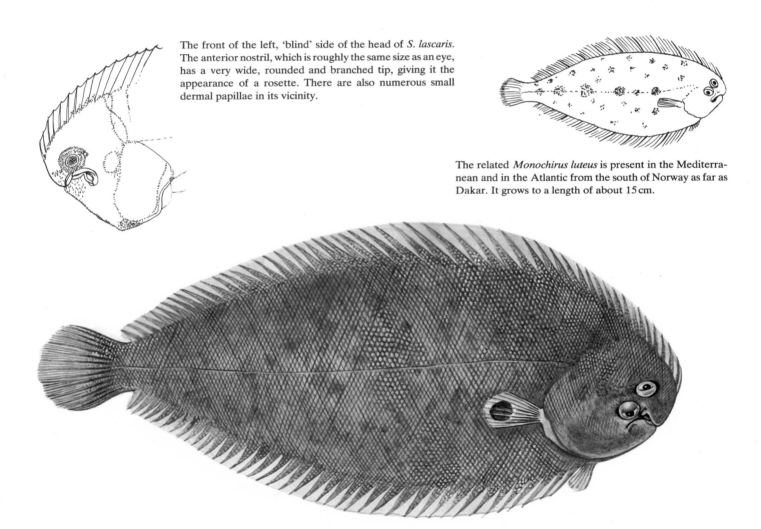

The order Gobiesociformes is a specialized group of small marine fishes with very broad heads and characteristic suction discs formed on the ventral surface of their bodies by transformation of the ventral fins. The family Gobiesocidae has five species living in European coastal waters.

Shore Clingfish
Lepadogaster lepadogaster

Despite its small size, *Lepadogaster lepadogaster* is one of the larger members of the family. It has a dorsoventrally flattened body, a relatively large head and a long snout with anterior nostrils, surmounted by long feelers especially in males. The dorsal and anal fins are connected with the caudal fin and the ventral suction disc is well developed. The colouring of the fish varies with locality from pink to dark red, but it can also be cinnamon brown or green. On the top of the head, behind the eyes, there are always two or three blue spots with yellow or brown borders and other darker spots may be seen on the back and sides.

Shore Clingfishes live mostly in the intertidal zone, attached to the undersides of stones amongst seaweeds and may occur in large numbers. Not even the strongest breakers can loosen the hold of the suction disc. Spawning occurs between April and the end of July and the female lays her eggs in empty mollusc shells. The adult fish are active mainly at night, searching for prey like polychaete worms and crustaceans. They can survive for quite a long time out of water, but die fairly soon (in 12—15 hours) in fresh water. If the salinity of the water is reduced slowly however, over a period of several days, they can survive in it for several months.

Commonest synonym: Cyclopterus lepadogaster
Size: 6—8 cm, exceptionally up to 10 cm
Weight: 20—80 g
Fin formula: D 15—20, A 9—12
Fecundity: 200—300 eggs
Distribution: In the coastal waters of the Atlantic from the British Isles in the north to Dakar in the south, in the Mediterranean and the Black Seas.

Diagrammatic view of the head of both *Lepadogaster* species from above: *L. lepadogaster* (1) and *L. candollei* (2).

The related Common Clingfish, *L. candollei*, lives in the Mediterranean and the Black Sea and in coastal waters of the Atlantic from the British Isles to Dakar. It can be distinguished from the Shore Clingfish by the fact that its anterior nostrils have no long feelers and its dorsal and anal fins are separate from the caudal fin. It grows up to 10—12 cm long.

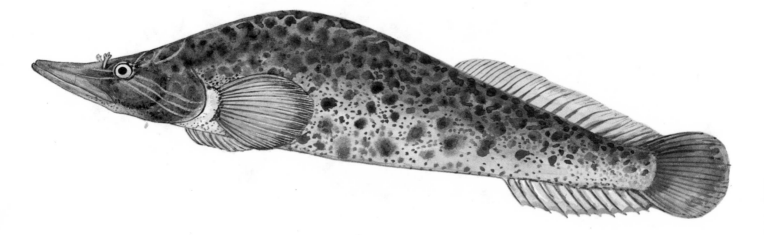

The order Lophiiformes contains about 225 species of marine fishes with characteristic, dorsoventrally flattened bodies. The family Lophiidae contains about four genera with twelve benthic species living in the great oceans from temperate to tropical waters. They are somewhat inactive fishes, have large, flat heads and strikingly large jaws and are often to be found at great depths.

LOPHIIDAE

Common Angler Fish

Lophius piscatorius

This fish has a characteristically wide head and wide mouth well armed with large curved teeth; above the mouth is a well-developed 'lure', actually the first spine of the dorsal fin. There are five other spines of this fin, widely spaced down the midline of the back. Round the lower jaw and on the sides of the fish is a row of tassel-like outgrowths imitating tufts of seaweed. The fish is scaleless and is covered instead by small bony plates on the loose skin.

Angler Fishes generally live in the shallow coastal waters and spend most of the time buried in the sand on the bottom or amongst seaweeds with only the lure exposed. This is twitched regularly and small fishes like sand eels, sculpins, flatfishes, which come to investigate, are swallowed. Lobsters, crabs and squid are also taken. In the autumn the fish migrate from European coastal waters to the deeper water in the Atlantic, to depths of usually 1,000–2,000 m. Spawning takes place in January and February and the pelagic eggs are laid in slimy hexagonal clusters, joined together in ribbon-like sheets which may measure up to nine metres long and 90 cm wide. After a complicated initial development lasting about four months, the larvae adopt a benthic mode of life.

Angler Fish are known as Monkfish to fishmongers. They have fairly tasty flesh and in recent years have become profitable. The total annual catch has been about 40,000–60,000 tons.

Size: 1.5 m, exceptionally up to 2 m
Weight: 30–40 kg
Fin formula: D_1 2 + 1 + 3, D_2 11–13, A 9–11
Fecundity: 1,3000,000 eggs
Distribution: Atlantic coastal waters of Europe and North Africa, the Mediterranean and the Black Seas.

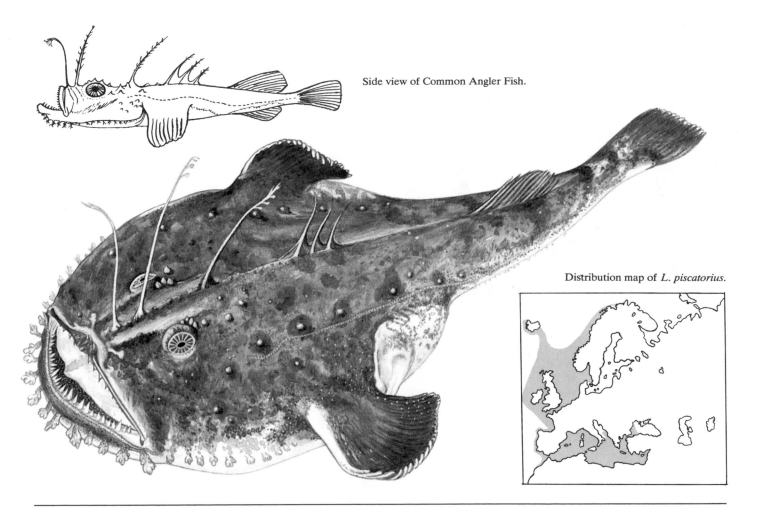

Side view of Common Angler Fish.

Distribution map of *L. piscatorius*.

295

The Tetraodontiformes are a large group of tropical and subtropical fishes with powerful teeth in both their jaws. The members of the family Molidae have characteristic, flat-sided bodies convexly truncated at the back as a result of atrophy of the end of the spine and the tail.

Sunfish
Mola mola

This is a massive fish, immediately recognisable from its strange truncated shape. It is brownish grey with a lighter belly and has a scaleless body covered with extremely thick, elastic skin. It has long dorsal and anal fins, both joined to the rudimentary caudal fin.

Sunfishes often swim at the surface of the sea, with just the dorsal fin showing, but are known to descend to considerable depths. Many of the individuals seen at the surface have been found lying on the water and are thought to have been weak or dying. Little is known of their spawning habits. The larvae live in the deep layers of the open sea; they are coloured differently from the adult fish and their bodies are covered with large spines which protect them against predators but which disappear in adults. Sunfishes feed mostly on soft-bodied invertebrates like jellyfishes and comb-jellies, but also on crustaceans, cephalopods and occasional eel larvae.

They are rarely seen in fishermen's catches and the flesh, though not poisonous, is virtually inedible.

Commonest synonym: Tetraodon mola
Size: 2.5 m, exceptionally up to 4 m
Weight: 1,400 kg, maximum 2,000 kg
Fin formula: D 16—18, A 14—18
Fecundity: up to 300,000,000 eggs
Distribution: In open water in all tropical and subtropical seas; carried by the Gulf Stream as far as the southern coast of Norway.

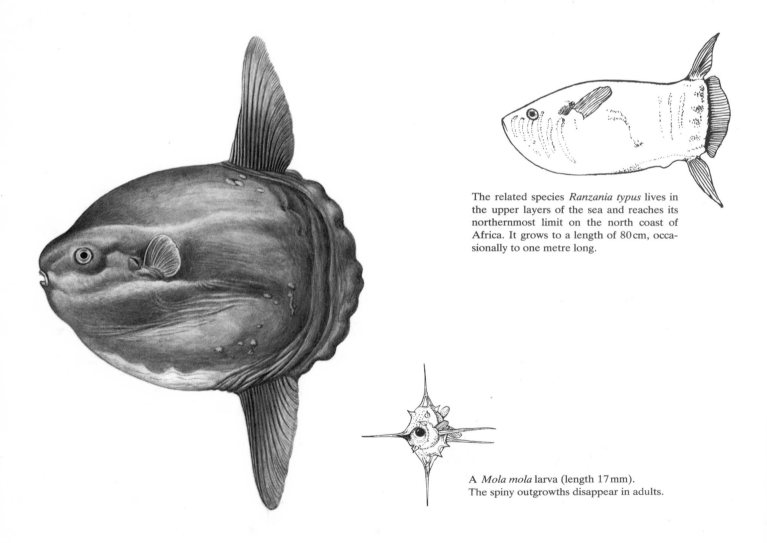

The related species *Ranzania typus* lives in the upper layers of the sea and reaches its northernmost limit on the north coast of Africa. It grows to a length of 80 cm, occasionally to one metre long.

A *Mola mola* larva (length 17 mm).
The spiny outgrowths disappear in adults.

Bibliography

Hureau, J. C. & Th. Monod, Eds. 1973. Checklist of the Fishes of the North-eastern Atlantic and of the Mediterranean. Unesco.

Maitland, Peter S. 1977. Guide to the Freshwater Fishes of Britain and Europe. Hamlyn

Midgalsi, Edward C. & George S. Fichter. 1977. The Fresh and Salt Water Fishes of the World. Octopus.

Muus, Bent J. & Preben Dahlstrøm. 1974. Guide to the Sea Fishes of Britain and North-west Europe. Collins.

Philips, Roger & Martyn Rix. 1985. Freshwater Fish. Pan.

Smith, Margaret M. & Philippa C. Heemstra. 1986. Smith's Sea Fishes. Springer-Verlag.

Wheeler, Alwynne. 1969. Fishes of the British Isles and North-west Europe. MacMillan.

Wheeler, Alwynne. 1975. The World Encyclopedia of Fishes. MacDonald.

Wheeler, Alwynne. 1978. Key to the Fishes of Northern Europe. Frederick Warne.

Whitehead, P. J. P., Bauchot M.-L., Hureau, J.-C. & E. Tortonese, Eds. 1984. Fishes of the North-eastern Atlantic and the Mediterranean. Vols. I–III. Unesco.

Index of scientific names

Numbers in bold type refer to main entries

Index of common names

Numbers in bold type refer to main entries